Aristotle's Quarrel with Socrates

SUNY series in Ancient Greek Philosophy

Anthony Preus, editor

Aristotle's Quarrel with Socrates
Friendship in Political Thought

JOHN BOERSMA

Published by State University of New York Press, Albany

© 2024 State University of New York

All rights reserved

Printed in the United States of America

No part of this book may be used or reproduced in any manner whatsoever without written permission. No part of this book may be stored in a retrieval system or transmitted in any form or by any means including electronic, electrostatic, magnetic tape, mechanical, photocopying, recording, or otherwise without the prior permission in writing of the publisher.

For information, contact State University of New York Press, Albany, NY
www.sunypress.edu

Library of Congress Cataloging-in-Publication Data

Name: Boersma, John, author.
Title: Aristotle's quarrel with Socrates : friendship in political thought / John Boersma.
Description: Albany : State University of New York Press, [2024] | Series: SUNY series in Ancient Greek Philosophy | Includes bibliographical references and index.
Identifiers: ISBN 9781438496702 (hardcover : alk. paper) | ISBN 9781438496726 (ebook)
Further information is available at the Library of Congress.

10 9 8 7 6 5 4 3 2 1

*Dedicated to my wife,
Jennifer Driscoll Boersma*

Contents

Acknowledgments		ix
Introduction	Politics, Philosophy, and Friendship	1
Chapter One	Socratic Friendship and Man's Desire for the Good: *Lysis*	17
Chapter Two	Socratic Citizenship	45
Chapter Three	Aristotle's Friendship of the Good	85
Chapter Four	The Metaphysical Foundations of Friendship	117
Chapter Five	Friendship and the Practice of Politics	161
Conclusion	Friendship in the American Constitutional Republic	185
Notes		197
Bibliography		241
Index		253

Acknowledgments

I owe a great many thanks to many people. This book has its origins in the first political theory seminar course I took at Louisiana State University, taught by my committee chair, Professor James R. Stoner. Professor Stoner's approach to teaching not only introduced me to the complexity and intricacy of ancient political thought but also instilled in me a desire to make sense of that complexity. The guidance and wisdom I've received from my dissertation committee members—James Stoner, Cecil Eubanks, Alexander Orwin, Mary Sirridge, and Christopher Sullivan—has been invaluable. I would also like to acknowledge Richard Avramenko at the Center for the Study of Liberal Democracy at the University of Wisconsin-Madison for providing me the time and space to revise my dissertation and make it ready for publication while I was a Fellow at the Center. In addition, I would like to thank the students at the University of Wisconsin-Madison who took a course with me on Aristotelian political theory. Their incisive questions led to great discussions, and I learned much from them. Part of chapter 4 originally appeared in revised form as "'Two Going Together': The Alliance of Politics and Philosophy in Aristotle's *Ethics*," *Political Science Reviewer* 45/1 (2021): 39–68, and I thank the editors and anonymous reviewers for their very helpful comments.

I would also like to express my gratitude to my editor at State University of New York Press, Michael Rinella, for his support of the manuscript, and the anonymous reviewers whose comments and suggestions made for a better book. In addition, I would like to thank my parents. Aristotle writes that one can never repay the debt one owes to one's parents. This is undoubtedly true in my case, as my parents have been a constant source of support and encouragement. My father patiently read and edited each chapter, providing helpful feedback and criticism. Finally, words cannot express the gratitude I have toward my wife and children for their love, support, and patience. Jennifer is my dearest friend, and her constant support and devotion made the writing of this book possible.

Introduction

Politics, Philosophy, and Friendship

Reflecting on his friendship with Étienne de La Boétie, Michel de Montaigne famously asserted that if asked why they were friends, he would be unable to provide an answer other than to say "because it was he, because it was I."[1] While Montaigne's answer appears to be somewhat glib, it does reveal something important about their friendship. Montaigne believed it hinged upon the particularity of their respective characters. The two of them were so constituted that it seemed as if they had been made for one another. In fact, Montaigne goes on to declare that their friendship was so all encompassing that he and La Boétie became thoroughly entwined with one another, so that they became "of one piece," such that there was "no more sign of the seam by which they were first conjoined."[2] Montaigne and La Boétie were fused into one.

While Montaigne's description of his friendship with La Boétie is beautiful, it may also give us pause. Few of us, I believe, can claim to have so close a friendship that we can argue to have become as one with the other. The closest such friendship that many of us might be able to point to is a marriage or other amorous relationship. However, Montaigne explicitly characterizes his relationship with La Boétie as a friendship, rather than a relationship of amorous love. If we take Montaigne's standard as the guide, a fair number of us might claim never to have had such a friend. In the *Lysis* (the dialogue analyzed in the first chapter of this book), Socrates asserts that despite his great desire for a friend "he is so far from the possession" of such a thing that he does not know "the manner in which one person becomes a friend of another." (*Lysis*, 212a3–4).[3] Socrates's desire for a friend—someone who can complete him—becomes an important theme in the dialogue, as Socrates is skeptical that anything other than the good itself could provide such completion for man. Taking Montaigne's friendship with La Boétie as the governing standard, many of us can probably relate to Socrates's elusive quest for a friend. While beautiful, the completion that Montaigne claims to have found in his friendship with La Boétie is not something with which most of us are familiar.

At the same time, friendship is largely recognized to be an integral component of human flourishing, and it would seem odd to say that those with whom we are close are not worthy of the term *friend*, but are, in the words of Montaigne, "mere acquaintances."[4] The elusive character of friendship is neatly encapsulated by the famous quip attributed to Aristotle, "Oh my friends, there is no friend!"[5] This paradox speaks to the difficulties attending the use of the term *friend*. In common parlance, the term *friendship* is used to describe a whole range of relationships, from the sense of brotherly camaraderie that can exist among teammates engaged in a common enterprise to the intimate love between spouses, and in the Christian tradition, a believer's personal relationship with Christ. Some even maintain that the relationship between merchant and customer can be considered friendship in some loose way. As a result, we often distinguish between distant friendships, ordinary friendships, and close friendships.

According to Aristotle, there is nothing strange about the disparate meanings we colloquially assign to the term *friendship*. In his treatise on friendship in *The Nicomachean Ethics* (analyzed in chapters 3 and 4), he divides friendship into three types: friendships of utility, friendships of pleasure, and friendships of virtue. Friendships of utility are characterized by the use each party obtains from the relationship—we can think here of commercial friendships—and last only as long as each party benefits from the relationship. In contrast, friendships of pleasure are premised on the enjoyment each party obtains from being with their friend. Aristotle explains that these friendships are prevalent among the young and typically dissolve quickly. The last type of friendship exists only among those who are good and alike in point of virtue and, because it is based on the excellence of each party to the friendship, it is the only one of the three that can be described as a friendship of the good. I once had some students ask if the study group they had created for the upcoming test was a friendship of utility. I teased in return that Aristotle believed friendships of the good are often marked by having shared in suffering together. The truth is that while we are able to distinguish between these three conceptual types of friendship, Aristotle believes that the friendship of virtue includes both pleasure and use and that there is movement between the three types—friendships of mere use or pleasure can develop into friendships of virtue. Thus, the confused way in which we use the term *friendship* reflects the complexity of the phenomenon.

In addition to the three friendships described above, Aristotle also describes the relationship that exists among the citizens of the polis. While this relationship is often described as *civic friendship* and compared to the friendship of utility, I prefer the Greek term *homonoia* employed by Aristotle, which means "sameness of mind," as he expressly distinguishes this relationship from friendship (*Nicomachean Ethics [NE]*, 1155a24).[6] While Aristotle provides only a brief description of what "sameness of mind" entails in *The Nicomachean Ethics*, he indicates that it relates to the conception of justice, equity, and norms shared by the citizens of a particular regime. In chapter five, I analyze Aristotle's description of the best regime in the *Politics*, to see how it reflects *homonoia* and whether Aristotle has any advice for cultivating these shared norms.

Despite the confused way in which we ordinarily speak of friendship, Aristotle believes that only the highest type of friendship—friendship of virtue—is friendship in the authoritative sense. This friendship, while not identical to Montaigne's account of friendship, shares some affinities with Montaigne's description of his own friendship with La Boétie. For Aristotle, the highest type of friendship, like Montaigne's friendship, is dependent upon character. Specifically, the highest type of friendship is based on excellence of character. Aristotle describes this type of friendship as *sunaisthetic*, which in Greek means "joint perception."[7] In the Aristotelian friendship of virtue, each party is good and alike in point of virtue and, as a result, they are each able to perceive the excellence in the other's character. Such friendships are rare because excellence of character is rare. Friendship in the authoritative sense is described as an important aspect of human existence without which human life would be lacking. Friendship of virtue, therefore, appears to be of great moment to Aristotle, while remaining somewhat elusive.

The Decline of Friendship

However elusive friendships of virtue might have been in antiquity, it seems that modern democracy has witnessed a decline even in the number of friendships Aristotle would have termed friendships of pleasure, as well as the sense of *homonoia* he describes. There is a general sense that the relationships and associations that used to be a staple of life in democracy are disappearing. The decline in such relationships is not simply a symptom of nostalgia or an attitude of pessimism toward the present times. Numerous studies have documented the disintegration of civil bonds and friendships that were characteristic of an earlier democratic age. Robert Putnam's observations documenting the decline of such bonds in his book *Bowling Alone* are well known.[8] Compared to a short while ago, the civic associations and groups that populated the American landscape have declined precipitously.

The disappearance of these meaningful relationships has left us with only the more transient and thin friendships of utility. While these friendships are no doubt important, they are characterized primarily by necessity rather than as something good and beautiful in their own right. Adam Smith describes these friendships as follows: "Colleagues in office, partners in trade, call one another brothers; and frequently feel towards one another as if they really were so. . . . The Romans expressed this sort of attachment by the word *necessitudo*, which . . . seems to denote that it was imposed by the necessity of the situation."[9] The decline in relationships that are founded on shared sentimentality, pleasure, or virtue means that the primary bonds of society are founded on necessity, rather than on anything that is good and beautiful in its own right.

We might wonder why a decline in relationships founded on shared sentimentality, pleasure, or virtue is problematic. After all, if necessity is that which keeps society together as Adam Smith suggests, we might do well to build on this low but seemingly solid foundation, rather than to spurn that which nature provides. However, Putnam amply shows the way relationships based on shared sentimentality provide the social capital that facilitates ease of interactions and affords society with the trust that enables utilitarian exchanges to take place with minimal friction.[10] In sum, the shared sentimentality, pleasure, and occasionally virtue that characterize civic associations have a use of their own. Of course, to justify nonutilitarian relationships on the basis of their use may be the last refuge of scoundrels, and it might be better to simply acknowledge that the decline in relationships founded on shared sentimentality has resulted in the loss of something beautiful in its own right.

The explanations often provided for the decline in relationships and associations of shared sentiments are varied. Some point to the rise in technology, suggesting that the proliferation of weak online relationships is the culprit of the destruction of meaningful in-person friendships—our social circles are widened at the expense of their depth. Others point to the rise in individualism, suggesting that the focus on individual liberties, self-expression, and a preoccupation with autonomy have led to the decline of friendships beyond mere utility, as people have shunted group activities, perceiving them to be stifling their independence. Finally, others have suggested that globalization and neoliberalism are to blame, whereby the prioritization of profit over the protection and enhancement of social cohesion destroyed associational tendencies.

I think there is truth to all these explanations. What they all have in common, however, is a shift in values. The last few centuries have witnessed a shift that has deprioritized traditional virtue as espoused in different forms by Aristotle, Cicero, Thomas Aquinas, and others, in favor of utility, autonomy, and profit. The virtues necessary for commercial society have been substituted for traditional virtues. Of particular influence in this regard were the writers of the Scottish Enlightenment, such as Adam Smith, Francis Hutcheson, and Thomas Reid, who sought to refashion the virtues and sentiments of society to make them congruent with the aims of a modern society based on commerce.[11] Considering this substitution of commercial virtue, it is not surprising that we see a decline in the traditional friendships of virtue as well and, as I hope to make clear in subsequent chapters, a concomitant decline in friendships of pleasure and civic friendships.

Why Study Friendship?

There has been a resurgence of scholarly interest in the topic of friendship, and many of the books written have explored the writings on friendship that date from classical antiquity to help further their own inquiries into the concept of friendship.[12] However, while the relevance of civic friendship to politics is straightforward—as noted, civic friendship, in addition to being pleasing in its own right, provides the thick social bonds necessary for political cohesion and action—the relevance of friendships between two virtuous individuals in the manner of Aristotle's *sunaisthetic* friendship of the good (or the relationship between Montaigne and La Boétie for that matter) to the field of political philosophy is not immediately apparent.

Friendship seems, at first glance, to be decidedly nonpolitical. Contemporary conventional understandings of friendship seem to suggest that it is more fundamental than politics. Not only are friendships able to transcend political boundaries (and in fact often do), but our understanding of political relations also ordinarily entails concepts of rights and duties that seem to be foreign to our conception of friendship. Friendship appears to be outside of the realm of politics or relegated to the private sphere. Consequently, it may seem more appropriate to the field of sociology than political science. If friendship is largely conceived of as a private affair, why should it be the object of study for political philosophy?

The political philosophers of antiquity, including Plato and Aristotle, discuss the concept of friendship in detail. As I hope to explain in subsequent chapters, these writers saw the friendship between philosopher and statesman as constituting the height of friendship and believed it to have important political ramifications. This same political view of friendship held practical and theoretical influence in the Christian tradition as is evidenced by the treatise on friendship written by Aelred of Rievaulx, the theological writings of Thomas Aquinas, and the epistle on education addressed to the young Prince Charles of Spain by Desiderius Erasmus.[13] While the modern era is still witness to a number of treatises on friendship, Montaigne's essay being among the most influential, the provenance of these treatises is decidedly less political, and friendship is presented primarily as one of the pleasures of private life.[14]

By relegating friendship to the private sphere, these writers of the early modern period point toward the political philosophy of Thomas Hobbes, who sought to establish politics on a solid scientific and mechanistic basis rather than on what he saw to be the unstable ground of friendship.[15] Travis Smith makes the case that a principal motivation for Hobbes's system of government is his concern over the problems posed by friendship. According to Smith, Hobbes's embrace of the all-powerful Leviathan is borne out of a belief that human society "cannot sustain itself on the basis of friendship alone without suffering 'a great deal of grief.'"[16] In fact, friendships pose a danger to the security of society, as Hobbes views them as "partial associations" that are inclined toward self-interest. Accordingly, an important goal for Hobbes is to weaken these relationships to ensure that they pose no danger to the state. Smith concludes that Hobbes's attempt to weaken friendship entails a concomitant attempt to "transform the state into something impersonal and procedural."[17] For Hobbes, a politics reduced to procedure and contract is superior to that practiced in classical antiquity, which was sustained by the fickle bonds of friendship.

This history may go some way to explaining the resurgence of interest in friendship. Perhaps the rise in scholarship devoted to friendship is undertaken in response to the perceived inability of social contract theories to explain deep commitments. Michael Walzer has documented the way in which the social contract theory underpinning liberalism is felt to inadequately respond to man's deepest metaphysical needs, leaving people feeling isolated and alone.[18] As abstract rights and duties begin to be perceived as incapable of providing a solid foundation for politics, people may be turning to friendship to provide an alternative source of meaning, commitment, and stability.[19] However, a majority of the recent scholarship is primarily sociological and is devoted to exploring friendship's capacity to provide meaning and purpose to private life. While there is certainly merit in these studies, they proceed in a manner conditioned by modern political thinking: friendship is analyzed as a private association that operates independent of and subordinate to the realm of politics. I propose that the history of friendship provides a justification for analyzing friendship from the standpoint of political philosophy. If the modern approach to politics is seen as being incapable of providing a solid foundation for politics, it may make sense to turn to ancient conceptions of friendship to uncover why friendship was seen as foundational for politics, rather than something belonging to the private realm into which individuals can retreat for the sake of comfort and fulfillment.

The purpose of this book is to explore why seemingly private friendships between two individuals was seen to be foundational to the practice of conventional politics according to both Socrates and Aristotle. Through a comparison of Plato's *Lysis* and *Gorgias* with books VIII and IX of Aristotle's *Nicomachean Ethics* as well as his discussion of the best regime in the *Politics*, I hope to explore friendship's relationship to political life. There are good reasons for pairing these texts together. The *Lysis* and the *Gorgias* form a pair, as the former reveals the Socratic conception of friendship, while the latter reveals the effect this conception of friendship has on politics. Furthermore, recent scholarship has suggested that the dramatic date of these dialogues indicate that the *Gorgias* takes place immediately after the *Lysis*.[20] Aristotle's reflections on friendship in books VIII and IX of *The Nicomachean Ethics*, in turn, are dependent on many of the strands of argumentation abandoned by Socrates in the *Lysis*. Aristotle develops an account of friendship in these books and, in the *Politics*, explains how friendship animates the polis and orients it toward the good.

While readers might wonder why I have chosen to focus on Socrates rather than Plato, the reason is fairly straightforward: Plato places the arguments developed in the dialogues in the mouth of his characters, and while Plato does not himself speak in the dialogues, it is possible to uncover what he wants to show his readers by paying close attention to the characters, setting, and topics of the dialogues.²¹ For example, in the *Lysis*, Plato presents Socrates engaging with the youngest interlocutors of the entire Platonic writings, employing a number of sophistic arguments, and concluding with an account of friendship that stresses its basis in need. Similarly, in the *Gorgias*, we witness Socrates seeking to (unsuccessfully) persuade Callicles to avoid politics on the basis of a conception of friendship that had been examined, and found wanting, in the *Lysis*. While these arguments and dramatic details may not enable us to derive a full-blown conception of Platonic friendship, when combined with other similar indications, they enable us tentatively to conclude that Plato saw the Socratic approach to friendship and politics as leaving something to be desired. The lacunae that Plato identifies in the Socratic approach to friendship and politics provide a space, or ground, upon which it is possible to construct an alternative account of friendship and politics. It is my contention that Aristotle grapples with many of the same philosophical puzzles that had rendered Socrates's inquiry into friendship aporetic but, in contrast to Socrates, is able to uncover an account of friendship that provides a solid foundation for politics. It is my hope that the book reveals that although Socrates and Aristotle reach different conclusions as to the nature and purpose of friendship, both provide invaluable insights into the extent to which friendship should inform our political life and provide an alternative to the modern conception that approaches politics from a strictly mechanistic perspective.

The City and the Philosopher

Socrates's death at the hands of his political community, famously recounted in Plato's *Apology*, illustrates the inherent tension that seems to exist between the philosopher's devotion to a life of contemplation and the political community. Socrates's famous assertion that "the unexamined life is not worth living" generates criticism among the Athenian political elite and the poets who point out that his life of constant inquiry calls into question the conventional practices of Athens (*Apology*, 38a6–7).²² The tension between philosophy and the polis pervades much of subsequent philosophy, with the result that many political philosophers since Socrates—particularly in the modern era—have recognized this tension and sought to reduce it in various ways.²³

This theme of the tension between philosophy and politics pervades Aristotle's *Nicomachean Ethics* as well—albeit in a nuanced form—and has recently been the focus of a renewed interest in Aristotle's *Ethics*.[24] However, in contrast to Socrates, Aristotle makes his peace with politics. Not only does Aristotle devote an entire treatise—the *Politics*—to the different possible regimes and the manner in which such regimes might be improved, but he also famously collected constitutions alleging that these collections of laws and regime types would be of good use to those who are capable of determining which laws would be beneficial for the various types of regimes (*NE*, 1181b8–10). As a result, some have persuasively argued that the *Politics* is intended to be the counterpart to the *Ethics*, and that the one is meant to lead seamlessly into the other.[25]

Furthermore, Aristotle's interest in politics was not limited to strictly theoretical concerns but extended to practical engagement with politics. Aristotle's relation to the Macedonian rulers has long been acknowledged—in particular his relationship with Alexander the Great, whom he was hired to tutor in 343 BC. While the exact extent to which Aristotle acted as a political advisor to Alexander is debated, most scholars agree that Aristotle had an influence on Alexander's political and ethical undertakings.[26] Whatever the extent to which his advice had a practical impact on Alexander's policies, it is generally agreed that Aristotle was politically active. Thus, in contrast to Socrates, who eschewed the practice of politics as an enterprise that entailed the exercise of injustice (cf. *Apology*, 31d–32e) and inquired into political matters only to show the inherent limits of politics, Aristotle inquired into and engaged in the practice of politics in a concrete manner.

How is it that Aristotle alleviated the tension between politics and philosophy in a way that Socrates chose not to? Can it be that Aristotle was simply more of a realist than Socrates when it comes to political life? Did Aristotle understand the harsh necessities of politics and condone them in a way that Socrates did not? Many political interpretations of Aristotle's *Ethics* have adopted precisely this argument.[27] Leo Strauss and others have put forward an interpretation according to which Aristotle recognized the tension between philosophy and politics but sought to alleviate it in various ways while maintaining the superiority of the philosophical life.[28] According to this interpretation, Aristotle's concern with the political community was primarily practical—he recognized that the philosopher's good is in some way dependent on the political community, and as a result he attempted to foster a favorable disposition towards philosophy among the educated political class.[29] In essence, the Straussian interpretation of the *Ethics* holds that at best Aristotle's presentation of the moral virtues was intended to point out that they are merely a pale imitation of the philosophical life of contemplation, while at worst his presentation may simply be an elaborate ruse, the goal of which is to ensure that the city is made safe for philosophy.

The standard Straussian reading of the *Ethics* has much to offer. According to this reading, Aristotle sought to present the life of moral virtue so as to emphasize its nobility, while also exposing its limitations. In this way, the well-bred Greek gentleman (καλοσκάγαθος), if he is a sufficiently attentive reader, will recognize that the true benefit of moral virtue is that it points beyond itself toward philosophical virtue, which is self-sufficient and capable of being practiced alone.[30] This interpretation accords nicely with the general consensus that perceives Socrates as the idealist who doggedly pursues the good and holds Aristotle to be the realist who moderates his pursuit of the good in order to concern himself with political matters.[31]

While there is certainly an element of truth to the idealist/realist dichotomy that scholars have imposed on Socrates and Aristotle, I will argue that their differing evaluations of political life stem instead from their different conceptions of friendship. While the interpretation of Aristotle's *Ethics* described above provides much purchase, its greatest difficulty is that it struggles to incorporate much of books VIII and IX into the overall inquiry of the book. These books, both of which deal with friendship, are largely treated by the standard Straussian approach as an exhortation preparing the reader for Aristotle's somewhat startling claim that the philosophical life is the happiest life.[32] In contrast, I will argue that these two books, which together comprise a fifth of the entirety of the *Ethics*, entail a direct response to Socrates's inquiry into friendship in the *Lysis* and are meant to make clear the deficiencies of Socrates's understanding of friendship, as well as of his approach to politics as described in the *Gorgias*. As I will make clear, Socrates has a largely negative understanding of friendship, according to which friendship acts as an impediment to one's advancement toward what is good. It is this understanding that causes Socrates to treat philosophy and the pursuit of the good as occurring outside of the political realm. In contrast, Aristotle sketches a positive account of friendship. This positive view, I will argue, caused Aristotle to present politics in a favorable light and enabled him to use philosophy as a measure that can order the political realm toward the good.

Friendship, Necessity, and the Polis

It may perhaps seem odd to explain the differing stances Socrates and Aristotle take toward the polis as the result of their differing concepts of friendship. After all, neither Plato nor Aristotle discuss friendship at length in their most obviously political works.[33] Furthermore, as noted, friendship is often conceived as a private relationship that transcends politics or as being somewhat more fundamental than politics. Many of us likely have friendships and familial relationships that transcend partisan political positions, and it is not uncommon for friendships to transcend political boundaries. As a relationship that is more fundamental than politics, we might say that it is anchored in nature rather than in the conventional world of politics and is therefore primarily a pre-political relationship. Why would Socrates and Aristotle regard friendship as a field of inquiry for political philosophy if it is a pre-political relationship?

The answer is that for both Aristotle and Socrates pre-political relationships have an important effect on politics. Their respective accounts of how the polis comes into existence manifests this important effect. On the surface, it seems that for both Socrates and Aristotle it is pre-political relationships—specifically, relationships developed to fulfill a felt need, or lack—that give rise to the polis.[34] In book II of *The Republic*, Socrates relates to Adeimantus that a city "comes into being because each of us isn't self-sufficient but is in need of much" (*Republic*, 369b6–7).[35] What follows is an analysis of the way in which different parts of the city come together to provide one another with various necessary goods. Aristotle's account of the development of the polis appears to be similar to that of Socrates. The polis seems to emerge from a variety of parts that come together to counter necessity. The most basic unit of the polis, states Aristotle, is the individual, who joins with other individuals to form the household. This is done to provide "for the needs of daily life," as these individuals "cannot exist without one another." In turn, several households come together to form a village, so as to provide for the sake of "non-daily needs." Finally, the "complete community, arising from several villages, is the city" (*Politics*, 1252a26–30).[36] Thus, Socrates and Aristotle both suggest that the polis has its origin in the pre-political relationships that are ordered toward countering necessity.

There is, however, a subtle difference between the two philosophers' accounts of the city's formation. While Socrates is quite clear that the city arises from the pre-political relationships that are ordered toward countering necessity, Aristotle's account goes beyond this. As Aristotle presents it, the daily and non-daily necessities are countered at the level of the household and the village respectively. In contrast, the city—the complete community— comes into being "for the sake of living well" (1252a30). However, Aristotle remains silent about what it is that *causes* the city to be ordered towards this end. As a result, it seems that for Aristotle there is some force other than a desire to relieve man's estate that orders the city towards living well.

I hope to show that the differences bewtween Socrates's and Aristotle's accounts of the city's development have their roots in their disparate understandings of friendship. If the pre-political relationship of friendship has its basis in a felt need or lack, then Socrates is correct: the entirety of the political community is founded on pre-political relationships of desire and need. Political communities are, at bottom, little more than economic associations meant to provide for man's necessities. Friendship and political community are simply arrangements of convenience designed to facilitate mutual, utilitarian advantage; only the desire to overcome the harsh necessities of nature causes human beings to form communities. However, if individuals are liable to enter into friendships with one another wholly independent of need, then Aristotle's account may be correct. Political communities have their basis in pre-political relationships that are based on an appreciation of another's virtues or goodness, rather than individual deficiency. Political communities are ordered toward an end that is more noble than mere utilitarian advantage.

It is precisely this difference in understanding of friendship that causes Socrates and Aristotle to adopt differing stances to politics. Socrates's belief that friendship, and by extension the political realm, has its basis in necessity causes him to take a negative, abstentious approach to politics. Placing philosophy in the service of politics would be a degrading and humiliating exercise that is beneath the dignity of the philosopher. In contrast, Aristotle's understanding of friendship and politics as based on self-sufficiency and a recognition of another's virtues allows philosophy to play the crucial function of ennobling politics; philosophy can have a positive guiding impact on politics. For Aristotle, friendship grants dignity to politics, a dignity that relationships based on necessity alone do not provide. Viewed in this perspective, the concept of friendship developed in the *Ethics* not only affects politics but may also be precisely that which prompts Aristotle to offer the practical, political advice contained in the *Politics*.

The following five chapters and conclusion proceed in a comparative manner. In chapter 1, I detail Socrates's understanding of friendship as presented in the *Lysis*. I make the case that a close reading of the *Lysis* reveals a number of problems with Socrates's conception of friendship. Plato presents Socrates as using eristic arguments and sophisms, while engaging his youngest interlocutors in the entirety of the Platonic *corpus*—Menexenus and Lysis—in a discussion concerning the definition of friendship. At one point, Socrates adopts a sophistic argument that is strikingly similar to an argument used by the two Sophists, Euthydemus and Dionysodorus, in the *Euthydemus*. The ultimate presentation of Socrates's argument in the *Lysis*, I argue, collapses the distinction between friendship and eros such that both are characterized by a felt need or desire. According to Socrates, there is no such thing as a friendship based on self-sufficiency and an appreciation that two people may have of one another's good qualities. The *Lysis* intimates not only that Socrates is incorrect in suggesting that all friendship has its basis in need but also that there are dangers attending his conception of friendship.

Chapter 2 presents the political implications of Socrates's conception of friendship by examining the *Apology* and the *Gorgias*. The *Apology* shows Socrates's relation to the practice of politics to be one of negation and abstention. As he attests in his defense speech, Socrates never puts forward a positive teaching but instead questions the Athenian citizens' settled convictions, exposing their ignorance. The result, I argue, is an approach to politics that is entirely negative or dissolvent of people's opinions. In addition, Socrates's approach is characterized by an unwillingness to involve himself in conventional politics. In his defense speech, Socrates claims that he entirely avoids the practice of politics due to its incompatibility with justice. While Socrates does not explain with precision why he believes the practice of politics to be incompatible with justice, this connection is made clear in the *Gorgias* and, as I make clear, hinges on Socrates's understanding of friendship. At a critical juncture of the dialogue, Socrates directs his interlocutor, Callicles, away from the practice of politics precisely on the basis of a definition of friendship that had been proposed—but found wanting—in the *Lysis*. I show that Socrates believes the conventional practice of politics depends on a false conception of justice and friendship.

The third chapter analyzes Aristotle's discussion of friendship in book VIII of the *Ethics* in light of his understanding of the virtue of magnanimity. I argue that Aristotle's friendship of the good is intended to describe the friendship between two magnanimous individuals. Turning first to Aristotle's presentation of magnanimity in the *Posterior Analytics*, in which Aristotle suggests that there may be two types of magnanimity—one that is political and another that is philosophical—I show that Aristotle views the virtue of magnanimity to be problematic. The two types of individuals who are held up as being potentially magnanimous are presented as being self-sufficient and aware of the honor and respect they deserve. Nevertheless, when they fail to attain the honors they rightly deserve, they tend to act in a socially destructive manner. I go on to argue that Aristotle's presentation of magnanimity in the *Ethics* suggests that the cure for the socially destructive tendencies of such magnanimous individuals is friendship. If the magnanimous philosopher were to befriend the magnanimous statesman, they would not only temper one another's socially destructive tendencies, but also their alliance—the alliance of power and wisdom—would be capable of bestowing great benefits on the political realm.

While chapter 3 shows that Aristotle's friendship of the good is intended to describe friendship between two magnanimous individuals, chapter 4 explains why it is that such individuals will choose to befriend one another. Aristotle recognizes that philosophers are not likely to become friends with individuals who hold positions of power, as those in power may well have had to engage in nefarious tactics to attain their position and therefore cannot be described as virtuous or good. Nevertheless, in book IX Aristotle uses a protreptic address to convince the philosopher to engage with the statesman. As I make clear, Aristotle induces the philosopher to interact with the statesman and to activate his potential for virtue. The friendship that develops is a *sunaisthetic* friendship. As noted, the Greek noun *sunaisthesis* means "joint perception." Those sharing in a friendship of the good perceive the good together or, more specifically, they perceive the excellence in one another's character. As Aristotle presents it, each partner to the friendship is actualized by the other and takes delight in the other's virtue. This type of friendship between the philosopher and the statesman ensures that philosophy will have an indirect, guiding effect on the practice of politics.

In the fifth chapter, I examine the practical effects that Aristotle's *sunaisthetic* account of friendship has on political life. While the *sunaisthetic* friendship of the statesman and the philosopher seems somewhat detached from the everyday practice of politics, I explain how this friendship comes to have a unifying influence on the city. In the *Politics*, Aristotle is clear that unity in the city is necessary, but he is relatively pessimistic concerning the ability of impersonal institutions to achieve such unity. In book II of the *Politics*, for example, he details at length the inadequacies of law, and it is not until books VII and VIII, that Aristotle reveals that it is the musical education system established by the city's founders (i.e., the magnanimous statesman and philosopher) that actualizes the citizens' capacity for moral virtue by instituting a common way of life or unity in the city. Through their shared perception of the music (*nomos*) of their regime, the citizens come to share in the *sunaisthetic* friendship of the city's founders.

I conclude with a brief analysis of the role friendship played in establishing the American Constitutional Republic. I show that while the American founders had realistic insight into the self-interested aspect of human nature, they were nevertheless sufficiently convinced of their fellow citizens' intelligence and good sense to entrust political decisions and constitutional design to public discussion and choice. As a result, using the philosophic ideas of the day, they sought to convince one another and the public of the merits of their proposed designs for government. I argue that the ratified Constitution reflects elements of both the Socratic and Aristotelian conceptions toward friendship. Finally, I provide a brief account of the troubled friendship between John Adams and Thomas Jefferson, to show the practical benefits and limits of seeking to ground politics in constitutional procedures alone. I show that the commitment of the two statesmen to the principles of the Constitution was insufficient to maintain their friendship. Instead, what was needed was the prudent intervention of their mutual friend, Benjamin Rush. Through intimate knowledge of his friends' characters, passions, and prejudices, Rush was able to reconcile the two former friends before their passing. The dramatic rupture in their friendship, along with the reconciliation effected through the wisdom of Benjamin Rush, reveals that politics will always require the leavening effects of prudence and friendship. I conclude that the sensible approach to politics adopted at the time of the American founding, which was sufficiently attentive to the Socratic insight concerning man's deficiencies while maintaining an Aristotelian appreciation of man's capacity for virtue, provides us with a model worthy of emulation.

Chapter One

Socratic Friendship and Man's Desire for the Good

Lysis

In his "Second Letter," Plato informs us that his writings present a Socrates "become young and beautiful" (*Letters*, 2.314c). If this is the case, Plato's writings present at least some difficulty in distinguishing the true "historical" Socrates from the Socrates made young and beautiful. This difficulty is only heightened by Socrates's well-known self-deprecation and irony. Thus, not only do we receive a portrait of Socrates that is potentially highly idealized, but we are also further hampered in our efforts to attain a portrait of the "real" Socrates due to his dissembling dialectics. However, Plato chooses to write nine dialogues in narrative form, four of which are narrated in their entirety by Socrates (*The Republic*, *Lysis*, *The Lovers*, and *Charmides*).[1] In these dialogues, Socrates himself conveys not only the conversations in which he engages, but his activities and reflections as well. As a result, although these dialogues may not obviate the problem of distinguishing the "historical" Socrates from the Socrates made young and beautiful, they may enable us to distinguish more clearly Socrates's dialectical arguments from his true intentions. These dialogues provide us with a window into Socrates's character in a way that most other dialogues do not, granting us a particularly clear picture of who Plato believed Socrates to be.[2]

In the *Lysis*, Socrates recounts to an unnamed audience how he happened to encounter a group of young men and boys at a palaestra—the site of a wrestling school—and, upon being invited to join the group, engaged in a short, but consequential conversation with two young boys about the topic of friendship. Despite the fact that the *Lysis* has been called *the* Platonic dialogue on friendship, what it teaches about friendship has been highly contested. Some scholars have argued that it is simply aporetic and contains no positive teaching. Pointing to Socrates's last line of the dialogue, in which he concludes, "What he who is a friend is we have not yet been able to discover" (*Lysis*, 223b9–10), these scholars maintain that the *Lysis* is one of Plato's earlier dialogues and presents a failed attempt at defining friendship. Others maintain that amidst the false starts and inconclusive arguments, the *Lysis* does present a coherent account of friendship or, at the very least, points toward what a friend is. For example, taking her bearings from the dramatic date of the dialogue, which she places at 406—occurring between the *Euthydemus* and the *Gorgias*—Catherine Zuckert argues that by showing the boys "that they did not know what a friend is," Socrates acted as a friend toward them.[3] Still others, such as David Bolotin, have pointed toward the inconclusive ending of the dialogue in order to show that it contains a teaching pertaining to man's metaphysical neediness. According to this argument, Plato holds that all friendship and desire have their roots in man's need for completion.[4]

What is it about this dialogue that lends itself to such different, even contradictory, interpretations? Partly it is that at least some of the arguments raised and eventually refuted by Socrates are neither fully fleshed out nor conclusively refuted. In fact, one of the possible definitions of friendship that Socrates raises is hardly even explored. As a result of the dialogue's elementary, and at times, even specious arguments some scholars in the nineteenth century went so far as to label it spurious, contending that Plato could not have written something containing so many eristic arguments.[5] Today, the authenticity of the *Lysis* is no longer disputed, but it is by and large agreed to be a genuine work.[6] However, the difficulty posed by the sophistic arguments remains: why would Plato present Socrates as failing to properly refute arguments and engaging in sophistic arguments, all while speaking to what are likely the youngest interlocutors in the entire Platonic corpus?

Diogenes Laertius relates that "on hearing Plato read the *Lysis*, Socrates exclaimed, 'By Heracles, what a number of lies this young man is telling about me!' "[7] To assume that Diogenes's recounting of Socrates's reaction to the dialogue is accurate would not prove Plato's depiction of Socrates to be erroneous. However, assuming its truth *would* point to a difference of opinion between Plato and Socrates on the topic of friendship. The contention that Plato's thought differs from that of Socrates and that Plato alludes to the differences between them in his dialogues has been suggested by a variety of authors. Gregory Vlastos makes the case that Plato's views developed over time and that while the dialogues composed earlier in his life are more Socratic in character, the dialogues written later represent Plato's independent thought.[8] In contrast, Catherine Zuckert has pointed to the limitations of this approach and makes the case that it is possible to distinguish Platonic and Socratic thought based on the dramatic content in and across the dialogues.[9] Zuckert describes her approach in the following way: "Plato's understanding is to be found in what he shows, first in individual dialogues, taken as a whole, and then in his corpus, read as a whole."[10] According to this approach, one cannot simply assume that Socrates speaks for Plato but must instead analyze the drama of the dialogue to ascertain the relationship between the two philosophers.

Applying Zuckert's interpretive framework, it is my contention that Plato intends for the *Lysis* to elucidate the disagreement between himself and Socrates on the topic of friendship, and that in the *Gorgias*—the dialogue Zuckert dates as immediately following the *Lysis*—he chronicles the political implications of Socrates's understanding of friendship. To this end, Plato writes the *Lysis* in such a way that it both points toward a more complete understanding of friendship, while also revealing a deficiency in Socrates's understanding of friendship. Specifically, Plato shows that in his haste to direct the young toward a life of contemplation, Socrates fails to give the concept of friendship the proper regard it deserves; a failure that has extremely negative political consequences. Plato presents Socrates raising serious arguments, but rejecting them in a facile, sophistic manner. Through this process, Plato leaves enough of a trail from which one can develop a fully coherent understanding of friendship.[11]

The Introduction: Panops, Hermes, and a Sleight of Hand

The *Lysis* begins by introducing the reader to characters and details that seem superfluous to what appears to be the dialogue's main inquiry: what is friendship? Socrates relates, "I was on my way from the Academy straight to the Lyceum, along the road outside the wall" (203a1–2). Both the Academy and the Lyceum are located outside of the walls of the city: the Academy to the north, and the Lyceum to the southeast. Socrates is therefore taking the circuitous route outside and around the city rather than choosing to go directly through the city itself. While we are not told *why* Socrates makes this choice, we are told that the road he was walking along was "outside the wall and close under the wall itself," and it is here that he chances upon Hippothales, Ctesippus, and some other youths outside the palaestra near the spring of Panops (203a2–7).[12] Panops, whose full name is Argus Panoptes, was the name of a local deity, whose name means all-seeing. According to Greek mythology, Panops was famous for his watchful gaze. Thus, the dialogue takes place near the edge of the city under watchful eyes.

Hippothales tries to induce Socrates to come inside the palaestra and talk with them. Plato seems purposefully to direct our attention to the location in which the conversation about friendship will take place, describing it as "a kind of enclosure set against the wall" and informing us that it was "built recently" (203b7–204a3). A palaestra is a place of instruction in both wrestling and other matters. Thus, the setting of the dialogue on friendship is a place of instruction—together the disputants will wrestle with one another in an attempt to come to a conclusion as to who or what a friend is.[13] The fact that Socrates needs to enter the palaestra to engage in the discussion concerning friendship may suggest that he himself is in need of instruction. This interpretation is bolstered by the fact that Hippothales informs Socrates that the teacher at the palaestra is Socrates's "companion" and "praiser," Miccus (204a7). Socrates responds with an oath and relates that "the man is not an inferior one, but a capable sophist" (204a8–9). That the dialogue on friendship occurs in a place of instruction under the guidance of an instructor suggests that Socrates is not in an unambiguous position of superiority in this dialogue. Of course, Miccus does not instruct the participants of the conversation, but the fact that he is mentioned in the prologue and is recognized by Socrates as "a capable sophist" may suggest that Socrates's understanding is in some way deficient.[14]

Hippothales suggests that Socrates pass time with the group. He proposes that the group might share their speeches with him and that, together, they could observe the "good-looking" boys. Hippothales thus sets up the invitation as one in which all will share in the good things equally. Hippothales's invitation tells us that he has a relatively sanguine view of friendship. Indeed, the idea that they might share their speeches with Socrates brings to mind the adage that will come to impact the conversation later: "Friends have all things in common" (cf. 207c9–11). In contrast, Socrates's response indicates the opposite. While interested, he replies that he would prefer first to hear "what terms [he is] to enter on and who the good-looking one is" (204b1–2). Socrates's wariness of friendship is on display already at the beginning of the dialogue. He will not accept Hippothales's friendly invitation without knowing precisely what he is entering upon; Socrates suspects that friendships may involve a quid pro quo and are not something simply gratuitous or given solely for the sake of the other.

While Socrates's skepticism may be disconcerting, Plato points out that it is not—at least in this case—completely unwarranted, as it soon becomes clear that Hippothales likely has an ulterior motive in inviting Socrates to join the group. Hippothales is quickly revealed to be "in love" (ἔρωτος) with one of the good-looking ones. Indeed, when Socrates pushes him to reveal whom *he* believes the good-looking one to be, Hippothales blushes, apparently out of modesty or bashfulness. Socrates then tells Hippothales that he can see that Hippothales is not only in love, but that he is also "far along the way in love already" (204b8–9). Thus, the dialogue on friendship begins with a young man who is *in love*. In fact, the term *love* (ἔρως) enters into the discussion prior to the term *friend* (φίλος), implicitly suggesting that for Socrates love takes primacy over friendship. Socrates continues, making note of his knowledge of erotic matters: "I am inferior and useless in other things, but this has somehow been given to me from a god—to be able quickly to recognize both a lover and a beloved" (204b9–c2). Socrates refers to his divine gift and suggests that his knowledge of erotic matters is his *only* area of expertise. Later on, he will tell us that he has no knowledge of what a friend is. Given Socrates's distinction between friendship and erotic love, we may wonder whether he is useless when it comes to friendship, or whether perhaps his sole fixation on erotic love causes him to give short shrift to the concept of friendship.

Socrates points out that his capacity to recognize lover and beloved is a useful one. In response, Hippothales blushes "still much more" (204c3). This time however, it is not clear that he blushes from bashfulness alone; perhaps Hippothales blushes from the shame of having his friendly invitation to Socrates uncovered as having an ulterior motive; enlisting his help in discerning whether his beloved is endeared toward him.

In any case, Ctesippus breaks in, noting that all this false modesty is a little much coming from a man who is so in love with the young boy, Lysis, that he constantly sings his praises, much to the annoyance of his friends. Ctesippus goes on to detail how Hippothales sings songs of praise about Lysis that include songs regarding Lysis's family's past exploits, and his family's mythical connection to the gods. When Socrates hears this, he rebukes Hippothales, strongly declaring his actions to be "ridiculous." He notes, "Whoever is wise in love-matters . . . does not praise his beloved before he catches him" (206a2–3), for in doing so, the lover simply fills the beloved with "proud thoughts and bragging," making him "harder to capture" (206a4–5). After this, Hippothales finally confesses to his ulterior motives in conversing with Socrates, noting, "It's because of these things, Socrates, that I'm consulting with you. And if you have anything else, give your advice as to what to say in conversation or what to do so that someone might become endeared to his favorite" (206c1–4). Socrates agrees to make a "display" of what it is Hippothales needs to say to Lysis to ensure his love is requited, and the group begins to design a scheme whereby they may induce Lysis into conversation.

It is at this point that we are informed that the dialogue on friendship is taking place during the Hermaea, a festival in honor of the god Hermes. Hermes was not only the patron of the palaestra, but he was also known as the god of tricks who would commit thefts and other shameful acts, the god who transgressed boundaries, and the god who would outwit other gods in order to help human beings.[15] In fact, it is precisely this penchant for crossing boundaries that allows Socrates and the other older youths to associate with Lysis. As part of their scheming, Hippothales notes that "since they're observing the Hermaea, the youths and the boys are mingled in the same place" (207d1–3). The rules, or boundaries, surrounding appropriate relations are relaxed during the Hermaea, allowing the older youth to associate with the younger boys.[16] Thus, the setting for the dialogue has been carefully constructed: the very dialogue in which Plato is scrutinizing Socrates's understanding of friendship occurs during a festival in honor of a deity who deceives other deities in order to help humans transgress their limits.

That the dialogue occurs during the Hermaea is significant not only because of Hermes's status as the god who helps human beings transgress their limits, but also due to Hermes's relation with Panops. As will be recalled, at the very beginning of the dialogue, Socrates relates that he was stopped near the "spring of Panops." The references to Panops and Hermes—the only references to deities (aside from oaths) in the entire dialogue—is not accidental. As it turns out, the two deities figure prominently in the Greek myth of Io. In this myth, Io the river goddess is transformed by Zeus into a cow and is being guarded by Argus Panoptes (Panops)—a deity whose one hundred eyes never all sleep at the same time—to ensure that she does not transform from a cow back into a deity. Hermes rescues Io by telling Argus Panoptes incredibly long tales until he falls asleep, at which point he cuts off Panoptes's head, setting Io free.[17] Why would Plato allude to this story—a story recounting the primordial crime of the first murder among the gods—in the dialogue concerning friendship? As the remainder of the dialogue indicates, Socrates effects a similar transformation to that effected by Hermes. Through the use of sophistic arguments, Socrates manages to transform friendship into love under the watchful eyes of Plato.

A False Start

When the group enters the palaestra, Socrates relates that the boys are all dressed up, playing knucklebones, a game of chance. The fact that these boys are all dressed up and seem to take their game of chance quite seriously may indicate that friendship in general, or at least the carefree friendship of children, is taken much too seriously. The scene also reinforces the fact that the boys in the palaestra are quite young. The boys' young age makes Socrates's subsequent conversation with them all the more scandalous. Indeed, in what follows, he engages in a conversation with the boys that can be broken up into three parts: First, he speaks with both Lysis and his friend Menexenus as to the nature and purpose of their friendship. Next, he speaks with Lysis alone, questioning the love Lysis's parents have for him. Last, he again speaks with both Lysis and Menexenus as to who or what a friend is. In the course of the latter two portions of the conversation Socrates makes use of a variety of questionable claims and eristic arguments. These claims and arguments are used to question not only the young boys' relationship with one another, but also their other relationships, such as those they have with their parents and with the city itself. Socrates seems to be using sophisms and eristic arguments to undermine the children's existing attachments. Based on the depiction of Socrates in this dialogue, one gets the sense that the charge of corrupting the youth leveled against him in the *Apology* may not have been unwarranted.

The conversation begins with a false start. Once Lysis and Menexenus have come over to join the conversation—a mini-drama itself, which requires the more forthright Menexenus first to join the group before his more bashful friend Lysis summons the courage to join them—Socrates begins by asking them which of them is older. Rather than beginning the inquiry into friendship with a "what is" question, as he is prone to do in other dialogues, Socrates begins by exposing a quality of friendship.[18] Indeed, the question posed is seemingly designed to uncover a source of conflict between the two young boys, who are roughly the same age. Menexenus confirms this, stating, "We dispute about that" (207b13). Socrates's question suggests that he seems already to have some idea of what friendship is.

Socrates continues to ask questions that bring out the competitive nature of their friendship, including who is more *noble* (γενναιότερος) and who more *beautiful* (καλλίων). Last, he asks them about their wealth. Citing the well-known adage, he states, "Well the things of friends are said to be in common, so you [two] won't differ in . . . respect [to wealth], if indeed you [two] are speaking the truth about your friendship" (207c9–11). Both Lysis and Menexenus agree. Doubt has already been raised implicitly earlier on in the dialogue as to whether friends have all things in common, and it seems that Socrates is pursuing this line of inquiry. As friends who are similar to one another in age and nobility, Lysis and Menexenus naturally compete with one another, and while it is certainly possible for them also to compete about who is more wealthy, the boys seem to be sufficiently wellborn to recognize that competition in such matters is unseemly. Thus, Socrates's probing questions have uncovered that at the heart of their friendship lies a desire in each of them to strive after what is good for themselves. Socrates is about to pursue the inquiry into whether all things are held in common by asking them "which one was juster and wiser," but is interrupted when Menexenus is called away (207d1–4).

The question of which of the two boys is juster and wiser is a potentially fruitful avenue of inquiry for *who* or *what* a friend is. Indeed, are justice and wisdom, like age and nobility, things about which friends compete? Socrates sought to frame the question in a compound manner—"I was attempting to question them as to which one was juster and wiser" (207d1–4)—thereby giving the boys the option to agree that while the one is more just, the other is wiser. In this way, justice and wisdom would *not* be like the other things about which friends compete. Indeed, the two would not simply strive against one another in a bid to outdo each other, as they do when they argue about who is older or more noble but would instead recognize each other's strengths. Perhaps, their differing strengths could even be recognized as complementary.[19] The complementarity of Lysis and Menexenus is intimated at various points of the dialogue. Recall, for example, that the bashful Lysis would not join the group until the more forthright Menexenus had joined (207a3–b5). Similarly, later in the conversation, after Socrates perplexes Menexenus, and Lysis volunteers to take over for him, Socrates notes, "Since I wished to give Menexenus a rest and was also pleased by [Lysis's] love of wisdom [φιλοσοφία], I turned to Lysis and began to make my arguments to him" (213d8–e1). Plato draws our attention to the fact that the brash Menexenus and the wise and bashful Lysis have complementary strengths. However, Socrates's attempt to ask which one is "juster and wiser" is frustrated, as Menexenus is called away "to supervise the sacred rites" as part of the Hermaea (207d–4). Before the inquiry into the nature of friendship continues, Hermes, the god of tricks and transgression of boundaries, receives a sacrificial victim.

Socratic Sophisms and a Sacrificial Victim

At this point, the conversation takes a sharp turn. From the conversation that follows, it seems that the sacrificial victim Hermes requires as payment for helping man transgress his boundaries and have a share of the divine lot is Lysis's friendships. Indeed, rather than discovering the complementarity of Lysis and Menexenus, Socrates's line of questioning causes Lysis to question all his existing friendships. In stark contrast to Hippothales's love songs, which speak of the exploits of Lysis's family, Socrates immediately sets Lysis against his family. First, by means of a faulty argument, Socrates intimates that Lysis's parents do not love him. He begins by asking Lysis whether his parents love him and whether they want him to be happy. Lysis predictably answers that of course his parents love him and want him to be happy. Next, Socrates asks him whether it would be possible to be happy if one were a slave, "and if it were not possible for him to do anything he desired" (207e1–3). When Lysis answers no, Socrates, asks whether his parents, therefore, allow him to do whatever he desires, since he avers that they want him to be happy. Of course, Lysis relates that they do prevent him from doing a great number of things. Socrates drives the point home by purposefully asking Lysis about various activities that he knows his parents will not allow him to do, such as riding his father's chariots in a competition, driving the mules, or even ruling over himself. Socrates further elicits from Lysis that his parents trust hirelings or slaves with these tasks, while preventing Lysis himself from undertaking them. It seems that Socrates's point in pursuing this line of questions is to suggest to Lysis that his parents do not love him and seek to prevent him from doing what he desires. Socrates seems purposefully to be driving Lysis to resent his parents on the grounds that they don't love him.

The implied conclusion of Socrates's line of questioning is obviously false. It is not true that if Lysis's parents desire him to be happy, they would allow him to do whatever he wants. Following one's desires, whatever they happen to be, does not lead to happiness. This is made eminently clear in *The Republic*, where Socrates depicts the tyrannical soul as a destructively desirous soul that acts against its own wishes by following its every desire (*Republic*, 579a–c). Lysis likely does not recognize what is at stake philosophically in Socrates's line of argumentation and instead asserts in conformity with what is conventionally appropriate that his parents prevent him from engaging in various activities because he is not yet old enough for these tasks. Socrates, however, skillfully directs Lysis away from the topic of age and leads him to recognize that it is because of his lack of understanding that his parents prevent him from racing chariots and driving the mule team. Whereas they grant him autonomy in such things as reading, writing, playing the lyre, and other activities of which he has an understanding, they deny him autonomy in the activities of which he lacks understanding.

Socrates continues, using Lysis's recognition that his parents prevent him from engaging in various activities to suggest that when his father recognizes Lysis is not only capable, but also superior to him in the things he is currently prevented from doing, his father will entrust himself and his entire estate to Lysis's management. At this point, Socrates begins to straightforwardly appeal to Lysis's ambition and desires. Not only will his father entrust his estate to him, but once his neighbor believes Lysis's household management skills are superior to his own, his neighbor will do so as well. In fact, once Lysis has the requisite skill and knowledge, the Athenians will hand over the keys of the city to him—the only thing preventing Lysis from ruling in the city is that he does not yet have the knowledge. Socrates concludes:

> With regard to the things in which we become prudent, everyone—Greeks as well as barbarians, and both men and women—will entrust them to us. . . . But with regard to those things in which we don't acquire good sense, no one will entrust [them to us] . . . but everyone will obstruct us as much as is in his power—not merely aliens, but even our father and mother and whatever may be more closely or akin to us than they are. (*Lysis*, 210a9–c3)

Good sense, Socrates argues, is all that is required for imperial rule. Of course, Socrates's argumentation fails to acknowledge the possibility that others may not recognize Lysis's good sense. Good sense alone is not enough to obtain power. What is most striking, however, is Socrates's statement that to the extent we do not have good sense, "everyone will obstruct us as much as is in his power." One *could* charitably interpret Socrates's overall intention in this part of the dialogue to be an attempt to make Lysis recognize his own deficiency and thereby spur him toward self-improvement and the acquisition of "good sense." However, this particular line of the argument seems to cast doubt on this interpretation, as it introduces an antagonistic element into all of Lysis's relationships that would seem to be unnecessary if Socrates's sole intention was to cause Lysis to recognize his deficiency. The implication is that no one loves another for his own sake, but only in so far as he has good sense and will be beneficial.

Thus far, Socrates has appealed to Lysis's competitive and ambitious nature to cause him radically to question his existing relationships and to view them all in terms of utility and need. However, after having fed Lysis's vanity and ambition, Socrates cuts him down to size. He relates, "Now, therefore, not even your father loves you, nor does anyone else love anyone else insofar as he is useless" (210c8–9). Friendship, Socrates argues, depends upon wisdom. If Lysis becomes wise, he will be useful and good, but if he fails to do so "no one else will be your friend, and neither will your father, nor your mother, nor your own kinsmen" (210d2–4). It is important to note that according to Socrates, not only will his father and his mother not love him, but his entire political community will also disown him. While the main point is to humble Lysis, we can see here that Socrates's understanding of friendship is somewhat problematic, as political friendships are equated with the love parents have for their children, with no distinction.

At this point in the conversation, Lysis has been shown to have knowledge in some areas (reading, writing, and playing the lyre), and to lack knowledge in others (chariot racing and mule driving). However, Socrates drives home Lysis's lack of wisdom by means of another fallacious argument, which ends with the conclusion that Lysis does not have *any* knowledge. He asks Lysis, "Is it possible . . . for someone to think big, in regard to those matters in which he's not yet thinking?" (210d4–5). Lysis responds that it would be impossible. Socrates follows up by stating (not asking), "And if you require a teacher, you're not yet thoughtful" (210d6–7). When Lysis concurs, Socrates concludes that "your thoughts are not [too] big, if indeed you're still thoughtless" (210d7–8).

In making this argument, Socrates is engaging in a deliberate sophism, in the same way and regarding the same topic as the Sophists in the *Euthydemus*. It will be helpful to relate the scene from the *Euthydemus* to emphasize the similarity between Socrates's argument and that of the Sophists. In the *Euthydemus*, two Sophists named Euthydemus and Dionysodorus heckle a young boy named Cleinias with eristic arguments, designed to tangle him up in knots, by equivocating on the term *to learn*. Euthydemus asks Cleinias whether those who learn are the wise or the ignorant. No matter which way Cleinias answers, the two Sophists are able to refute him. When Cleinias first answers that the wise learn, the Sophists point to the fact that those students who learn from their teachers are "unlearned" at the time of their learning. However, when Cleinias agrees that the ignorant are the ones who learn, the Sophists immediately point out that when the teacher dictates things, it is the wise boys, rather than the unlearned boys, who learn the dictation. No matter how Cleinias answers, the Sophists are able to refute him. After this display of sophistry, Socrates consoles Cleinias:

> Our two visitors are pointing out this very thing, that you did not realize that people use the word "learn" not only in the situation in which a person who has no knowledge of a thing in the beginning acquires it later, but also when he who has this knowledge already uses it to inspect the same thing. . . . Now this, as they are pointing out, had escaped your notice—that the same word is applied to opposite sorts of men, to both the man who knows and the man who does not. . . . These things are the frivolous part of study . . . and I call these things "frivolity" because even if a man were to learn many or even all such things, he would be none the wiser as to how matters stand. (*Euthydemus*, 277e4–278b5)

By equivocating on the term *to learn*, the Sophists have refuted Cleinias. It is precisely this same tactic that Socrates uses against Lysis.[20] The statement "if you require a teacher, you're not yet thoughtful" can be either true or false depending on what the term *thoughtful* (φρονεῖν) means. The ambiguity of the term renders Socrates's question sophistic, as it can mean both "to understand" and "to think."[21] Indeed, if thoughtful means "to understand," then it would be correct to state that the fact Lysis needs a teacher means he does not yet "understand." However, if thoughtful simply means "to think," then the syllogism would be incorrect. It is not true that simply because Lysis needs a teacher, he does not yet "think." As Benjamin Rider points out, "A student spends a lot of time *thinking* about his subject; he just thinks deficiently and needs a teacher to help him *understand* it."[22] Socrates equivocates on the term φρονεῖν in a manner that is strikingly similar to the way the Sophists equivocate on the term *to learn*.

After this sophism, the demonstration is finished. Socrates has led Lysis to the conclusion that he is not wise. In addition, he has caused him to question his existing relationships—primarily, but not exclusively, his relationship with his parents. At this point, Socrates looks over at Hippothales and nearly blurts out, "This, Hippothales, is how one needs to converse with his favorite, by humbling him and drawing in his sails instead of puffing him up and spoiling him, as you do" (*Lysis*, 210e3–6). Hippothales's gratification of Lysis through constant songs of praise only has the effect of spoiling him and leads to vanity. To "catch" one's beloved, Socrates shows, it is necessary to shake him from his complacency and show him that he is *not*, in fact, self-sufficient.

Why does Plato present Socrates as using sophistic arguments to make his point? According to James Rhodes, Socrates is not being serious either when he questions whether the boy's parents love him or when he suggests that all friendships stem from the utility they obtain. Instead, Rhodes insists that these arguments are simply a dialectic ploy meant to "bamboozle" Lysis and are part of a larger attempt to correct a moral failing on the part of Lysis. He writes, "when we mean to take the wind out of a person's sails, we need not resolve that every word we utter be true. It suffices to contrive that our speech, true or false, will deflate our victim."[23] Thus, according to Rhodes, Socrates uses sophistic arguments simply to cut Lysis down to size and cause him to recognize that utility cannot be the basis of friendship.[24] While this is possible, it seems to be only a partial answer, as it fails to account for why sophistic arguments are necessary for this purpose. Presumably, Socrates would be capable of constructing non-sophistic arguments that have the effect of belittling Lysis. Furthermore, it fails to account for the striking similarity between Socrates's approach and the approach adopted by the Sophists in the *Euthydemus*; Plato seems to go out of his way to a draw a parallel between these two dialogues.[25]

To avoid this problem, Benjamin Rider argues that Socrates makes use of sophistic arguments in an effort to draw Lysis into the philosophic life. Focusing on Lysis's competitive character, Rider argues that Socrates uses Lysis's penchant for eristic games by raising "interesting and worthy problems," so as to encourage him to apply his "skills in competitive argument to doing real philosophy."[26] While this may seem to be a plausible interpretation, one of the difficulties with it—one with which Rider does not contend—is that it is not clear that Lysis is ever led to pursue "real philosophy" or the life of contemplation. If Lysis has not been led to pursue the life of contemplation but has instead simply been led to question his existing relationships, Socrates may be acting in a reckless fashion; a recklessness that the end of the dialogue intimates.[27]

The recklessness of Socrates's activity is revealed more immediately when Menexenus rejoins the conversation. Upon his return, Lysis turns to Socrates and whispers to him, asking him to repeat the conversation to Menexenus. Presumably Lysis desires Menexenus to go through the same humiliating experience he has just undergone. Socrates counsels Lysis to tell Menexenus himself, instructing him to remember everything clearly: "Try, then . . . to remember it as well as possible, so you can tell him everything clearly. And if you forget any of it, ask me again, when you first happen to come across me" (211a10–13). Curiously, this type of regurgitative teaching is not in keeping with Socrates's ordinary style, which is to consider the character and soul-type of his interlocutor.[28] Might Plato be suggesting that Socrates is too quick to disabuse the young of their existing conceptions of friendship? In any case, the fact that Socrates's conversation with Lysis has had an effect on him becomes clear when Lysis reveals that his overriding concern is for Socrates to "chasten" Menexenus. As Bolotin notes, "In order to overcome his own humiliation, he arranges by stealth to have the returning Menexenus chastened, and not just ridiculed, in his presence. This is no mere continuation of their friendly rivalry. Lysis's action, while playful and harmless enough, contains the seeds of betrayal."[29] It seems that Socrates's earlier conversation has, in fact, caused Lysis to turn on his friend.[30]

What Is Friendship?

Socrates agrees to Lysis's demand that he converse with Menexenus and initiates the conversation by delivering a long speech about his desire to have a friend. He congratulates the boys on their friendship, noting, "I am so far from the possession that I don't even know the manner in which one becomes a friend of another" (212a3–4). Socrates's disclamation of any knowledge regarding friendship sits in stark contrast with his claim to have a divine dispensation concerning erotic matters. At this point, friendship and erotic love seem still to be clearly distinguished, although Socrates's disquisition concerning his desire to have a friend may perhaps foreshadow Socrates's conflation of the two terms, given the association of erotic love with desire.

Calling on Menexenus's "expertise" in friendship, Socrates asks him the following question: "When someone loves (φιλῇ) someone, which one becomes a friend (φίλος) of the other, the loving (φιλῶν) of the loved (φιλουμένου), or the loved (φιλούμενος) of the loving (φιλοῦτος)? Or is there no difference?" (212a10–b2). What seems to be straightforward question is in fact a minefield of ambiguity. As A. W. Price points out, Socrates's initial interaction with Menexenus contains three senses, or usages, of the term φίλος:

> (i) Reciprocal and equivalent to our "friend"; usually conveyed by a pair of correlative pronouns (212a6, c8), once by a conjunction of the active and passive moods of the verb *philein* (213a6–7), and once simply by the plural "the *philoi*" (213a7). (ii) Neuter and passive, meaning "dear"; often followed by a personal dative (most explicitly at 212e6, and introduced by a list of *philo*-compounds (for instance, "horse-lover," "dog-lover," 212d5–7). (iii) Masculine and active, meaning "fond"; often followed by a genitive (most explicitly at 213b5–6).[31]

This dizzying array of different usages of the term φίλος allows Socrates to switch between the various meanings of the term throughout his first colloquy with Menexenus, leading to their failure to adequately define what a friend is.

Menexenus answers that in his opinion it makes no difference which of the two loves the other; so long as one of the two individuals loves the other, the two will both become friends. Socrates notes that this cannot be. Using the verb φιλεῖν (to love), Socrates notes that it is possible for one to love and not be loved in return. To explicate this, he provides the example of a lover (ἐραστής) who, even though he loves (φιλοῦντες) as much as possible, supposes that he is not loved in return (οὐκ ἀντιφιλεῖσθαι). While Socrates's example seems to be simply a particularly acute case of non-reciprocal friendship, his use of the term ἐραστής is significant, as it connotes a more passionate love bound up with desire than the term φίλος (friend) ordinarily implies. As will be made clear, Socrates's use of ἐραστής is not simply to provide an acute example of non-reciprocal love, but it again foreshadows the way in which the ordinary sense of the term friendship or φιλία will ultimately be transformed into love or ἔρως by the end of the dialogue. In any case, because it would be ridiculous to say that there is friendship between the ἐραστής and his indifferent beloved, Socrates and Menexenus tentatively conclude that love must be reciprocal.

Shortly afterwards, Socrates notes that it would then be improper to call those who love inanimate objects lovers. Using the masculine noun φίλοι,

Socrates asks whether the poet Solon was lying when he said, "Prosperous is he who has children as friends (φίλοι), together with single-hoofed horses, Dogs for the hunt, and a guest-friend in a foreign land?" (212e3–4). Using the masculine noun, Socrates is able to show that in everyday discourse, people speak—in a colloquial way—of being friends not only with animals but also with inanimate objects: lovers of dogs, lovers of wine, or lovers of wisdom. Thus, according to Solon's approach, friendship need not be reciprocal, and can exist even if the one who is loved does not return the love, but in fact hates his lover. Assuming that Solon did not speak incorrectly, they tentatively conclude, now using the neuter noun, that "that which is loved . . . is a friend (φίλον) to the lover . . . whether it loves or even if it hates" (212e6–8). According to this account, "it's not the one who loves who is a friend but the loved one" (213a5–6). However, this definition proves to be obviously problematic as well, as it leads to the conclusion that "many . . . are loved by their enemies and hated by their friends" (213a8–b2). Socrates and Menexenus agree that this conclusion is absurd but, given the way Socrates has framed the question, there is no evident path forward.

Socrates suggests that they turn away from the semantic difficulties associated with the concept of friendship and seek help from the poets instead. Doing so clears the way to get at the *ground* of friendship. Indeed, the poets assert that "always a god leads [the one who is] like to [the one who is] like" (214a8). Thus, for the poets, the gods are the cause of friendship, and they lead those who are alike to become friends. Ostensibly, Socrates turns to the poets because they are, "as it were, our fathers in wisdom and our guides" (214a1–2). However, a short while later, Socrates will invoke a second poet, Hesiod, in support of a completely contradictory principle: those who are most alike to one another are "most filled with envy, love of victory, and hatred toward each other," while those most unlike one another are filled with friendship (215d1–4). According to Socrates's interpretation of Hesiod's poetry, those who are opposite will be friends. If fathers are, indeed, like the poets as Socrates suggests, they would also say contradictory things (cf. *NE*, 1180a19–29). Socrates's point in invoking the poets as "our fathers in wisdom" seems to be a further attempt to undermine Lysis's trust in his parents; neither a parent's love nor the veracity of his claims ought to be taken as a matter of trust. Instead, recourse to philosophy is necessary.

Perhaps as a result of the unreliability of the poets, Socrates invokes the authority of certain philosophers "who converse and write about nature and the whole" in support of the contention that "like is always necessarily a friend to its like" (*Lysis*, 214b2–6).[32] However, in bringing up these philosophers, Socrates engages in a somewhat curious dance regarding how they should react to the statement that like is a friend to like. He first notes that perhaps the philosophers only speak well in half of what they say, because it would be impossible for those who are wicked to be friends with one another, as they would do injustice to one another. Next, he alternatively suggests that perhaps the philosophers speak well in all of what they say, "only we don't understand them" (214b8–10). Why would Plato present Socrates as uncertain of the soundness of the philosophers' statement? Could it be that Plato is suggesting that Socrates does not understand these philosophers? In the *Phaedo*, when he recounts Socrates's famous turn from investigations concerning nature and the whole to what is distinctively human, Plato tells us that Socrates had "no natural aptitude" for natural philosophy (*Phaedo*, 96c1–2). Similarly, in the *Metaphysics*, Aristotle informs us that Socrates ignored the study of nature (*Metaphysics*, 987b1–4).[33] It may be that by presenting Socrates as unsure of the philosophers' statement, Plato is pointing to a flaw in Socrates's intellectual capacity, a flaw that influences his understanding of friendship. To understand the human things, one must understand human nature.

In any case, accepting that the wicked cannot be friends with one another—as they are at variance with even themselves—Socrates and the boys posit that the philosophers must mean that it is the good who are friends to one another. However, Socrates complicates this possibility as well, asking, "Is he who is like, insofar as he is like, a friend to his like, and is such a one useful to such a one?" (*Lysis*, 214e6–7). This difficulty cuts to the heart of the dialogue. By juxtaposing "the good" with "the useful," Socrates is able to uncover the fundamental question concerning friendship. Is it possible to have a friendship that is based solely on self-sufficiency, where both parties to the friendship admire and love one another for their own sake? Or are all friendships rooted in deficiency and need? The difficulty is that in so far as a person is good, he would be self-sufficient and would not be in need of any other individual. As Socrates notes, "Would anything whatsoever which is like anything whatsoever have the power to hold out any benefit to it, or to do it any harm, which that couldn't also do itself to itself?" (214e8–10). A completely self-sufficient individual, Socrates suggests, would have no need of anyone else and, hence, would have no reason to treasure another individual. Because it would be absurd to claim that friendship exists among those who do not treasure one another, Socrates and Menexenus conclude that the basis of friendship cannot be the extent to which the parties are the same.

At this point, Socrates tries to take another tack and suggests that two individuals who are good might be friends with one another insofar as they are good and *not* insofar as they are alike. The idea seems to be that two people who are good, but nevertheless differ in some other respect, may be friends. However, Socrates quickly points out that the difficulty with this proposition is, again, that as self-sufficient individuals who are "in want of nothing," these good individuals would have no reason to treasure one another, and as such would not love one another (215a7–9). As a result, because such individuals have no use for one another, they would not be friends. In his earlier conversation with Lysis alone, Socrates had suggested that all of Lysis's friends—including his parents and fellow citizens—are friends with him only to the extent to which he is useful. Now, Socrates again asserts that it is need that causes one to befriend another. Before he turns to the next possibility of who may be friends, Socrates asks Lysis, "Consider then, where we have gone astray. Are we somehow being deceived in the whole?" (214c3–4). Plato again seems to draw our attention to the fact that Socrates may not have a full grasp of "the whole," or that his knowledge is only partial. Perhaps there is something in the saying of the "wisest ones" who study "nature and the whole" that Socrates does not fully understand.[34]

Socrates now brings up another possibility for the basis of friendship, noting that he once heard someone say "that what is like was most hostile to its like, and that those who are good [were most hostile] to the good" (215c4–7). According to this understanding of friendship, it is precisely those who are most unlike who will be friends with each other; the poor and the wealthy will be friends, as will the weak and the strong. In fact, according to Socrates's source, the principle that all opposites desire one another extends to all of nature, such that "what is dry desires [something] wet, [and] what is cold [something] hot" (215e3–5). In contrast, those who are alike can derive no use or advantage from one another and are not friends.

Socrates asks Menexenus whether this "oppositional" account of friendship seems to be a correct understanding of friendship. When Menexenus agrees, Socrates immediately points to the obvious difficulty with this conception of friendship: if opposites are friends, then it would be the case that an enemy—the opposite of a friend—would be "a friend to the friend" (216b3–4). It would, of course, be absurd to claim that an enemy is a friend. However, the proposition that all opposites desire one another, would seem to entail this conclusion. As a result of this absurd but logically necessary consequence, Socrates concludes that the "oppositional" account of friendship is incorrect: friendship does not exist between opposite entities.

However, in his depiction of this exchange, Plato seems to present Socrates as being much too quick to dismiss the "oppositional" conception of friendship. Introducing the refutation of the "oppositional" conception of friendship, Socrates asks, won't the "all-wise men, the ones skilled in contradicting, be pleased to leap upon us straightway and ask whether hatred isn't most opposite to friendship?" (216a8–b1). Plato seems to go out of his way to emphasize that only eristic debaters and the "all-wise" who are "skilled in contradicting" would try to exploit this linguistic difficulty rather than get to the root of what the "oppositional" conception of friendship entails.[35] Plato suggests that by accepting the linguistic objection, Socrates is, in fact, acting like one of these eristic all-wise men who are skilled in contradicting.

Socratic Friendship

Given the failure of the two previous definitions, Socrates now proposes his own definition, suggesting that "whatever is neither good nor bad may thus at some times become a friend of the good" (216c2–4). He continues noting: "I am really dizzy myself from the perplexity of the argument, and it may be[36]—as the old saying goes—that what is beautiful is a friend. It seems, at any rate, like something soft, smooth, and sleek. And that is why, perhaps, it easily slides past us and gives us the slip, inasmuch as it is such" (216c5–d2). A number of indicators suggest that this is not simply another definition, but is, in fact, a turning point in the dialogue. First, Socrates's definition drops the requirement that the friendship be reciprocal. He only states that "whatever is neither good nor bad" becomes a friend of the good; he does not state that the good becomes a friend in return. Furthermore, Socrates recognizes that friendship has been giving them the slip and admits that the perplexity of the argument has left him dizzy. In fact, he's so dizzy that he settles on the *possibility* "that what is beautiful (τό καλόν) is a friend." Why would Socrates be content with a mere possibility? The answer, I believe, is that by suggesting that the beautiful is a friend, Socrates is admitting defeat as to the question of what "friendship" is. At this point in the dialogue, Socrates is beginning to lay the groundwork for transforming friendship into erotic love. Indeed, in the *Symposium* Socrates recounts how Diotima sought to initiate him into erotic matters by explaining to him how the beautiful acts as a spur to philosophical contemplation of the form of the good and the beautiful (*Symposium*, 210a4–b6). Diotima develops a "ladder of love," whereby one's initial encounter with the beautiful in the form of a particular person gives way to increasingly abstract encounters with the class of beautiful things until at last one contemplates the form of the beautiful. As we will see, Socrates's suggested definition of friendship is very much akin to this "ladder of love."

Socrates finally elaborates on his definition of friendship. Noting that he is speaking "as a diviner"—we are not told whether his divination comes from a friendly source or not[37]—he states that "whatever is neither good nor bad is a friend of the beautiful and good" (*Lysis*, 216d3–8). By finding a middle category—a neutral state between good and bad—Socrates avoids the difficulties that beset the previous definitions of friendship. Of course, it is precisely the existence of this neutral, middle state that Diotima discloses to Socrates in the *Symposium*. Diotima tells Socrates that Eros (the δαίμων of desire) is something between the good and the bad, or between the beautiful and the ugly (*Symposium*, 202b1–5). This parallel seems further to indicate that the transformation from friendship to erotic love is underway.

At this point none of the logical problems that hindered the previous definitions of friendship threaten to undermine Socrates's proposed definition. However, it is not yet clear *why* the neutral would seek out the good. This difficulty is brought to the fore when Socrates analogizes human desire for friendship or love to the human body's desire for the medical art. A healthy body has no need of the medical art due to its "sufficient" condition (*Lysis*, 217a6). It is only insofar as the body is diseased that it seeks out the medical art. Socrates emphasizes, however, that when the disease is in its initial stages the body itself remains neutral—it has not yet become bad. As a result, the body (neutral) seeks the medical art (good) because of the presence of a disease (bad). Similarly, an individual only has need of the good when some evil is present, causing it to desire the good. However, if the evil has been allowed to fester and caused the individual to become bad, it "deprives [him] of the *desire*, at the same time as the *friendship*, of the good," because what is good cannot be a friend of what is bad (217b7–c1; emphasis added). At this point, we can see Socrates effecting the transformation of friendship into erotic love, as he strings together desire (characteristic of ἔρως) and friendship, indicating that Socrates believes them to be in some way related.

Next, Socrates extends this formulation to an individual's relation to wisdom. Neither those who are already wise nor those who are so ignorant as to be bad would love wisdom. Instead, it is only those "who while having this evil, ignorance, are not yet senseless or stupid as a result of it, but still regard themselves as not knowing whatever they don't know. And so therefore, the ones who are not yet either good nor bad love wisdom"

(218a7–b2). Why would Socrates extend his formula of "the neutral being a friend to the good" to cover the one who is partially ignorant as being a friend to wisdom? Socrates's primary purpose is to hold up the philosophic life and the pursuit of wisdom as that which can most fulfill one's desire for the good. However, in making this argument, he is also providing a response to the sophistic argument he had earlier used to belittle Lysis. During the earlier part of his conversation with Lysis, Socrates made use of the ambiguity of the term φρονεῖν (thoughtful) to belittle Lysis in front of Hippothales, suggesting that Lysis did not have any knowledge. Here, Socrates shows how one might be partially ignorant, and that a recognition of that ignorance is the first step to wisdom. In addition, Socrates shows how it was necessary for him to belittle Lysis, in order to make him aware of his ignorance. It is only once Lysis becomes cognizant of his ignorance that he may be impelled to the pursuit of wisdom.

In any case, Socrates concludes that they have "discovered that which is the friend. . . . For we assert . . . that whatever is neither bad nor good is itself, because of the presence of an evil a friend of the good" (218b8–c3), and he rejoices as a result. However, Socrates's happiness at having discovered "that which is the friend" is short-lived, as "some most strange suspicion came over me—from where, I don't know—that things we had agreed to were not true" (218c7–9). Socrates explains that the difficulty with this definition of friendship is that all friendships are pursued "for the sake of something" (218d8–9). Just as the body (which is neutral) becomes friends with the medical art (which is good) for the sake of health (which is also good), so a friend becomes a friend for the sake of a further friend. Socrates establishes a "ladder of friendship" that is strikingly similar to the "ladder of love" that Diotima develops in the *Symposium*. Of course, the implication is that no one becomes a friend to another for the sake of the other individual, but only so that the other can spur him on to higher friendships. Socrates notes that it is necessary "for us to renounce going on like this or else to arrive at some beginning principle," so that they might "come to that which is a friend in the first place" (219c).[38] Just as all the beautiful objects one encounters on the ascent up the "ladder of love" are pursued only for the sake of contemplating the "beautiful itself" (*Symposium*, 211d1), so the ordinary friendships that one has are for the sake of the "first friend."

In contrast to the *Symposium*, however, Socrates concludes not only that the lower objects on the "ladder" are for the sake of the "first friend," but also that they are, in fact, phantoms of the "first friend." Ordinary friends cannot even be considered friends as they are, in fact, "deceiving us," as they are qualitatively different from the first friend (*Lysis*, 219d1–5). Socrates's denunciation of ordinary friendship seems especially harsh. However, immediately after this, Socrates employs an analogy that pulls back on this harsh appraisal of friendship. He notes that upon discovering that his son has drunk hemlock, a father who "values his son more highly than all his other possessions" would treasure not only wine, which acts as an antidote to hemlock, but also the jar that carries the wine (219d5–220a1). These things are treasured, not for any intrinsic value they have, but only insofar as they are useful for the final good of healing the son. A father who recognizes the instrumental value of the wine and the jar, values them correctly. In the same way, an individual who recognizes the instrumental value of his ordinary friendships will value them correctly.

Why would Socrates first suggest that ordinary friendships involve only deceptive phantom friends, and then indicate that these friendships have the potential to be useful? Through this juxtaposition, Socrates seems to be suggesting that while friendships have the *potential* to spur one on to higher friendships, and ultimately to the contemplative life, they are also potentially debilitating. If a friendship leads to a sense of complacency or a false sense of self-sufficiency, the friendship will act as an impediment to the philosophic life. Thus, to the extent that any friendship is not directed toward the *first friend*, that is, toward the good, it is a phantom image of friendship. Socrates's implicit lesson here seems to be that friendship ought to impel one toward the good, and that friendships are *never* for their own sake.

While Socrates's introduction of the first friend theory calls into question many existing friendships, there is a logical difficulty with his introduction of the first friend theory as well. Indeed, this theory violates one of the principles established earlier; like cannot be a friend to its like. By formulating the ladder of friendship in such a way that the body (neutral) becomes a friend with the medical art (good), and that the medical art accepts the friendship for the sake of health (good), Socrates intimates that the medical art (good) desires health (good). Of course, because health and the medical art are both good, this would be a case of like becoming a friend to its like, which they had previously asserted to be impossible. While Socrates recognizes this problem, he states "this I allow to go by" (219b7–9).[39] Why would Socrates allow this to go by? Whereas previously he invoked the violation of this principle as a reason to discard a definition of friendship (214e6–215a5), now this violation is allowed to go by. It seems that Plato is, again, suggesting that Socrates is less interested in getting to the root of what friendship is than in driving forward a definition of friendship—a definition that encompasses friendship within the ambit of erotic love.

By establishing the first friend as the only *true* friend, Socrates has made clear that all friendship aims at the good, and that it does so because of the presence of something bad; all friendship has its roots in some deficiency or need. To explore whether this is, in fact, the only basis of friendship, Socrates engages in a thought experiment. First, he asks whether "that which is good is a friend" (220b7–8). When Menexenus agrees, Socrates follows up with a hypothetical question: Supposing that what is bad did not afflict us, would the good still be useful to us? If it is, in fact, the case that the first friend is a friend solely on account of the evils present in us, it would seem to be "of no use itself for its own sake" (220d7–8). When Menexenus responds that based on what has been said, it doesn't appear that the first friend would remain a friend to us in the absence of evil, Socrates responds with an oath. He asks whether in such a situation all desires would cease as well. Indeed, if that which is bad ceases to exist, would there still be hunger, thirst, or other desires?

The question, of course, cannot be answered, and Socrates—in recognition of this fact—asks, "Is the question ludicrous—what will be or will not be then? For who knows?" (221a1–6). What we do know, he suggests, is that even now it is possible for those with desires to desire in a manner that is beneficial for them (good desires), or in a manner that is detrimental to them (bad desires). For example, someone might have a desire for healthy foods or for unhealthy foods. As a result, if all bad things ceased to exist, only good desires would remain.[40] Having come to the conclusion that there may still be desires in the absence of evil, Socrates asks whether "it is possible for one who desires and who loves passionately (ἐρῶντα) not to love (φιλεῖν) [as a friend] that which he desires and loves passionately." When Menexenus answers that this would not be possible, Socrates concludes that "there will be, then, as it seems, some [things that are] friends, even if evils cease to be" (221b3–10). At this point, it seems that Socrates has found a basis for friendship that is *not* dependent on some evil, although it does have its basis in desire, and is therefore not distinguishable from erotic love.

Socrates picks up this thread of the argument, asking, "Is desire . . . really a cause of friendship?" (221d3–6). Securing Menexenus's agreement, Socrates asks whether it is the case that "that which desires desires whatever it is in want of?" and, if so, whether "what is in want, [is,] therefore, a friend of that which it is in want of?" (221d8–e3). Menexenus responds affirmatively to both questions. At this point, Socrates has secured the boys' agreement that all friendships have their basis in some perceived want or lack. Recall that the background assumption of Socrates's investigation at this point is that there is a basis for friendship independent of any evil. Thus, the want or lack that desire is responding to cannot be considered to be bad. In any case, Socrates continues, addresses Menexenus and Lysis by name, and tells them that it appears "passionate love, friendship and desire happen to be for what is akin" (221e4–6). Now, this is a curious statement. Why would one have a desire for what is akin (οἰκεῖον)? The difficulty resolves itself when we understand that the term οἰκεῖον can also be translated as "one's own." Thus, one desires what is one's own. As David Bolotin notes, the desire discussed here is not "like any desire or need, to acquire what belongs naturally to a single human being; instead, the desire or longing of each being is to belong to a larger whole of which he is merely a part."[41] Socrates notes that if Menexenus and Lysis are friends, they are "by nature in some way akin to each other" (221e7–8). If they are friends, Menexenus and Lysis *belong* to one another in some way; together they make up a composite whole. Both Menexenus and Lysis agree to this statement. It is perhaps not surprising that they do, as it seems to confirm that their friendship has its basis in nature.

Socrates concludes, "If someone desires another, boys, or loves him passionately, he would never desire, nor love passionately, nor love [as a friend] unless he happened to be akin in some way to his passionately beloved" (222a1–3). This time only Menexenus agrees, whereas Lysis falls silent. Socrates's statement—which broadens those who are akin to include not only those who are friends but also those who love passionately—may have prompted Lysis to ponder Hippothales's passionate love for him. Whether or not Lysis takes Socrates statement this way, it seems that Hippothales certainly does, for when he hears Socrates state that because it is "necessary for us to love what is akin by nature" it is necessary "for the passionate lover, who is genuine, and not pretended, to be loved by his favorite(s)," he "radiate[s] all sorts of colors as a result of his pleasure" (222a6–b3). At this point, it seems clear that Socrates has completed the transformation of friendship into passionate love. He has made clear that just as it is necessary for one to return the friendship (φιλία) of one who is akin by nature, it is equally necessary for one to return the love (ἔρως) of one who is akin by nature.

At this point, Socrates narrates to the reader that he "wish[ed] to examine the argument [for himself]" (222b4–5). Two things are important about this narration. First, Socrates expressly states that he now wishes to examine the argument for himself. This suggests that previously he was pursuing the argument, not for his own sake, but for the sake of his interlocutors. Perhaps Socrates has been conducting the argument in a particular way to lead the boys to this understanding of friendship. Second, Plato draws our attention to the fact that Socrates is in some way curious about the argument that friends might be akin to one another, or that he does not yet fully understand the argument, and therefore wishes to examine it further. Socrates turns to Lysis and Menexenus and states: "If what is akin differs in some respect from the like, we might be saying something, in my opinion, concerning what a friend is. But if it happens that like and akin are the same, it isn't easy to reject the previous argument, which says that what is like is useless to its like insofar as there is likeness" (222b4–9). Conceding that they are "drunk" from the argument, Socrates suggests that they simply grant and declare that "what is akin is something other than the like" (222c1–4). Thus, they do not even investigate whether this is, in fact, the case, but simply assume it. Again, Plato seems to be hinting at sloppy reasoning by Socrates. Socrates continues, "Shall we also, then, posit that what is good is akin to everyone, and that what is bad is alien? Or else [shall we posit] that what is bad is akin to the bad; that what is good is akin to the good; and that whatever is neither good nor bad is akin to whatever is neither good nor bad?" (222c4–8). The boys opt for the latter, and Socrates notes that this leads them back to the difficulties that plagued their earlier definitions of friendship; the bad and unjust will be friends with each other, no less than the good.

Socrates continues, suggesting that they avoid this difficulty by restricting what is akin to what is good—thereby excluding those who are bad. However, he quickly notes that this avenue also would not work, as "on this point, too, we supposed that we had refuted ourselves" (222d8). However, as Bolotin points out, the refutation that the good cannot be friends to the good was refuted only on the supposition that the good were self-sufficient, and therefore would be of no use to each other. As it is, the present argument rests on the presupposition that those who are akin are also good, and yet are *not* in every respect alike (222c1–3). Thus, it is not clear that the previous refutation holds as applied to the present argument. Could it not be that two individuals who are akin (or who belong to each other), are both good—and yet are good each in his own way, or according to his own *nature*?

Socrates initially began the conversation with Menexenus and Lysis by asking which of them was "juster and wiser." It was earlier posited that this was a potentially fruitful line of inquiry, as it allowed the boys the option of suggesting that one of them was more just, while the other was wiser. Furthermore, it was noted that throughout the dialogue Menexenus is presented as the more spirited or forthright of the two, while Lysis is presented as the more thoughtful. If the virtues of justice and wisdom are both within the class of what is good, each boy would be self-sufficient in his respective field, and yet they would not be identical to one another. As a result, despite the fact that the two boys are both good and self-sufficient, they would nevertheless still be useful to one another.[42]

Friendship and Desire

Socrates's assumption that the earlier refutation suffices to dispose of the proposed definition of friendship without reexamining it ensures that they do not discover a friendship between two self-sufficient individuals that is independent of need. Thus, the inquiry seems to conclude in a state of aporia. However, it is not the case that the dialogue is wholly without any development whatsoever. Indeed, one fundamental change that occurs throughout the course of the dialogue is the character development of Lysis. Socrates's interrogation on the nature of friendship has had an effect on Lysis, such that he begins not only to question his existing friendships, but also to recognize the benefit of erotic relationships. While no proposed definition of friendship is ever successfully maintained, through the course of the dialogue Socrates has transformed friendship into erotic love. Lysis has come to recognize that he suffers from some sort of metaphysical lack or need, which only the good, or the first friend can fulfill. Socrates suggests that to the extent that Lysis's ordinary friendships—his friendship with Menexenus, his friendship with his parents, or even the more extended friendship he has with the other members of his polis—leave him feeling sufficient and complacent, they are phantom friends that impede his access to the good. By forcing Lysis to confront and recognize that at their root all his friendships are, in some way, based in desire, Socrates turns him toward erotic love and, therefore, toward the good.

That Socrates's goal has been to turn Lysis toward erotic love and the good from the start of their conversation is borne out by the end of the dialogue. He concludes the inquiry into friendship by recounting the proposed definitions of friendship they have put forward—a method he rejects elsewhere.[43] He lists nearly every definition of friendship that they have proposed, noting that "I, at least, don't remember any more because of their multitude—if nothing among these is a friend, I no longer know what to say" (222e7–9). Socrates seems to suggest that he is at a loss. However, Plato has Socrates narrate to the reader the following: "But as I said these things, I already had in mind to set in motion someone else among the older fellows" (223a1–2). Socrates is not nearly as much at a loss as he lets on, but is, in fact, very much in control of the argument. What precisely is it that Socrates has in mind to set in motion among the older fellows? While we are never explicitly informed as to what Socrates has in mind, the preceding action of the dialogue leaves little room for doubt. Socrates has prepared Lysis for passionate love by causing him to question his existing friendships and inculcating in him a desire for the good. Given that Socrates views ἔρως as an impetus to philosophic contemplation, it seems that what Socrates has in mind is to bring Lysis and one of the older fellows together. In this way, the *Lysis* can be seen as a prelude to the *Symposium*, with its focus on ἔρως.[44]

Throughout the dialogue, not only has Plato shown Socrates to be somewhat hasty and too quick to dismiss possible definitions of friendship, but he has also shown him to have engaged in a rather reckless manner. Socrates has used a variety of sophistic arguments to undermine the friendships of perhaps the youngest interlocutors in the entire Platonic corpus.[45] Indeed, first, Socrates indicated to Lysis that a person is only happy if he follows his desires, regardless of what those desires may be (207e1–3). Next, he intimated that Lysis's parents only love him to the extent he is useful (210d2–4). Finally, in an effort to belittle Lysis, Socrates employed a specious argument that equivocated on the term "to understand," showing him that he knows nothing (210d4–8).[46] Socrates seems to have been depicted as a rather irresponsible individual.

One might want to absolve Socrates of his recklessness, given that his intention appears to have been to awaken in Lysis a desire for the good and to spur him to the contemplative life. However, Plato draws our attention to the fact that the dialogue does not have such a happy conclusion. Before Socrates can "set in motion someone else among the older fellows" as he had intended, the attendants and brothers of Menexenus and Lysis come forward "like some daemons," to bring the boys home (223a1–4). Socrates relates that "we and those standing around tried to drive them away" (223a6–7). The scene is striking, in that it is the only time in all the Platonic dialogues that Socrates is depicted as engaging in something more than a verbal dispute. As Bolotin notes, "Socrates directed or at least assisted Lysis and Menexenus in a rebellion against the guardians appointed by their fathers."[47] This little rebellion makes clear the effect that Socrates's discussion has had on the boys. While Socrates has sought to initiate at least one of them into the philosophic life, in the process of doing so, he has instilled in them a spirit of rebellion.[48] By finding that friendship has no basis apart from desire, Socrates has devalued existing attachments and friendships, including the friendships that exist between a parent and a child, and thereby the friendships that provide the foundation for traditional authority. The rebellion with which the *Lysis* ends points toward the difficulty that Socrates's approach poses to traditional authority and, by extension, to political cohesion. Ultimately, the rebellion is unsuccessful; the attendants, we are told, were impervious to reason as they "had been drinking quite a bit at the Hermaea" (223a8–b2). Hermes, the god of tricks, appears once again to have frustrated Socrates's intentions.

Given Socrates's inability to match Lysis with one of the older fellows, we are left wondering about Lysis's fate. On the one hand, Lysis has been led to awareness of his own insufficiency, an awareness that leaves him desirous of completion—a completion that perhaps only philosophic contemplation and the pursuit of the truth can attain. On the other hand, Socrates has also instilled within Lysis a rebellious streak that causes him to be dismissive of existing friendships and open to erotic relationships.[49] These two outcomes suggest that Plato is aware of the dangers of Socrates's approach. The Socratic approach, he suggests, may lead an individual to pursue the contemplative life. However, it may equally induce a hubris that is destructive of the friendships that are at the basis of political life.[50] The name of the dialogue itself suggests as much. "Lysis" (Λυσις) can be translated both as "to loosen" and "to destroy."[51] Thus, while Socrates seeks to loosen Lysis from the strictures and standards of the city, he is at the same time destroying his preexisting friendships in a way that may be harmful to the health of the polis.

Chapter Two

Socratic Citizenship

In his "Seventh Letter," Plato relates that he gave up on political reformation because he found the task to be impossible without friends (*Letters*, 7.325d). For Plato, friendship seems to be a sine qua non for political action. This is noteworthy, as it suggests that Plato's depiction of the Socratic approach to friendship has implications for politics. What does Socrates's treatment of friendship tell us about his relationship to politics? We have seen that in the *Lysis*, Plato presents Socrates as giving short shrift to the phenomenon of friendship and transforming it into erotic desire. Socrates takes his interlocutors' friendships—which were thought (perhaps erroneously) to be full and self-sufficient—and substitutes for them something that has its basis in desire, lack, or incompleteness. In the *Lysis*, Socrates fails to discover a definition of friendship that entails an appreciation between two people solely for the other's good qualities. Nevertheless, at the end of the dialogue, Socrates indicates that he considers himself to be the boys' friend. Through the process of refuting the boys, Socrates has, in some way, become their friend. In addition, we have seen that Plato seems to be skeptical of Socrates's approach to friendship. Not only does he seem to point to an oversight or misunderstanding in Socrates's understanding of friendship, but he also indicates that dangerous political effects attend the Socratic approach to friendship. The rebellion that Socrates inspires at the end of the dialogue is indicative of this, and it hints at the deleterious effect Socrates's understanding of friendship can have on politics.

Having uncovered Socrates's understanding of friendship by way of a close analysis of the *Lysis*, it is now necessary to explicate the way this understanding impacts his approach to politics. In contrast to his presentation of Socrates's conception of friendship, which covers only a single dialogue, Plato's depiction of the Socratic approach to politics is covered in a variety of dialogues, each of which reveals only an aspect of this approach.[1] The two dialogues that are most apposite for uncovering Socrates's relationship to the political community are the *Apology* and the *Gorgias*.[2] In the course of his trial recounted in the *Apology*, Socrates documents his relationship with the polis. As will be made clear, the *Apology* shows that Socrates's interaction with the political community is essentially one of negation and abstention. However, the trial takes place in a very public manner, in front of an audience consisting of five hundred jurors who are largely hostile to Socrates's way of life. As a result, the reasons adduced by Socrates in defense of his peculiar stance toward the political community do not convey the totality of the reasons for his seemingly antagonistic relation to the political community. Thus, while the *Apology* provides a succinct overview detailing the *facts* of Socrates's relationship to the political realm, it does not adequately get to the heart of *why* the facts are the way they are.

In order to get to the heart of why Socrates's stance toward political life is one of negation and abstention, it is necessary to turn to the *Gorgias*. Not only does the *Gorgias* allude to and foreshadow Socrates's trial and death numerous times, but it also deals with the same theme as the *Apology*. Socrates's way of life is explicitly put at issue and is contrasted with the active life of politics.[3] However, in contrast to the highly public character of the *Apology* in which the political community makes Socrates's way of life the focus of debate, the *Gorgias* is a private discussion among learned individuals, including one of the leading rhetoricians of the time, in which Socrates himself puts his way of life under discussion. It is in this private setting amongst learned individuals that Socrates feels free to uncover what "he professes and teaches," or "who he is" (*Gorgias*, 447c–d).[4] As Socrates makes clear, it is his opinion on the nature of friendship that causes his approach to the conventional practice of politics to be one of avoidance and negativity.

The *Apology*: A Life of Principled Abstention

In the *Gorgias*, Socrates tells Chaerephon to begin the conversation with the great Sophist Gorgias by asking him "who he is" (447d). By means of this question, Socrates aims to determine Gorgias's relation to the polis. Socrates points out that one can easily determine who a person is and what his function is in the polis based on the craft in which he engages. By asking this question, Socrates indicates (as does the remainder of the dialogue) that the rhetoricians' relation to the polis is questionable. However, we may equally ask the same question of Socrates himself: "Who is he?" What is Socrates's relation to the polis? Does the philosopher have a defined role in the city like any other craftsman? An examination of the *Apology* does not definitively answer these questions. However, it does reveal two essential characteristics about Socrates's way of life that point toward an answer: Socrates's way of life is both private and negative. Socrates abstains from a public role in the city, and when a public role is forced upon him, his public activity is essentially negative in character.

In the course of his trial, Socrates explains his way of life as a kind of divine mission designed to reveal the paucity of human wisdom. He recounts his perplexity at the fact that, in response to a question posed by Chaerephon, the oracle at Delphi stated there was none wiser than Socrates (*Apology*, 21a).[5] Why, Socrates wonders, would the oracle make this statement, given that he was in fact very conscious of his lack of wisdom? This perplexity, he asserts, caused him to set out to test the oracle's statement by speaking to the politicians, poets, and craftsmen of the city to test their wisdom. He relates that those most reputed to be wise among these three classes turned out to be ignorant of the "greatest things" (22d).[6] In fact, after speaking to one of the politicians, Socrates tells the jurors that he reasoned with himself as follows: "I am wiser than this human being. For probably neither of us knows anything noble and good, but he supposes he knows something when he does not know, while I, just as I do not know, do not even suppose that I do. I *am* likely to be a little bit wiser than he in this very thing: that whatever I do not know, I do not even suppose I know" (21d). Socrates has no knowledge of the "greatest things" and is eminently aware of his ignorance. As a result, he paradoxically concludes that he must be the wisest.

In recounting his activities, Socrates reveals that the entire approach he adopts is negative. This emphasis on negativity is consistent with what are held to be Plato's early dialogues, in which Socrates employs dialectical argumentation to dissolve his interlocutors' opinions about the various virtues. In none of these dialogues does Socrates ever arrive at a definition of the virtues. As Dana Villa notes, Socrates does not claim to have any knowledge of the virtues. Instead, all his energies "are devoted to dissolving the crust of convention and the hubristic claim to moral expertise."[7] Thus, the Socratic method seems to be entirely negative.[8]

In the *Apology*, after emphasizing that he possesses no knowledge of the "greatest things," Socrates argues that his negativity and his practice of dissolving conventional opinion nevertheless benefit his fellow citizens. He states that as a result of his divine mission, "I always do your business, going to each of you privately, as a father or an older brother might do, persuading you to care for virtue" (31b). By forcing them to examine their opinions concerning the "greatest things," Socrates exposes his fellow citizens' ignorance, purges them of their opinions, and opens them up to the possibility of true knowledge by perplexing them, or leading them to a state of confusion.[9] What is revealing about Socrates's statement is that it shows not only the negative character of his teaching, but also the private form it takes. Socrates dissolves his fellow citizens' opinions, and he does so by going around to each of them *privately* and by "being a busybody in private" (31c).[10]

The negative, private approach that Socrates adopts ensures that he does not involve himself in the democratic institutions of Athens. Instead, he purposefully seeks to avoid political activity (31c–d). By Athenian standards, Socrates's choice is, at best, peculiar. Indeed, in choosing to eschew public life, Socrates is acting in a way that is not only contrary to what was customary for Athenians, but also in a way that was decried as unpatriotic. For example, in his famous *Funeral Oration*, Pericles describes the public life of the Athenian citizens as follows: "Here each individual is interested not only in his own affairs but in the affairs of the state as well. . . . We do not say that man who takes no interest in politics is a man who minds his own business; we say that he has no business here at all."[11] Socrates's private, abstentious approach seems to be directly contrary to the Athenian ideals posited by Pericles.

Why would Socrates choose to proceed in a purely private manner that is contrary to the ideals and practices of his polis? Much of the extant literature emphasizing Socrates's negative and abstentious relation to the polis in the *Apology* suggests that his stance towards politics stems from his unique moral integrity and a commitment to avoiding injustice. In fact, this reading of the *Apology* has become so ubiquitous that its characterization of Socrates's stance toward the polis has been labeled *Socratic Citizenship*.[12] This commentarial tradition suggests that Socrates resolves the tension between his commitment to justice and the seemingly unavoidable injustice required by politics by abjuring the practice of politics. Scholars point to Socrates's own argument for political abstention:

> Know well, men of Athens, if I had long ago attempted to be politically active, I would long ago have perished, and I would have benefitted neither you nor myself. . . . For there is no human being who will preserve his life if he genuinely opposes either you or any other multitude and prevents many unjust and unlawful things from happening in the city. Rather, if someone who really fights for the just is going to preserve himself even for a short time, it is necessary for him to lead a private rather than a public life. (31d–32a)[13]

Socrates seems to ground his abstention from politics in the belief that one cannot be both politically involved and committed to justice without endangering his own life. Socrates's moral integrity would seem to require political abstention.

Political abstention, however, is not always possible. As a result, those who emphasize Socrates's moral integrity and commitment to justice posit that when political action is unavoidable, Socrates maintains it is best to act in an almost entirely negative fashion so as to avoid being complicit in injustice. Pointing to the two instances Socrates mentions where he was forced to involve himself in politics, these scholars maintain that Socrates chooses the negative stances of dissent and noncompliance in order to avoid being party to acts of injustice. The first example Socrates provides is when he was elected by lot to serve on the council, the administrative body overseeing the domestic political affairs of the city during Athens' democratic period. Socrates was elected during the Peloponnesian war and, as part of his duties, was called upon to judge the conduct of ten generals who had been accused of neglecting their duties during the war.[14] Socrates relates that although the council wished to judge the ten generals "as a group," which was contrary to Athenian law, he alone opposed the council and voted against its action (32b). On this basis, George Kateb concludes that "Socrates risks life and freedom in situations in which no one else does. He stands alone, as one person, as his naked moral self. He has only himself to fall back on. His courage is for the sake of refusing to be an instrument of injustice."[15] According to Kateb, Socrates's negative morality mandates that he oppose the unjust political action of the council by choosing to dissent boldly from their action. Although Socrates's dissent may be ineffectual, Kateb concludes that he would rather maintain his moral integrity than lend support to their injustice.

The second example where Socrates acts in a negative manner is the arrest of Leon the Salaminian, which occurred during the oligarchic reign of the Thirty Tyrants. Socrates relates that the Thirty ordered him and four others to arrest Leon, a man reputed to be perfectly just, and bring him from Salamis to die.[16] Socrates relates, "That government, as strong as it was, did not shock me into doing anything unjust. . . . The other four went to Salamis and arrested Leon, but I departed and went home. And perhaps I would have died because of this, if that government had not been quickly overthrown" (32d). Here, rather than engage in what he considers to be an unjust act, Socrates refuses to comply with the order. Dana Villa writes that Socrates's noncompliance bespeaks "the seriousness with which he takes the imperative of avoiding injustice, while reflecting the awareness of how the life of active citizenship . . . constantly generates injustice."[17] Avoidance of injustice seems to be the primary driver of Socrates's negative and abstentious relation to politics.

Based on Socrates's stance toward politics, advocates of the Socratic Citizenship interpretation suggest that Socrates evinces a type of citizenship that is "moderately alienated" from the polis. For the most part, these readings emphasize that it is Socrates's commitment to avoiding injustice that leads him toward a politics of abstention and negation. For example, Hannah Arendt argues that Socrates's approach to politics paralyzes political action. For Arendt, Socrates's negative, dissolvent approach to politics "slows people down in their potentially unjust pursuits."[18] Similarly, George Kateb argues that when Socrates "engages in worldly action in acts of citizenship, his whole concern is to avoid injustice."[19] Finally, Dana Villa suggests that "the avoidance of injustice, where the sense of injustice is plain and reflects widely held standards, is the heart of Socratic virtue."[20] According to these commentators, Socrates's strong commitment to avoiding injustice leads to a "moderately alienated citizenship" that is inherently skeptical of existing claims to justice. While not each of these scholars agrees that Socratic Citizenship is possible or desirable, all see in the figure of Socrates the archetype of a politics of negation and abstention that is based on the avoidance of injustice.[21]

The notion that Socrates's stance to politics stems from a desire to avoid injustice is, as far as it goes, correct. However, it fails to present the full picture of why Socrates employs the stance toward politics that he does. It is noteworthy that in the *Apology*, no definition of either justice or injustice is ever advanced. Furthermore, in this same dialogue, Socrates never claims that his abstention from political activity *results* from a clash between his commitment to avoiding injustice and the inevitable injustice that the practice of politics involves. Instead, he notes that his abstention is a product of the daimonic voice: "The cause of this [abstention from politics] is what you have heard me speak of many times and in many places, that something divine and daimonic comes to me, a voice.... This is something which began for me in childhood: a sort of voice comes, and whenever it comes, it always turns me away from whatever I am about to do, but never turns me forward. This is what opposes my political activity" (31c3–d6). It is the daimonic voice that is specifically credited with opposing Socrates's political activity. Socrates's avoidance of injustice seems to be simply an *effect* of the daimonion's counsel to abstain from politics.

If the daimonion is Socrates's individuated conscience, as numerous scholars have suggested, then it is possible that Socrates's desire to avoid injustice is simply the product of his daimonion, or conscience.[22] However, a number of factors indicate that the relation between Socrates's daimonion and his desire to avoid injustice is somewhat more complex. First, while the daimonion is cited as being the *cause* of Socrates's abstention from political activity, Socrates's contention that one cannot both act justly and preserve one's own life while engaging in political activity is only cited as evidence that the daimonion's opposition is "altogether *noble*" (31d; emphasis added).[23] He does not cite this fact as the *cause* of his abstention for political activity. In fact, in introducing the two examples from his own life that show that one cannot be both committed to opposing injustice and politically active without endangering one's life, Socrates states, "I for my part will offer great proofs of these things for you—not speeches, but what *you* honor, deeds" (32a; emphasis in original). He goes on to say, "I will tell you vulgar things, typical of the law courts, but true" (32a–b). While the examples that Socrates provides of his commitment to moral integrity are honorable according to Athenian standards, they are in his estimation vulgar and paltry.[24]

Socrates's depiction of the Athenian conception of justice as vulgar, combined with the fact that the *Apology* contains no definition of justice, raises the questions: what is Socrates's real reason for abstaining from politics? Why does the daimonion oppose his involvement in politics? And what is Socrates's conception of justice? The Platonic corpus as a whole provides little information about Socrates's daimonion. However, the *Gorgias* offers a suggestion as to why Socrates's daimonion may oppose his involvement in politics. As noted, the *Gorgias*, like the *Apology*, deals with Socrates's relation to the polis, but it does so in a more private setting, among learned intellectuals. In the *Gorgias*, Socrates claims, in what appears to be a stark contrast with the *Apology*, that he is the only person in all of Athens who practices politics (*Gorgias*, 521d). While on the face of it, Socrates's claim appears to contradict the negative and abstentious stance he takes towards politics in the *Apology*, the claim makes sense in light of the *Gorgias*'s teaching concerning friendship and justice. Specifically, the *Gorgias* shows that the Socratic understanding of friendship affects Socrates's approach to politics, rendering it an exclusively negative and private matter.

Gorgias Part I: Phantom Friends and Phantom Politics

The *Gorgias* is ordinarily considered to be Plato's dialogue concerning rhetoric. However, a closer look reveals that the dialogue is nearly equally concerned with friendship and justice, or the way one ought to treat a friend. As Roger Duncan points out, friendship features prominently in "the third and longest section of the dialogue where Socrates and Callicles confront each other."[25] Catherine Zuckert makes the case that the *Gorgias* follows the *Lysis* dramatically and points to the thematic affinity of the two dialogues: "The tension between the philosophical friendships Socrates attempted to form with the young and the political friendships among citizens that emerges at the end of the *Lysis* becomes thematic in the *Gorgias*, particularly in the concluding exchange between Socrates and a young Athenian named Callicles. Claiming to be his friend (499a), Callicles urges Socrates to give up philosophy and enter the political arena."[26] The theme of friendship pervades the *Gorgias* just as it does the *Lysis*. However, as we shall see, Socrates draws out the connection between friendship and justice in the *Gorgias*.

The *Gorgias* is divided into two parts. In the first part, Socrates engages with the well-known Sophist Gorgias and his pupil Polus who are visiting Athens; in the second part, he converses with Callicles, the Athenian at whose house Gorgias and Polus are staying. While their conversations cover similar topics, Socrates treats his interlocutors very differently. At the end of the first part of the dialogue, he seems to send Polus back into the city, armed with a rhetoric designed to challenge the city's conventions. In contrast, toward the end of the second half of the dialogue, Callicles is counseled to avoid the conventional practice of politics altogether. The disparate treatment Socrates affords his interlocutors has long been the source of scholarly debate. I will argue that the difference in approach Socrates takes with his interlocutors stems from his understanding of friendship. Furthermore, I will show that

Socrates's understanding of friendship also makes sense of Socrates's negative approach to politics and his abstention from the conventional practice of politics. An analysis of Socrates's discussion with Polus reveals that Socrates's understanding of friendship necessitates a negative approach to politics in which rhetoric is used to purge the city of injustice. However, Socrates also invokes friendship as grounds for Callicles to avoid the conventional practice of politics altogether. Thus, the *Gorgias* reveals that friendship lies behind both Socrates's negative and his abstentious approach toward politics.[27]

The connection between the themes of rhetoric and friendship comes to the fore near the beginning of the dialogue. Socrates and Chaerephon arrive late at Callicles's house, and Callicles states, "In war and battle, they say, one must take part in this manner" (447a). We soon learn that Gorgias, a Sophist visiting from Leontini, has been regaling the crowd inside with rhetoric, and that Socrates and Chaerephon have come too late to hear the display of the speeches. Callicles's remark suggests that rhetoric is war—that is, rhetoric necessarily contains a conflict in which one side emerges victorious. Socrates responds with his own proverb, "Oh, so have we then come, as the saying goes, after the feast and too late?" (447a). In contrast to Callicles's statement, the proverb quoted by Socrates implies that rhetoric is not like war but is more like a feast of which all friends can partake. The opening colloquy sets up the fundamental question of the dialogue: Is rhetoric akin to war with its clash of opposing interests, or is it more like a feast shared among friends that leaves everyone satisfied?

Socrates informs Callicles that he would prefer to skip the feast and learn instead from Gorgias "what the power of the man's art is, and what it is that he professes and teaches" (447c). What is the power of Gorgianic rhetoric? Socrates wishes to know to what extent rhetoric can truly reconcile opposing interests and satisfy all parties.[28] To begin the inquiry, Socrates instructs Chaerephon to ask Gorgias "who he is" (447d). Perhaps in a bid to put on his own display, Polus interjects with an oath, "By Zeus, Chaerephon, test me, if you wish!" (448a). Chaerephon obliges and asks Polus what it is that Gorgias ought to be called; just as one who knows the art of medicine is called a doctor, and one experienced in the art of painting is called a painter, so Chaerephon wishes to know, on the basis of Gorgias's art, what he should be called. As noted, the question of who Gorgias is has to do with his relation to the city—what is Gorgias's contribution to the city? Or, how does he fit into the whole?[29] In providing the examples of a doctor and a painter, Chaerephon—perhaps unwittingly—anticipates Socrates's discussion with Gorgias and gets to the heart of the dialogue. Is rhetoric akin to the *knowledge* of a doctor or is it merely an *experience* or skill that imitates reality?

Polus responds with comic prolixity, saying nearly nothing.[30] He simply praises Gorgias's art as "the best," without saying what it consists of. However, Polus does choose between the two options provided by Chaerephon, "knowledge" and "experience," noting that art is simply experience and that art (as experience) conquers chance (448c).[31] He suggests that in the absence of the skills obtained through experience, our lives would proceed according to the vagaries of fortune. Rhetoric, indicates Polus, is one of the skills that can conquer chance. At this point, Socrates interjects, noting that Polus has engaged in rhetoric—that is, he has simply praised Gorgias's art, without answering *what* it is. Socrates knows enough about rhetoric to know that it consists in assigning blame and praise, and that it commonly does so without knowledge of its object. Because of Polus's failure, Socrates begins to engage Gorgias directly. After quickly establishing that Gorgias claims to practice the art of rhetoric and that, as such, he can rightly be called a rhetor, Socrates asks him, "What of the things that are (τα ὄντα), does rhetoric happen to be about?" "About what . . . is it a science?" (449d). By characterizing Gorgias's practice in this way, Socrates skillfully shifts the category under which rhetoric falls from art to science, and from experience to knowledge.[32] By shifting rhetoric's categorization in this way, Socrates suggests that he wants to probe the extent to which Gorgias's practice is directed towards truth or towards "the things that are."

Gorgias responds that rhetoric concerns speeches and, when pressed for more specificity, he states in a manner reminiscent of Polus's vacuous response, that the rhetoric of speeches is concerned with "the greatest of human affairs . . . and the best" (451d). Socrates points out that opinions vary on what is "the greatest of human affairs," and to illustrate he quotes a quatrain from a popular drinking song, which enumerates the various goods people claim are best: " 'Being healthy is best, and second is to have become beautiful and third' as the poet who wrote the song says, 'is being wealthy without fraud' " (451e). However, Socrates omits portions from the song. The full quotation concerning the second good is "to have become beautiful *in one's nature*." In addition, Socrates completely omits the song's fourth good, namely, "to be in the prime of youth with friends."[33] Both of these omissions are significant because, as I will make clear, they go to the heart of the issue of the *Gorgias*: to what extent is rhetoric akin to a war, and to what extent is it akin to a feast shared by friends?

Gorgias responds that rhetoric has the power to obtain *all* the goods mentioned by Socrates in the drinking song. Rhetoric is "able to persuade by speeches" in any political setting, enabling one to obtain power over the artisans who produce health, beauty, and wealth (452e). He thus sets up rhetoric as architectonic; it is able to command all other arts and sciences and is able to satisfy all bodily desires. However, rhetoric's relation to friendship—the fourth good of the drinking song that was left unstated by Socrates—remains open. Is friendship a good like health, beauty, and wealth, which can be obtained through rhetoric? Or is friendship something altogether different? Rhetoric's relation to friendship will soon be raised directly by Gorgias himself.

Perhaps as a result of Gorgias's response, Socrates shifts the category again, adopting the language of art: "You're saying that rhetoric is a *craftsman* of persuasion" (453a; emphasis added). It seems that while Socrates is willing to grant Gorgias the benefit of the doubt in describing it as a science, Gorgias's response causes Socrates to relegate it again to the status of art. By switching the status of rhetoric from art to science and back again, Socrates signals his ambivalence about the status of rhetoric; it may theoretically be possible for rhetoric to be a science, but as described by Gorgias, rhetoric is at most an art.

The notion that rhetoric is concerned with persuasion is not precise enough for Socrates. He notes that while he has a *suspicion* as to what Gorgias means with this notion, he would like to ask Gorgias to clarify it for him by responding to his questions. The reason he chooses to proceed in this manner rather than stating his suspicion outright is, according to Socrates, "not on account of you, [Gorgias], but on account of the argument, in order that it may go forward so as to make what is being talked about as manifest as possible to us" (453c). Socrates declares, perhaps somewhat rudely, that his concern is not for Gorgias, but rather for the truth of the argument. Socrates's *primary* interest in speaking with Gorgias is not to improve Gorgias in some way, but is instead self-interest.[34] Socrates's own good—that is, his inquiry into the power of rhetoric—rather than a concern for Gorgias's good is the primary driver of the conversation.[35] A short while later, Socrates will state forthrightly that he would rather be refuted if he were to say something false than refute another's false statement, for "it is a greater good to be released oneself from the greatest evil than to release another" (458a).

Upon prompting, Gorgias makes clear that rhetoric is about "persuasion in law courts and in other mobs . . . and about those things that are just and unjust" (454b). Socrates indicates that this is precisely the suspicion he had, but that he had asked for clarity, "not on account of you" (i.e., not for Gorgias's interest), but instead so that the argument can "be brought to a conclusion in a consequential manner" (454c). Again, Socrates makes clear that he is pursuing the argument for his own sake, or to attain truth. This time, however, after noting that he is pursuing the argument for the sake of truth rather than for Gorgias's sake, Socrates adds, "so that we may not become accustomed to guessing and hastily snatching up each other's words" (454c). Socrates makes clear that while his *primary* concern is with the truth, he would like to remain on friendly terms with Gorgias. Socrates is exploring the main theme of the dialogue: What is the power of Gorgianic rhetoric? Can Gorgianic rhetoric be directed toward the truth (Socrates's interest) and at the same time maintain friendships?

Having made clear to Gorgias that he would like their conversation to proceed in a friendly manner *and* to aim at the truth, Socrates continues his questioning, extricating from Gorgias the concession that rhetoric, in contrast to didactic persuasion, "provides belief without knowing" (454e). Socrates concludes by diplomatically stating the conclusion to their colloquy: "The rhetor, therefore, is not didactic with law courts and the other mobs about just and unjust things, but persuasive only; for he would not be able, I suppose, to teach so large a mob such great matters in a short time" (455a).[36] Upon Gorgias's acceptance of this summary, Socrates once again presses Gorgias to define precisely what it is that rhetoric is able to obtain. Surely, it is engineers and architects (those with knowledge), not rhetors, who are responsible for the walls and harbors of the city. Therefore, concerning what—aside from the just and unjust—does rhetoric give counsel? (455d). Gorgias counters by noting that it *is* the rhetors, rather than the craftsmen, who are responsible for the "coming into being" of walls, harbors, and the like. Socrates does not dispute Gorgias's claim, but encourages him, noting that rhetoric "appears to me as a power demonic in greatness" (456a).

Gorgias responds to this flattery by giving in to his propensity for loquacity and delivers a disquisition on the benefits and purpose of rhetoric, a disquisition that will make clear his confused understanding of rhetoric. Socrates subtly points out that gratification or flattery leads another into error. By encouraging or gratifying him, Socrates goads Gorgias into delivering a long disquisition on the powers of rhetoric. As it turns out, it is precisely this disquisition that brings to light Gorgias's confused and contradictory understanding of rhetoric.

To prove the power of rhetoric, Gorgias points to his ability to persuade those unwilling to do what is best. Gorgias notes that when accompanying doctors to visit the sick, he is able to persuade these patients to take their medicine for their own benefit, despite their reluctance do so, through the power of rhetoric, even while the doctors are incapable of doing so. Therefore, rhetoric is all-powerful and can be used to ensure that people undertake what is good for them, even if they don't recognize it as good (456b). Yet, despite this power, Gorgias quickly cautions that it should be used only against one's enemies, not against one's friends and family. Just as one who has become skilled in boxing ought not use those skills to "beat . . . his father and mother or some other relative or friend" but ought instead to use those skills against "enemies and doers of injustice," so rhetoric ought to be used in the same manner (456d–456e). In this statement, Gorgias exposes his understanding of justice—an understanding that calls to mind Polemarchus's definition of justice in *The Republic*: one ought to do good to friends and harm enemies.

Three fundamental and connected themes emerge from Gorgias's disquisition: the good, justice, and friendship. Gorgias's statement that rhetoric can persuade those who are unwilling to take their medicine reveals a recognition that rhetoric can and should be aimed toward the good. However, Gorgias also displays a devotion to friendship, or the principle that one ought to be loyal to one's own. Tellingly, however, Gorgias allies justice only to friendship, and not to the good. Indeed, he asserts it would be unjust to use rhetoric against one's friends.[37] The rhetor is placed in somewhat of a quandary. According to Gorgias's description, the rhetorician has two incompatible goals. On the one hand, the rhetor is capable of administering treatment to his patients, ensuring that those who are unwilling to do what is best for them will nonetheless do so. On the other hand, Gorgias believes that justice dictates that the rhetor ought not to use his skill against his friends. Of course, if a friend were to fall ill and be in need of medicine, the rhetor's goals would come into conflict. Friendship, or the desire to gratify one's friends, may well impede the rhetor's ability to administer medicine in a manner that is conducive to the patient's health.

Socrates very likely realizes that Gorgias's conception of justice and friendship is in tension, if not outright opposition, with his belief that rhetoric ought to aim for the good. However, rather than set the good and the just against each other directly, Socrates instead shows that the rhetorician could never do an injustice. After coaxing Gorgias to admit that the rhetorician must necessarily know what justice is, Socrates is able to show (not altogether convincingly) that as a knower of justice, the rhetorician must therefore be just, do just things, and never wish to do injustice (460b–c). When Gorgias agrees, Socrates concludes that Gorgias must have been mistaken in asserting that the rhetor would ever use his art in unjust manner.

What is noteworthy about this exchange is that neither Gorgias nor Socrates offers any definition of justice. As Polus will later assert, Gorgias likely does not know *what* justice is, but is shamed into asserting that he is concerned with justice. As a rhetorician who travels from place to place, Gorgias has likely seen that different cities have different conceptions of justice. Further, as a rhetorician who sells his services, Gorgias likely adapts his speeches (and thereby his conception of justice) to the city he happens to be visiting. Socrates appeals to Gorgias's sense of shame, inducing him to concede (perhaps falsely) that he is concerned with justice. As a result, Socrates's refutation of Gorgias contains no direct conflict between justice, or a commitment to one's friends, and the good.

Through an appeal to Gorgias's shame, Socrates manages to save the phenomenon of justice. However, the relationship of justice to friendship and to the good has not yet been resolved. Is justice allied with friendship (as Gorgias indicates) and therefore opposed to the good? Or is justice allied with the good, and therefore something that undermines friendship? The question of where justice stands in relation to the good and friendship comes to the fore in the next section of the dialogue, which takes place between Socrates and Polus. Upon witnessing Socrates refute Gorgias, Polus interjects with force, arguing that Gorgias is simply ashamed to admit that the rhetorician does not also know the "just, noble, and good things" (461b), and that it is his sensitivity to shame that has led to his refutation.[38] Socrates responds, telling Polus that it would be just for Polus to correct him and Gorgias if they have been "tripped up in the speeches on some point" (461d).[39] Polus agrees and begins to question Socrates on what rhetoric is. Through a series of exchanges in which Socrates tells Polus what questions to pose to him, Socrates reveals that he believes rhetoric to be a sort of flattery that is, in fact, a "phantom of a part of politics" (463d).

When Gorgias intervenes, expressing confusion, Socrates elaborates, noting that the art that is directed to the soul is called politics, and that it is comprised of two parts—the legislative art and justice (464b–d). Justice, therefore, is directed toward the improvement of the soul. Socrates continues, stating that flattery (the phantom art of politics) is itself divided into two parts; sophistry and rhetoric, which are meant to mimic the legislative art and justice. Flattery, he states, "slipped in under each of the parts" of the art of politics (the legislative art and justice) and pretends to be that which it has slipped under. Thus, sophistry pretends to be the legislative art, while rhetoric pretends to be justice. The problem, Socrates notes somewhat perfunctorily, is that neither of these parts of flattery gives heed to "the best," and that both "hunt . . . after folly with what is ever most pleasant" (464d).

The distinction, therefore, between rhetoric and justice is that while justice aims at what is best, rhetoric aims at what is most pleasant. While Socrates does not yet declare what "the best" is, we can surmise that between the two contenders, friendship and the good, Socrates means that justice aims at the good. This supposition is borne out when Socrates invokes the analogy to the medical art that Gorgias had raised earlier, noting that justice is akin to the art of the doctor in that it aims at what is best: the health of the patient. By invoking this analogy, Socrates finally dissociates justice from friendship and allies it instead with the good. It seems at this point that rhetoric, which aims only at what is pleasant or that which gratifies, is allied with friendship. However, while Socrates suggests that justice aims at what is best and, therefore, at the good, we still do not know what justice is. In fact, Socrates remains almost cryptic about what justice is.[40]

Polus, not knowing quite what to make of Socrates's depiction of rhetoric, seeks to burnish the reputation of rhetoric by focusing on the supposedly powerful *deeds* that the person skilled in rhetoric is capable of accomplishing. He asks: Don't rhetors, like tyrants, have the capacity to "kill whomever they wish, and confiscate possessions and expel from the cities whomever it seems good to them" (466b–c)? Rather than explain precisely what justice is, Socrates explains that Polus has, in fact, asked two questions: "Do rhetors do whatever they wish?" and "Do rhetors do what seems good to them?" (466c–d). Through a series of dialectical moves, Socrates shows that the rhetor who engages in these deeds does them only to pursue what he perceives to be good for him. Therefore, if the rhetor engages in one of these acts under the mistaken belief that he is doing something good for himself, he does nothing of what he wishes, although he certainly does what seems to him to be best (466e). Given that Polus had earlier agreed that having power is good for the person who wields it, Socrates is able to refute Polus's conception of power, concluding, "Do you then think it is good, if someone who does not have intelligence does those things that seem to him to be best? And do you call this having great power?" (466e).

In response, Polus reveals his commitment to what is pleasant as opposed to what is best. He protests indignantly that Socrates himself would "welcome the possibility of doing what seemed good" to him, whether it was just or unjust (468e). In recognition that Polus has not been convinced by his refutation—that is, by what is *best*[41]—Socrates attempts to gratify him by appealing to his desire for punishment. First, he tells Polus that one ought not admire those who do injustice but instead ought to pity them for their wretchedness. When Polus asks how the rhetor who commits great acts of injustice is wretched, Socrates compares the rhetor to a common criminal who kills citizens in the marketplace. In response, Polus protests that this is not the type of power he has in mind, because "it is necessary for someone who acts in this manner to pay a penalty" (470a).[42] This reply reveals that Polus's earlier shameless disregard for justice was feigned; Polus is not so shameless as to praise a petty criminal. While Polus admires rhetors and tyrants who are able to engage in injustice on a grand scale, he has no admiration for the common criminal.

Having exposed Polus's shame or sense of decency by appealing to his desire for punishment, Socrates seeks to refute Polus on two points. The first is Polus's notion that it is better to do injustice than it is to suffer injustice (469b), and the second is Polus's belief that the individual who escapes punishment is better off than the individual who pays the penalty for his injustice (472e). In order to prove the first claim, that doing injustice is a greater evil than suffering injustice, Socrates begins by establishing that all fine or noble things are called such on the basis of either use or pleasure, while the shameful are defined by the opposite, namely, pain and badness. Because Polus agrees that doing injustice is more shameful than suffering injustice, the former must surpass the latter either in pain or in badness, or in both. Furthermore, because doing injustice cannot possibly exceed the suffering of injustice in the realm of pain, it must surpass it in badness (474e–475b). As a result, doing injustice must be worse than suffering injustice (475d).[43]

Next, Socrates seeks to prove that it is a greater evil to avoid paying the penalty for injustice than to be punished for an injustice. First, he obtains Polus's agreement that "all just things are fine" or noble insofar as they are just (476b). After this, he asserts that in any action that is undertaken, the entity undergoing the action undergoes it in whatever way the action is inflicted. Thus, if someone beats violently, the object that has been beaten will have been beaten in a violent manner (476c). Having secured Polus's affirmation, Socrates extends this to suffering a penalty. If someone suffers a penalty from one who justly inflicts the penalty, the penalty must also be suffered justly. And, if the penalty is suffered justly, it must also be noble or fine to suffer such penalties (476e). Socrates concludes that it is beneficial to suffer punishments, as it releases one from "badness of soul" (477a).

By appealing to Polus's desire for punishment, Socrates partially reintegrates Polus into the city. Polus's attack on justice has been uncovered as insincere, and Socrates seems to reestablish the ties of justice between Polus and the city. However, he does so in a manner that ensures that Polus does not simply uncritically accept the city's conventions. Indeed, if it is better to suffer punishment than to escape punishment, it is necessary that one seek to administer justice—and therefore punishment—both on oneself and on one's friends. The relationship of justice to friendship is finally revealed. While Socrates had earlier revealed that justice is allied with the good, we now see that it is allied with the good *against* friendship. One ought to act like a doctor that administers medicine. To act justly means removing injustice from one's own soul and from the souls of one's fellow citizens. As a result, Socrates states the following concerning rhetoric:

> For speaking in defense of one's own injustice, therefore, or that of parents or comrades or children or fatherland when it does injustice, rhetoric will be of no use to us, Polus; except if someone takes it to be of use for the opposite purpose, supposing that he must most of all accuse himself, and then whoever else of his relatives and friends happens at any time to do injustice, and not hide the unjust deed but bring it into the open so as to pay the just penalty and become healthy, and compel both himself and others not to play the coward but to grit his teeth and submit well and courageously as if to a doctor for cutting and burning. (480b–c)

Socrates appeals to Polus's desire to punish, noting that if rhetoric is to have any use at all, it would be to accuse oneself, one's friends, and one's own city.

Because Socrates suggests that one ought to accuse oneself, one's friends, and one's own city, some scholars have suggested that Socrates is sending Polus back into the city to administer justice and purge it of its unjust practices.[44] However, a close look at Socrates's statements concerning justice reveals that this is only partially correct. Socrates does not seem to be particularly concerned with what are conventionally or vulgarly considered to be the unjust practices of politics.[45] For example, when Socrates demurs from Polemarchus's assertion that Archelaus, the ruler of the Macedonians, is unjust, Polus responds incredulously, "But how on earth could he not be unjust?" (471a). Polus then conveys a litany of conventionally unjust practices that Archelaus has committed, including the illicit attainment of the throne of Macedonia and the killing of both his master and his master's bloodline (471a–c). Socrates responds, "I certainly do not agree with you on any one of these things that you are asserting" (471e).[46] Socratic justice, seems to be different from, or beyond, a conventional, vulgar understanding of justice that eschews the practices engaged in by Archelaus. Thus, it cannot be that Socrates simply sends Polus back into the city to purge it of practices that are conventionally considered to be unjust.

If Socratic justice differs from the vulgar, common conception of justice with which Polus is concerned, what does it consist of? While Socrates does not provide a definition of justice anywhere in his discussion with Polus, he intimates throughout that it is connected to speech. For example, when questioning Gorgias what *precisely* concerns rhetoric or in what areas it persuades, Socrates asks, "Since, therefore, not [rhetoric] alone but also other [arts] achieve this work [i.e., persuasion] . . . we might after this *justly* ask the speaker further, 'Of what sort of persuasion, and of persuasion about what, is rhetoric the art?' Or doesn't it seem to you *just* to ask further?" (454a; emphasis added). Similarly, when Polus angrily interrupts Socrates's conversation with Gorgias, Socrates tells him it is *just* for him to correct himself and Gorgias if they have been "tripped up in the speeches on some point" (461d). Justice is connected to speech; speaking truthfully is just, while falsity (and flattery) are unjust.[47]

This conception of justice also helps to make sense of Socrates's argument that it is better for one to pay the penalty for injustice than to escape punishment. According to Socrates's understanding of justice, escaping punishment simply ensures that one maintains a false conception of what *is*, whereas undergoing punishment ensures that one's false convictions are refuted. This interpretation of Socrates's understanding of justice is borne out in the dialogue, when Polus tells Socrates that even a child could refute him. Socrates responds, "I shall feel much gratitude to the child then, and equal gratitude to you too, if you refute me and release me from drivel. So don't tire of doing good *to a man who's a friend*, but refute" (470c; emphasis added). Similarly, immediately before refuting Gorgias, Socrates states, "And of what men am I one? Those who are refuted with pleasure if I say something not true, and who refute with pleasure if someone should say something not true. . . . For I think that nothing is so great an evil for a human being as false opinion about the things that our argument now happens to be about" (458a–b). Last, sometime after Socrates has refuted Polus, Socrates states, "Don't shrink from answering, Polus; for you will suffer no harm. But submit yourself in a nobly born manner to the argument as to a doctor, and answer" (475d). Socrates does not believe that justice primarily consists either in performing actions that are vulgarly considered to be just deeds or in avoiding unjust deeds. Rather, justice consists in refuting others' opinions about what *is*, for it is by refuting another—and thereby leading him to a state of perplexity—that a person is *released* from falsity.[48]

Socrates's conception of justice and his approach to Polus mirror the approach undertaken in the *Lysis*. It will be recalled that in the *Lysis* Socrates refutes Lysis in a manner that causes him to question all his pre-existing friendships. Socrates leads Lysis to understand that his friendships have not been sufficient and that, to the extent that Lysis believed them to be sufficient, they were simply "phantom friendships." Therefore, through refuting him, Socrates releases Lysis from a state of complacency and opens him up to an awareness of need and, perhaps, to the good life of contemplation. In the *Gorgias*, Socrates undertakes a similar approach with Polus. He refutes Polus and releases him from his erroneous conception of justice and rhetoric. For Socrates, justice is allied not with friendship but with the good. As a result, justice—and rhetoric, if it is to be just—ought to question friendships and the conceptions of justice that uphold them. According to Socrates, a true friend (as opposed to a "phantom friend") is one who questions and exposes the false or "phantom" conceptions of justice, friendship, or whatever else that *is*. In contrast, a "phantom" friend is one who engages in flattery, preserving a false conception of what *is*. In both dialogues, Socrates can be seen acting as a true friend (under the Socratic conception of friendship), who releases his interlocutors from a mistaken conception of what *is*. While refutation is a painful process—much like the taking of medicine or punishment—it leaves one better off, as it leaves one perplexed and therefore desirous of true wisdom.

Socrates's negative approach to politics, therefore, is explained by his conception of friendship and justice. His belief that justice consists in refuting a friend in order to free him from an erroneous conception of what *is*, means that Socrates's approach to politics and the practice of justice takes a negative form. In the name of friendship and justice, Socrates dissolves his fellow citizens' preexisting conceptions of who a friend is and what is just or noble. In this way, Socrates's claim to be the only person to practice politics is understandable, despite his complete avoidance of conventional politics. This negative approach is not primarily due to Socrates's commitment to avoiding acts that the many consider to be unjust (i.e., vulgar justice), nor is it due to a desire to preserve his own life. Rather, when Socrates relates in the *Apology* that he has never "conceded anything contrary to the just" (*Apology*, 33a), what he means is that he has never engaged in flattery but has instead always acted justly by dissolving his fellow citizens' erroneous conceptions of what *is*.

Through his refutation of Polus, Socrates is able to show both Gorgias and Polus why their practice of rhetoric is unjust. Flattery, as the phantom part of justice, preserves phantom friendships. Together, flattery and phantom friendships lead to complacency. Just as the phantom friendships described in the *Lysis* lead one to a false sense of self-sufficiency and impede one's access to the good, so flattery, the phantom part of justice, maintains a false conception of what *is* and keeps those who have been lied to in a state of ignorance and complacency (cf. *Republic*, 382b–c). In contrast, Socratic justice involves dissolving false conceptions of what *is*. Of course, by doing so, one also dissolves that which undergirds phantom friendships. In Socrates's view it is by dissolving another's false conception of justice and by dissolving his phantom friendships that one truly acts as a friend. Thus, it his understanding of friendship and justice that prompts Socrates to act as a gadfly who wakens his fellow citizens from their slumber by dissolving their preexisting conceptions of what is (*Apology*, 30e). It is only by dissolving another's false conceptions of what *is*, thereby leading him to a state of perplexity, that one can open him up to a life of contemplation. Socrates's approach to politics is negative because politics, as it is practiced in Athens—and likely as it is practiced in all places at all times—relies on flattery (cf. *Republic*, 414b–c).

Gorgias Part II: Socratic Eros and the Private Life

While Socrates's conception of friendship and justice explains his negative approach to politics, it does not yet explain why Socrates chooses to do this privately, but not in the public manner befitting an Athenian citizen (cf. *Apology*, 31c). That is, why does Socrates not choose to engage himself in the world of politics and publicly dissolve his fellow citizens' conceptions of what *is*? Some have maintained that it is simply because of the incompatibility of philosophy and politics.[49] However, Socrates's discussion with Polus has made clear that rhetoric can potentially be used to dissolve people's false conceptions of justice and of what *is* (*Gorgias*, 480b–c). To understand why Socrates abstains from publicly engaging in his negative approach to politics, it is necessary to turn to his discussion with Callicles, which comprises the second half of the *Gorgias*. As we shall see, the basis of Socrates's abstention is found in his conception of friendship.

Having heard Socrates explain to Polus that if rhetoric is to have any use in the city at all, it ought to be used to punish oneself, one's friends, and one's fatherland, Callicles cannot contain himself. He bursts in, asking Chaerephon whether Socrates is serious.[50] Somewhat curiously, Socrates responds to Callicles by first pointing to something he and Callicles share: "Callicles, if human beings did not have some feeling that was the same—some having one and others another—but if some one of us suffered some private feeling different from what the others feel, it would not be too easy to point out one's own affection to the other. I say this bearing in mind that you and I now happen to have suffered something that is the same: we are two lovers" (481c–d). Socrates points out that he and Callicles are similar in that they are both erotic individuals. Given the distinction between phantom friends and erotic desire formulated in the *Lysis*, Socrates seems to be indicating that Callicles, like he himself, is aware that he is in some way incomplete and in need. Neither Socrates nor Callicles suffers from the complacency brought on by the illusions of self-sufficiency associated with phantom friendships. Like Socrates, Callicles is a desirous individual. Thus, we can already surmise that Socrates's interaction with Callicles will not consist of a simple refutation designed to perplex him and lead him to a state of desire.

After this initial statement pointing out their similarities, Socrates quickly goes on to explicate the differences between them by pointing to the objects of their love. While Socrates loves Alcibiades and philosophy, Callicles is in love with the Athenian people and with Demos the son of Pyrilampes.[51] It seems that in their desirous nature, Socrates and Callicles are similar but not identical to one another. Of course, this was the final definition of friendship tentatively put forward, yet not fully explored, at the end of the *Lysis*. As I will make clear, by having Socrates emphasize both their similarities and their differences, Plato alludes to the possibility of a rapprochement, perhaps even friendship, between these two individuals.

However, Socrates does not seek a rapprochement between himself and Callicles. Instead, he confronts him in a very personal way by suggesting that his own philosophic way of life is superior to the active life practiced by Callicles, due to the stability of philosophy. While the fickleness of the Athenian people causes Callicles constantly to say different and discordant things, Socrates's own love, philosophy, always says the same thing. Socrates challenges Callicles to refute the philosophic principle that has come to light in his discussion with Polus, "by showing that doing injustice and not paying the just penalty when one does injustice are not the utmost of all evils" (482b). He concludes that if Callicles fails to refute this principle, he will continue to say discordant things and "will be dissonant in his whole life" (482b). It is only by either proving the superiority of his life or redirecting his desires from a love of the people to a love of philosophy that Callicles's soul will be made harmonious (cf. *Republic*, 443c–e).

Taking up the challenge, Callicles responds by appealing to a sense of natural justice. He asserts that the only reason Socrates has been able to refute both Polus and Gorgias was that he shifted the grounds of the debate from what is natural to what is conventional, thereby appealing to his interlocutors' sense of shame. It was their shame that caused Gorgias and Polus to shrink from saying what they truly believe and compelling them to say contradictory things.[52]

To avoid the fate of Gorgias and Polus, Callicles seeks to blunt the power of convention by attacking it at its roots. He asserts in what seems to be a proto-Nietzschean fashion that the conventional or the lawful is simply a creation of the "weak human beings and the many" (*Gorgias*, 483b). The lawful, according to Callicles, is simply a tool by which the weak frighten away the strong so that the many may have an equal share. In contrast to what is conventionally lawful, Callicles holds that the law of nature reveals that it is just "for the better to have more than the worse and the more powerful than the less powerful" (483d). A truly great individual, asserts Callicles, is one who transcends the conventional morality of the weak and rises up "to be revealed as our master" (484b). Thus, by engaging in the greatest of illegalities, an individual is only acting in accordance with what is *naturally* just.[53]

Callicles continues, arguing that it is only once Socrates gives up the philosophic life in favor of the political life that he will come to recognize the truth of natural justice. He warns of the dangers of devoting oneself exclusively to philosophy, noting that a person who does this will lack experience in political affairs and, as a result, will necessarily appear ridiculous when he attempts to engage in them, just as a man who devotes himself exclusively to political practices will appear ridiculous when he seeks to engage in philosophy. The individual who avoids public life, he intimates, is unable to help himself or his friends. He concludes, in a manner that is likely meant to foreshadow Socrates's trial and death, that Socrates's way of life is shameful. If anyone ever seized Socrates, claiming that he was doing an injustice, he would be left "dizzy and gaping, without anything to say"

(486a–b). Thus, Callicles urges him to "stop refuting" and to "'practice the good music' of affairs" (486c).

In the middle of his harangue, Callicles quotes a line from Euripides's lost play *Antiope*. Noting that those who exclusively pursue philosophy appear ridiculous when they enter into political action, and similarly that political men appear ridiculous when they enter into philosophic pastimes, Callicles states: "For Euripides' saying comes to pass: each one is brilliant in this, and presses on to this, 'allotting the greatest part of the day to this, where he happens to be at his best.' And he flees from wherever he is undistinguished and reviles this, but praises the other thing out of goodwill toward himself" (484e–485a). The quotation cited by Callicles is the first of many references in the *Gorgias* that comes from *Antiope*.[54] Why would Plato draw our attention to this play? The significance of these references is revealed by the play's dramatic plot, which centers on the tension between the active life and the contemplative life. According to the existing fragments, two brothers, Zethus and Amphion, sons of Antiope, the rightful Queen of Thebes, must rescue their mother from their murderous uncle. However, before they are capable of doing so, they must put aside their disagreements as to which of their two ways of life is superior. While Zethus maintains that the practical life devoted to political affairs is superior, Amphion holds that the life of philosophy and music is superior. Zethus's powerful arguments win, and Amphion accedes that the active life is better. Together they arrange their mother's rescue, and Amphion, having been won over to the active life, is just about to put their uncle to death when the god Hermes intervenes as a deus ex machina. Hermes reestablishes order by restraining the brothers and establishing them as rightful joint rulers of Thebes.[55]

The dramatic struggle between Zethus and Amphion depicted in *Antiope* mirrors the struggle between Callicles and Socrates. Not only does Callicles explicitly invoke Zethus as representative of his type of life, but the two also value many of the same things, including hard work, manly strength, and the ability to help oneself and one's family.[56] In contrast, Socrates, who leads a life of political abstention and pursues the pleasurable practice of philosophy, is akin to Amphion. According to one of the extant fragments, Amphion states that "anyone who engages in many activities that he need not engage in is foolish, when he can live free from business in a pleasant fashion."[57] Nightingale suggests that both Amphion and Socrates believed that despite their political abstention, they were capable of providing the greatest benefit for the city through their philosophy.[58] Furthermore, Socrates later forthrightly identifies himself with Amphion when he informs Callicles that he would have liked to give "him back the speech of Amphion for the speech of Zethus" (506b). Thus, it seems that Plato refers to Euripides's play to suggest that Zethus and Amphion are representative of Callicles and Socrates, respectively.

However, the resemblance between Euripides's *Antiope* and Socrates's encounter with Callicles is limited to this similarity between the characters. The conclusion of Euripides's play differs significantly from the conclusion of the debate between Socrates and Callicles. The conclusion of *Antiope* suggests that it is best for active and for contemplative individuals each to perform that to which they are by nature predisposed. The establishment of Zethus and Amphion as joint rulers at the end of the play points toward the necessity of both character types. As John Gibert notes, Zethus and Amphion "express complementary ideals, neither of which, in the partial and undeveloped form in which it is presented and exemplified by the inexperienced young men, is conspicuously beneficial to the polis."[59] The play, therefore, points toward the coincidence of power and wisdom in the figures of Zethus and Amphion. Both are in some way good and necessary for the city. As noted, this notion also characterizes the definition of friendship that was raised, but not fully explored, in the *Lysis*. As will be recalled, near the end of the *Lysis*, Socrates suggests that friendship may exist between those who are akin to one another.[60] The implication (an implication Socrates ignores) is that friendship may consist in the relation of two individuals who are akin (or who belong to each other) and who are both good *in their own way*, or according to his own *nature*.[61] By alluding to *Antiope*, Plato may be drawing our attention to a potential reconciliation between Callicles and Socrates that may serve as a foundation for political life.

As we shall see, however, no reconciliation between power and wisdom is forthcoming in Socrates's encounter with Callicles, as neither of them agrees with Euripides's assessment. For his part, Callicles argues that it is precisely the predilection to favor one's strengths and ignore one's weaknesses that leads to ridicule. To avoid the ridicule, Callicles argues that it is best for a serious man to gain experience in political affairs. While it is fitting and noble for a free man to partake of philosophy when he is young, beyond this he ought to focus on becoming highly distinguished in political affairs. For Callicles, if someone fails to practice philosophy when young, he "will never deem himself worthy of any fine and noble affair" (485d). That Callicles believes one ought to practice philosophy when young shows that he is not completely oblivious to its merit and its use. However, by recognizing its *use* in preparing men for "fine and noble affair[s]" (485d),

Callicles relegates philosophy to an inferior status. For Callicles, philosophy ought to be ministerial to the practice of politics.

In response to Callicles's disquisition, Socrates exclaims his good fortune in having fallen in with Callicles. He goes so far as to proclaim Callicles to be a touchstone on which he will be able to test his soul. Callicles, Socrates asserts, has the three characteristics of "knowledge, goodwill, and outspokenness," by which he will be able to "make a sufficient test of a soul's living correctly" (487a). While Gorgias and Polus were wise and friendly toward Socrates, they were "too sensitive to shame" (487b). In contrast, Socrates notes that Callicles is sufficiently educated, has goodwill toward him, and is outspoken, or not entirely restricted by a sense of shame. The extent to which Socrates's praise of Callicles is ironic has been a source of much debate because Plato appears to suggest that Callicles's character is the linchpin on which hinges the question of whether Socrates is correct in exclusively practicing the philosophic life.[62] Indeed, Socrates relates that because Callicles has all three of these qualities, his agreement with Socrates on the things Socrates has *opinions* about (not knowledge) would signal that Socrates's way of life is correct. In contrast, his disagreement would either signal that Socrates's way of life is incorrect, or that Socrates is insufficiently persuasive to convince Callicles of the truth of his opinions. Of course, at the end of the dialogue Socrates has not persuaded Callicles of the things he has opinions about.[63] Thus, if Callicles possesses these three qualities, it would suggest that, as presented by Plato, Socrates's way of life is in some way deficient.

The first quality, Callicles's knowledge, seems to be immediately called into question by Socrates. After calling Callicles knowledgeable, Socrates tells him that he has "been sufficiently educated, as many of the Athenians would say" (487b). Furthermore, Socrates relates that he once overheard Callicles urging his friends not to become "wise . . . beyond what is needful" (487d). Many scholars agree that Socrates's appeal to what "the many" would say, as well as Callicles's admonition not to become overly wise, suggests that his characterization of Callicles as knowledgeable is ironic. However, while Callicles may not have wisdom, this does not preclude him from having a certain type of knowledge, or intelligence, in the form of potential prudence. Callicles may lack wisdom, he does not lack a concern for the *human* things, as is evidenced by his concern for Socrates's safety, which is an aspect of prudence.[64] Of course, prudence in the authoritative sense of the term is governed by wisdom, and, in the absence of this governing virtue, the decisions made concerning the human things would be mere cleverness.

Nevertheless, Callicles's concern suggests that he at least possesses prudence in its potential form. In this way, Callicles can be seen to have knowledge, the first characteristic necessary to test Socrates's way of life.

Socrates further relates that Callicles does have goodwill toward him and is outspoken. As evidence of Callicles's goodwill, Socrates points to the fact that he has heard Callicles give his friends the same counsel that he had just conveyed to him, namely, to stop philosophizing beyond what is necessary, and to take greater care for his own safety. Some scholars point to the fact that later in the dialogue, Callicles will act in a way that causes Socrates to revoke whatever friendship he believed they had (499b–c). However, goodwill and friendship are distinct.[65] Thus, while Callicles likely is not Socrates's friend, this does not preclude him from showing goodwill toward him. In addition, Socrates suggests that Callicles's outspokenness, or immunity to shame, has been established by his speech praising natural justice whereby the strong rule the weak. Thus, Callicles appears to possess the characteristics necessary to test Socrates's way of life.

In any case, Socrates begins by taking on Callicles's assertion that according to what is naturally just the stronger and the superior ought to rule and have more than the inferior. The obvious difficulty with this position is that according to nature the many, when joined together, are stronger than the one. As a result, the laws they institute, including the laws that "doing injustice is more shameful than suffering injustice," are not only just by convention, but are just by nature as well (489a–b). In response, Callicles asserts that by superior he does not exclusively mean stronger but refers to those who are more intelligent (φρόνιμος). Thus, asserts Callicles, the more intelligent individual ought to rule and ought to have more than the ruled. Socrates seizes on this contention and asks whether a doctor, having intelligence concerning a person's diet, ought to have more food than others or whether, through his ruling, he ought to distribute the food to everyone, according to his intelligence. Earlier in the dialogue Socrates had compared justice to the art of medicine—while the art of medicine concerns the body, justice is directed toward the health of the soul. Socrates's example is intended to expound on this corollary, while also pointing out that Callicles is overly preoccupied with external goods such as food, rather than with what is good for the soul.

Displaying his lack of philosophic acumen, Callicles retorts, "You are talking of food and drink and doctors and drivel; but this is not what I mean" (490c–d). At this point, perhaps in recognition of Callicles's philosophic ignorance, Socrates becomes ironic with Callicles. He asks him whether those who are most intelligent and superior in weaving or cobbling ought to have the biggest cloak or the biggest shoes. In frustration, Callicles asserts that by those who are more intelligent and stronger he means "neither cobblers nor cooks, but those who are intelligent in regard to the affairs of the city and in what way they may be well governed" (491a–b). Callicles does not leave it at this, however, adding that the intelligent and strong are "not only intelligent but also courageous, being sufficient to accomplish what they intend" (491a–b). It is precisely these individuals—those who are intelligent in regard to the affairs of the city and courageous—who ought to rule. Callicles concludes, "The just is this, that these, the rulers, have more than the others, the ruled" (491d).

Devin Stauffer notes that by asserting that it is just for the superior to rule and for the rulers to have more than the ruled, Callicles provides a natural segue for the conversation to turn to the question of justice.[66] However, rather than do so, Socrates instead turns to the question of moderation, asking whether the ruler also ought to rule his own desires (491d). Why does Socrates turn to the topic of moderation? As will be made clear, part of the reason is Callicles's excessive concern with external goods, or the goods of the body. By turning to the issue of moderation, Socrates seeks to show Callicles not only that there is a greater good than these external goods, but also that the acquisition of these external goods necessarily requires some involvement with evil. Socrates seeks to redirect Callicles's desires from external goods to an unalloyed good that is not dependent upon evil.

In response to Socrates's suggestion that rulers ought to be moderate, Callicles asserts vehemently that one who controls his desires and appetites is a slave. Instead, he argues that one ought to allow one's desires to be as great as possible and that the ability to satisfy these desires leads to happiness. Socrates, in turn, praises him for his outspokenness before asking whether Callicles believes that in order to satisfy these desires one ought to "prepare satisfaction for them from any place whatsoever" (492d–e). When Callicles agrees, Socrates in turn asks whether those who are in need of nothing are, therefore, not happy. Callicles responds, "No, for in this way stones and corpses would be happiest (492e).[67] Surprisingly, Socrates does not deny the charge, but instead points out the equal wretchedness of those who continuously need to satiate their desires without end. He compares the life of the intemperate man to a man with perforated and decayed jars. In a quest to fill his jars, the intemperate man continuously works to fill them and is in pain when they are not filled. In contrast, the life of the orderly and moderate man is like a man with healthy jars who, upon having filled his jars, gives them no more thought and is at rest (493a–d). Callicles remains unpersuaded, noting again that the life of the moderate man is like that of a stone, for "when one has been filled up," he no longer rejoices nor feels pain (494b). Unable to convince Callicles, Socrates seeks to shame him, comparing the life described by Callicles first to a stone curlew, a bird who excretes as he eats, and next to a life of constant scratching (494b–c). In the face of both examples, Callicles remains outspoken and unashamed, asserting that "he who scratches, too, would live pleasantly" (494d). However, when Socrates finally turns to the "culmination of such things as these, the life of catamites," Callicles exclaims, "Are you not ashamed, Socrates, to lead the arguments into such things?" (494e). While some have maintained that this betrays Callicles's sense of shame, it is equally plausible that Callicles is attempting to shame Socrates. If so, Callicles can be seen to be turning Socrates's own tactics against him. Just as Socrates had appealed to conventional justice and shame to refute Gorgias and Polus, Callicles now seeks to use shame to refute Socrates. Again, Plato seems to be pointing to the similarity between Socrates and Callicles.

Socrates, of course, is impervious to Callicles's attempt to shame him. Instead, he simply notes that Callicles is the one who has led the argument to this point by refusing to distinguish between good and bad pleasures. Socrates now turns to the question of whether the good and the pleasant are the same or different. If the good and the pleasant are the same, the shameful examples provided by Socrates could, perhaps, be classified as good, whereas if the good and the pleasant are different, the examples would be classified as pleasurable, but not as good. In a bid to remain consistent, Callicles asserts that he will hold to the position that the good and the pleasant are the same. While Callicles's answer suggests that Socrates's examples have convinced him that the pleasant and the good are *not* the same, he asserts that he will maintain his former argument. Callicles is not willing to be shamed into abandoning his position. Rather, he will follow the argument to its conclusion. Callicles's desire leads the way; he is not held back by shame.

What follows is a somewhat odd colloquy, in which Socrates tells Callicles that if he is speaking contrary to his own opinion, he would be "corrupting the first speeches" and "would no longer be sufficiently examining with me the things that *are*" (495a; emphasis added). When Callicles replies, "And you too," Socrates coyly responds, "Well then, I too am not doing what's correct, if indeed I do this, nor are you" (495b). Through a series of dialectical moves, Socrates will go on to elicit from Callicles that the good and the pleasant are different. Of course, earlier in his conversation with Polus, Socrates led Polus to the conclusion that the good and the pleasant are the same. It seems that Socrates and Callicles agree that neither of them is going to be examining what *is*. Callicles will assert contrary to his true belief that the pleasurable and the good are the same, while Socrates, perhaps in contrast to his true beliefs, will attempt to lead Callicles to the belief that the pleasurable and the good are different.

As part of his refutation, Socrates distinguishes between the good and the bad on the one hand, and the pleasant and the painful on the other hand. According to Socrates, the good and the bad are completely distinct—that is, they are obtained and lost separately. As evidence, he points to health and sickness; when one becomes healthy, he is released from sickness. It is impossible to suffer what is good (health) and bad (sickness) at the same time. In contrast, the pleasant and the painful are necessarily mixed. When one obtains pleasure from eating or drinking, for example, this implies the need and desire of hunger or thirst, which is painful.

Socrates's ostensible purpose is to critique Callicles's apparently thoroughgoing hedonism by pointing out that pleasure cannot be identical to the good because pleasure is necessarily mixed with pain, while the good is wholly free of need, or lack. However, Socrates's critique suffers from a number of flaws. As Devin Stauffer points out, it is not true that health and sickness cannot coexist, as one can suffer varying degrees of sickness and health throughout life.[68] Furthermore, Socrates never proves that an unalloyed good, free of any bad, can exist. In fact, as was shown above, in the *Lysis* Socrates calls into question whether such a good can exist at all in the present life. However, Callicles does not raise these problems. Instead, when Socrates asks him whether he agrees that there is a good, independent of bad, Callicles asserts emphatically, "I do agree, extraordinarily so" (496c). Callicles's assertion is significant, as it reveals his desire for a good that is free of evil.[69]

The desire that Socrates and Callicles both have for an unalloyed good, independent of evil, points to a kinship between them. However, their desires differ in a fundamental point. Socrates seems to believe that if this unalloyed good exists at all, it transcends the present life and, as we've seen, this belief inclines him toward a denigration of existing relationships. In contrast, Callicles's concern for the human good and his insistence on the importance of the political life suggest that his desire for an unalloyed good is immanentist in character—Callicles might be said to be guilty of wishing to immanentize the eschaton. Despite the divergent directions in which they direct their desire, their kinship indicates that they may be compatible in some way. As indicated in chapter 1, in the *Lysis* Plato subtly raises the possibility that friendship between two individuals who are good, each in his own way, may be an unalloyed good. To the extent that such friendship is founded on the virtue of each partner rather than necessity, we might conclude that it operates as an instantiation of the unalloyed good.

Neither Socrates nor Callicles recognizes the kinship between them. Focused solely on the logical rigor of the argument, Socrates refutes Callicles by distinguishing the pleasant from the good. Through a series of moves, Socrates shows that if the pleasant and the good are indeed the same, then the intelligent and the courageous (those revered by Callicles as good and deserving to rule) are no different from the foolish and the cowardly, as both experience the same amount of pleasure. Callicles is shown to have no basis on which to ground his admiration for intelligence and courage. At the end of this exchange and in response to the refutation, Callicles asserts that he had not been forthright with Socrates in asserting that all pleasures are the same, but that he was, instead, joking. In response, Socrates cries out:

> Oh! Oh! Callicles, how all-cunning you are and how you treat me like a child—at one time claiming that things are this way, and at another time that the same things are otherwise, deceiving me! And yet I did not think at the beginning that I was to be deceived by you voluntarily, since you were my friend. But now I have been played false, and it looks like it's necessary for me—according to the old saying—to make do with what is present and to accept from you this that is given. (499b–c)

Socrates points out that Callicles has deceived him and, therefore, can no longer be considered a friend. Of course, as noted above, Callicles was never said to have friendship with Socrates; he was only credited with having goodwill toward him.

In any case, while Socrates claims to have exposed Callicles's friendship as fraudulent, it is significant that almost immediately prior to this, Socrates uncovers Callicles's desire for an unalloyed good. We have already seen that near the beginning of their discussion, Callicles shows himself to be a desirous individual. However, his desire was directed solely to the external goods that rhetoric and the conventional practice of politics are able to provide. At this point in the dialogue, Callicles's desire for the good is revealed to be so great that he believes in the existence of a good independent of any evil. In the next portion of the conversation, Socrates will lead Callicles to the conclusion that the attainment of such a good is, in fact, impossible.

Based on Callicles's distinction between good and bad pleasures, as well as his belief in the existence of an unalloyed good, Socrates steers Callicles to accept the proposition that pleasures and pains are good only to the extent that they are directed toward the good. Next, Socrates asserts that it requires an *artful* man to distinguish pleasant things that are good from pleasant things that are bad. Tying the conversation back to the theme of rhetoric, he reminds Callicles that he had earlier designated rhetoric as an experience rather than an art, on the basis that rhetoric concerns itself only with flattery, or pleasure, irrespective of whether the pleasure aims at the good. He concludes by asking Callicles whether the "rhetoric directed toward the Athenian people and the other peoples of free men in the cities" is anything other than simple flattery aimed at gratifying the people (502e). In response, Callicles asserts that it depends on the rhetor; some care for the citizens, while others are precisely as Socrates describes.

Perhaps surprisingly, Socrates does not deny the existence of the art of rhetoric Callicles describes, instead noting that if such an art were to exist, its goal would be to make the "citizens' souls to be as good as possible" (503a). However, Socrates quickly follows up on this comment by noting that this rhetoric has never yet come to pass. He continues his description of this "noble" rhetoric by noting that the rhetorician who "speaks with a view to the best" would seek to arrange and order the citizens' souls in a healthy way, namely, by instilling justice and moderation into them, and by removing injustice and intemperance (504d–e). Socrates notes, however, that moderation is not chosen simply for its own sake. Rather, just as doctors "allow a healthy man to satisfy his desires" and deny the same to a sick man, so the rhetor will allow healthy souls to pursue their desires, while keeping base souls from attaining their desires. By keeping the base soul away from these desires, the rhetor will improve it. When Callicles agrees, Socrates concludes by asking him to agree also to the proposition that keeping the base soul "away from the things it desires" is punishment and that being punished is "better for the soul than intemperance" (505b). Of course, by leading Callicles to this conclusion, Socrates has bested him. Socrates has shown Callicles to be unable to meet the challenge posed at the beginning of their conversation: to show that doing injustice and not paying the just penalty when one does injustice are not the utmost of all evils.

Callicles, however, refuses to be refuted, claiming that he does not know what Socrates is saying. In response to this feigned ignorance, Socrates states, "This man here does not abide being benefitted and suffering for himself this thing that the argument is about, being punished" (505c). Despite the logic of Socrates's argument, Callicles remains unpersuaded and refuses to take his medicine. Socrates now indicates that his argument is only half over because Callicles's intransigence is frustrating its development. At this point the dialogue takes a turn. Socrates asserts it is "not righteous to abandon even myths in the middle" and proposes to take over the argument by posing questions and answering them in turn (505c–d). In what follows Socrates shifts from a dialogic style of argumentation to a disquisitional, or rhetorical one, to finish the argument. However, Socrates explains that what he is about to say is *not* said with knowledge. Furthermore, he indicates that he would have preferred to continue speaking with Callicles until he had "given him back the speech of Amphion for the speech of Zethus" (506b). In this way, Plato suggests that the disquisition that Socrates is about to deliver cannot be characterized as Socrates's true belief—or that he is unsure of its truth.

Socrates begins by fairly accurately recounting the conversation he has just finished with Callicles. He distinguishes the pleasant from the good and states that the pleasant must be done for the sake of the good. Furthermore, he notes that things are made good by the presence of some virtue and that the virtue of the soul is moderation. At this point, however, Socrates deviates from the conversation he has had with Callicles. Whereas up to this point, Socrates has held that moderation is directed *toward* the good, he now holds that the moderate soul *is* good (507a). Given Socrates's insistence that philosophy always says the same thing, we may conclude that Socrates does not truly believe the rhetorical display he is delivering and that what he is about to say is simply a noble myth (505d).[70] As we shall see, this rhetorical display is designed to appeal to Callicles's desire for an unalloyed good.

Socrates continues by noting that the ordered, moderate soul is the basis for the ordered whole of nature, as moderation leads to happiness between men and the gods. The moderate man, Socrates states, would do "fitting things concerning both gods and human beings," and he would, in fact, be "the completely good man" (507a–b). Therefore, if one wishes to be happy and good, he must "pursue and practice moderation, and each of us must flee intemperance as fast his feet will carry him" (507d). At the center of this noble myth are the virtues of justice and moderation. Wisdom and its concomitant desire are not even mentioned.[71]

Socrates then ties the noble myth back to the philosophic principle that he has maintained throughout the dialogue; one ought to avoid the practice of injustice, and one must punish the evildoer, even if the evildoer is oneself or "some other of one's own" (507d). Invoking the wise (οἱ σοφοί), Socrates states that "heaven, earth, gods, and human beings are held together by community, friendship, orderliness, moderation, and justness; and on account of these things, comrade, [the wise] call this whole an order, not disorder and intemperance" (507e–508a). As a result, the immoderate evildoer, who is incapable of friendship and community, ought to be punished if this happy state of order is to be established: "If oneself or some other of one's own—whether private man or city—needs it, one must apply the just penalty and punish, if he is to be happy" (507d). According to the myth put forward by Socrates, a natural harmony obtains between the whole and the human soul; the soul is a microcosm of the whole. Although Socrates's account is simply a myth, the philosophic principle he has maintained throughout the dialogue remains the same: injustice ought to be avoided, and the evildoer must be punished. Thus, Socrates constructs a myth that is as close to the truth as possible.[72]

Socrates's myth, which holds out the possibility of a wholly ordered and wholly good universe, is designed to appeal to Callicles's desire for an unalloyed good. Socrates himself, however, does not actually believe in the existence of such a universe. As we shall see, for Socrates there is no natural compatibility between the individual soul and the whole; the soul is not, in fact, a microcosm of the whole. As a result, in contrast to Callicles, Socrates does not believe in the existence of an unalloyed good.

As noted, Socrates's myth is based on an understanding of nature and the whole articulated by *the wise* (οἱ σοφοί). This reference to the wise is significant because, as indicated above, these same wise (οἱ σοφοί), who "converse and write about nature and the whole," are invoked in the *Lysis* in support of the proposition that "like is always necessarily a friend to its like" (*Lysis*, 214b2–6). As argued above, Plato suggests in the *Lysis* that Socrates does not quite fully understand these "wisest ones." As will be recalled, Plato's purpose in the *Lysis* is subtly to imply that Socrates's inattention to nature and the whole causes his inquiry into the definition of friendship to flounder. It is perhaps no surprise, then, that almost immediately after providing this appealing account of an ordered whole of nature Socrates implicitly denies its possibility by appealing to the concept of friendship.

Socrates begins his denial of the myth by recounting Callicles's charge against him. Let us examine, he says, on the basis of the myth "whether what is said is fine or not: that I am unable . . . to help either myself or anyone of my friends or relatives, or to save them from the greatest dangers, but am at the mercy of whoever wishes" (*Gorgias*, 508c). As the myth has indicated, and as Socrates has continuously maintained, doing injustice and failing to pay the just penalty is the greatest evil or harm that can befall a person. Furthermore, he contends that the greatest help one can provide for oneself and for one's friends is to turn away the greatest harm; in turn, the second greatest benefit "would be help against the second evil, third against the third, and so on" (509b–c). The nobility of the benefit corresponds to the greatness of the evil turned away. When Callicles assents, Socrates notes that it is, therefore, necessary to prepare a power so as neither to do injustice nor to suffer injustice.

He begins by analyzing the power necessary to avoid suffering injustice. The power consists in either taking up rule in the city (perhaps even as a tyrant) or being a friend of the existing regime (510a). Not surprisingly, Callicles agrees emphatically. Next, Socrates asks whether Callicles also agrees that "each man is the friend of another to the greatest possible degree, who the ancient and wise said was the friend: like to like" (510b). As will become evident, the introduction of friendship and, in particular, the introduction of this definition of friendship, is crucial. In the *Lysis*, Socrates's understanding of this concept is depicted as, at best, incomplete. Not only does Socrates there deny the possibility of two individuals having a self-sufficient friendship that entails an appreciation for each other simply on account of one another's goodness, but he also guides the conversation in such a manner that at its end friendship is subsumed within the ambit of erotic desire or love (ἔρως).

When Callicles agrees to the definition of friendship provided by the wise—like is friend to like—Socrates continues, stating that neither a good nor a lowly man would be able to become the tyrant's friend "with his whole mind" (510b–c). The tyrant would either fear the good man or despise the lowly. The only individual who could be a friend with the tyrant, suggests Socrates, is the man "who, being of the same character and praising and blaming the same things, is willing to be ruled and to be submissive to the ruler. This man will have great power in that city" (510c–d). As a result, the only way an individual is able to obtain power in a city ruled by a tyrant—and thus be able to prepare a power to avoid injustice—is by becoming as much like the tyrant as possible. The obvious result of preparing such a power, concludes Socrates, is that great injustices will also have been committed and, therefore, the greatest evil will have befallen the individual who has obtained power in the regime. Such an individual will have harmed "his soul through imitation of the master and through power" (511a).

In effect, Socrates's understanding of friendship denies the possibility of the unalloyed good he had earlier proffered in the form of the noble myth. At the end of the *Lysis*, Plato points toward the unsettling political ramifications that the Socratic understanding of friendship entails. In the present dialogue, Plato makes clear how the Socratic understanding of friendship unsettles the cohesion of the regime. The myth of an ordered and complete whole depends on the phenomenon of friendship: "The wise say . . . that heaven, earth, gods, and human beings are held together by community, *friendship*, orderliness, moderation, and justness" (507e–508a; emphasis added). If political community and the order of the cosmos depend on friendship, Socrates's understanding of friendship implies that the myth does not adequately describe reality. Indeed, Socrates's understanding of friendship suggests that there is, in fact, no harmony between the individual soul and the political community. As a result, he counsels Callicles to avoid the life of politics and instead to pursue the Socratic way of life; the private life of contemplation. While the life of politics (including befriending the demos) may protect one from the lesser evil of suffering injustice, it does so only "at the cost of the things dearest to us" (513a). The Socratic life is unable to ensure that one does not *suffer* injustice; it does ensure that one avoids committing injustice, which is the greatest harm that can befall a person.

Upon the conclusion of Socrates's speech, Callicles seems to be only partially persuaded. He states, "In some way, I don't know what, what you say seems good to me, Socrates; but I suffer the experience of the many—I am not altogether persuaded by you" (513c). In reply, Socrates states, "If we investigate these same things often, and better, perhaps you will be persuaded" (513c–d). Perhaps a better rhetorician would be capable of persuading Callicles. In any case, as noted above, Socrates began the conversation with Callicles by noting that due to his goodwill, outspokenness, and knowledge, Callicles could serve as the touchstone for Socrates's way of life. Socrates had declared that if he could convince Callicles to agree with him on the thing about which he holds opinions, it would vindicate his way of life. Now, near the end of the dialogue, Callicles remains unpersuaded, suggesting that perhaps Socrates's way of life has *not* been vindicated. By drawing our attention both to Callicles's character and to the fact that Callicles remains unpersuaded, Plato seems to be suggesting that Socrates's approach to the debate between politics and philosophy—or the debate between Zethus and Amphion—is either not the correct approach or is a debate that is insoluble by Socratic rhetoric. Given Plato's critique of the Socratic understanding of friendship leveled in the *Lysis*, as well as the role that Socrates's understanding of friendship plays in the *Gorgias*, it is fair to conclude that the Socratic understanding of friendship is not only incomplete but also negatively impacts his relation to the polis.

The manner in which Socrates introduces the second and final myth at the end of the *Gorgias* bolsters this interpretation. The myth Socrates relates concerns the judgment of human beings in the afterlife, and it explains how it came to be that men are judged on the basis of their soul alone, rather than on account of their wealth, beauty, or political connections.[73] The myth is meant to underscore the message Socrates has conveyed throughout the dialogue: the care for one's soul ought to come before a concern for the external goods provided by politics, and, to the extent that the external goods are obtained at the expense of an upright soul, they ought to be considered worthless. Socrates introduces the myth by alluding to a passage in the *Iliad* concerning the division of rule among the gods. He states, "As Homer says, Zeus, Poseidon, and Pluto divided the rule among themselves, after they took it over from their father" (523a). James Nichols points out that this is a reference to book XV of the *Iliad*, in which Poseidon complains of being unjustly stripped by Zeus of his right to jointly rule the land. According to the account in the *Iliad*, Zeus orders Poseidon to leave the fighting at Troy. In response, Poseidon angrily states that he is of equal honor to Zeus. Poseidon recounts that he, along with Zeus and Pluto (Hades) had divided up the rule they had taken over from their father Cronos, such that while Pluto would have control of the underworld, Zeus would have control of the heavens, and Poseidon would have control of the seas. Meanwhile, they would all have equal access to the land and to Mount Olympus. As a result, Poseidon suggests that Zeus is committing a grave injustice by ordering him to stop interfering in the land battle between the Achaeans and the Trojans, as they have an equal title to jointly rule the land. Despite this fact, Poseidon leaves the battle on account of Zeus's superior force.

Why does Plato allude to this story? Of course, it introduces the myth in a way that sets up Zeus's ability to unilaterally alter the method by which human beings are judged without interference from Poseidon so that they are judged on the basis of their soul alone. Throughout the dialogue, Socrates has attempted to convince his interlocutors that the soul alone is important, suggesting that Zeus, as depicted in the myth, is representative of Socrates. Like Zeus, Socrates changes the standards of judgment such that the soul alone is of importance, while external or necessary goods are counted as worth nothing. Socrates believes that only his way of life is good.

Plato's allusion to Zeus's banishment of Poseidon through the myth told by Socrates at the end of the dialogue seems to offer a substitute ending to that of *Antiope*, the Euripidean play alluded to at earlier points in the dialogue. It will be recalled that in *Antiope*, Zethus, the political man of action (who is meant to represent Callicles), and Amphion, the philosophic man of contemplation (who is meant to represent Socrates), argue about whose life is superior. At the end of the play, Hermes enters and restores order by granting them the power to rule jointly. Of course, this is decidedly *not* how the dialogue between Callicles and Socrates ends. While Socrates does not persuade Callicles of the superiority of his way of life, he is unambiguously the victor of the conversation. Socrates ensures that the standards by which his way of life is judged, are recognized as the *only* standards. The fact that Plato introduces the final myth told by Socrates by alluding to Zeus's unlawful act of depriving Poseidon of his share in their joint rule suggests that he believes that Socrates also commits an injustice in denying any merit to Callicles's concern for the external (or necessary) goods. Could it be that Plato believed that some sort of joint rule is necessary between politics and philosophy? Or that the coincidence of power and wisdom is necessary?

Conclusion: Friendship and the Coincidence of Power and Wisdom

The *Gorgias* details the way in which the Socratic understanding of friendship developed in the *Lysis* directly impacts Socrates's approach to politics. At the end of the *Lysis*, Socrates's ambivalence about friendship is made clear. On the one hand, he tells Lysis and Menexenus that he counts himself as one of them, suggesting that they have become friends. On the other hand, he immediately follows this up by stating that they have not yet discovered what a friend is. It was earlier noted that the conclusion of the *Lysis* suggests that at the end of the dialogue Socrates considers himself to be a friend of the boys only because he has "refuted them" and has inculcated in them an awareness of their deficiency and of their metaphysical incompleteness—he has stoked in them a desire for the good.

In the *Gorgias*, Socrates's understanding of friendship is seen to impact his approach to politics. In the first half of the dialogue, Socrates's understanding of friendship, as well as his declaration of friendship to

Polus and Gorgias, leads him to refute them. By refuting them he seeks to remove their false conceptions of what *is*. First, he refutes Gorgias by exposing his deficient and contradictory understanding of the nature and purpose of rhetoric. Next, he refutes Polus, showing him that it is better to suffer injustice than it is to do injustice, and that it is better to pay the just penalty for injustices committed than it is to escape punishment. In the same way that Socrates refuted Lysis, he refutes Polus and Gorgias. Furthermore, just as in the *Lysis*, in which Socrates's refutation of the boys caused them to rebel against the established authorities, so in the *Gorgias*, Socrates sends Polus back into the city armed with a rhetoric designed to refute the city rather than flatter it. For Socrates, it is just to refute both oneself and one's friends; friendship consists in removing the lie that exists in one's soul. This ensures that a Socratic approach to politics is necessarily negative and destructive of the bonds of the city. Socrates's interaction with Gorgias and Polus shows how his conception of friendship has the effect of destroying the city's conception of justice (and thereby the bonds that hold the city together) and how his conception of friendship causes his interaction with it to be negative.

In the second half of the dialogue, Socrates counsels Callicles to avoid politics on the basis of the understanding of friendship he had developed in the *Lysis*. How is it that Socrates's understanding of friendship can cause him both to send Polus back into the city armed with a rhetoric meant to refute it *and* to counsel Callicles to avoid politics altogether? The answer is related to the difference in character type represented by Polus and Gorgias, on the one hand, and Callicles, on the other. In some ways Callicles is very similar to Socrates. While Polus and Gorgias both suffer from a strong sense of shame, Callicles and Socrates are both more outspoken. As a result, while Polus and Gorgias are not *capable* of overcoming the conventional understanding of justice due to their shame, Callicles and Socrates—perhaps to differing extents—*are* able to overcome these conventions. Indeed, both are shown to be highly erotic individuals, and it is their erotic desire for what is good that enables them to "shake . . . off and break . . . through all" the conventional taboos that stand in their way (484a). In fact, Callicles's desire for the good is so great that he believes in the existence of an unalloyed good independent of any evil. As a result, under the Socratic conception of friendship, which holds that like is a friend to its like, Callicles ought to avoid politics altogether—it is only by becoming like the regime that Callicles will come to have power in the city. Gorgias and Polus are both wedded to conventional conceptions of justice. Therefore, Socrates is not depriving them of the good by undertaking a life that requires them to challenge and refute the existing conventional understanding of justice. In contrast, Callicles's erotic desire and his devotion to natural justice suggest that he ought to avoid politics altogether.

Neither Socrates's negative approach to politics nor his attempt to avoid politics altogether is due primarily to a desire to avoid the conventional vulgar conception of injustice as is suggested in the *Apology*. Rather, the Socratic approach to politics stems from his conception of friendship. While the destructive effect of his understanding of friendship is hinted at near the end of the *Lysis*, it is made explicit in the *Gorgias*. There is no self-sufficient basis for friendship that is grounded in a simple conception of another's goodness. Rather, to the extent that friendship exists, it consists in refuting the lie in another's soul and in awakening in him a desire for completeness—a completeness that lies outside the realm of friendship and politics altogether.

Plato's treatment, however, suggests that the Socratic conception of friendship may be mistaken. In the *Lysis*, Plato alludes to the fact that there may be a basis for friendship between two people, both of whom are good, *each in his own way*. The friendship between Lysis and Menexenus is portrayed as a potential instantiation of such a friendship. The soft-spoken, thoughtful Lysis is contrasted with the more brash (potentially courageous) Menexenus. This allusion to a self-sufficient friendship independent of need is continued in the *Gorgias*. Socrates and Callicles are depicted as being in some way similar to one another. Both are erotic, relatively shameless individuals who have a strong desire for the good. However, each is devoted to a different mode of life; Callicles to the active the life of politics and Socrates to the quiet life of contemplation. Furthermore, their respective desire for an unalloyed good extends in different directions. While Callicles's desire is directed toward the imminent world, Socrates's desire seems to be more transcendent. By presenting Socrates and Callicles in this way—as similar, yet in some ways different—Plato seems to be suggesting that each might be good in his own way. The different way of life to which each of them is attracted might be complementary. If the goodwill they display toward one another were to develop into friendship, that friendship might operate as an instantiation of the good.

Given both Plato's depiction of the Socratic understanding of friendship in the *Lysis* and the way that friendship works to destroy the myth of an ordered, harmonious cosmos in the *Gorgias*, it seems that for Plato the seeds for a reconciliation between power and wisdom lie in a correct understanding of friendship. In both the *Lysis* and the *Gorgias*, Plato points to the danger the Socratic understanding of friendship poses for politics. The manner in which Socrates subsumes friendship into the ambit of erotic desire for the good ensures that there is no friendship independent of need. A friendship that appreciates another solely for the other's own good qualities is, for Socrates, simply a myth. As a result of this understanding of friendship, the pursuit of the good through philosophic contemplation becomes a personal endeavor, and the phantom friendships of politics interfere with that endeavor. Socratic philosophy, in its attempt to discover the right way of life through dialogue with others, has the (perhaps inevitable) effect of being parasitic on politics, as it questions the conventions and practices that hold a city together. At the same time, Plato's purpose in these dialogues is not *simply* to point to the danger of philosophy—a teaching certainly worth bearing in mind—for he simultaneously points toward a reconciliation between politics and philosophy through the medium of friendship, a reconciliation that is taken up in earnest by Aristotle.

Chapter Three

Aristotle's Friendship of the Good

Politics and Philosophy: An Unresolved Tension

In book I of the *Politics*, Aristotle traces the emergence of the polis, or how the polis comes to be established. In the overview provided, Aristotle stresses the role that necessity plays in the process. He notes that the most basic unit of the polis, the individual, unites with other individuals in order to counter necessity. As evidence of this, he points both to the natural coupling of male and female, who come together "from a natural striving to leave behind" offspring, and to the conjoining of master and slave, each of whom use their distinct functions to preserve themselves as well as the other. From these relationships arises the household, which exists in order to satisfy "the needs of daily life" (*Politics*, 1152b13). The household exists to counter day-to-day necessities. However, Aristotle continues by noting that a household is not on its own self-sufficient but is still subject to necessity of "non-daily needs" and, as a result, various households join together to constitute the village. In turn, several villages come together to comprise "the complete community"—the polis. The polis, Aristotle states, is completely self-sufficient and exists "by nature." From this brief sketch it seems that for Aristotle the rise of the polis is a natural process that occurs in response to the press of necessity. Man is by nature a political being because his nature is not, on its own, self-sufficient.

If, however, necessity is the only basis for the development of the polis, it is not entirely clear *why* several villages would come together to form a polis. As Aristotle makes clear, the household and the village together already provide for both man's daily and non-daily needs. At the level of the village necessity is already overcome. To what end do villages join together to form a polis? In his brief depiction of the development of the polis Aristotle hints that the polis has an end beyond the simple countering of necessity; while the polis comes "into being for the sake of living, it exists for the sake of living well" (1252b25–30). The city, therefore, has an end beyond merely securing the existence of its members and countering necessity. Aristotle initially suggests that the end of the city is justice. Pointing to man's capacity for speech, he notes that man, in contrast to other herd animals, has the ability to distinguish between good and bad, justice and injustice, and that he further has the capacity to institute his judgments concerning the just into custom and law. Justice seems to be the natural end of the city.[1]

Based on the city's complete and full self-sufficiency, Aristotle argues that it is "prior by nature to the household and to each of us" (1253a20). The whole is prior to the part. As a result, man's full existence depends on his relation to the polis in the same way that a foot or a hand depends on the existence of whole body. Aristotle seems to suggest that it is in the city that man finds completion or perfection as a human being. Specifically, it is by being an active participant in the shaping and promulgation of the city's laws concerning what is just and unjust, and furthermore by obeying these laws, that man fulfills his purpose. In contrast to Socrates, Aristotle presents the individual as having the same end as the city. In book I of the *Politics*, Aristotle seems to imply that there is a natural harmony between the individual and the city. The remainder of the *Politics*, however, complicates this picture. In book VII, Aristotle specifically raises the question of what the best life is for the individual and whether it is the same for the individual as for the city. We are again told that the city has an end beyond itself; it aims at living well, not mere existence. Both the city and the individuals that comprise it ought to aim at living well, but whether this end is the same for both the individual and the city is subject to debate.

What it means to live well is not entirely clear. While Aristotle is clear in book VII of the *Politics* that living well means living a life of virtue, he notes there is debate over *which* virtue.[2] At this point, Aristotle deals head-on with the question that had been debated by Callicles and Socrates in the *Gorgias*: "There is dispute among those who agree that the most choiceworthy way of life is that accompanied by virtue as to whether the political and active way of life is choiceworthy, or rather that which is divorced from all external things—that involving some sort of study, for example—which some assert is the only philosophic way of life" (1324a26–29). The political and the philosophic life are here juxtaposed, and, after spending some time distinguishing the various modes of the active life, Aristotle involves himself in the debate between the proponents of these two types of life.[3] Aristotle lays out the various opinions before investigating them. He first puts forward a position that is nearly identical to the Socratic position as presented in the *Gorgias* before contrasting it with the position held by Callicles. He notes that some eschew the active life on the grounds that "the way of life of the free person [is] different from that of the political ruler and the most choiceworthy of all," and that the political life is an impediment to one's own well-being (1325a17–22). In contrast, others consider the active life to be best due to the fact that "it is impossible for one who acts in nothing to act well, and that acting well and happiness are the same thing" (1325a22–24).[4] The debate between Socrates and Callicles is taken up in the seventh book of the *Politics*.

In the last book of *The Nicomachean Ethics*, Aristotle conspicuously concludes that the philosophic life is superior to the political life. This same conclusion is expressed in book VII of the *Politics* as well. Thus, while Aristotle's statement that "happiness is a sort of action" may seem to settle the debate between the two lives in favor of the active life of politics, Aristotle famously redefines the life of philosophy to be a life of action. The active life, he states, is "not necessarily in relation to others" (1325b17). Aristotle suggests that the active life can also be practiced in a *private* manner, rather than simply in a public or political manner, as philosophic thought is a type of activity. In fact, Aristotle goes so far as to say that those thoughts "that are complete in themselves, and the sorts of studies and thoughts that are for their own sake" are "much more" active than those thoughts that are pursued for some other activity (1325b18–21). This statement mirrors Aristotle's argument in book X of the *Ethics* that the philosophic life is the happiest due to its greater self-sufficiency and to the fact that it is sought as an end in itself. The *Politics* and the *Ethics* come to the same conclusion: the philosophic life is the *most* active life.

While Aristotle is explicit in his assertion that the philosophic life is superior to the political life, in the *Politics* he nevertheless emphasizes that cities can *also* partake in the action of thought. Positing the existence of an "isolated city" that intentionally chooses to live alone, he writes that this type of city is also active, "for activity can come about relative to a city's parts: there are many sorts of shared activities undertaken by the parts of the city in relation to one another" (1325a3–4). While this passage is somewhat cryptic, what Aristotle seems to have in mind is education. As Susan Collins notes, Aristotle "suggests that the political community may be organized so that its highest aim is action understood in [the] sense" of study and thinking.⁵ The life of political rule—understood as the improvement of souls—shares in the active life of the philosopher by aiming at the life of study and thought. It is for this reason that the last book of the *Politics* covers the education that ought to be instituted in the best regime. Aristotle concludes that in this way the aim of the best regime and the aim of the individual are the same; both partake of the activity of thought.

A number of indicators suggest, however, that harmony between the individual and the city is not so easily achieved. First, the education described by Aristotle is not *simply* philosophic. In fact, Aristotle's views on philosophic education mirror those of Callicles. It will be recalled that Callicles believed that while some education in philosophy was necessary and suitable for the young, one ought not to pursue education beyond what is necessary. Aristotle relates similarly that one ought not to "persevere overly much in the [liberal sciences] with a view to proficiency" (1337b17). Commenting on the education in Aristotle's best regime, Collins writes that the education Aristotle lays out aims at "a life of leisure in which the arts and music figure most prominently. This life is neither wholly political nor wholly philosophic—neither wholly devoted to the city nor separated from it."⁶ Of course, this seems to be in stark contrast to book X of *The Nicomachean Ethics*, where the life of theoretical contemplation is unambiguously held to be the best life, for the sake of which all other actions are undertaken. Robert Bartlett concludes that "the discussion of 'leisure' in [book] VII is arguably the peak of the *Politics*, not because it outlines the genuinely satisfactory end of life but because it points to the true peak, the truly satisfying and altogether private activity of philosophic contemplation."⁷ If Bartlett is correct, it would seem that the aim of the individual and the aim of the city are *not* the same, as the aim of the city is not strictly philosophic in the way it is for the individual.⁸

Furthermore, to the extent that education in the best regime *is* philosophic, we have to wonder what causes the city to be concerned with philosophy. That is, while the necessity that characterizes the pre-political state is the impetus that animates the city's concern for justice, it remains an open question what it is that animates and orients the city toward philosophy. Last, Aristotle fails to make clear why the philosopher should be concerned with the well-being of the city. It will be recalled that in his discussion concerning the relative worth of the political and philosophic life, Aristotle had raised the Socratic objection to the political life that political rule is simply an impediment to one's own well-being (1324a38–39). However, he does not (in the *Politics*) directly respond to this criticism. Given that Aristotle spends the last book of the *Politics* giving political advice on how to institute an educational system that is concerned with the improvement of the souls of *other* people, it would seem fair to question whether Aristotle's pursuit of the good is undermined or tainted in some way by political concerns.[9] We may conclude, therefore, that in the context of the *Politics* Aristotle's attempt to resolve the tension between the philosopher and the city appears to be at most a superficial solution. Analogizing the leisure of the city to the theoretical speculation of the philosopher does not fully reconcile the philosopher to the city.

The *Politics* does, nonetheless, hint at a resolution to the problem regarding the philosopher's estrangement from the city. In introducing the educational system of the best regime, Aristotle raises the question of why one would do, or learn, something if it does not directly benefit oneself. He writes: "It makes a difference, too, for the sake of what one does or learns something. What is for one's own sake or for the sake of friends or on account of virtue is not unfree, while the person who does the same thing on account of others would often be held to do something characteristic of the laborer or the slave" (1337b18–22). It seems that the philosopher needs to obtain some benefit from instituting the educational system if he is not to be doing something "characteristic of the laborer or the slave." As the quotation indicates, it is the concept of friendship that is able to answer the questions of why the city is concerned with philosophy and why the philosopher is concerned with the education of his fellow citizens. As will later be made clear, friendship is concerned both with one's own good and the good of another. Like the city itself, friendship is ordered toward two ends.

Friendship and the Structure of Aristotle's *Nicomachean Ethics*

Fully to understand the way in which friendship mediates the tension between the political and philosophic life, it is necessary to turn to *The Nicomachean Ethics*, in which Aristotle unpacks his conception of friendship in detail. It is a discussion that has traditionally received little attention. This lack of attention is curious, given that the two books on friendship, books VIII and IX, together constitute a full fifth of the *Ethics*. To see how Aristotle's discussion of friendship figures into the debate between proponents of the life of politics and those who champion the private life of contemplation, it will be helpful to look to the structure of *The Nicomachean Ethics* as a whole. The first book of the *Ethics* states Aristotle's intention "in outline." In this book, Aristotle notes that his goal is to find "the human good" (*NE*, 1094b7). Based on an argument that assumes the teleological character of the entirety of nature, Aristotle holds, somewhat ambiguously, that the human good is "an activity of soul in accord with virtue, and if there are several virtues, then in accord with the best and most complete one" (1098a17–18). Of course, as the *Ethics* continues it quickly becomes clear that there is more than one virtue; Aristotle distinguishes the moral virtues, discussed in books III through V, from the intellectual virtues discussed in book VI.

The ambiguity surrounding the human good—and whether it consists in the practice of moral virtue or the practice of intellectual virtue—does not appear to be resolved until book X, the last book of the *Ethics*, in which Aristotle straightforwardly states that the philosophic life of contemplation is the highest life, while the life of moral virtue is happy "only in a secondary way" (1178a8–9). Given Aristotle's somewhat abrupt conclusion and the apparent ambiguity surrounding the way in which his discussion of the moral virtues fits together with his account of the philosophic life described at the end of the *Ethics*, some scholars have despaired of finding any unity at all in the *Ethics*.[10]

Many political interpretations of the *Ethics* have sought to resolve these difficulties by reading the *Ethics* in light of the debate raised in the *Politics*; the relation between the active life devoted to politics and the private contemplative life of philosophy.[11] One standard political interpretation of Aristotle's *Ethics* holds that Aristotle recognizes the tension between philosophy and politics but seeks to alleviate it in various ways, all the while maintaining the superiority of philosophy.[12] According to this interpretation, the *Ethics* can be seen as containing two complementary parts. While the first half deals with the political life characterized by moral virtue, the second half is concerned with the philosophic life. This interpretation has much to offer in that it is able to make sense of the way the moral virtues relate to the life of philosophic contemplation. Specifically, this reading holds that Aristotle presents the life of moral virtue in a way that emphasizes its nobility while also exposing its limitations. This ensures that the well-bred Greek gentleman (καλοσκἀγαθος), if he is a sufficiently attentive reader, will recognize that the true benefit of moral virtue is that it points beyond itself toward philosophic virtue, which is self-sufficient and capable of being practiced alone.[13]

While this interpretation provides much purchase, it suffers from two drawbacks. First, it struggles to make sense of Aristotle's stated intention in book I to define the human good. In describing his intention at the outset, Aristotle argues that the end of human action—the human good—falls under the architectonic art of politics and that the good of a nation or city is "nobler and more divine" than the good of any single individual (1094b10–11). How can the good of the city be "nobler and more divine" than the good of a single individual if the *Ethics* ends with the conclusion that the solitary life of contemplation is the human good? Second, it runs into a difficulty similar to that noted above concerning the conclusion of the *Politics*—namely, if the human good is the solitary life of contemplation, why does Aristotle concern himself with the activity of directing the Greek gentleman toward the life of contemplation? Last, and perhaps most problematically, this political interpretation gives short shrift to Aristotle's two books concerning friendship. The standard political approach typically treats these two books as an exhortation meant to prepare the reader for Aristotle's somewhat startling claim that the philosophic life is the happiest life.[14]

It is my contention that, in light of Aristotle's discussion of friendship, the *Ethics* does *not* end with the conclusion that the solitary life of contemplation constitutes the human good. Rather, I will show that Aristotle views the political life of moral virtue and the philosophic life of contemplation as complementary. Focusing on Aristotle's account of friendship not only allows us to see the *Ethics* as a single, unified work, but it is also able to account for why Aristotle asserts that the philosopher is concerned with the political realm.

The Ascent to Friendship via Magnanimity

Aristotle famously holds that true friendship, or friendship in the primary sense, is the friendship of good human beings (1157a30–32). If so, it would seem that the highest friendship would be a friendship between those who are characterized by magnanimity or those who are "great-souled" (μεγαλοψυχία), as Aristotle considers these individuals to be completely virtuous (1123b36–1124a2). Therefore, when we turn to Aristotle's discussion of magnanimity, we are perhaps unsurprised to see that friendship makes an appearance. At the same time, however, its appearance in the discussion of magnanimity is striking given Aristotle's depiction of the great-souled man. He is described as haughty and somewhat aloof (1124a20). One commentator has gone as far as to say that Aristotle's magnanimous man is "self-absorbed."[15] And yet, Aristotle writes that the magnanimous man "is incapable of living with a view to another—except a friend—since doing so is slavish" (1124b28–1125a1). Why does the topic of friendship appear at this juncture of the *Ethics*? Even more curiously, why does it appear as part of the description of an individual who seems to be most self-sufficient and is "incapable of living with a view to another"? The question is related to Socrates's inquiry in the *Lysis*: what need could a self-sufficient, good individual have of another?

The answer, I hope to make clear, will become apparent once we understand who Aristotle's magnanimous man is. However, the identity of the magnanimous man is itself a vexing question as Aristotle never provides a definition of the virtue of magnanimity; nor does he give an unambiguous indication in the *Ethics* of who the magnanimous man is. To understand the identity of Aristotle's magnanimous man requires that we look outside the confines of the discussion of magnanimity in the *Ethics* and examine first the virtue of courage, as well as Aristotle's depiction of the magnanimous man in the *Posterior Analytics*. As will be made clear, Aristotle's account of courage reveals the need that a city may occasionally have for an individual who is capable of transcending its standards. While the great-souled man would seem to fit the mold of an individual who is not beholden to the city's standards, Aristotle's depiction of the great-souled man in the *Posterior Analytics* shows the dangers such a man poses to the city.[16] I contend that when Aristotle's account of magnanimity in the *Ethics* is read in the light of these other passages, it becomes clear not only *who* the magnanimous man is, but also why friendship is introduced at this point of the *Ethics*, and what role friendship plays in Aristotle's political philosophy in general.

Courage is the first moral virtue that Aristotle covers in the *Ethics* and, contrary to what some have insisted, his discussion of this virtue is far from a conventional retelling of the Greek conception of courage.[17] On the contrary, as we shall see, Aristotle's account of courage in book III is meant subtly to bring into focus the limits of the conventional Greek understanding of courage. Aristotle seeks to expose these limits in order to make clear to the reader the need for the virtue of magnanimity, which is introduced in book IV.

Aristotle initially indicates that courage "is a mean with respect to fear and confidence" (1115a7–8). However, what this mean entails is never fully resolved in Aristotle's discussion of courage. This lack of resolution is due, in part, to the interrelation between two aspects of courage: (1) the courageous man's desire for honor; and (2) his lack of concern for ill-fortune. The courageous man's desire for honor is initially portrayed as laudable—indeed, one *ought* to be fearful of disrepute (1115a10–15). The courageous man's lack of concern for ill-fortune is similarly suggested to be laudable (1115a15–17). Aristotle suggests that perhaps one should not be fearful of things such as poverty or sickness, as these are outside of one's control. It seems, then, that courage is primarily concerned with pursuing that which is noble and honorable and remaining impassive in the face of the vicissitudes of fortune.

As Aristotle's account of courage develops, however, he indicates that the relationship between honor and ill-fortune is somewhat troublesome and that the common conception of courage is problematic. Toward the end of the first chapter on courage, Aristotle defines courage "in the authoritative sense," by noting that "a courageous man could be said to be someone who is fearless when it comes to a noble death and to *any* situation that brings death suddenly to hand," such as illness or death at sea (1115a33–35). This seems simply to bolster the observations made earlier—the courageous man is concerned with honor and is unmoved in the face of ill-fortune. Aristotle, however, follows this definition of courage "in the authoritative sense" by noting two things. First, when faced with the prospect of death at the hands of ill-fortune, the courageous man "despairs of his preservation" (1115b3). Of course, this pulls back on the observation that a courageous man ought to remain impassive when confronted with ill-fortune. Rather than remain unaffected by ill-fortune, the courageous man "despairs of his preservation" and ought to be "disgusted with [the] sort of death" brought on by ill-fortune (1115b2–3). Second, Aristotle notes that while "the courageous act like men (ἀνδρίζονται) in circumstances where prowess in battle is possible or dying is noble," in situations of illness or sea, "neither such prowess nor nobility is possible" (1115b6–7). Aristotle subtly suggests that the virtue of courage is not exhausted by the manly acts of valor that are considered noble—true courage seems to extend beyond that which the many consider noble. For Aristotle, neither excessive concern with honor nor a disregard of one's fate in the face of ill-fortune is indicative of true courage.

This interpretation receives added credence from Aristotle's depiction of the five types of specious courage that merely resemble courage in the authoritative sense. The first of these types of specious courage is the "courage found in the citizen" who "endures dangers" for the sake of honor (1116a17–20). Aristotle uses Hector and Diomedes from Homer's *Iliad* as examples of this type of courage. According to the lines Aristotle selects to portray Hector and Diomedes as exemplars of civic courage, both warriors indicate that they will maintain their stations in battle so as to avoid reproach or scorn. These are, of course, somewhat odd examples of *specious* courage, as both Hector and Diomedes are warriors undertaking great acts of valor on the battlefield—precisely the situation described by Aristotle as that in which the courageous man is able to display his virtue. Why are these examples used to illustrate the courage that only *seems* like virtue in the authoritative sense, when they seem to fit all the criteria for a courageous act?[18]

The answer becomes evident when one examines the wider context in which these lines are spoken. The first line is part of a dialogue Hector has with himself as he is preparing to face Achilles on the battlefield: "Polydamas will be the first to lay a reproach upon me" (1116a24). The ending of the line—which Aristotle does not quote—is as follows: ". . . for that he bade me lead the Trojans to the city during this fatal night, when goodly Achilles arose. Howbeit I hearkened not—verily it had been better far!"[19] Hector is portrayed as a hero with a tragic flaw. His devotion to reputation and honor is so great that he cannot heed the advice of others and, as a result, puts the welfare of his entire city at risk. Hector's good (as he perceives it) conflicts with that of his city. This tragic flaw prevents him from acting for the welfare of his city, as he places his own sense of honor above that of the common good.

The second example Aristotle provides is that of Diomedes, who states, "For Hector will one day declare among the Trojans, speaking in the assembly, 'The son of Tydeus, by me . . .'" (1116a25). Diomedes makes this statement as he is attempting to pursue Hector on the battlefield. Each time he attempts to do so, however, Zeus thwarts his advance with a "white lightning-bolt."[20] When Nestor recognizes that the gods are against them and advises Diomedes to turn and flee, Diomedes initially refuses because of a concern about what Hector will say of him. Like Hector, Diomedes is incapable of heeding advice because his reputation and honor are at stake. Aristotle uses the example of Diomedes as an instance in which pride and concern for honor can result in a failure to acknowledge one's limitations. Diomedes's pride and his excessive concern for honor cause him initially to spurn Nestor's advice in favor of the belief that he can oppose the will of the gods, or challenge fortune. Diomedes's failure to heed Nestor's advice evinces equanimity in the face of ill-fortune of a kind that is destructive of his own self-preservation and serves as a detriment to his fellow Greeks.

These two examples, coupled with what follows, indicate why civic courage is not the same as courage in the authoritative sense. Aristotle immediately follows up these examples of civic courage by comparing them to examples of men whom it is necessary to *compel* to fight. He writes,

"Someone might put in the same category also those who are compelled by their rulers [to fight]" (116a30–31). The only difference between those operating under the auspices of civic courage and those who must be compelled to fight is that while the former fight out of a sense of shame, the latter fight on account of fear of the penalties involved. The city, it seems, has two ways to induce men to fight for its interests: by holding out honor or by the threat of penalties.

While Aristotle flatly states that having to be compelled to fight by the threat of penalties is not noble (1116b4), he indicates that the former method—fighting for the sake of honor—is also problematic. Indeed, the very concern for honor that the city seeks to inculcate in its citizens so as to induce them to fight for its security and continued existence can undermine that same goal as well. The corollary of honor is shame and, as the examples of Hector and Diomedes make clear, an excessive concern with honor and shame (the standards of the city) can cause men to act in ways that are contrary to the good of the city. While Hector and Diomedes may obtain honor and glory by facing their foes on the battlefield (and avoid the shame that attends leaving the battlefield), their conduct is destructive to both themselves and the city. Through these examples, Aristotle makes clear that the very sense of honor and shame that the city inculcates in its citizens can lead to its ruin as well. To secure its existence, it seems that the city may at times require an individual who is capable of transcending the city and its standards. Aristotle's depiction of civic courage as deficient points to the need for a more developed account of the proper relation to honor and fortune, one that is *not* tied to the standards of the city.

Aristotle's account of civic courage directs the reader's attention to the need for an individual who is capable of transcending the standards of the city. It is precisely this individual whom Aristotle describes in his portrait of the great-souled man in book IV of the *Ethics*. However, while Aristotle's account makes clear that the magnanimous man transcends the city and is capable of bestowing great benefits on the city, the question of who this magnanimous man is, and therefore what type of benefits he provides, has long been the subject of debate. Some have argued that the great-souled man represents the height of moral achievement that is capable of being attained by an individual devoted to the life of politics, such as a statesman or general.[21] Others have suggested that Aristotle is referring to the philosopher who is devoted to the life of contemplation.[22]

Strong arguments have been raised in favor of both positions. For example, those insisting that Aristotle's great-souled man is intended to depict a man of great moral or political achievement point to Aristotle's placement of this virtue among the so-called moral or political virtues and to the fact that the magnanimous man is concerned with great actions. In addition, the magnanimous man is said to be eager to help others and willing to face great dangers.[23] In contrast, others have suggested that the great-souled man is the philosopher par excellence, with some going so far as to maintain that he is intended to represent Socrates. Pointing to Aristotle's statement that magnanimity is a "kind of ornament" that only attends those who have complete virtue (1123b36–1124a2) and to his statement that the life of theoretical contemplation is the happiest life (and hence the most virtuous), these scholars conclude that the magnanimous man is meant to represent the philosopher.[24] In addition, some have noted that the magnanimous man's idleness and proclivity to irony also favor the view that magnanimity is at root a philosophic virtue.[25]

Further debate has surfaced as to whether Aristotle views the magnanimous man as unambiguously good or whether he presents him as suffering from a tragic flaw.[26] For example, Harry Jaffa suggests that the fault of the magnanimous man is his "overweening" concern with "his own greatness."[27] In contrast, Carson Holloway argues that this "overweening concern" is "compatible with and may arise from his moral seriousness and not from a merely personal preoccupation with his own status."[28] Others, such as W. F. R. Hardie, have suggested that the tragic fault of the magnanimous man lies not in his intolerance of insults but in his refusal to recognize "the contribution of luck and nature to his achievement."[29] According to this view, the tragedy of the magnanimous man is his inability to recognize his indebtedness to fortune.

It is my contention that in his account of the virtue of magnanimity in the *Ethics* Aristotle proposes to describe *both* the philosopher and the statesman. Building on Aristotle's discussion of magnanimity in the *Posterior Analytics*, in which Aristotle suggests the possibility that there may be two types of magnanimity, I will argue that his depiction of the great-souled man in the *Ethics* is intended as a response to the difficulties posed by the virtue of magnanimity in the *Posterior Analytics*.[30] Specifically, I will argue that the *Posterior Analytics* suggests that magnanimity can be ascribed to the apex of the moral life exemplified by the politically active man as well as to the height of the philosophic life exemplified by the philosopher. As depicted by Aristotle in the *Analytics*, both these individuals, who attain the apex of their respective ways of life, have a correct estimation of the great benefits they are capable of providing to the city. At the same time, they both suffer from a tragic flaw that causes them to act in a socially destructive manner. Last, I will argue that in the *Ethics* Aristotle provides a solution to this tragic flaw in the form of friendship. It is through friendship and the recognition of each other's virtue that Aristotle is able to reorient the magnanimous man's lack of concern with the standards of the city for the common good.

Aristotle's discussion of the virtue of magnanimity in the *Posterior Analytics* occurs in a passage that is ostensibly meant to provide a simple overview of how to attain the definition of a genus that covers more than one species. The virtue of magnanimity is provided as an example (*Posterior Analytics* [*PA*], 97b7–28).[31] Aristotle maintains that to obtain a definition of magnanimity it would be necessary to compare two groups of individuals who are held to be magnanimous on account of different traits to see what they have in common. If we take our bearing from Alcibiades, Achilles, and Ajax, we are led to the conclusion that magnanimity consists in an intolerance of dishonor, as it was intolerance that caused Alcibiades to go to war, roused Achilles's wrath, and drove Ajax to commit suicide (97b20–21). In contrast, if Lysander and Socrates are held to be magnanimous, it seems that magnanimity consists of being indifferent (ἀδιάφορος) to good and ill-fortune.[32] Aristotle concludes his brief discussion of magnanimity by stating that to obtain a definition common to these two groups, it would be necessary to "inquire what common element have equanimity (ἀπάθεια) amid the vicissitudes of life and impatience of dishonor" (97b23–26). If they have nothing in common, Aristotle concludes that there would be two genera of magnanimity.

If Aristotle's discussion of magnanimity in *The Nicomachean Ethics* is intended as an attempt to discover a common trait that applies to both groups of men mentioned in the *Posterior Analytics*, it would initially seem to have failed. Indeed, as Howland notes, "If one reads the passage from the *Posterior Analytics* at face value, such an attempt [to find a common trait] must fail: anyone who is intolerant of insults after the manner of Alcibiades, Achilles, and Ajax is not truly indifferent to fortune."[33] However, before making a judgment as to whether the *Ethics* does, in fact, apply to both groups of magnanimous men, it is necessary to inquire into the two groups themselves to discover *all* the commonalities that the members of each respective group share. Aristotle provides the following advice for attaining a common, universal definition:

> It is also easier by this method to define the single species than the universal, and that is why our procedure should be from the several species to the universal genera—this for the

> further reason too that equivocation is less readily detected in genera than in *infimae species*. Indeed, perspicuity is essential in definitions . . . and we shall attain perspicuity if we can collect separately the definition of each species through the group of singulars which we have established . . . and so proceed to the common universal with a careful avoidance of equivocation. (97b28–38)

Thus, Aristotle states that we must first inquire into *all* aspects that members of each respective group share in common with one another, maintaining an especial vigilance for equivocation, before examining what it is that the members of both groups have in common.

When we turn to the individuals who comprise the first type of magnanimity—those intolerant of insults—their commonality seems straightforwardly political. As Tessitore notes, Alcibiades, Achilles, and Ajax were all great Greek warriors who "embody a conception of greatness that expresses itself in action and battle. Each is characterized by a desire for glory that exhibits itself in conquest and implacable resistance to dishonor."[34] Thus, it is clear that the first type of magnanimity is, at root, political. All the individuals that comprise this group are capable of providing great benefits in war and battle for their respective political communities. However, as Aristotle intimates, while their concern for honor can lead them to confer great benefits on their community, it can also lead them to inflict great harm on their community due to a tragic flaw (ἁμαρτία): stubbornness and an inability to listen to advice.

A brief analysis of each of the three politically magnanimous men shows that knowledge of their own greatness and of the honors they are due, combined with an inability to heed advice, causes them to inflict great damage on their community. Ajax is famous for attempting to kill the Greek generals Menelaus and Agamemnon after they fail to grant him the honor he feels he is due. According to Sophocles's rendering of the story, as Ajax prepares to leave his tent to avenge his dishonor, his concubine, Tecmessa, attempts to dissuade him. Ajax replies, "Woman, silence is the grace of woman."[35] Later, when the plan goes awry due to the intervention of the gods, Ajax plans to kill himself. Again, Tecmessa seeks to dissuade him, asking, "Wilt thou not heed?"[36] Again Ajax spurns her advice, telling her, "Too much hast thou spoken already."[37] Ajax commits suicide shortly after a fit of delusional rage.

Similarly, when Agamemnon deprives Achilles of the war prize he believes he has rightly merited during battle, Achilles refuses to continue fighting with the Greeks against the Trojans, thereby depriving them of their greatest warrior.[38] When Odysseus and Phoenix seek to persuade him, Achilles refuses to be reconciled with Agamemnon, recounting instead the dishonor that Agamemnon had done him.[39] This failure to heed their advice results not only in the death of a great many Greeks, but also of his dear friend Patroclus.[40] Last, Alcibiades's failure to listen to Socrates's moderating advice leads to his notorious political enterprises.[41] In his pursuit of political glory, Alcibiades betrayed the Athenians by aiding the Spartan forces in their war efforts against the Athenians during the Peloponnesian War.[42] All three of these great warriors were very much attuned to the honors they were due, and this self-knowledge, combined with an incapacity to heed moderating advice, caused them to inflict great harm on their community.

While it is relatively straightforward to determine what connects the individuals comprising the first type of magnanimity, it is more difficult to discern what holds Lysander and Socrates together. Socrates the philosopher and Lysander the Spartan general initially appear to have little in common, aside from an ability to bear the ill-fortune of poverty with equanimity.[43] As a result, some have maintained that Lysander's love of honor and supposed intolerance of dishonor suggest that he actually belongs with Alcibiades, Achilles, and Ajax, while Socrates comprises a class all on his own.[44] Others have suggested that Lysander is merely included as "a more accessible but less perfect introduction" to the philosophic magnanimity of Socrates.[45]

The inclusion of Socrates as representative of the second type of magnanimity suggests that Aristotle intends to draw our attention to the fact that this type of magnanimity can take a philosophic form. However, while Aristotle may seek to draw our attention to the philosophic form that this type of magnanimity can take, it is still necessary to account for the reason Aristotle chooses to include Lysander the Spartan general (who was not known in any way for his philosophic acumen) as opposed to some other philosopher. If we follow Aristotle's advice and proceed "from the several species to the universal genera" while maintaining an eye for "equivocation," we will see that Lysander and Socrates have more in common than simply an ability to bear poverty with equanimity. Following Aristotle's method allows us to avoid the premature conclusion that Aristotle has either misplaced Lysander or has included him as simply a "more accessible" introduction to philosophic magnanimity.

In addition to having an ability to bear the ill-fortune of poverty with equanimity, Lysander and Socrates share an experience of having been excluded from rule on account of their status in society.[46] However, in contrast to their easy acceptance of poverty, both Socrates and Lysander did *not* easily accept the ill-fortune of their lowborn status. Instead, each believed himself to be superior to others and deserving of honor and rule. We have already seen in our analysis of the *Gorgias* and the *Apology* that Socrates views his manner of life to be superior to the political life due to his commitment to avoiding injustice, and that he thinks he is worthy of honor for the benefits he is capable of bestowing on the city.[47] Callicles tells Socrates that his philosophizing causes him "to become unmanly (ἀνάνδρῳ)" as he flees "the central area of the city and the agoras" (*Gorgias*, 485d5–7). He presciently declares that Socrates's preoccupation with philosophy at the expense of practicing the more manly art of rhetoric and politics ensures that if he is ever accused of doing an injustice, he would stand in the law-court "dizzy and gaping, without anything to say" (486b1–2). Of course, in the *Apology*, Socrates does attempt to use rhetoric to make the case that his way of life is superior to the active life. As part of his defense speech, he seeks to justify his way of life by telling the jurors that he constantly philosophizes because the oracle at Delphi had ordered him to do so, but he fails to persuade the requisite number of jurors of his innocence.[48] Given the depiction of Socrates in the *Gorgias*, as well as Socrates's inability to persuade the jurors in his trial, we can conclude that Socrates's failure was largely the result of his inability to take seriously the necessity of courage and rhetoric in political affairs.

Lysander's lowborn status similarly prevented him from obtaining the honor and privilege that he deserved. To rectify this perceived injustice, Plutarch relates that Lysander "formed a design to remove the government from [those who ruled Sparta], and to give it in common to all . . . Spartans," so that he might have a share in ruling.[49] The plan, as recounted by Plutarch, is strikingly similar to the story that Socrates relates at his trial concerning the oracle at Delphi. According to Plutarch, Lysander sought to trick his fellow citizens into believing that it was the will of the gods that political rule ought to be decided on the basis of merit rather than nobility. To this end, he conjured up oracles from Apollo to "alarm and overpower the minds of his fellow-citizens by religious and superstitious terrors, before bringing them to the considerations of his arguments."[50] However, as Plutarch relates, Lysander's plan fell through due to the lack of courage on the part of one of its participants.[51] Thus, both Lysander and Socrates audaciously sought to use the religious customs of the people to implement great change in the order of the city, and both failed due to a lack of courage on the part of the participants involved in the plan.

The commonality between Lysander and Socrates is all the more striking in light of the fact that the term ἀδιάφορος is equivocal and can mean different things in different circumstances. When paired with *poverty*, ἀδιάφορος describes one who is *indifferent* to poverty.[52] However, when paired with *adversity*, it means to be *steadfast* or *unwearying*.[53] In light of Aristotle's advice that one ought to avoid equivocations when making the requisite comparisons necessary to arrive at a common definition, it seems that we have to choose from among the two meanings of the word *indifferent*. Aristotle means to draw our attention either to the capacity of Lysander and Socrates to be indifferent to poverty or to their ability be steadfast and persevere in the face of their lowborn status.

It is likely that Aristotle intends to highlight the ability of Lysander and Socrates to persevere in the face of their lowborn status, as this seems to be a more fitting basis for magnanimity than their ability to suffer poverty with equanimity.[54] In addition, viewing Socrates and Lysander from this perspective not only elucidates what they have in common, but it also makes clear what unites the first type of magnanimity with the second, allowing us to obtain a common, universal definition of magnanimity. Indeed, the members of both groups believe themselves to be great and, therefore, to be worthy of great things.[55] Achilles, Ajax, and Alcibiades were all outstanding in battle, and because of an awareness of their own great worth, they spurned their political community when it deprived them of the honor that they were due. Socrates and Lysander were similarly aware of the outstanding benefits they were capable of bestowing on their political community.[56] To ensure that they, or their way of life, would be accorded the honor it was due, each attacked the foundations of their respective regimes.[57] If the second group of magnanimity is intended to be, at root, philosophic, Aristotle seems to indicate that while those who are philosophically magnanimous may have the capacity to undertake great deeds for their community, their awareness of this fact, coupled with adverse fortune, can lead them to attempt to conquer fortune in a way that is inimical to the well-being of the city.

The men who are provided as examples of the two types of magnanimity (political and philosophic) in the *Posterior Analytics* have a correct estimation of their worth. However, while they rightly recognize that their virtue is worthy of great honor, they mistake their own virtue for the whole of virtue. Those who are politically magnanimous mistake their courage and the benefits it provides for the city as the whole of virtue. Therefore, when they are not afforded the honor they are due, they fail to take advice from those who have knowledge and end up acting in a socially destructive manner. Similarly, those who are philosophically magnanimous fail to recognize the necessity of political courage and, therefore, they seek to usurp the existing order of the city. As great-souled individuals, all five of the magnanimous men listed in the *Posterior Analytics* stand above the standards or conventions of the city; yet each has a tragic flaw causing him to be destructive of the health of the city.

Curing the Magnanimous Man

Based on the portraits he provides of civic courage in the *Ethics* and of magnanimity in the *Posterior Analytics*, Aristotle seems to be in a bit of a quandary. On the one hand, his portrait of civic courage points to the need for a type of courage that transcends the conventions and standards of the city. Indeed, the excessive concern with honor and shame that the city fosters in its citizens causes Hector and Diomedes (both of whom embody civic courage) to spurn advice and act in a way that is inimical to the well-being of their respective cities. On the other hand, the magnanimous men described in the *Posterior Analytics* do transcend the standards of the city. While they are not motivated by shame (as are Hector and Diomedes)—instead, they have an accurate knowledge of their own worth—they also end up acting in socially destructive ways when they fail to receive what is their due. Perhaps it is the destructive tendency of these magnanimous men that causes Aristotle to conclude his discussion of magnanimity in the *Posterior Analytics* by suggesting that if there is one definition of magnanimity, the medical treatment for each will be the same. He states, "Besides, every definition is always universal and commensurate: the physician does not prescribe what is healthy for a single eye, but for all eyes or for a determinate species of eye" (*PA*, 96b26–28). As we shall see, in the *Ethics* Aristotle hints that the prescription for the socially destructive propensity of magnanimous men is friendship.

An initial reading of Aristotle's account of magnanimity in the *Ethics* reveals a number of contradictions, particularly in regard to the magnanimous man's orientation toward honor and fortune. Aristotle does not begin his discussion by disabusing the magnanimous man of the notion that he is worthy of great honor, but instead reaffirms his worth. The magnanimous man "deems himself worthy of great things and *is* worthy of them" (*NE*, 1123b3–4). However, as Aristotle continues, his focus shifts from the honors that attend greatness to the underlying basis of that honor, namely, virtue. As Ryan Hanley notes, "As the account of the magnanimous man's attitude to honour develops it becomes clear that greatness of soul consists not in equal parts claiming and deserving honour; true magnanimity has instead everything to do with the latter and little to do with the former."[58] In fact, near the end of his discussion of honor, Aristotle forthrightly states that the magnanimous man's virtue is so great that no honor could be worthy of it (1124a8). It seems that Aristotle transitions from a concern for honor to a concern for virtue.

Based on this shift, some have suggested that Aristotle's purpose is to cast the virtue of magnanimity initially in such a light as to appeal to ambitious honor-loving individuals. Once this appeal is made, Aristotle subtly shifts the emphasis from honor to the underlying virtues that accompany honor. According to this interpretation, Aristotle is simply preparing the reader for the claim that is to come later in the *Ethics*: the life of theoretical virtue is the best life.[59] One of the difficulties posed by this interpretation, however, is that the shift from honor to virtue is not sharply drawn. Indeed, while the magnanimous man is said to have "complete contempt" for honors that come from people at random, or for small honors, the magnanimous man has a moderate disposition toward the honor that comes from "serious human beings," taking pleasure from such people in a measured way (1124a5–12). Thus, it is not the case that Aristotle unambiguously and absolutely shifts the magnanimous man's concern from honor to virtue alone. Aristotle remains purposefully ambiguous.

Similar ambiguity surrounds Aristotle's depiction of the magnanimous man's orientation to fortune. First, we are told that the magnanimous man takes a measured approach to good and bad fortune as well as to wealth and political power, neither being overjoyed by good fortune nor despairing of ill-fortune (1124a12–17). Next, he connects the gifts of fortune to honor, stating that the magnanimous man "is not disposed even toward honor as though it were a very great thing, and political power and wealth are choiceworthy on account of the honor they bring" (1124a17–18). On the basis of this statement the magnanimous man seems to be concerned with fortune because of the honors that attend good fortune. However, Aristotle soon shifts, noting that "in truth only the good human being is honorable" (1124a25–26). This would seem to suggest that one ought not to direct any attention to the gifts of fortune or the honors they bring, as it is only the underlying character trait or virtue that is of real worth. Rather than ending with this conclusion, however, Aristotle instead follows up by noting that "he who has both goodness and good fortune is deemed even worthier of honor" (1124b26–27). That Aristotle calls attention to the fact that some people *believe* those with good fortune are more worthy of honor than those with ill-fortune, suggests that the beliefs of these people matter. Thus, in the same way that the magnanimous man ought to accept honor from those who are "serious," he also needs to dispose himself to fortune in a proper manner, since fortune is productive of honor.

Why would Aristotle maintain such an ambiguous stance on the magnanimous man's relation to honor and fortune? If it is truly only the magnanimous man's underlying virtue that is good, rather than the honors that attend this virtue, why does Aristotle go out of his way to maintain that the magnanimous man is concerned with honor from those who are serious and to suggest that good fortune can affect other people's perceptions of one's magnanimity? The answer has to do with the phenomenon of friendship. As noted above, friendship makes a curious appearance in Aristotle's discussion of magnanimity. Indeed, Aristotle states that the magnanimous man is "incapable of living with another—except for a friend—for to do so is slavish" (1124b31–1125a1). As will shortly be made clear, Aristotle believes that the two types of magnanimous men listed in the *Posterior Analytics* are well-suited for friendship.

As noted in chapter one, in the *Lysis* Socrates fails to arrive at a definition of friendship. Nevertheless, in that dialogue, Plato intimates that friendship may come to exist between two individuals who are similar yet different in some way from one another. It is precisely this type of friendship that Aristotle suggests as the cure for the socially destructive tendencies of the two types of magnanimous men listed in the *Posterior Analytics*. The two groups of magnanimous men listed in the *Posterior Analytics* are similar in that they are all magnanimous and capable of bestowing great benefits on their community, though the benefits they are capable of bestowing differ in kind. As we have seen, however, the individuals that comprise the two groups of magnanimous men all suffer from a tragic flaw. Their awareness of the honors they are due causes Alcibiades, Achilles, and Ajax to spurn prudent advice, leading them to act in socially destructive ways. Similarly, while Socrates and Lysander have the knowledge and wile to reform the social order, their plans result in failure due to a lack of a particular type of courage. It seems, therefore, that each type of magnanimous man is well-suited to befriend the other, as each makes up what is lacking in the other.

Bearing in mind the suitability of friendship between these two types of magnanimous men helps to make sense of the apparent contradictions in Aristotle's account of magnanimity in the *Ethics*. Aristotle's account of honor and fortune both indulges and tempers the magnanimous man's excessive concern with honor and his perseverance in the face of adversity. Aristotle indulges the magnanimous man by insisting that he is great and is deserving of great things. In this way, the magnanimous man avoids the strictures and standards of the city; he is not beholden to the city's standards concerning honor and shame in the way that Hector and Diomedes are. At the same time, the magnanimous man is not a law unto himself. Aristotle tempers the destructive tendency of the magnanimous man by ensuring that he be concerned with the honor of a few serious people. In the case of those magnanimous men that are "intolerant of insults," Aristotle's method ensures that they will maintain a concern for the opinion and, indeed, the *advice* of serious people, while thinking nothing of the honors or dishonors that come "from people at random" (1124a10). To the extent that he is concerned with the opinion of other serious or magnanimous individuals, Aristotle's magnanimous man is open to persuasion and advice.

Similarly, Aristotle's ambiguous treatment of the magnanimous man's relation to fortune is meant to both indulge and temper those magnanimous men who have the ability to persevere in the face of ill-fortune. Aristotle's statement that "in truth, only the good human being is honorable" indulges the magnanimous man's belief that he is worthy of honor (and perhaps rule) independent of any ill-fortune regarding birth, status, or wealth. At the same time, Aristotle draws attention to the fact that some people esteem those with good fortune. To the extent that the magnanimous man cares for the honor of "serious people," Aristotle's remark has the effect of tempering the magnanimous man's desire to upend the social order in his pursuit of that which is his due. Aristotle's account of magnanimity in the *Ethics* can be seen as an attempt to lead these magnanimous men to recognize the social conventions that honor those who are wellborn, powerful, and courageous. The magnanimous man must, to some extent, *accept* the existing social order. According to Aristotle, fortune is something that ought to be worked with rather than conquered. Of course, being able to recognize the good attributes of another is the definition of a friendship based on the good.

When read in light of the topic of friendship, Aristotle's discussion of magnanimity can be seen as part of his "cure" for the magnanimous men listed in the *Posterior Analytics*. By being complete or self-sufficient *in their own nature*, each type of magnanimous man described in the *Analytics* is good. Yet, to the extent that these magnanimous men mistake their own virtue for the whole of virtue, they are tragic figures that cause grief for their communities. It is only by recognizing the virtues and claims of other magnanimous men who are similar to themselves, yet differ in some point of virtue, that the magnanimous man is able to avoid tragedy.[60] By indulging his concern for honor, Aristotle ensures that the magnanimous man stands above the conventions of the city. At the same time, Aristotle tempers the magnanimous man's concern for honor such that he is concerned only with the honor of "serious people." In this way, Aristotle sets the ground for friendship, which alone can act as the cure for the socially destructive tendencies of the magnanimous man; a cure that is more fully developed in books VIII and IX.

Friendship: Book VIII—A Self-Sufficient Friendship

Already in the first chapter of book VIII, it becomes apparent that Aristotle's discussion of friendship seeks to engage in the same inquiry as that undertaken by Socrates in the *Lysis*: is there a friendship that is *not* rooted in each friend's deficiencies, but instead is based on an appreciation of one another solely for their own sake? Yet, in contrast to Socrates, who was unable to discover a definition of friendship and, therefore, placed it within the ambit of erotic relationships characterized by desire and need, Aristotle does provide a definition of friendship. Building on the framework of Plato's *Lysis*, Aristotle develops an understanding of friendship that is based not on a lack or need, but instead on a reciprocal appreciation of another's goodness.

In stark contrast to Socrates's decision to preface his inquiry into friendship by setting two friends against one another, Aristotle begins his discussion of friendship in book VIII of the *Ethics* with a sort of panegyric to the advantages and uses of friendship. Indeed, he tells us that friendship is "most necessary with a view to life" and that "without friends, no one would choose to live" (1155a5–6). Friends provide a beneficiary for whom one can perform good deeds, and they can help guard the prosperity of the wealthy or act as a source of solace for the poor (1155a7–12). Friends can save the young from error and can provide care for the old (1155a12–14). Last, right near the end of this introduction, Aristotle states that friendship is also useful for those who are in their prime and wish to perform noble actions. In support of this contention, he cites the *Iliad*: "For 'two going together' are better able both to perceive and to act" (1155a15–16).

Why does Aristotle provide a citation from the *Iliad* in his opening statement on friendship? While much scholarship simply glosses over this citation as simply forming part of Aristotle's opening encomium to friendship that will later be qualified or developed,[61] some scholars have argued that this passage is intended to bring out the competitive, or rivalrous aspect of friendship. For example, Anne Marie Dziob argues that Aristotle's purpose is to point out that what inspires one to perform noble actions is the spirited competitive rivalry that can exist among friends.[62] Patrick Cain and Mary Nichols go even further in emphasizing the rivalrous nature of friendship, arguing that Aristotle means to convey that "noble friends do not readily 'go together' in support of each other's noble deeds" because their "very competition with each other for nobility means that their nobility competes with their friendship."[63]

However, the difficulty with these interpretations that highlight the rivalrous aspect of friendship is that the very citation "two going together" (σύν τε δύ' ἐρχομένω) implies that the friends work together in a spirit of aid or cooperation rather than a spirit of competition.[64] I propose that the context in the *Iliad* from which the citation—σύν τε δύ' ἐρχομένω—is drawn reveals Aristotle's intention to highlight the importance and benefit of complementarity in friendship. The citation is taken from the *Doloneia*, the episode in the *Iliad* in which Diomedes and Odysseus conduct a reconnaissance mission at night to seek information concerning the movement of the Trojan troops.[65] The *Doloneia* is a telling example of two individuals whose complementary strengths work together in harmony, rather than a competitive rivalry in which they seek to outdo each other.

The citation "σύν τε δύ' ἐρχομένω" is spoken by the courageous and powerful Diomedes as he is selecting a partner to accompany him on the expedition. Diomedes selects Odysseus, describing him as being "wise above all . . . in understanding."[66] In large part because of their complementarity, their excursion is wildly successful. They not only learn of the Trojan troop movements but are also able to sneak into the Trojan camp and abscond with some fine horses.[67] Odysseus's wile proves indispensable in extorting information from Dolon, the hapless Trojan soldier the two warriors encounter on their expedition, while Diomedes's ruthless courage ensures that Dolon does not reveal their presence to the Trojan captains. Together, the wily Odysseus and the courageous Diomedes are able to provide great benefits for the city, which redound to their own honor.[68] By alluding to this vignette, Aristotle intimates the great political benefits that can be attained if power and wisdom are able to work together effectively.

This interpretation gains additional credence from Aristotle's investigation into the question of what friendship *is*. Aristotle initially puts forward two potential options. He notes that while some argue that friends are "those who are alike," others stress the complementarity of opposites (1155a33–1155b7). Of course, both options were explored and found wanting in the *Lysis*. In the *Lysis*, Socrates found that neither provides the means for elevating the basis of friendship beyond mere utility or need. However, Aristotle provides a further definition of friendship—a definition that was raised but not fully explored by Socrates in the *Lysis*: Aristotle notes that aside from those who cite the previous two definitions of friendship, there "are still others, including Empedocles, who claim that like aims at like" (1155b7–9). Of course, in the *Lysis*, this quotation—"like aims at like"—was used as the launching pad for much of the inquiry into friendship. However, while in the *Lysis* the expression is interpreted as suggesting that those who are identical to each other are friends, in the *Ethics* the quotation appears to describe a middle approach between the friendships of those who are identical to one another and the friendships of those who are opposites. This middle approach suggests that those who are similar but not identical to one another would be friends.[69] That Aristotle introduces a third possible definition of friendship, one not fully explored by Socrates, suggests he intends to add to Socrates's inquiry into friendship, or that he considers Socrates's inquiry deficient in some way.[70]

After raising these three possible definitions of friendship, Aristotle informs us that he intends to turn aside from these "perplexing questions bound up with matters of nature" to focus instead on those questions that are "bound up with what is distinctively human" (1155b9–10).[71] As we shall see, however, the "distinctively human" approach that Aristotle adopts is very much bound up with nature. In fact, throughout his discussion of friendship Aristotle will on several occasions lapse into a discussion of nature almost as if to remind his audience of friendship's connection to nature. In this way, Aristotle can be seen to be building on the framework established in the *Lysis*.

To see how Aristotle responds to the problems raised in the *Lysis*, it will be useful briefly to recap the difficulties Socrates encounters in his attempt to define friendship. It will be recalled that Socrates first raises the problem of reciprocity. While it seems natural that if friendship is to exist between two people they need to love one another, Socrates notes that it is common to speak of lovers of wine, lovers of gymnastics, or lovers of wisdom, all of whom love objects that are incapable of reciprocating their love. However, accepting that friendship need not be reciprocal would result in the absurd conclusion that those who do not reciprocate love, or even hate their lover, are nevertheless friends of their lover. Taking a different tack, Socrates suggests that perhaps the wise—those who inquire into nature and the whole—are correct in holding that "like is always necessarily a friend to its like" (*Lysis*, 214b5).

The difficulty posed by this definition is twofold. First, Socrates argues that it is impossible for the base to be friends. Second, even if it is assumed that the wise are talking not about the bad at all, but only about the good befriending the good, Socrates notes that these would not be useful to one another. To the extent that the good are sufficient in themselves, they will not be in want of anything and, therefore, will not have any desire for their friend. Finding this definition inadequate, Socrates takes another approach and suggests that perhaps those who are opposite and wholly unlike are friends with each other. This suggestion immediately runs into the difficulty that hatred is the opposite of friendship. Finally, Socrates raises the possibility that the neutral (those who are neither good nor bad) are friends with the good. As the dialogue continues, it becomes clear that this definition would destroy the phenomenon of friendship, because it would mean that, in comparison with *the* good (which Socrates terms the *first friend*), all one's friends would simply be phantom friends.

Aristotle begins by critiquing the notion that there would be a single *form* of friendship. According to Aristotle, there are three forms of friendship, which correspond to the three things that are loveable: the good, the pleasant, and the useful.[72] Almost immediately, Aristotle points to a difficulty: in their love of what is good, "is it the good, then, that people love or is it the good for themselves?" (*NE*, 1155b22–23). This question recalls Aristotle's discussion of Plato's theory of the forms in book I, in which he investigates whether the good is one and universal, or whether the good differs for different entities. Aristotle does not fully resolve this question in book I, but he does note that the way in which various things are said to be good are in some way *similar* to one another. In the present discussion of friendship, Aristotle again suggests that both are possible (i.e., that the good is both universal and differs for various objects or people). He writes, "It seems that each person loves what is good for himself and that, while in an unqualified sense the good is what is lovable, what is lovable to each is what is good for each" (1155b23–25).[73] Aristotle suggests that different people are by nature directed toward different things; while the good may be unqualified and universal, the way in which people pursue the good may be different or unique.

After raising the distinction between the universal good and that which is good for each individual—a distinction that will inform nearly the entirety of the rest of his discussion on friendship in book VIII—Aristotle goes on to address the difficulties associated with friendship that Socrates raises in the *Lysis*. First, he emphasizes the reciprocal nature of friendship. He notes that friendship must involve reciprocated goodwill—that is, one must wish for good things for one's friend, for his own sake. Explicitly alluding to Socrates's objection that one can be a friend to inanimate objects, Aristotle states, "It is perhaps laughable to wish for good things for the wine, but, if anything, one wishes that it be preserved so that one may have it" (1155b29–30).[74] Friendship, Aristotle suggests, must be between people. However, goodwill alone is not sufficient to form a friendship and preserve it; rather, each friend must also be aware of the other's existence.[75] People might well feel goodwill for another they have not met but suppose is decent. It would be absurd, Aristotle argues, to suggest such people are friends without knowing of each other's existence. Again, Aristotle emphasizes the phenomenological and, thus, human aspect of friendship. Based on these characteristics, Aristotle provides the following description of friendship: "Friends must, therefore, have goodwill toward each other and not go unnoticed in their wishing for the good things for the other, on account of some one of the [lovable] things mentioned" (1156a3–5).

Based on this definition, Aristotle in chapter three distinguishes the three forms of friendship from one another. The first two types of friendship—friendships of utility and pleasure—exist only on the basis of some advantage or pleasure that each individual comes to have from the friendship. The parties to these types of friendship "do not love each other in themselves but only insofar as they come to have something good from the other" (1156a10–13). As a result, once the purpose for which the friendship was entered into ends, these types of friendship are prone to dissolve. In contrast, friendships between "those who are good and alike in point of virtue" love each other on account of *who* they are (1156b7–8). Aristotle writes that these friendships are "stable," since the underlying basis for the friendship, virtue, is a stable thing (1156b12–13). Thus, in contrast to Socrates, who held that all friendships are based on a lack, Aristotle holds that there is a self-sufficient friendship based on an appreciation of the good characteristics of each party to the friendship. The good, or those who are virtuous, love one another solely for the other's sake, insofar as he is good.[76]

Of course, while Aristotle arrives at the precise opposite conclusion from that of Socrates, he does not yet explain how he resolves the fundamental obstacle to his definition of friendship. Specifically, why would two good individuals be friends to each other if they are both "good and alike in point of virtue"? What benefit could they provide one another? Or, as Socrates asserts, "How . . . will those who are good be at all friends to the good, since neither do they long for each other when absent—for even apart they are sufficient for themselves—nor do they have any use for each other when present?" (*Lysis*, 215b). Why would these two virtuous individuals desire each other's company? Indeed, Aristotle simply asserts that good people are both beneficial and pleasant to one another, without explaining the basis for this assertion.

It has already been noted in the discussion on magnanimity above that Aristotle believes those who are magnanimous in the mold of Alcibiades, Achilles, and Ajax to be well-suited for friendship with those who are magnanimous in the manner of Lysander and Socrates. The members of the two groups are different from each other; yet they are all self-sufficient and good with respect to their own character or virtue. Moreover, if the second type of magnanimity is at root philosophic, then the wisdom it evinces would be well-suited to complement the courage that is emblematic of the first type of magnanimity. If these two types of magnanimous men were capable of amicably ruling together, wisdom and power would coalesce in a way that benefits the entire political community. However, as Aristotle subtly indicates in the *Posterior Analytics*, these magnanimous men are not likely to recognize each other's virtues. As noted above, these magnanimous men suffer from the tragic flaw of mistaking their own virtue for the whole of virtue. Furthermore, we have seen that these two types of magnanimous men stand *above* the standards of the city and, as a result, a utilitarian appeal to the city's well-being is unlikely to have the persuasive effect necessary to lead them to recognize each other's virtue or claim to rule. Thus, while the two types of magnanimous men may be well-suited to become friends with one another, it seems that they have little inclination to do so.

In chapters four through six of book VIII, Aristotle presents a somewhat cryptic argument to explain why it is nonetheless in their *own* interest for these magnanimous individuals to recognize each other's virtue and claim to rule. In chapter four, Aristotle sets up the basis that will undergird his explanation as to what benefit friendship holds out for magnanimous, self-sufficient men. He begins by reasserting that friendships that are complete are both pleasant and useful as well. However, as he continues, Aristotle begins consistently to elevate friendships of pleasure, such that the good and the pleasant turn out to be nearly indistinguishable from one another. Aristotle begins by noting that "among those who seek pleasure or utility, friendships endure especially whenever each attains the same thing from the other—for example, pleasure—and not only this but whenever it comes from the same type, as in, for example, those who are witty" (*NE*, 1157a4–6). By way of this example, Aristotle points to the overlap between the good (virtue) and the pleasant, as wit was identified as one of the social virtues articulated in book IV. He immediately contrasts this example with the relationship of lover and beloved, who do not receive pleasure from the same thing: the lover is "pleased by seeing the beloved, the beloved [is pleased] by being attended to by his lover" (1157a6–8). While Aristotle initially seems to disparage this type of relationship by stating that it sometimes fades "when the bloom of youth fades" (1157a8), he continues by noting that these types of friendships can become stable if, through the time spent living together, they begin to develop affection for one another's character (1157a10–12). Thus, the time spent together can cause two lovers to delight in one another's character.

Turning to complete friendships, Aristotle underscores the way that erotic friendships can evolve into friendships of virtue by pointing to the way in which the time spent together stabilizes friendship. He writes, "Only the friendship of the good is secure against slander, for it is not easy to trust anyone when it comes to slander about someone who has been tested by oneself over a long time" (1157a21–22). He then concludes that only friendships based on the good are complete friendships and that the other two friendships are friendships "only by way of a resemblance" (1157a32). However, Aristotle follows this up by noting that "what is pleasant is a good for the lovers of pleasure" (1157a33). Here Aristotle seems almost unequivocally to suggest that pleasure and the good are, for some, the same.

Why does Aristotle elevate friendships of pleasure, such that they become nearly identical with friendships of the good? The answer becomes apparent in chapter five, where Aristotle subtly reveals his solution to the difficulty that Socrates encounters in the *Lysis*: what would cause those who are good and self-sufficient to desire another? Aristotle begins chapter five by noting that "just as in the virtues, so too in friendship: some people are spoken of as good in reference to the characteristic they possess, others as good in reference to the activity they engage in" (1157b5–7).[77] Aristotle informs us that virtue or goodness expresses itself in different ways. Some are good in reference to their virtuous characters (i.e., their possession of moral virtues), while others are good in reference to their activity (i.e., their practice of philosophy). As we shall see, this differentiation in goodness provides the basis for friendship in a way that avoids the difficulty encountered by Socrates in the *Lysis*.

After these initial steps towards a solution to Socrates's dilemma, Aristotle makes a small detour, reiterating what he had stated previously, namely, that living together is important to friendship. Those who live together, he states, "delight in and provide good things to one another" (1157b8). Again, pleasure comes to the fore as an important aspect of friendship. He continues, noting that if friends remain separated for an extended period of time, the friendship itself can be destroyed. Thus, Aristotle suggests that even among those who are good, friendship cannot exist and be maintained on the basis of the good alone. Friendship, Aristotle suggests, needs the leavening effect of pleasure. Turning to the elderly's indisposition to form friendships, this point is made even more starkly. The elderly and the sour, he states, are unlikely to form friendships, "for there is little that is pleasant in them" (1157b14–15). He concludes, "Nature appears to avoid most of all what is painful and to aim at what is pleasant" (1157b17). With this short statement, Aristotle both reminds the reader of friendship's connection to nature (or that friendship is natural), and that the basis for friendship cannot be the good alone, but that pleasure is a necessary component of friendship—perhaps even more so than the good.[78]

After having again emphasized the importance of pleasure, Aristotle directly touches upon the Socratic dilemma. He restates the dilemma as follows: "The friendship of those who are good, then, is friendship most of all, just as has been said many times. For what is good *or pleasant* in an unqualified sense seems to be lovable and choiceworthy, whereas what is good *or pleasant* to each individual seems to be such only to that person. But a good person is lovable and choiceworthy to a good person on both accounts" (1157b25–29; emphasis added). Aristotle here restates Socrates's question of how it can be that someone who is good or pleasant in an unqualified sense can also be good or pleasant only for a certain individual. Would it not instead be the case that the good in the unqualified sense be good for all good individuals?

Aristotle's solution to the dilemma is best understood against the backdrop of the introductory statement of chapter five: "Some people are spoken of as good in reference to the characteristic they possess, others as good in reference to the activity they engage in" (1157b5–7). Aristotle seems to suggest here that in a friendship of the good each individual is unqualifiedly good—and, we may add in light of the subsequent discussion, such individuals are also pleasant—and is therefore loveable and choiceworthy. While it is true that in a friendship based on the good, both parties to the friendship are unqualifiedly good and pleasant, each party is also different from the other in some way—some being good in character, others in philosophic activity. Each party can therefore be good and pleasant specifically for the other party to the friendship. In this way, Aristotle is able to resolve the Socratic dilemma of why those who are good and self-sufficient would ever treasure or love another.

The sort of individuals that Aristotle has in mind as being both good unqualifiedly and good for the other party to the relationship seems to be those who best exemplify the moral virtues and those who practice the intellectual virtues. This interpretation is bolstered by the following paragraph, where Aristotle delineates the role played by each party in a friendship based on the good. He writes, "Friendly affection is also like a passion, whereas friendship is like a characteristic: friendly affection exists no less toward inanimate things, whereas people *reciprocate* love as a matter of choice, and choice stems from one's characteristic" (1157b28–32). In this statement, Aristotle indicates that each party will have a different role. The fact that friendly affection is akin to a passion that one may have towards an inanimate object is meant to recall the philosopher's passionate love of wisdom.[79] In this way, Aristotle suggests that one party to the friendship acts as the passionate philosopher.[80] In contrast, the party who reciprocates love does so as a matter of choice, which stems from a characteristic.[81] Aristotle's terminology here is meant to bring to mind the moral virtues, which are characteristics marked by choice. Aristotle indicates that a friendship based on the good involves an exchange of pleasure or delight between the practitioner of the intellectual virtues and the practitioner of the moral virtues.

It seems therefore, that in a friendship based on the good, one party to the friendship will have a *passionate* love for his friend similar to that which a philosopher has for wisdom, while the other party will reciprocate love based on his characteristic. In this succinct statement on friendship, Aristotle points toward a resolution to the Socratic dilemma concerning friendship. Each party to the friendship brings a specific good or pleasure to the relationship that is both good in and of itself and is also good or pleasant in some *specific* way for the other party. He concludes, "Each [party], then, both loves what is good for himself and repays in equal measure what they wish for the other and what is pleasant. For it is said, 'friendship is equality'" (1157b35–37).[82]

In the following chapter (chapter 6), Aristotle discusses the political implications of this type of friendship. Regarding the friendships of "people in positions of authority," he states the following: "It has been said that the serious person is at once pleasant and useful; yet such a person does not become a friend to someone who exceeds him [in power], unless [the person in power] is also exceeded [by the serious person] in virtue. But if this does not occur, [the serious person] is not rendered equal [to the person of greater power], since he is exceeded in the relevant proportion" (1158a33–37). Aristotle indicates that the powerful, owing to their superiority in power, are unlikely to be friends with those who are "serious." In fact, it is only when the serious person exceeds the person in power in point of virtue that a friendship may develop, as the differential in virtue is able to compensate for the power differential between the two parties. Again, Aristotle points toward a solution to the fundamental political problem: how power and wisdom might coincide to realize the best regime possible. Those who are politically powerful ought to befriend those who are "serious." The magnanimity of an Alcibiades requires the complementary magnanimity of a Socrates. Of course, Aristotle knows that Alcibiades spurned Socrates's advice and that the powerful are unlikely to befriend the wise. As a result, he concludes this brief reveal of the political implications of his discussion of friendship with the observation that "[those in positions of authority] are not much accustomed to becoming these sorts [of friends to the virtuous]" (1158b38–39).

In his discussion of friendship, Aristotle has made clear that magnanimous men who are politically powerful, wellborn, and courageous are well-suited for friendship with philosophically magnanimous men who, despite their lowborn status, have great benefits to offer the city. Aristotle suggests that the fundamental political problem identified by Socrates and Plato—how to ensure the coincidence of power and wisdom—can potentially be resolved by the phenomenon of friendship. Through an appreciation of one another's virtue, two individuals who are self-sufficient and good in their own nature can together ensure the existence of the best possible regime. However, not a few difficulties remain. First, while Aristotle has hinted that pleasure is that which causes the one individual in such a friendship to appreciate the good qualities of the other, he has not yet indicated how or why this mutual exchange of pleasure will take place. In fact, the most he has indicated is that those in positions of authority are *not* much accustomed to becoming friends of the virtuous. It is not until book IX, in which Aristotle finally tackles the fundamental political problem regarding the coincidence of wisdom and power, that he explicates *how* this mutual exchange of pleasure will occur.

Chapter Four

The Metaphysical Foundations of Friendship

Aristotle believes the fundamental problem of politics—attaining the coincidence of power and wisdom—may be capable of resolution through the medium of friendship. Specifically, by way of friendship, the philosopher can impact the policies of those in power. However, while Aristotle hints that friendship is a solution to the difficulty of attaining the coincidence of power and wisdom, he states quite frankly that those in power and those who are philosophically inclined are not disposed to become friends with one another. The goal of book IX of *The Nicomachean Ethics* is to show how such individuals may become friends with one another. By way of a discussion of the giving and receiving of benefits, Aristotle explains how, despite initial misgivings, a friendship between the philosophically inclined and those with power may be developed.[1]

Aristotle's intention in taking up the discussion of how those in power may become friends with those who are philosophically inclined is indicated in the first sentence of book IX, which states that its subject matter is heterogeneous friendships in which the goal of each party is different.[2] Aristotle begins by providing an example of a political or market friendship between different craftsmen.[3] This type of friendship is easily equalized through the medium of commerce, as each party exchanges his wares according to their value, and Aristotle has discussed this type of friendship at length in book V in connection with justice.[4] In contrast, the following example that Aristotle provides is a decidedly non-political friendship, which is more difficult to equalize and, as a result, is susceptible to dissolution: the erotic friendship consisting of a lover and beloved who enter into the relationship for different purposes. Aristotle notes that such relationships will dissolve "when the lover loves the beloved for the pleasure involved, the beloved his lover for his usefulness to him, and when both parties do not have what each wants" (*NE*, 1164a6–10). Because neither party to the relationship receives what he desires, the relationship ends.

By introducing the example of a political or market friendship that is easily equalized alongside that of a decidedly non-political relationship that is difficult to equalize, Aristotle subtly raises the question of whether relationships may exist that are both political *and* difficult to equalize. Are some political relationships beyond the realm of proportional justice? The answer, it turns out, is yes. The relationship between those who are in power and those who are wise—that is, the relationship between those with political ambitions and those who are philosophically inclined—is a relationship that is political in nature and is beyond proportional justice.

That Aristotle has this particular relationship in mind is borne out by his subsequent discussion concerning the giving and receiving of benefits. He uses an erotic relationship, in which neither party receives what it wishes, as a springboard to launch into the question of who is to decide the worth of what is given in a friendship. Ought the person who "takes the initiative in giving" assess the gift's worth, or should it be "the one who is first in receiving" the gift? (1164a23–24). Aristotle answers that "he who takes the initiative in giving appears to entrust this assessment to the receiver, which is in fact what they assert Protagoras used to do" (1164a24–25). Aristotle's example of Protagoras is revealing and introduces the subject matter that will subtly come to dominate the rest of book IX. Protagoras, of course, was the philosopher who claimed to have the unique ability to teach men "the political art" and how to "make men good citizens" (*Protagoras*, 319a4). By using Protagoras as an example, Aristotle draws attention to the classic theme of the relationship between politics and philosophy, a relationship that is both political and difficult to equalize.

Protagoras, asserts Aristotle, would "bid the learner to estimate how much he held [his teachings] to be worth knowing, and that is the amount he used to take" (*NE*, 1164a25–27). In describing Protagoras's conduct, Aristotle distinguishes him from the Sophists, "who take money in advance and then do nothing of what they claimed, because their promises were excessive" (1164a27–31). While the Sophists are rightly accused by those with whom they contract for failing to deliver what they promised, those who take the initiative in giving advice for the benefit of their partner "do not give cause for accusation" and may instead be practicing the highest type of friendship (1164b34–35).[5] Thus, Aristotle implies that the philosopher who advises with the intention of benefitting the one who receives the advice—perhaps by teaching him "the political art" or by making him a "good citizen"—may, in fact, be practicing the highest form of friendship (1164a35–36).

While the introduction to book IX strongly suggests that Aristotle intends this section of the *Ethics* to cover the friendship between philosophers and those who hold power, several obstacles prevent the easy attainment of this type of friendship. First, as noted above, Aristotle indicates that those in power and those who philosophize are not likely to befriend one another (cf. 1158a32–39). Those who are in power may have had to engage in decidedly nefarious tactics to attain their position and, as a result, cannot be described as virtuous or good. Thus, it can fairly be asked: What would dispose the philosopher to dispense advice to such a person? As will be made clear, in this section of the *Ethics*, Aristotle seeks to appeal to his philosophically inclined audience by way of a protreptic address to prepare them for the potentially difficult character of the politician. Second, if the friendship between these two magnanimous individuals is a friendship based on the good, Aristotle will have to make clear *how* the philosopher will turn the politician toward virtue, such that they may appreciate and take pleasure in each other's excellence. Third, even if Aristotle's protreptic address is capable of preparing the philosopher for the politician's difficult personality, it remains to be seen what benefit these magnanimous individuals receive from their friendship with one another. If the magnanimous man is "incapable of living with a view to another" (1124b31–1125a1), as Aristotle states in book IV, why would the magnanimous statesman and the magnanimous philosopher enter into friendship with one another? As will be made clear, Aristotle addresses each of these issues in turn, explaining how and why the friendship of the philosopher and the politician can be attained, thereby securing the coincidence of wisdom and power necessary for political flourishing.

Taming the Philosopher

In the *Rhetoric*, Aristotle presents the following advice regarding political oratory: "Those present [at the address] may be inclined to treat the matter either more or less seriously than you wish them to. You may accordingly have to excite or dispel some prejudice" (*Rhetoric*, 1415b35–37). Aristotle adopts this approach in his protreptic address in the first three chapters of book IX. If he intends to bring about a friendship between the philosophically inclined and the politically powerful, he needs to inculcate a friendly disposition in his philosophically inclined audience, as they are likely to have an instinctive disdain for those who hold authority in the city.[6] In order to prepare the philosopher for the possibility that those in power may not be receptive or appreciative of his advice, Aristotle seeks to ground the philosopher in his community, or to tame his hubristic demeanor. He does so in the first three chapters of book IX. First, he humbles his reader, indicating that the value his philosophically inclined audience place on their advice may be mistaken. Second, he reminds his audience that those in power and the political community more generally have certain claims that ought to be taken seriously. Finally, almost as if by way of last resort, Aristotle appeals to the philosopher's superiority, entreating him to be patient with those who, due to their limited capabilities, are unable to recognize either the benefits of the advice or the good character of the one who bestows the advice. Only after this protreptic address does Aristotle provide, in chapters four through six, an explanation as to why his audience should befriend those who seem noble and courageous.

Aristotle begins his address by suggesting that the philosopher who provides political advice with the intention of conferring a benefit may deserve some sort of repayment from the one who receives the advice. However, the issue of repayment is difficult, as it is not evident what could possibly count as adequate repayment for the benefit of learning "the political art" and becoming a "good citizen."[7] It would perhaps not be surprising that the philosopher, in recognition of the value of his benefit, might feel slighted either if the benefit he bestows remains unrecognized or if the repayment does not appear to be adequate.

The issue of repayment is complex, and Aristotle remains—perhaps purposefully—vague in discussing the issue. Initially, he notes that the gift of philosophy is invaluable and, as such, the repayment afforded cannot be satisfied by either money or honor. Instead, he notes cryptically, "Whatever it is possible to repay would be sufficient" (1164b3–5). Aristotle continues, however, noting that "if the giver receives as much as the recipient is benefited (or however much in return the recipient would have given in choosing the pleasure involved), the giver will have received what was merited from the recipient" (1164b10–13). The meaning of this somewhat abstruse explanation of repayment will later be revealed, but at present it suffices to note that Aristotle suggests that repayment depends, in part, on the efficacy of the philosophical advice rendered.

Before Aristotle expounds on what may count as adequate repayment, he seeks to prepare the philosopher for the possibility that those in power may not be receptive or appreciative of his advice. In order to forestall the sullen and bitterly ironic reaction of a philosopher who, in response to having his advice rejected, retreats to his own private realm to criticize the political community, Aristotle seeks to ground the philosopher in his community, or tame his hubristic demeanor.[8] As we shall see, he uses a number of tools to accomplish this task. First, he indicates that the value the philosopher places on his advice may be mistaken; that is, the philosopher may not have an accurate understanding of his worth, or the worth of his advice.[9] Second, he reminds the philosopher that those in power and the political community more generally have certain claims that ought to be taken seriously. Last, he appeals to the philosopher's superiority, entreating him to be patient with those who, due to their limited capabilities, are unable to recognize either the benefits of the advice or the good character of the one who bestows the advice.

Aristotle begins his protreptic approach at the end of chapter one by unequivocally stating that in the absence of an express agreement of the gift's worth, the one who receives the gift—or advice—ought to assess its worth in determining repayment. The rationale, according to Aristotle, is that "many things are not valued equally by those who possess them and by those who wish to receive them, since *what is one's own* and what one gives *appears* to everyone to be worth a great deal" (1164b17–19; emphasis added). The reference to "one's own" (οἰκεῖον) is the second of two references in the totality of the *Ethics* in which "one's own" is explicitly contrasted with philosophy or the truth. The first reference occurs in book I, where Aristotle begins his famous critique of Plato's theory of the forms. Prefacing his critique, Aristotle notes that it will be a difficult undertaking "because the men who introduced the forms are [friends]" (1096a13–14). He continues, however, stating that for philosophers in particular, it may be necessary to "do away with even one's own things," in order to preserve the truth (1096a14–16). Thus, while gaining a truthful account of things may be difficult, Aristotle leaves us with the impression that such an account of things is possible. The second reference to "one's own," which occurs here in book IX, seems to pull back on the idea that one will ever be able to achieve a full, truthful account of things. Indeed, the fact that the philosopher ought to entrust the assessment of the worth of his advice to the recipient indicates that even the philosopher is incapable of attaining complete objectivity and may have a preference for what is "one's own," or for his own teaching.[10] Ever so subtly, Aristotle suggests that the philosopher may not be impartial as to the worth of his teaching, and that the love of "one's own" may cloud his assessment of the worth of his teaching.

In this way, Aristotle humbles his audience. Not only may his philosophical readers be mistaken about the worth of their teaching or advice, but Aristotle suggests that his readers ought also to entrust the assessment of the worth of their advice to those to whom the advice is directed. Aristotle thus calls into question his readers' capacity to attain complete objectivity. Even his philosophic readers, he suggests, may have a preference for what is "one's own," or for their own teaching. Ever so subtly, Aristotle suggests that his readers may not be impartial as to the merit of their teaching and that the love of "one's own" may cloud their assessment of their teachings' worth.

In chapter two, having humbled his audience, Aristotle continues his protreptic address by suggesting to his reader that he owes something to the political realm. He does so by raising the question of what obligation one has to one's father. Ought one "render everything to one's father and obey him in everything?" (1164b22). The claims of the ancestral are raised in light of the preceding discussion regarding the advice rendered by the philosopher—that is, the philosopher and his penchant for innovation are weighed against the claims of established customs. Similar political questions are raised in conjunction with the claim of the ancestral: must one "serve a friend more than a serious man?" and "must one repay a favor to a benefactor rather than give away something to a comrade?" (1164b26–28). Each of these questions raises the issue of how one ought to be disposed towards the claims of "one's own" and towards the claims of philosophic truth.[11]

In dealing with these questions, Aristotle proceeds delicately, employing a paromologia—a rhetorical device whereby one concedes his audience's point of view before raising important objections to this point of view—to convince his audience. Indeed, Aristotle initially provides an answer that would not shock his more philosophically inclined readers: "That someone ought not to give back everything to the same person is not unclear; nor is it unclear that, for the most part, he must repay good deeds more than gratify his comrades, just as a person must pay back a loan to someone he owes, more than he must give away something to a comrade" (1164b30–34). This answer provides the philosophically inclined reader with precisely what he would expect: not everything is owed to the ancestral; the good ought to take priority over one's comrades; and the repayment of a loan (i.e., repayment for the philosophical advice one has received) ought to come before one undertakes to give any gift to one's comrades. Truth takes precedence over political and familial loyalties.

No matter how axiomatic this answer may seem to the philosopher, Aristotle immediately calls it into question. Perhaps, suggests Aristotle, "not even this is always so" (1164b34). What follows is a somewhat cryptic example regarding ransoms. Ought a person who has been ransomed from pirates pay in return the ransom to his ransomer? Aristotle indicates that while the general rule holds that an obligation is incurred, the obligation is relieved under certain circumstances. For example, if a person owes his ransomer money while at the same time his father is being held ransom, he ought to ransom his father first (11643b–1165a3). On its face, Aristotle's example is not overly controversial; if one's father is in danger, one ought to help one's father before settling one's debts. However, by using the example of ransoming one's father, Aristotle elevates the claim of the ancestral and suggests that the philosopher's axiomatic preference for the good over the ancestral may not always be warranted.

Last, Aristotle appeals to his reader's superior position relative to those to whom he gives advice. If his reader will be neither humbled nor persuaded by the claims of the established political authorities, perhaps Aristotle can appeal to his reader's hubris. He writes, "Sometimes the repaying of a previous service is not even equal—when someone benefits a person he *knows* (εἰδώς) to be serious, but the repayment is to one whom the serious person *supposes* (οἴεται) to be corrupt" (1165a4–7; emphasis added). Ann Ward interprets this passage to mean that "the requirements of justice do not always hold in our relations with bad men, to whom we should not repay good deeds."[12] She goes on to interpolate that Aristotle intends to "raise doubts concerning our obligations to our father," should he be a "bad man."[13] While Ward rightly points out that Aristotle is raising the question of conflicting obligations, she does not account for the different terms—(εἰδώς and οἴεται)—that Aristotle employs. Indeed, in the scenario posited by Aristotle, the service is rendered by a knower (i.e., a philosopher), who has a correct assessment of the recipient's character, while the recipient (i.e., a political authority)—although serious—only has an opinion of the philosopher's character. Through an appeal to the philosopher's superior knowledge, Aristotle seeks to exhort him to be patient with those to whom he gives advice, as they may be incapable of recognizing either the soundness of the advice or the philosopher's virtuous character and may be under the false impression that the philosopher is corrupt.

Only after having called into question the philosopher's axiomatic preference for the good over the ancestral and after having exhorted the philosopher to be patient with those who lack knowledge, does Aristotle make clear the implications of his teaching. He writes that different relations ought to be accorded different honors. Again, Aristotle places the philosophic and the ancestral in explicit contrast to one another: "Honor too we owe to parents, just as to the gods—though not every honor. For we do not owe the same honor to a father as to a mother; nor, in turn, do we owe them the honor proper to a wise man or general" (1165a24–26). As Ann Ward notes, "Aristotle . . . suggests that although we owe honour and affection to our parents as the source of our bodily being, albeit in distinct ways, we also owe persons honor and affection if they are wise."[14] We might add here, that according to Aristotle, we also owe honor and affection to those, such as generals, who are politically powerful. Thus, Aristotle finally raises the notion that honor may be due to a wise man—i.e., someone who gives advice—but it is only after he has elevated the claims of the ancestral that the possibility of such honor is mentioned, and it is further only mentioned in conjunction with the honor owed to a general. The chapter concludes by noting that while a relative assessment of what honor belongs to each relation is difficult, "one must not, on this account, give up the attempt but rather make the relevant distinctions, to the extent possible" (1165a34–36). Aristotle thus remains coy about what honor is, in fact, owed for the philosophic advice rendered.[15]

In chapter three, Aristotle continues the theme of the obligations that exist among relations. Having cautiously presented his belief that members of the political community have an obligation to the ancestral in the previous chapter, Aristotle now introduces the far more radical contention that the philosopher himself may have certain obligations toward the political community. Perhaps in recognition of the fact that the philosopher will likely have an instinctual aversion to the idea that he has obligations to the political community, Aristotle introduces the topic tentatively. He begins by simply reiterating the relatively uncontroversial assertion that friendships based on what is useful or pleasant tend to dissolve when they no longer serve the purpose for which they were entered. However, the focus soon shifts to the more difficult—and for the philosopher, perhaps, more controversial—question of whether a friendship based on the good can be dissolved if the character of one of the parties undergoes a change: "If someone accepts another person as good, and that other becomes corrupt or seems so, must he still love him? Or is it not possible, if indeed not everything is loveable but only the good?" (1165b12–15).

Aristotle has, of course, already prepared his reader for the answer to this question in the previous two chapters by suggesting that the ancestral is loveable. If the good and the ancestral are distinct—as they usually (perhaps always) are—this would imply that the ancestral is loveable *despite* the fact that it is distinct from the good. In this way, Aristotle has tacitly signaled his answer: while the good may be preeminently loveable, the philosopher owes something to the ancestral as well. This comes to light most clearly in the hypothetical friendship presented by Aristotle in which one individual stays the same while the other "greatly surpasses him in virtue" (1165b23). Ought the more virtuous individual treat the one who has remained the same as a friend? Alternatively, if an individual comes to a greater awareness of the good and thereby recognizes the flaws and failings of the city in which he was raised, how ought he respond to the city that raised him? Should he actively seek to undermine the conventions and opinions that hold the city together? In contrast, Aristotle argues that while friendship may no longer exist in such situations, the philosopher still owes something to his former friend.[16] Rather than altogether dismissing his former friend, "one ought . . . to remember the life lived together with him" and on this basis "render something to those who were once friends" (1165b33–36). Thus, even in the event that the distance becomes so great as to dissolve the friendship, Aristotle nevertheless finds that something is still owed.

Having introduced the possibility of an individual who so surpasses his friend in virtue that the two can no longer remain friends, Aristotle turns, in chapter four, to the question of whether it is possible for such an individual to be a friend to himself. While the question is no doubt provocative, it seems to be a logical development from the previous chapter. If one's superiority to those around him is so great that he can no longer remain friends with them, then perhaps such a person can fulfill his desire for friendship by being friend to himself.[17] This topic is introduced by noting that four attributes appear to be most characteristic of friendship: (1) wishing and doing things that are good (or at least appear good) for the sake of the other; (2) wishing that the friend exist and live, for the friend's own sake; (3) going through life together and choosing the same things as the friend; and (4) sharing in life's sufferings and joys (1166a1–10). Aristotle goes on to state somewhat tersely that these four characteristics can all pertain to oneself. He writes, "Each of these [attributes] belongs to the decent person in relation to himself, and . . . he stands in relation to a friend as he does to himself—for the friend is another self" (1166a29–32). Aristotle's famous statement that a friend is "another self" (ἄλλος αὐτός) is somewhat curious and does not receive much in the way of elaboration.

Much of the scholarship that focuses on the rhetorical quality of the *Ethics* have taken Aristotle's curious description of the friend as an ἄλλος αὐτός to mean that, at this point, Aristotle is referring to the friendship one can have "with oneself" based on the composite nature of human beings (1166a34–1166b2).[18] What these accounts overlook, however, is that Aristotle's description of the manner in which the second of the four characteristics of friendship applies to oneself—wishing that a friend exist and live—contains a compact discussion of what it means to exist:

> He also wishes that he himself live and be preserved, and especially that [part of himself] with which he is prudent. For existence is a good to the serious person, and each wishes for the good things for himself. Yet no one chooses to possess every good by becoming another—for even now, the god possesses the good—but rather by being whatever sort he is; and it would seem that it is the thinking part that each person is or is most of all. (1166a18–23; square brackets original)

A serious person, argues Aristotle, finds his existence to be both desirable and good and, as a result, he will seek to *preserve* his existence. By invoking the notion of preservation, which hinges on the virtue of prudence (φρόνησις), Aristotle focuses on man's existence as a mortal entity—that is, *as a human being*. No one, he tells us, would choose to possess every good by becoming another. Just as the god would not stoop to become mortal in order to attain the characteristically human virtue of prudence, so the philosopher does not wish to concern himself with merely human affairs. Nevertheless, in contrast to the god, the philosopher is human and, as such, needs to concern himself with merely human affairs, if only to ensure his own preservation. By emphasizing prudence, Aristotle reminds us that even the individual who is preeminent in virtue is merely human and, as such, needs to preserve his existence. In the very argument in which the friend is famously declared to be "another self," Aristotle seeks to tame the philosopher by reminding him of his humanity, and that his virtue, while it may be self-sufficient, is not the *whole* of virtue. In this way, Aristotle reveals to the philosopher that he may in some sense be in need of a friend. Given Aristotle's discussion in book VIII concerning the importance of complementarity in friendship, we can surmise that the philosopher's friend will be an individual whose characteristics complement those of the philosopher. Together, the philosopher and his friend could, perhaps, possess the entirety of virtue.

Forming a Friend

Together, chapters three and four point toward a difficulty. On the one hand, chapter three raises the possibility that the philosopher may be so vastly superior to others that he is incapable of friendship with them. On the other hand, chapter four reiterates the philosopher's limited nature as a human being and strongly suggests that he is nonetheless in some sense in need of a friend. What ought the magnanimous philosopher to do in such a situation? It seems that the only path forward would be to seek out a *potential* friend, whom one can form or educate with a view to virtue, such that he may *become* good and pleasant.[19]

Chapters five and six are devoted to identifying *who* the philosopher ought to become friends with. The transition from chapter four to chapter five confirms that this is, indeed, Aristotle's intention. At the end of chapter four, after having warned that the base person seeks to spend time with others only so as to escape his own misery, Aristotle tells the reader he must "flee corruption with the utmost effort and attempt to be decent, since in this way he would both be disposed toward himself in a friendly way and become a friend to another" (1166b27–29). In turn, chapter five focuses on goodwill (εὔνοια), which Aristotle defines as "the beginning of friendship" (1167a3). Aristotle begins chapter five by distinguishing εὔνοια from friendship proper. While εὔνοια is similar to friendship, it differs in that it "arises suddenly" and is "without intensity or longing" (1166b34–1167a3). Peter Hadreas argues convincingly that εὔνοια is best rendered in English as the "recognition of another's worthiness."[20] Aristotle emphasizes that this recognition is a necessary precursor to friendship and that if it is "prolonged over time and [is] carrie[d] over into the habit of living together . . . [it] becomes friendship" of the highest kind (1167a13–14). As noted previously, in the *Gorgias*, Socrates and Callicles are described as having goodwill for one another, and yet later in the dialogue, it becomes evident that the initial goodwill they feel toward one another is an insufficient ground for friendship. Thus, Aristotle makes explicit what Plato had implied in the *Gorgias*: εὔνοια, or the recognition of another's worthiness, may become the grounds on which a friendship can be started, but friendship itself requires time and trust.

Aristotle concludes chapter five by indicating to whom the philosopher might look in his search for a potential friend. He writes, "On the whole, goodwill arises on account of virtue and a certain decency, whenever someone appears to another as *noble or courageous* or some such thing, just as we said in the case of competitors as well" (1167a18–21; emphasis added). Thus, Aristotle suggests that when looking for a potential friend, his philosophically inclined audience ought to seek out those who appear to be noble or courageous. By pointing to the noble (καλός) or courageous (ἀνδρεῖος), Aristotle seems to be directing his audience to those who can be said to embody or protect the ideals of the polis, or those who have an authoritative political role. Philosophically inclined individuals will complement such individuals, and together they will be able to accomplish great good.

The introduction to chapter six further underscores the importance of complementarity in friendship. Aristotle notes that "like-mindedness . . . appears to be a mark of friendship" (1167a22). However, he quickly clarifies that this like-mindedness does not pertain to just anything but must concern matters of common advantage and action. As a result, he states that "those who are of like mind concerning the things in the heavens" are not friends (1167a26). Those concerned with speculative matters will not become friends solely on account of their theoretical agreement.[21] As Lorraine Smith Pangle notes, "It would seem to be only in response to some problem or need . . . that the crucial element of friendship, sharing in choices, comes into play."[22] True friendship, Aristotle intimates, requires some level of differentiation.

That complementarity, or differentiation, is a key ingredient to friendship is borne out by the example that Aristotle chooses to illustrate the importance of like-mindedness in friendship. The citizens of Mytilene, he notes, were like-minded when they resolved to have Pittacus rule. Each Mytilenean citizen agreed that the good should rule, and this like-mindedness among them contributed to the common good. In contrast, a like-mindedness based on identicality, for example, "when each person wishes that he himself rule," results in "civil faction" (1167a30–35). By stressing the complementarity of the partners in a friendship, Aristotle is clear that friendship is not marked by identicality, but instead by a like-mindedness that concerns "what is advantageous," aims at "what has been resolved in common," and pertains to "matters of action" (1167a26–30). Aristotle informs his philosophically inclined audience that by building on latent goodwill, and by spending time with one another, it is possible for them to develop a friendship with those who hold power.[23]

By stressing the complementarity of the partners in a friendship, Aristotle subtly indicates to the reader why Socrates's search for a definition of friendship in the *Lysis* results in failure. It will be recalled that Socrates had initially interpreted the phrase "like to like" as requiring identicality. In contrast, Aristotle suggests that friendship is not marked by identicality, but instead by a like-mindedness that concerns "what is advantageous," aims at "what has been resolved in common," and pertains to "matters of action" (1167a26–30). By looking for identicality, Socrates's inquiry was bound to fail.[24] Indeed, interaction between those who seek the exact same benefits or honors is more likely to result in factious disputes than harmony. Aristotle indicates that the final definition of friendship that Socrates puts forward (but fails adequately to pursue) in the *Lysis* is, in fact, the one that is most characteristic of friendship between the good. The highest form of friendship, for Aristotle, is that which exists between those who are similar to one another yet differ in a point of virtue.

Aristotle's distinction between goodwill and friendship is important. The notion that goodwill is only *potential* friendship, or friendship that lies idle, suggests that the individual described in chapter five as one who *appears* noble or courageous to the philosopher, has the potential to become friends with the philosopher. Much of the *Ethics* can be read as an attempt by Aristotle to actualize the potentiality of those of his readers who appear to be noble. No less than four times in the *Ethics* does Aristotle remind his readers that his intention is to make his reader "good" (1094b11; 1095a4–6; 1103b26–30; 1179b1–4). Furthermore, in the introduction to book II of the *Ethics*, Aristotle states that "none of the moral virtues are present in us by nature, since nothing that exists by nature is habituated to be other than it is. . . . [The moral virtues] are instead present in us who are of such a nature as to receive them, and who are completed through habit" (1103a19–26).[25] Thus, Aristotle's task in the portions of the *Ethics* discussing the moral virtues can, in large measure, be interpreted as that of "forming a friend."

To comprehend well the manner in which Aristotle's *Ethics* is an attempt to "form a friend" by actualizing his potential for virtue, it is necessary to turn to Aristotle's inquiry into the nature of "being" in the *Metaphysics*, where Aristotle discusses the forces of potentiality (δύναμις) and actuality (ἐνέργεια) in detail. In the first book of the *Metaphysics*, Aristotle recounts the history of philosophy, or the history of the investigation into the "first causes and the principles of things" (*Metaphysics*, 981b29). He notes that most of the pre-Socratic philosophers believed that "the principles which were of the nature of matter were the only principles of all things" (983b7–8). Aristotle describes this belief as inadequate, as it fails to account for the existence of artificial or conventional things. He states, "It is not likely either that fire or earth or any such [material] element should be the reason why things manifest goodness and beauty both in their being and in their coming to be" (984b11–13). Aristotle argues that there needs to be something beyond the simple material elements that accounts for change and causes things to exhibit goodness and beauty.

This question concerning the origin of the artificial and conventional, as well as of the origin of goodness and beauty, is similar to the question Aristotle implicitly raises in the *Politics* concerning the origins of the polis. It may be recalled that while Aristotle argues that the household comes into existence to deal with day-to-day necessities, and the village comes into being to provide for the non-daily needs, he never indicates what it is that causes the polis to come into existence. Indeed, it seems that with respect to material necessity alone, the village is self-sufficient. Nevertheless, Aristotle maintains that the polis is natural and serves the purpose of "living well," without providing much in the way of explanation as to why this is so. In the *Metaphysics*, in his recounting of pre-Socratic philosophy, Aristotle provides the early pre-Socratic answers to the question of why things manifest goodness or beauty, or what causes things to progress and develop beyond the bare necessity dictated by nature. He notes that according to Empedocles, friendship is the cause of order, beauty, and goodness, and strife is the cause of what is bad, disordered, and ugly (cf. 984b8–985a9). Thus, for Empedocles, friendship and strife are the sources of movement or change and account for what is conventional or artificial. However, Aristotle states that while Empedocles correctly identifies the sources of movement or change as friendship and strife, he does so in a vague and unscientific manner (985a22–985b3).

It is not until book IX of the *Metaphysics*, when Aristotle describes the forces of potentiality (δύναμις) and actuality (ἐνέργεια), that he scientifically describes the way friendship and strife act as the sources of movement or change. At the beginning of book IX, Aristotle explains that potentiality and actuality are the originative sources of motion. However, he is quick to note that these terms do not refer *simply* to motion but are also used in another sense (1045b28–1046a4). Thus, while potency and actuality are, indeed, the cause of motion, they are also the cause of something else. As I hope to make clear, these forces are, in fact, that which cause things to exhibit either goodness, beauty, and order, or disharmony and ugliness.

To understand how the forces of potentiality and actuality cause things to exhibit either goodness, beauty, and order, or disharmony and ugliness, it will be useful first to look to Aristotle's criticism of the Megaric school's understanding of potency and actuality. In the third chapter of book IX of the *Metaphysics*, Aristotle states that "there are some who say, as the Megaric school does, that a thing 'can' act only when it is acting, and when it is not acting it 'cannot' act" (1046b28–30). Aristotle provides the example of a builder to elucidate this position. According to the Megaric school, "he who is not building cannot build, but only he who is building, when he is building" (1046b30–31). Potency and act are, for the Megaric school, unified and indistinct. The obvious difficulty with this view, states Aristotle, is that "a man will not be a builder unless he is building . . . and so with the other arts" and, indeed, all other capacities (1046b33–35). This leads to the absurd conclusion that an individual gains and loses the ability to conduct an art as many times as he commences and ceases acting with no account of how he comes to possess the art (1046b35–1047a4). According to the Megaric position, any time a capacity is not exercised, the capacity is lacking altogether. The consequence of the Megaric position, according to Aristotle, is that it does away with both "movement and becoming" (1047a14–15). As Edward Halper writes, the Megarians "appear to have pressed the results of logic despite the disagreement of these results with physics."[26] Aristotle, in contrast, maintains that because movement and becoming are processes that clearly do occur in the world, potency and actuality are distinct forces that account for these processes.

In chapter four of book IX of the *Metaphysics*, Aristotle introduces the notion of *pairs* of potentialities, which are dependent on one another. In a passage that is dense with formal logic, Aristotle makes the case that "if B's existence necessarily follows from A's, and if A is possible, B must be possible."[27] While it is initially unclear what role this discussion concerning pairs of potentialities plays in Aristotle's metaphysics, chapter five makes his intentions manifest. Aristotle begins by noting that all potentialities or capacities come from (1) nature; (2) habit; or (3) instruction (1047b31–34).[28] Potentialities from nature are nonrational and, as a result, always act in a particular way when they are brought into contact with that which has the potential to be affected. Aristotle makes clear that pairs of potentialities within nature have a certain regularity or necessity. For example, when fire comes to bear on a pot of water, the water will eventually boil and become steam. The water's potential to assume an altered state is actualized when it comes into contact with fire's potential capacity to cause the water to turn to steam. When these two potentialities come into contact, they are *both* necessarily actualized.[29]

In contrast to the nonrational potencies, which act in a predetermined and necessary way, rational potencies—those from habit and instruction—can act in different ways or produce contrary effects. Aristotle uses carving as an example: "We say that potentially . . . a statue of Hermes is in the block of wood . . . because it might be separated out" (1048a32–34). However, the block of wood can also potentially be something else, perhaps a table. The final form that the block of wood exhibits depends on the "desire or will" of the carver (cf. 1048a5–15). The rational potency of the carver comes to bear on the nonrational potency of the piece of wood to determine what artificial or conventional thing it might be. Indeed, we may say that the carver has the ability to bring order or beauty to nature. However, Aristotle makes clear that it is impossible for these potentialities to produce contrary effects at the same time. The carver can form the block of wood into a statue of Hermes or into a table, but he cannot form it into both simultaneously. Aristotle indicates that "desire or will" is determinative of what the rational potency will do when it is brought into contact with that which has the potential to be affected. Thus, potencies—including rational potencies—come in *pairs*, and it is through the interaction of these potencies that the artificial or conventional comes into existence.

Of course, human beings have both types of potencies—the nonrational potencies from nature, which are innate and "imply passivity," as well as rational potencies that come to be from either habit or learning (1047b31–34). The fact that human beings have each of these potencies is amply demonstrated in the *Ethics*. In book II, Aristotle notes that the moral virtues come into existence via a process whereby practice comes to bear on the innate passive potencies. He states: "Neither by nature, therefore, nor contrary to nature are the virtues present; they are instead present in us who are of such a nature as to receive them, and who are completed through habit" (*NE*, 1103a22–26). Thus, the innate potencies are realized, or come to be, through practice or habit, and they in turn give rise to another potency, or capacity: the capacity to act virtuously. However, as the *Ethics* demonstrates, if repeated practice is to result in the acquisition of a stable virtue, it needs be informed by reason. Thus, to act virtuously, one needs to be informed (or formed) by one who has knowledge—that is, by the philosopher. The philosopher's rational potency has the ability to form another individual in the same way that a carver's rational potency can form a statue of Hermes out of a piece of wood. When the philosopher's rational potency comes into contact with his friend's rational potency for habitual action, the result may well be the actualization of virtue. Of course, the crucial difference between the philosopher's ability to form another individual and the carver's ability to form a block of wood, is that the block of wood is wholly passive, whereas the individual the philosopher seeks to form is not a blank slate but has reason and will, as well as preexisting habits and dispositions, to which the philosopher ought to be solicitous. Nevertheless, Aristotle's discussion of potency and actuality implies that contact between the philosopher's rational potency and his friend's potency for habitual action can potentially be the cause of that which is good, beautiful, and orderly.

Aristotle's understanding of potency and actuality as explicated in the *Metaphysics* helps to clarify much of his discussion of friendship in the *Ethics*. Part of Aristotle's purpose in the *Ethics* is to "form a friend," by actualizing the potentiality of another individual. In chapter seven of book IX, Aristotle investigates the counterintuitive observation that those "who perform a benefit seem to love those who receive this benefit more than those who are the recipients of the benefit love those who perform it" (1167b16–19). While it may seem contrary to reason for the benefactor to love the recipient more than for the recipient to love his benefactor, Aristotle explains why this is so by analogizing the situation to the relationship between an artisan and his work (perhaps a carver and his statue). An artisan, states Aristotle, "is fond of his own work more than he would be loved by that work, should it come to have a soul. . . . The case of those who perform a benefit is like this too, for what has received the benefit is their own work" (1167b34–1168a4). This curious comparison suggests that by dispensing advice, the philosopher is, in some sense, acting like an artisan: the philosopher leaves his imprint on the one he has benefitted.[30] In fact, in words that mirror the division between the active and passive parts of friendship in book VIII, Aristotle reiterates that "friendly affection . . . resembles an active 'making,'" while "being loved resembles a passive 'undergoing'" (1168a19–20). Thus, it is through the dispensing of advice that the philosopher is able to form the character of another individual, such that the latter is able to act as an enlightened statesman.[31]

The format of Aristotle's presentation of the virtues in the first portion of the *Ethics* makes clear that his purpose is to dispose a potential friend to be receptive of the advice of the philosopher. As noted in the previous chapter, Aristotle begins with the virtue of courage, subtly making clear its limitations and pointing toward the need for magnanimity.[32] Magnanimity, in turn, points toward friendship as the cure for the magnanimous man's socially destructive tendencies.³³ Throughout his presentation of the social virtues, Aristotle points toward the need for an intellectual virtue or formative force that is capable of guiding these virtues. He states repeatedly that "one ought to choose the middle term—not the excess and not the deficiency—and that the middle term is what correct reason states it to be" (1138a18–21), but never once indicates what "correct reason" (ὀρθὸς λόγος) is. When he turns to the intellectual virtues in book VI, he makes clear that what he had previously stated regarding the ethical virtues is, "though truthful, not at all clear" (1138b25). As a result, he argues in book VI that it will be necessary also to examine the intellectual virtues, as it is the intellectual virtues that define the boundary or outer limits of ὀρθὸς λόγος. In his explanation of the intellectual virtues Aristotle finally forthrightly reveals that the statesman ought to be receptive to the formative advice of the philosopher. However, as I will make clear, Aristotle maintains an approach that is sensitive to the statesman's sense of self-worth, framing the philosopher's role in a manner that is as nonthreatening as possible.

The intellectual virtues, Aristotle tells us, are fivefold: art (τέχνη), science (ἐπιστήμη), prudence (φρόνησις), wisdom (σοφία), and intellect (νοῦς) (1139b15–18). Of these five, νοῦς receives the least attention. Notably, however, it is νοῦς that preeminently defines ὀρθὸς λόγος. Indeed, νοῦς is the most divine of the intellectual virtues and is specifically concerned with the outer limits or boundaries of correct reason.³⁴ In chapter six of book VI, in which Aristotle briefly describes the intellectual virtue of νοῦς, he distinguishes it from ἐπιστήμη, σοφία, and φρόνησις. While ἐπιστήμη "is a conviction concerning universals and the things that exist of necessity" (1140b31–32), νοῦς concerns the "principle of what is known scientifically" (1140b34). Νοῦς is, therefore, a grasp or comprehension of the principles of science itself, or a grasp of that which lies *beyond* science's demonstrable method. Aristotle explains that while that which is "known scientifically is demonstrable," the principles upon which ἐπιστήμη rests are not demonstrable but are beyond λόγος altogether; they *defy* ordinary discursive explanation.

Precisely because the principles with which νοῦς is concerned lie beyond λόγος they are, strictly speaking, beyond the capacity of man. Man is principally defined—and distinguished from the gods—by his capacity for speech. As Aristotle makes clear in the *Metaphysics*, the activity of pure intellect or νοῦς is characteristic of the god (*Metaphysics*, 1072a1–29). Nevertheless, while this sort of existence is not a possibility for man, this does not mean that nothing can be said about these principles. Aristotle indicates that through the exercise of certain intellectual capacities, man is capable of certain "νοῦς-like" activities.³⁵ Heidegger explains the νοῦς characteristic of man in the following way: "This νοῦς in the human soul is not a νοεῖν, a straightforward seeing, but a διανοεῖν [thinking through] because the human soul is determined by λόγος."³⁶ Man's capacity for νοῦς is therefore never pure intellection as it is for the god, but is instead discursive because it is bound up with λόγος.³⁷

In the *Posterior Analytics*, Aristotle provides a succinct account of the way in which man's capacity for "νοῦς-like" activities can give rise to knowledge of the principles with which νοῦς is concerned, despite the fact that they originate through the use of faculties that are, strictly speaking, independent of λόγος. He writes:

> All animals . . . have an innate power [*dunamin*] of discrimination called sense perception [*aisthēsin*]. But when sense perception is present in some animals, a retention of the thing perceived comes about. . . . And when many such things occur, forthwith, another difference emerges, so that for some, an account [*logon*] comes about from the retention of such things, for others not. Therefore from sense perception comes memory, as we call it, and from memory (when it happens repeatedly in connection with the same thing), experience [*empeiria*]. For memories that are many in number form a single experience. And from experience—that is from the whole universal [*tou katholou*] having come to rest in our mind, the one apart from the many, that which in all things is one and the same—there comes a principle of art [*technē*] or of science [*epistēmē*]. (*PA*, 99b35–100a9; square brackets original)³⁸

The first principles with which νοῦς is concerned are ultimately the result of a complex interaction of experience and memory brought about by sense perception (*aesthēsis*). As a result, to the extent that man is able to take part in noetic activities, it will take a form that is characteristically human and bound up with perception.

In book VI of the *Ethics* Aristotle indicates that the intellectual virtues capable of discerning the principles with which νοῦς is concerned are wisdom (σοφία) and prudence (φρόνησις). Through the exercise of these virtues man has the capacity to engage in dianoetic activity that approximates that of the divine νοῦς. What is it about σοφία and φρόνησις that sets them apart as man's "νοῦς-like" capacities? Σοφία, Aristotle explains, is "a science and an intellectual grasp [νοῦς] of the things most honorable by nature"

(*NE*, 1141b3–5). While science (ἐπιστήμη) concerns the demonstrable teaching that proceeds from certain eternal principles, σοφία goes beyond mere ἐπιστήμη in that it seeks "not only to know what proceeds *from* the principles but also to attain the truth *about* the principles" (1141a18–19). Wisdom, therefore, concerns the outermost principles that are capable of being discerned by wise human beings (οἱ σοφοί). Aristotle specifically distinguishes σοφία from φρόνησις, which concerns itself with human affairs. While prudence deals with that which is immediately given in our everyday existence, or that which concerns our human needs, σοφία has the ability to grasp intellectually (νοεῖν) the principles that are beyond merely human concerns and is able to demonstrate, or teach, that which proceeds *from* those principles. Thus, it is σοφία's concern with the outermost limits of ὀρθὸς λόγος that sets it apart as man's highest virtue.

Although Aristotle sets up σοφία as distinct and separate from φρόνησις on account of the former's concern with the principles that underlie science, φρόνησις also imitates—although to a lesser degree—the activity of the divine νοῦς. Φρόνησις, as noted, concerns itself with human affairs and, in contrast to science, concerns those things that can be otherwise. Aristotle defines it as "a true characteristic that is bound up with action, accompanied by reason, and concerned with things good and bad for a human being" (1140b5–7). Because of this somewhat expansive definition, φρόνησις comes in a variety of forms, including (1) the political art (πολιτική); (2) household management (οἰκονομία); and (3) φρόνησις in the specific sense, concerning the interests of the individual (cf. 1141b24–31). While these roles are all distinct, they are nevertheless similar to one another in that they all involve action in response to engagement with particular circumstances. Aristotle states the following: "Prudence concerns the ultimate particular thing, as was said, for the action performed is of this kind. Indeed, prudence corresponds to intellect (νοῦς), for intellect (νοῦς) is concerned with the defining boundaries, of which there is no rational account; and prudence is concerned with the ultimate particular thing, of which there is not a science but rather a perception" (1142a24–27). Φρόνησις, like σοφία, corresponds to νοῦς, because it is concerned with the "defining boundaries, of which there is no rational account." However, in contrast to σοφία, which is concerned with the most abstract principles, prudence is bound up with the most particular thing. Thus, both σοφία and φρόνησις involve an intellectual grasp of things that are at the opposite ends of the very limits of human comprehension.

Aristotle continues by noting that the perception of the "ultimate particular thing" involved in φρόνησις is a perception (αἴσθησις) "not of things peculiar to one of the senses, but a perception of the sort by which we perceive that the ultimate particular thing, in mathematics, is a triangle" (1142a28–29). Commenting on this passage, Heidegger suggests that Aristotle is referring to the perception of "states of affairs as a whole" as they are "commonly given in everyday existence."[39] When we are faced with a particular given situation, we may be able intuitively, without the need for further deliberation, to grasp the course of action that must be taken. In the same way that we can sense by simple perception that in mathematics the triangle is the most elementary shape that cannot be broken down any further,[40] so the prudent man (φρόνιμος) is able intuitively to perceive how he ought to act in a particular situation.[41]

As Heidegger points out, Aristotle holds that this same intuitive grasping occurs in the arts and sciences. For Aristotle, those engaged in the arts and sciences do not deliberate about the ends that ought to be pursued but only about the method that ought to be employed to pursue the end: "A doctor does not deliberate about whether he is going to heal; on the contrary, that belongs to the meaning of his existence itself, because as a doctor he has already resolved in favor of healing."[42] Thus, the doctor looks around at the given situation as it presents itself, and when he perceives "the first αἴτιον [cause] whence [he] can intervene," he then acts to bring about the end which is already posited.[43] In the same way, a politician or statesman does not deliberate about the *end* he ought to pursue (i.e., the good of the community), but instead looks at the political situation and simply perceives the best possible way that this end might be pursued. Thus, Aristotle frames φρόνησις—intuitive grasping of the situation at hand—as something that *precedes* action.

Both σοφία and φρόνησις are concerned with discovering the noetic principles at the boundaries of right reason. These noetic principles are discovered by the use of perception rather than reason and are to a certain degree beyond reason. The extra-rational means by which these principles are discovered to present a problem for conveying or sharing them with others, for as Aristotle notes in book I of the *Politics*, man is a rational being who communicates with others through speech or reason (*Politics*, 1253a8–10). The noetic principles discovered through σοφία and φρόνησις are grounded in perception (αἴσθησις) rather than λόγος and, as a result, will be incapable of being shared in a straightforwardly discursive manner. The account or λόγος of the noetic principles will have to be shared in a manner similar to that in which they were discovered—making use of man's capacity for perception. Aristotle's description of the way man discovers the noetic principles necessary for art and science—the markers of political society—points toward the need for an approach to politics that appeals not only to man's reason but also to his capacity for perception. While Aristotle develops such an approach in books VII and VIII of the *Politics*, for now it is sufficient to note that it is through the intellectual activity of σοφία and φρόνησις that man is capable of acting in a manner akin to the divine νοῦς.

Of these two intellectual faculties, σοφία takes priority over φρόνησις and, as a result, the philosopher can be described as the one who truly possesses the knowledge of political science. However, Aristotle does not straightforwardly assert this priority. Instead, he clarifies the relationship between these two intellectual virtues through an extended discussion of deliberation. This discussion reveals that good deliberation is a capacity of those who are held to be prudent and is dependent on σοφία. Good deliberation, Aristotle writes, is a sort of "correctness of deliberation," in which the end of the action being deliberated upon is correct (1142b16). Aristotle explains that while "the base person" may set before himself some ignoble goal and, with the use of calculation, attain that goal, he will not thereby have engaged in good deliberation. While he may have gotten ahold of what he sought, he cannot be said to have exhibited good deliberation, because good deliberation "is apt to hit on what is good" (cf. 1142b17–27). For deliberation to be considered "good," the end at which it aims must be good. Therefore, good deliberation—the characteristic of the prudent man—takes its bearing from σοφία, which establishes the end toward which the prudent man will be directed.[44]

On its face, this relationship between σοφία and φρόνησις appears to be problematic. Indeed, the magnanimous statesman is the jealous type not prone to listening. However, as pointed out, Aristotle has taken care throughout the first five books of the *Ethics* to point out the limits of the social virtues, as well as their need to be guided by some higher virtue. In this way, Aristotle has disposed his audience to be solicitous of any advice that may help guide these social virtues. At this critical juncture in book VI, where he finally forthrightly makes clear that φρόνησις takes its direction from σοφία, Aristotle frames his depiction of the relationship in terms that will be palatable to the magnanimous statesman. The virtue of φρόνησις is described as being for the sake of some further political action. In addition, the hero chosen as the archetype of this virtue is the great Athenian statesman Pericles (1140b9). The courageous individuals at whom Aristotle aims this description of φρόνησις will appreciate the life of action that Aristotle presents here. In contrast, his description of those who are wise is presented in a nonthreatening manner: Aristotle holds up the philosophers Anaxagoras and Thales who, while they "know things that are extraordinary, wonderous, difficult, and daimonic," are thought to be useless "because they do not investigate the human goods" (1141b3–8). Notably, Aristotle does not here dispute this assertion,[45] but instead follows up by contrasting their wisdom with the utility of prudence: "But prudence is concerned with the human things" (1141b9). By calling attention to what appears to be the uselessness of wisdom and immediately comparing it with the eminent practicality of prudence, Aristotle presents the two virtues in such a way that that the statesman will not feel threatened by the philosopher but will instead solicit his advice.

Aristotle makes clear that the philosopher is able to form the character of the statesman through the dispensation of advice. Although the greatest of his politically inclined readers are hubristic and by nature contemptuous of advice, Aristotle shows that it is nevertheless possible for the philosopher to gain an audience with these politically inclined readers by appealing to their desire for action and by presenting the philosopher in a nonthreatening manner. Nevertheless, several issues remain: first, by framing φρόνησις as being oriented and directed toward action, Aristotle has placed one of man's highest, νοῦς-like capacities in the service of political action. Furthermore, σοφία has been relegated to acting as a formative or guiding force for the statesman and the city. While Aristotle's presentation of the intellectual virtues suggests that great things may be accomplished for the sake of the city if the two types of magnanimous men were to become friends, the servile and utilitarian role σοφία appears to assume in this presentation seems to open Aristotle up to the charge that, in contrast to Socrates, he moderates his pursuit of the good in order to concern himself with political matters.

Pleasure and Self-Love

That the philosopher is able to form the character of another individual through the dispensation of advice raises a number of related issues. First, the fact that σοφία has priority over φρόνησις suggests that the relationship between the philosopher and the statesman will not be one of equality. Aristotle indicates a number of times that friendship is characterized by equality. Is it possible for true friendship to exist between two unequal individuals? Second, what does the philosopher gain from actualizing the potency of the gentleman? Why would the magnanimous philosopher, who has been described by Aristotle as being somewhat asocial and "incapable of living with a view to another" (1124b31), put his talents in the service of his friend and of the city? Would this not involve a certain degradation on the part of the magnanimous philosopher? Aristotle devotes chapters eight and nine to answering these issues.

He opens chapter eight by exploring the perplexing question "as to whether one ought to love oneself most or someone else" (1168a29). On the one hand, people commonly stigmatize those who are "fondest of themselves" as having "self-love" (αὐτοφιλία) on the understanding that the base person does "everything for his own sake" (1168a32). On the other hand, Aristotle notes that all the qualities of friendship are "present especially in the person in relation to himself," such that "he is most a friend to himself, and so [he] ought to love [him]self most" (1168b4–7). Aristotle proposes to investigate these common opinions to ascertain the extent to which they are true.

In the ensuing discussion, Aristotle clarifies both why self-love can be a good thing and how it can be made compatible with friendship. He begins by stating that those who are constantly grasping for a "greater share of money, honors and bodily pleasures" are seeking to gratify the nonrational part of their soul. Aristotle concludes that these individuals "bring self-love into reproach" (1168b15–21). In contrast, while those who pursue what is just, moderate, and noble may not commonly be characterized as self-lovers, Aristotle states that this type of person is, in fact, *more* of a self-lover. Indeed, he notes that those who pursue what is just, moderate, and noble are self-lovers, as they are seeking to gratify the most authoritative part of themselves (1168b36). Aristotle's argument mirrors Plato's comparison of the tyrannical man and the just man in *The Republic*. While the tyrannical man is grasping and has insatiable desires, the just man is self-restrained, and ensures that his desiring part is "neither in want nor surfeited—in order that it will rest and not disturb the best part by its joy or its pain, but rather leave that best part alone pure and by itself" (*Republic,* 571e2–572a2).

A number of indications suggest that Aristotle's praise of self-restraint is not absolute, or that it does not comprise his final thoughts concerning self-love. He observes that by being a self-lover, the good man will both "profit himself and benefit others by doing noble things" (*NE,* 1169a12–13). However, it seems that these "noble things" may be different for different people. Aristotle writes, "Every intellect chooses what is best for itself, and the decent person obeys the rule of his intellect" (1169a17–18). The serious person, he states, "does many things for the sake of both his friends and his fatherland, and even dies for them if need be: he will give up money, honors and, in general, the goods that are fought over, thereby securing for himself what is noble" (1169a19–22). This gentleman, as Aristotle describes him, can be said to "grasp" at what is noble. Of course, by this point in the *Ethics*, Aristotle can trust that his reader does not believe the noble to be whatever the community honors, but instead what "serious individuals" deem noble or honorable Thus, Aristotle suggests that the self-lover seeks out opportunities to undertake great deeds of noble self-sacrifice, not to attain honor from any "random person," but inasmuch as these deeds are considered noble by "serious individuals."

However, while noble self-sacrifice that has the effect of saving the fatherland may be best for some, it is not best for all serious persons. Aristotle notes that it is equally possible that the serious person would "forgo, in favor of his friend, the performance of certain [noble] actions, and that it is nobler for him thus to become the cause of his friend's actions than to perform those actions himself" (1169a33–34; square brackets original). Given his discussion of potentiality and actuality, it seems that Aristotle distinguishes two roles: while it may be best for those who are politically magnanimous to pursue the noble action of self-sacrifice, it is better for those who are philosophically magnanimous to be the cause of their friend's actions, or to actualize their friend's innate potentiality. Aristotle suggests that it is greater for the philosophically magnanimous man to give up honors and political offices to a friend, thereby becoming "the cause of his friend's actions," than to "perform those actions himself" (1169a29–34). In this way, Aristotle solves the unstated issue regarding the roles of the politically magnanimous man and the philosophically magnanimous man that had been left lurking in the background, namely, which of the two ought to rule. The philosopher's role is to enable the statesman to rule.

Although Aristotle resolves the unstated issue as to whether the philosopher or the statesman should rule, the question remains: What does the philosopher obtain in return for actualizing the ruling potential of his friend? If it is equality that characterizes friendship most of all, should the philosopher not obtain something in return for providing this great benefit to his friend? It would seem uncharacteristic of friendship if the friendship between the philosopher and the statesman resulted in the statesman's ability to gratify his most authoritative part by doing noble deeds, while the philosopher was left without any means to gratify *his* most authoritative part. Aristotle's statement that it may be "nobler" for the philosopher to "become the cause of his friend's actions than to perform those actions himself" seems to be an underwhelming reason for the magnanimous philosopher to commit himself to actualizing the potentiality of his friend for the benefit of the city. What benefit does the philosopher obtain from actualizing the potential of his friend? Furthermore, what if there are no opportunities for the politically magnanimous man to gratify himself? If the city is at peace—a condition that Aristotle will later endorse as being preferable to war (cf. 1177b7–12)—how will the politically magnanimous man have opportunity to gratify himself?

Aristotle provides answers to these questions in chapter nine of book IX of the *Ethics*. Here, Aristotle explains that the philosopher's friend, having been formed by the philosopher, is in turn able to actualize the potential of the philosopher. The way in which Aristotle explains this process of actualization is somewhat cryptic. To grasp Aristotle's answer properly, it is necessary to turn again to the metaphysical principles that undergird his explanation. Specifically, we must turn first to Aristotle's account of actuality, or complete reality, in the *Metaphysics*, as well as to his treatment of pleasure in book VII of the *Ethics*.

As noted, the *Metaphysics* makes clear that actuality is the opposite of potentiality, and that a person's or a thing's actuality can be realized when two potentialities come into contact. Just as the potentiality of the carver can come to bear on the innate potentiality of a block of wood, actualizing its potential to become a statue, so the philosopher's potentiality can come to bear on, and actualize, the innate potentiality of the statesman, such that the statesman may become an enlightened statesman. In chapter six of book IX of the *Metaphysics*, Aristotle notes that there are different types of actions or actualities. On the one hand, some actions have a limit or a definite end. As an example, Aristotle states that an exercise that makes the body thin is not a complete action, as the movement itself (i.e., exercise) is not the purpose of the action. The purpose, or end, for which the action is engaged (thinning out the body) is outside the activity itself (*Metaphysics*, 1048b18–23). Such actions are limited, or incomplete, as the end does not inhere in the action itself. On the other hand, actions in which the end *is* present in the action itself are complete actions. Aristotle provides the following examples: "At the same time we are seeing and have seen, are understanding and have understood, are thinking and have thought" (1048b23–24). Activities such as seeing, understanding, and thinking, Aristotle indicates, are whole and complete immediately upon being exercised.

Aristotle thus concludes by classifying the former actions (actions that have a definite end) as movements, and the latter actions (actions which contain the end in the activity itself) as actualities or "complete reality" (1048b28–34).

Aristotle's extended account of pleasure in book VII of the *Ethics* makes clear that pleasure is one of those types of actualities that is complete, or which contains its end in its action. Indeed, pleasure is similar to sight, understanding, and thought. Aristotle prefaces his investigation of the nature of pleasure with a brief description of the reasons that people posit for deprecating pleasure as being less than, and distinct from, the good. The central reason that people deprecate pleasure is that they view "every pleasure [as] a perceptible process of coming into its nature, [and] no coming-into-being belongs to the same class as the ends we pursue" (*NE*, 1152b13–14). According to this teleological argument, all actions or activities are pursued for the sake of some end or purpose. As a result, because pleasure is an activity, or a "coming-into-being," it cannot be the good or the purpose for which we act. According to the common opinion that Aristotle describes, pleasure exists for the sake of some other end.

Aristotle quickly notes his disagreement with this opinion. He states, "It does *not* turn out that, on account of these things, pleasure is not good, or even not the best thing" (1152b25). He begins by distinguishing different types of pleasures: incidental pleasures and unqualified pleasures. Incidental pleasures, Aristotle informs us, are restorative in nature. These pleasures are not "unqualifiedly pleasant," as they are pleasant *only* to the extent there is something lacking on the part of the individual enjoying the pleasure (1152b33–35). For example, eating and drinking are pleasant only because they are restorative in nature. However, once our nature has been restored (our hunger sated or our thirst slaked), continued eating and drinking are no longer pleasant. Thus, restorative pleasures are not unqualifiedly pleasant but are pleasant only by virtue of a deficient condition.

In contrast, "unqualified pleasures" are those that are pleasant in and of themselves. In support of this contention, Aristotle explains that contrary to common opinion, pleasure is *not* a process of coming-into-being but is an "activity and an end" (1153a10). Some pleasures, Aristotle contends, do not have something else as an end, but the end inheres in the activity itself. Aristotle indicates that pleasure is like one of the "complete activities" listed in book IX of the *Metaphysics*: seeing, understanding, and thinking. As a result, he defines pleasure as an unimpeded "activity of the characteristic that accords with nature" (1153a14), and he provides "the activity bound up with contemplation" as an example (1152b37). When one's nature is not deficient, the activity of contemplation is accompanied by neither pain nor desire but is pleasurable in and of itself. Thus, because the activity of pleasure that is "bound up with contemplation" is not impeded in any way when one's nature is not deficient, contemplation is unqualifiedly pleasant.

In the following chapter, Aristotle goes on to argue that pleasure is good and may in fact be "the best thing." He explains that if the unimpeded activity of each characteristic (i.e., pleasure) is most choiceworthy, it follows that "a certain pleasure would be the best thing" (1153b12). Of course, the term "best thing" implies that it is better than all others, or that it is the highest good. What is striking about this claim is that Aristotle explicitly seems to be pulling back on a claim he had made in book I. There he had critiqued Plato's theory of the forms on the basis that the good appears to be manifold; things such as pleasure, honor, and prudence, all of which are said to be good in themselves, are "distinct and differ in the very respect in which they are goods" (1096b24–25). In fact, Aristotle went on to note that even if there is some one thing that is separate all by itself, which we might term "the good" or the idea of the good, such a thing "would not be subject to action or capable of being possessed by a human being" (1096b33–34). Why would Aristotle now discuss this "best thing" after having claimed in book I that it is beyond the capacity of a human being to attain?

A possible answer is given immediately after Aristotle's criticism of the Platonic theory of the forms in book I. He notes that even though no human being can possess such a thing as "the good," it may be helpful to have the idea of the good "as a sort of model," or pattern, so that "we will to a greater degree know also the things that are good for us; and if we know them, we will hit on them" (1097a2–4).[46] Thus, while Aristotle seems to be ambivalent about the actual existence of this sort of good, he appears to think that it may nevertheless be useful for human beings to strive for, so that they may attain what is good for them.[47]

The fact that in book VII Aristotle states that pleasure may be "the best thing" may indicate that he views pleasure as the model, or pattern, on which human beings can base their life. In making the argument that the pleasures of contemplation may be "the best thing," Aristotle states that "*if* in fact there are unimpeded activities of each characteristic . . . a certain pleasure *would* be the best thing" (1153b7–13; emphasis added). The significance of the conditional nature of this argument is made clear near the end of Aristotle's account of pleasure, where he underscores the human limitations in achieving such pleasure. Because human nature, in contrast to that of the god, is not simple, "the same thing is not always pleasant" for human beings.⁴⁸ The pleasure that the god enjoys is, in the words of book I, "not subject to action or capable of being possessed by a human being" (1096b33–34). While the god can "always enjoy . . . a pleasure that is one and simple" (1154b26), such a pleasure is beyond the capacity of a human being to attain due to a certain "defective condition" (1154b29).⁴⁹

Why, if Aristotle has already in book VII arrived at the conclusion that the best life for a human being is the life of contemplation, does the *Ethics* continue for another three books? The answer has to do with our limited capacity for continuous pleasure. While human beings *are* capable of experiencing the sublime pleasures associated with contemplation that the god experiences, we are incapable of experiencing this pleasure *continuously*, due to our embodied and limited existence. As a result, Aristotle's concluding paragraph of book VII reminds the reader of his humanity: "'Change in all things is sweet,' as the poet has it, on account of a certain defective condition."⁵⁰

That Aristotle discusses the limitations of human nature immediately before launching into his two books on friendship may seem to suggest that it is precisely our limitations that cause us to engage in friendship. Much of book IX of the *Ethics* seems, at least at first glance, to bear out such a reading. As noted above, Aristotle indicates the manner in which the philosopher may seek out a courageous or noble individual in order to *form* a friend precisely because his status as a mortal human being requires him to have a friend. And in chapter nine of book IX, Aristotle explicitly links his insights concerning our limited nature in book VII to the philosopher's need for a friend who can actualize his potentiality. If this interpretation were to hold, Aristotle's attempt to find a basis for friendship that is rooted in self-sufficiency would be a failure. As I will make clear, however, towards the end of the *Ethics*, Aristotle does find a basis for friendship between two magnanimous individuals that is not rooted in deficiency but is instead based on a self-sufficiency, while enabling each party to the friendship to recognize and appreciate the good of the other.

Aristotle begins his analysis by raising the issue of whether the happy person needs friends. He mentions the Socratic opinion concerning self-sufficiency and friendship that was stated in the *Lysis*: "Those who are blessed and self-sufficient have no need of friends, since the good things are theirs already; and . . . since the happy are self-sufficient, they have no need of anyone in addition" (1169b4–7). The quotation that Aristotle invokes to summarize this position may give us an inkling of his valuation of the Socratic stance. Indeed, he cites the following line from Euripides's *Orestes*:

"When a *daimon* gives well, what need of friends?" (1169b8). In the play, the line is stated caustically by Orestes as he is being pursued mercilessly by the daimonic furies for having killed his own mother. This suggests that Aristotle is not entirely convinced of the Socratic stance, or that the Socratic stance may not convey the totality of the phenomenon of friendship.

Why, then, will the magnanimous, self-sufficient individual need friends? Furthermore, if he does need friends, does this not imply a deficiency on the part of the magnanimous man? Aristotle's response to the Socratic dilemma unfolds in three stages by way of a kind of crescendo, with each argument building upon and complementing the previous argument. Aristotle's first argument in favor of the philosopher's need for friendship is based on a number of conditions: if the actions of a serious person are good and pleasant, and if we can contemplate the actions of those near us better than our own, it follows that "the actions of serious men who are friends" will be "pleasant to those who are good" (1169b30–1170a1). Lorraine Smith Pangle points out that this argument is incomplete, as "a friend's activity [is] always ultimately his and not ours."[51] According to Pangle, any pleasure we receive from witnessing the good or noble acts of another "will always be a somewhat passive and vicarious pleasure."[52] However, as pointed out above, Aristotle views friendship to consist in an "active making." Thus, to the extent that the philosopher is the *cause* of his friend's good and noble actions, the pleasure received will not be simply passive and vicarious. Instead, the philosopher will have undertaken an active role in creating those good and noble acts.

The second argument draws our attention away from viewing the activity of a friend to the difficulty attending continuous activity. Aristotle tells us that life is hard for the solitary person, "since it is not easy to be active continuously by oneself" (1170a5–6). This recalls Aristotle's argument in book VII concerning the limits of human life. In contrast to the god, who is capable of constant contemplation, human beings are limited and are therefore incapable of constant contemplation. This conclusion is stated explicitly in book X of the *Ethics*, where Aristotle states that while the wise person is "the most self-sufficient," the life of constant contemplation "would exceed what is human" (1177a30; 1177b27). Read in this context, Aristotle's second argument for the need for friends seems to be that because the life of *constant* activity is impossible, the magnanimous man will, to this extent, need friends.

Finally, Aristotle's third argument is based on an understanding of the workings of nature. He notes that for a serious person, a friend is choiceworthy and good by nature, and that the things that are good by nature are "good and pleasant" in themselves (1170a13–16). In this way, Aristotle signals to the reader that his third argument will show friendship to be good not on account of some lack that it is able to fill, but inasmuch as it is good in itself, or on its own terms.

Aristotle begins by pointing out that for human beings, living is defined as "a capacity for perception or thought" (1170a16–18). This definition is striking in that it seems to go out of its way to include perception. At the beginning of the *Ethics*, Aristotle had insisted that what is distinctive about human beings is our capacity for thought, as it is our capacity for thought that distinguishes us from the animals. At this point, however, shortly after having pointed out that man is not a god, Aristotle includes man's particularly corporeal capacity of perception in his definition of man, thereby drawing our attention to man's distinct status as neither beast nor god. He continues, noting that "a capacity is traced back to its activity, and what is authoritative resides in the activity" (1170a18). As applied to perception and thought, this means that the authoritative status of a person or thing lies not in its potentiality, but in its activity. We have already seen that the philosopher actualizes the potentiality of the statesman by the dispensation of advice, causing him to act in accord with the moral virtues. At this point, as we will see, Aristotle intends to make the argument that while the philosopher actualizes the statesman, the statesman in turn also actualizes the potentiality of the philosopher.

To make the case that the statesman also actualizes the philosopher's potential, Aristotle states the following: "If living itself is good and pleasant . . . and if he who sees perceives that he sees . . . then there is something that perceives that we are active. The result is that if we are perceiving something, we also perceive that we are perceiving. . . . And to perceive that we are perceiving . . . is to perceive that we exist" (1170a27–34). This abstruse passage is meant to elucidate a fundamental aspect of Aristotle's understanding of friendship. His argument is that it is through the senses, and in particular the sense of sight, that we come to perceive (αἰσθάνομαι) or understand that we have sight. Since sight is a type of activity, it is through the medium of sight that we are capable of perceiving or apprehending that we are active. As a result, when we look at something, or apprehend something, we also come to realize that we are apprehending. Finally, to realize that we are apprehending something is to understand that we exist. This passage could appropriately be called the existential moment in Aristotle's *Ethics*. For Aristotle, it is through our sense perception, and specifically through our perception of a friend, that we become aware of our own existence.⁵³ Because the philosopher is the *cause* of his friend's noble actions, he is able to perceive the good present in himself by witnessing his friend's noble actions.

In this third and final argument as to why the philosopher needs a friend, Aristotle explains how the exchange between two friends takes place. It will be recalled that in the very first chapter of book IX, Aristotle had indicated that the philosopher is owed some kind of return for the philosophical advice he gives his friend. Nevertheless, Aristotle indicated that it is up to the recipient of the advice to determine its worth. Aristotle cryptically stated: "For if the giver receives as much as the recipient is benefited . . . the giver will have received what was merited from the recipient in question" (1164b11–13). In this third argument as to why the philosopher needs friends, Aristotle finally unpacks this statement regarding what the philosopher is owed: the philosopher receives *pleasure* in return for his philosophical advice.⁵⁴ By rendering efficacious philosophical advice, the philosopher actualizes the potential of his friend and is able to witness his friend's noble acts. Furthermore, because he is the proximate *cause* of his friend's noble actions, the philosopher is, in a sense, witnessing his *own* actions and is thereby taking pleasure in his own existence. The relationship between the statesman and the philosopher is made equal by the exchange of pleasure that occurs.⁵⁵

However, Aristotle does not stop at pointing out the benefits that the philosopher will obtain from actualizing the potential of the statesman. As noted earlier, Aristotle describes the statesman's prudence—specifically his ability to survey a given situation and intervene—as directed and oriented toward political action. We saw that this is problematic both because it subordinates a "νοῦς-like" function as if it were a mere instrument to achieving some political good, and because the opportunities to exercise this function are likely to be limited. Aristotle had already hinted at the lack of opportunity to exercise this "νοῦς-like" function in the service of political ends in his description of magnanimity in book IV.

In book IV, Aristotle noted that the magnanimous man's awareness of his own worth and greatness causes him to view most things as beneath him. As a result, he is slow to act; in fact, Aristotle goes so far as to characterize him as "idle" (1124b24). Not all small occasions will cause the magnanimous man to act, as these are inappropriate to his greatness. Instead, it is only when an opportunity arises that is equal to his greatness that the magnanimous man will take a great risk, and, in doing so, he will be unsparing of his life "on the grounds that living is not at all worthwhile" (1124b8–10). However, as long as no opportunity presents itself for the statesman to intervene, his overweening concern with his own worth culminates in a sort of sloth.⁵⁶ Susan Collins concludes that because the magnanimous man views only great enterprises as worthy of his action, "the 'activity' of magnanimity . . . could be described most simply as the magnanimous man's self-contemplation of his own great virtue."⁵⁷

Chapter 9 presents the solution to the difficulties posed by the fact that the statesman's "νούς-like" capacity is directed toward political action and that the magnanimous statesman may lack opportunity to contemplate his own great virtue. Aristotle not only indicates that the philosopher will obtain pleasure from witnessing the noble acts of his friend, but he makes clear that by actualizing the potential of his friend, the friend *also* becomes aware of his *own* existence. Aristotle writes, "Existing is . . . a choiceworthy thing because of a person's perception that he is good, and this sort of perception is pleasant on its own account. Accordingly, one ought to share in the friend's perception that he exists" (1170b8–12). The philosopher, Aristotle explains, becomes aware of his *own* existence by sharing in the friend's perception (συναισθάνομαι) that he exists. By actualizing his friend's potential, both the philosopher and the statesman become aware of their own goodness together.

How does this joint-perception of existence occur? It is in his explanation of this process that Aristotle finally makes clear that the friendship between the philosopher and the statesman will have political consequences. Aristotle explains, "This [joint-perception of existence] would come to pass by living together and sharing in a community of speeches and thought—for this is what living together would seem to mean in the case of human beings, and not as with cattle, merely feeding in the same place" (1170b12–14). Aristotle indicates that it is through the establishment of a "community of speeches and thought"—i.e., through the establishment of a polis—that the philosopher can share in his friend's perception that he exists. Thus, in the same way that the philosopher's potential is actualized by witnessing the noble deeds of his friend—deeds of which he is the proximate cause—so the statesman's potential is actualized by perceiving the regime that he has founded. With the help of the philosopher, the statesman will be able to form "a community of speeches and thought" and will become aware of his own virtue by looking at and deriving enjoyment from the regime he has helped to establish.

By linking the magnanimous statesman's ability to perceive his own virtue with the establishment of a regime, Aristotle resolves the difficulties that had initially appeared to complicate his depiction of the magnanimous statesman's prudence. The perception involved in φρόνησις is no longer oriented simply toward political activity, such as noble acts of valor, but is instead engaged in for its own sake. The magnanimous man perceives the regime he has formed, and, through this perception, he becomes aware of his own existence and his own virtue. The statesman's ultimate activity—the activity that is done for its own sake—consists in a pure onlooking. In addition, Aristotle obviates the difficulty posed by the lack of opportunity. The magnanimous statesman was initially beset by awareness of his own greatness, which caused him to refrain from acting. Unless a worthy opportunity presents itself, the magnanimous man will not act. As a result, in the depiction of the magnanimous man in book IV of the *Ethics*, the life of the magnanimous man appears to be a joyless quest for opportunities worthy of his effort. By pointing to the magnanimous man's ability to perceive the regime that he creates, Aristotle shows that the magnanimous statesman's ability to contemplate his own virtues need not be limited to those rare opportunities in which he can exercise his virile virtues.

In the *Politics*, Aristotle provides little justification as to why the polis emerges. It will be recalled that while the household and the village are sufficient to deal with the necessities of life, Aristotle nonetheless traces the emergence of the polis from several villages and argues that it is ordered towards the good. In book IX of the *Ethics*, Aristotle indicates that friendship is the cause of the city's coming-into-being. Specifically, it is the friendship between the philosopher and the statesman that leads to the formation of the city. While it is not incorrect to say that Aristotle's intention in the *Ethics* is to direct the statesman toward a higher form of life, the form this life takes is not the life of philosophic contemplation as many scholars have indicated.[58] Instead, it is the life of perception, which seems to be somewhat *analogous* to the life of philosophic contemplation.[59] Aristotle directs the gentleman to take an active role in the creation of a just and noble state such that he may then perceive his creation and, through that perception, become aware of his own goodness and take delight in his own existence. Together, the philosopher and the enlightened statesman are cocreators of the polis and are able to order it toward the good. It is their friendship—a friendship in which wisdom and power come together—that is the formal cause of the polis.[60]

Self-Sufficiency and Actualization

Aristotle's arguments concerning the need for friendship make clear that friendship between those who are good is a mutually beneficial arrangement for both the magnanimous philosopher and the magnanimous statesman, and that it will have beneficial political effects. Indeed, the philosopher and the statesman actualize each other's potentiality, such that each becomes aware of his own good and takes pleasure in that awareness. However, if their innate capacity to come to an awareness of their own existence lies dormant until it is actualized through the other's actions, would this not imply a certain deficiency? As Sarah Broadie notes, the motion from a state of potentiality to actuality "essentially arises from its subject's lack. The subject moves or is moved into a new condition because the latter is better than its previous states."[61] If it is true that the statesman and the philosopher play an actualizing role for each other—each actualizing the other's potential for pleasure—then Socrates's view of friendship would seem to be vindicated: friendship has its basis in deficiency, lack, or need. However, as will be made clear, Aristotle is eminently aware of this difficulty, and he confronts it directly in his final account of pleasure in book X.

Aristotle's final account of pleasure in book X begins in chapter four and is similar to his earlier treatment of pleasure in book VII.[62] In both accounts, Aristotle argues against the common opinion that pleasure is a process, or a coming-into-being. However, his method in each account is slightly different. In book VII, as part of his rebuttal of the contention that pleasure is simply a process, Aristotle emphasizes pleasure's status as an activity. In contrast, in book X he instead focuses on the wholeness, or completeness, of pleasure. In support of this contention, Aristotle contrasts pleasure with motion; while motion is never complete, as the entity in motion changes position over time, the form of pleasure "is complete at any moment" (1174b4–8). Furthermore, in contrast to motion, which we can experience only over time, we can experience pleasure in an instant. At any distinct moment in which we undergo the experience of pleasure, that experience is whole and complete. Why does Aristotle emphasize the completeness of pleasure and the fact that it exists independent of time? The reason is that he is attempting to point out that our inability to experience pleasure continuously is *not* a deficiency. Because pleasure is something that is whole and complete and "resides in the 'right now'" (1174b9), our human incapacity to experience this pleasure continuously in the manner of the god or First Mover does not imply a deficiency on our part.[63]

Furthermore, in both accounts of pleasure—the accounts in book VII and book X—Aristotle makes mention of the fact that there are distinct pleasures and activities that are appropriate to different individuals. Thus, he intimates that while the activity of contemplation and its accompanying pleasures may be best for some, it is not necessarily best for all. In fact, in book VII, Aristotle notes that "some of the base motions and processes seem to be base unqualifiedly, whereas for a particular person, they are not such but are even choice worthy for him, while some are not choice worthy for him but are such only on a given occasion and for a short time, though not unqualifiedly" (1152b29–32). Aristotle thus subtly indicates that the activities bound up with courage, or perhaps even violence—which in the absence of some sort of necessity would be base—may appear good to some people. According to Aristotle, different individuals choose different activities and pleasures that correspond to what is most authoritative in them. At various points of the *Ethics*, Aristotle points out that we *are* the part that is most excellent and authoritative in us. Thus, by perceiving the ultimate particular thing—the moment that he can engage and bring a task to completion—and then acting upon that perception by undertaking noble deeds of valor, the statesman engages and gratifies his most authoritative part. Similarly, by contemplating the outermost bounds of abstract thought, the philosopher engages and gratifies his most authoritative part. The pleasure that the statesman and the philosopher receive from engaging in their respective activities is whole and complete, even though they are incapable of being practiced continuously.

Aristotle's description of pleasure in book X as something whole and complete is meant to show that our human incapacity to experience pleasure continuously does not imply a deficiency on our part. While it is true that we cannot experience pleasure in the manner of the god—i.e., continuously—this is not indicative of any deficiency on our part, because pleasure is something whole and complete. However, Aristotle does not end his analysis of pleasure with this insight. Instead, he turns to address the specifically *human* element of our existence, namely, our capacity for sensation. He writes, "Every sense perception is active in relation to the thing perceived, and it is active in a complete way when it is in a good condition with a view to the noblest of the things subject to sense perception" (1174b14–16). Thus, after having explained that there is nothing deficient about our inability to experience pleasure continuously, Aristotle explains that a proper consideration of our existence as embodied human beings must take into account our material surroundings as well.

Aristotle continues by noting that the specifically human aspect of our existence is also capable of experiencing pleasure: "When both the thing perceived and that which perceives are of this most excellent sort, there will always be pleasure" (1174b30–32). While Aristotle is somewhat cryptic in describing the pleasure that accompanies perception, in light of his comments concerning friendship, it appears that what he has in mind is the pleasure that accompanies a friendship based on the good, specifically, the delight that one derives from perceiving the order and beauty that one has created. Thus, friendship is necessary as it completes, or activates, our existence as human beings.

Again, the fact that friendship is necessary to complete our existence as human beings may seem to vindicate the Socratic contention that all friendship is based on a metaphysical lack or need. However, because Aristotle has consistently maintained that we are defined by what is authoritative in us, he forestalls this conclusion. That friendship completes or activates our existence *as human beings* does not imply any deficiency on the part of the magnanimous statesman or philosopher. Neither the magnanimous statesman's capacity to perceive the ultimate particular thing and engage in noble courageous acts, nor the magnanimous philosopher's godlike capacity for contemplation requires actualization from another. As a result, Aristotle is able to maintain that while friendship completes our existence as human beings, we do *not* need a friend to complete that part which is most authoritative in us. Aristotle resolves the Socratic paradox concerning the good man's need for friendship by recognizing our limitations as human beings but refusing to acknowledge that we are *defined* by those limitations.

Aristotle makes clear that the limitations posed on us as human beings do not define us when he depicts the life of contemplation. After describing the superiority of the contemplative life to the life of political action, he points out that this contemplative type of life exceeds what is human. He writes, "It is not insofar as he is a human being that a person will live in this way, but insofar as there is something divine present in him" (1177b27–28). Nevertheless, Aristotle concludes: "One ought not—as some recommend—to think only about human things because one is a human being, nor only about mortal things because one is mortal, but rather to make oneself immortal, insofar as that is possible, and to do all that bears on living in accord with what is the most excellent of the things in oneself" (1177b32–1178a1). Thus, Aristotle recognizes that while the material, corporeal aspects of our existence ought to be of concern if we are to attain our full potential as human beings, one ought not to attend to these human concerns at the expense of our most divine capacities. While the perception of his friend and the political regime he founds may be pleasurable and necessary for the magnanimous philosopher's completion as a human being, he ought not devote himself to these pleasures at the expense of his more divine capacity of philosophic contemplation. Similarly, while the magnanimous statesman may derive pleasure from undertaking noble (and necessary) actions pertaining to politics and war, these pursuits should not be all-encompassing, or be pursued at the expense of his more divine capacity for perception.

This exhortation is echoed in the form of a warning at the conclusion of Aristotle's discussion of pleasure. He points out that the pleasures that complete the activities bound up with thinking differ from pleasures related to sense perception, and similarly the pleasures that accompany the various sense perceptions differ from another. While the pleasures that properly correspond to the activity act as an aide in the completion of the activity, pleasures foreign to the activity have the effect of impeding the activity. Thus, he writes, "Those who love the aulos are incapable of paying attention to speeches if they overhear someone playing the aulos, because they take greater delight in the art of aulos playing than they do in the activity before them" (1175b2–6). The delight that one derives from music can interfere with other more rational activities. This example is intended to show that the pleasures associated with lower-order activities can impede our ability to utilize our higher capacities. Just as the pleasures of music can interfere with our capacity to engage in rational activity, so the lower-order sensory pleasures can interfere with our theoretical (θεωρητικὴ) capacities. When this occurs, Aristotle seems to say, our lives become all too human.

Aristotle as Advisor

Having established the importance of friendship, while also warning his readers of its dangers, Aristotle devotes the last chapter of book X to explaining, in outline, how the statesman and the philosopher can order the regime toward the good, or how they may transcend mere nature. He notes that while all the relevant topics have been discussed—virtue, friendship, and pleasure—the inquiry is not yet complete, as the end in matters of action consists not simply in contemplating and understanding things, but also in *doing* them. To this end, Aristotle proposes to investigate the manner in which one may "possess the virtues and make use of them" (1179a3). Aristotle believes that possessing and making use of the virtues is dependent upon good law (or νόμος), as it is through the habituation and the cultivation of good judgment engendered by the law that a person may come to be capable of reasoned debate, persuasion, and ultimately self-government.

However, Aristotle also deals with the difficulty that arises when public care for the laws is lacking, explaining how one can become good in the absence of good laws. He posits private education and friendship as the method of reforming the law in such a situation. In this way, he reveals that the *Ethics* can operate as a handbook both to establish and to maintain public order.[64]

Speeches and rhetoric on their own are insufficient, argues Aristotle, to make the majority of people decent.[65] The use of reasoned persuasion is, in most cases, inadequate without a certain level of prerational education. In order for the majority of people to be capable of listening to reasoned advice, the "soul of the student must be prepared beforehand by means of habits" (1179b25–26). Here, Aristotle agrees with Plato's method of education: habituation must precede rational education. A correct upbringing in which one is taught what he ought to love and what he ought to dislike is necessary if he is later going to be open to reasoned persuasion. However, Aristotle notes that correct habits are difficult to obtain without proper laws. While people may have the potential to develop habit and thereby acquire a second nature, they are not disposed to act in a moderate manner before this potential is actualized. Left in their untutored state, most people are prone to act in an immoderate and uncontrolled manner. Because most people "obey the governance of necessity more than of speech, and of punishments more than of what is noble" (1180a4–6), Aristotle concludes that life as a whole is in need of law.

Despite the necessity of law in the formation and habituation of the citizens of the polis, Aristotle observes that most cities utterly neglect the law. What occurs in most cities is not the rational imposition of law, but instead the "command characteristic of a father" (1180a19). According to Aristotle, the problem inherent in this "command method" of order is that it leads to resentment; people begrudge those who impede them in their pursuit of their untutored desires. In contrast, the impersonal character of the law avoids this resentment and is not viewed as invidious. The rational, orderly, application of the law, Aristotle indicates, is superior to the personal, perhaps tribal, approach to justice that characterizes the pre-political realm.

Unfortunately, argues Aristotle, what holds sway in most cities is not the reason of the law. Quoting a line from Homer's *Odyssey*, Aristotle indicates that what happens instead is that each father " 'lay[s] down the sacred law for children and wife' in the manner of the Cyclops" (1180a28–30). Aristotle's invocation of the Cyclops—a race that appears as bloodthirsty cannibals in the *Odyssey*—is notable for two related reasons. First, Aristotle, suggests that untutored nature is nasty, brutish, and short. Without the imposition of the impersonal framework of the legal system, most individuals will fail to acquire the virtue necessary to ensure that life is pleasant, orderly, and good, and will instead act in the brutal manner of the Cyclops. In addition, the Cyclops appear to have spurned technical innovation, trusting instead in the forces of nature, or providence. In the *Odyssey*, in the line prior to the one invoked by Aristotle, we are told that "the Cyclopes neither plant nor plough, but trust in providence."[66] By trusting in providence or fortune alone, the Cyclops live a savage and bloodthirsty life. Nature, Aristotle intimates, is nasty and brutish.

How, then, can one rise above the severity of nature? Somewhat paradoxically, Aristotle indicates that the cure lies within nature itself. He states, "When cities utterly neglect the public care, it would seem appropriate for each individual to contribute to the virtues of *his own offspring and friends*" (1180a30–33; emphasis added). Aristotle paints a glowing portrait of the way in which a father's actions can come to influence his children: "For just as it is the laws and customs that hold sway in cities, so also it is the speeches and habits of the father that do so in households—and these latter to a greater degree, on account of the kinship and benefactions involved, for from the outset household members feel affection for one another and are readily obedient by nature" (1180b4–8). It may seem odd that Aristotle would point to private education and the care for one's own offspring and friends as the means of transcending the severity of nature after having just compared that approach to the life of the Cyclops. How can the love of one's own be characterized both as the cause of a harsh cycloptic existence *and* as the method by which man transcends that existence? Aristotle's Janus-faced depiction of paternal authority and friendship suggests that fortune or chance will never be completely conquered. In contrast to Socrates and Lysander, both of whom sought to conquer fortune altogether by subverting the established order, Aristotle suggests that one still needs to work with the material nature provides, such that it may be molded in the manner best conducive to human flourishing. As the examples of Socrates and Lysander show, attempts to confront fortune directly, without respect for prevailing conditions, will result in failure.

So, how does one accommodate oneself to nature, or to that which is given, so that the cycloptic existence that often characterizes pure nature might be transcended? Throughout the *Ethics*, Aristotle has subtly indicated that the answer lies in the phenomenon of friendship—that is, the natural forces of potency and actuality. As noted above, the actuality of a rational agent can come to bear on the potentiality of another rational agent, cultivating and actualizing the other's innate potentiality. In this last chapter of the *Ethics*, Aristotle indicates that friendship—and by extension the forces of potentiality and actuality—are natural, pre-political forces that exist in family life and in friendships. These natural forces, Aristotle contends, both can and should be cultivated when public care and education have broken down. When the established order is in a state of dissolution, fathers and friends ought to act as *informal* lawgivers and educate those in their care privately.[67]

The primary difficulty in establishing private education, however, is that if it is to be effective, the educator himself must already be properly formed. If the lawgiver is to institute (informal) laws that are conducive to the cultivation of virtue, he must be cognizant of the end at which these laws are aimed, and he must himself be oriented toward that end; in sum, the educator or lawgiver must—to a certain degree—already be virtuous. Aristotle had indicated earlier in the chapter that in the absence of the requisite laws, it is difficult for someone to obtain a correct upbringing leading to virtue. As a result, he seems to be in the position of a catch-22. On the one hand, when the city neglects the public care, it requires individuals to undertake private education so as to reform the public order. On the other hand, private education itself requires the preexistence of an individual that has been properly educated, which in turn depends on good laws.

Nevertheless, Aristotle notes, even in the absence of a formal system of public care, it is not impossible for select individuals to be self-taught on the basis of experience alone: "Nothing prevents someone—even someone without scientific knowledge—from exercising a noble care for an individual, provided that he has, through experience, contemplated in a precise way the results for each, just as even some people seem to be their own best doctors but are unable to aid another at all" (1180b16–19). Aristotle concedes that certain individuals are capable of being self-taught via experience. However, he immediately follows this concession by noting that this experience is, on its own, insufficient for educating others; self-taught individuals are "unable to aid another at all" (1180b19). He notes that if such a self-taught individual had the desire to educate others, he would have to concern himself with science, and "proceed to the universal and become also acquainted with this to the extent possible" (1180b21–22). Thus, if one wishes to become an educator, experience alone is insufficient; rather, one needs at least some level of acquaintance with universal, scientific, principles.

Aristotle next turns to the question concerning the source from which the legislator may attain the requisite scientific knowledge that is necessary for one to become an educator or skilled legislator. From where can the legislator attain the science of politics? The legislative skill, he argues, is different from that of the other sciences or capacities that people may develop. The other arts and sciences operate on a sort of apprenticeship system by which an individual who practices the art also transmits that capacity to others. However, in politics—of which the legislative art is a part—this does not seem to occur. Echoing Socrates's observation in the *Gorgias*, Aristotle notes that skilled politicians do not make "their own sons or any of their friends into skilled politicians," even though this would be a reasonable thing to do (11801a5–7). Aristotle observes that it is instead the Sophists who profess to teach "the political art" and how to "make men good citizens" (*Protagoras*, 319a4; cf. *NE*, 1180b35–1181a2). Like Socrates, Aristotle seems to be dismissive of their claims. In general, he notes, "they do not even know what sort of a thing [the political art] is or with what sorts of things it is concerned: otherwise, they would not have posited it as being the same thing as rhetoric—or even inferior to it" (1181a13–16).

However, in elaborating upon the Sophists' failure properly to teach the political art, Aristotle does not dismiss their claims of knowledge entirely. Instead, he insinuates that their art is incomplete, for they believe political science consists simply of "putting together a collection of the well-regarded laws" (1181a17). On its own, this collection is insufficient because the selection of *which* laws to implement is not an easy task but requires a particular skill. The Sophists, he concludes, fail to recognize that "selection [is] a part of the comprehension involved, and [act] as if the correct judging of them were not the greatest thing, just as it is in music" (1181a17–19). Aristotle's critique of the Sophists seems to be aimed not at their lack of scientific knowledge, but at their belief that this scientific knowledge is sufficient by itself and that the act of implementing that knowledge is an easy task.

Founding a regime and establishing good laws, Aristotle suggests, is not simply an endeavor that entails scientific knowledge or an intellectual grasp of the truth about eternal principles. Instead, these tasks require the full range of man's dianoetic capacities. In addition to an intellectual grasp of the outermost bounds in the direction of the most general universality, founding a regime requires an intellectual grasp of the ultimate particular thing as well. The former capacity belongs, of course, to the philosopher. The philosopher has the capacity to write treatises and "collections of well-regarded laws" based on an intellectual grasp of eternal principles. The latter capacity—a capacity to grasp the ultimate particular thing—belongs to those politicians or statesmen who have the relevant experience: "Those with the relevant experience in each thing," he writes, "judge the works involved correctly, and they comprehend through what or how the works are brought to completion" (1181a20–23). It is not the philosopher, but statesmen with political experience who have the capacity to observe a given political situation and discern the first instance or opportunity where they may intervene to bring a particular action to completion. Of course, in establishing the rule of law, or νόμος, the philosopher and the statesmen are not creating ex nihilo but are instead building on, and bringing to completion, what is already inchoately present in nature.[68]

Aristotle's twofold account of politics is depicted as requiring the capacity of both statesman and philosopher. The necessity of both actors stems from the contingency of political matters—a fact that Aristotle indicates the Sophists have forgotten. Political science is not *simply* a matter of laying out the best laws but also involves matching laws with actual existing conditions (1181a16–18). While assembling a collection of "well-regarded laws" is a science (ἐπιστήμη) fit for the philosopher, the selection of which law to apply in any particular regime requires the practical judgment proper to the statesman. It is perhaps for this reason that in book IV of the *Politics*, in which he discusses regime preservation and reformation, Aristotle asserts that it belongs to political science to study not only the best regime, but also the regime that is best under the existing circumstances (*Politics*, 1288b21–27). To simply describe the best regime without paying any attention to the conditions on the ground would be to practice political science in the manner of a Sophist. At the same time, to engage in political science without the knowledge of what laws are best is to act without the requisite theoretical knowledge.

The fact that regime preservation and reformation require the statesman's attention to what is possible under the circumstances suggests that the political *effects* of the highest type of friendship will be governed by existing conditions. It is likely for this reason that in book III of the *Ethics*, Aristotle leads the magnanimous men who transcend the standards and conventions of the city to maintain a solicitous regard for the city's standards (*NE*, 1124a20–25). While their friendship, founded on true virtue, transcends the standards and conventions of the city, they nevertheless must take into account the city's conventions, tailoring their political reforms to the circumstances on the ground, so that their reforms may have more efficacious results. The science of politics, Aristotle intimates, ought to be conducted with the eye of a philosopher attuned to what is best, and the eye of the statesman to what the conditions on the ground permit.

In the last chapter of the *Ethics*, Aristotle makes clear that forming or reforming a regime requires not only the scientific capacity of the philosopher, but also the practical reason of the statesman. The last chapter sheds much light on the purpose of the *Ethics* as a whole. The capacity of both the magnanimous philosopher *and* the magnanimous statesman are necessary for the formation of a polis that is ordered toward the good. While both types of magnanimous individuals are capable of bestowing great benefits on the community, their awareness of this fact also causes them to be a danger to their community. Aristotle shows that friendship of the good—that is, friendship between two magnanimous individuals who are self-sufficient and aware of their own greatness—can cultivate the public benefits magnanimity is capable of bestowing, while avoiding its attendant dangers. In this way, Aristotle solves the classic dilemma posed by political philosophy: friendship can attain the coincidence of wisdom and power that ensures that the regime and the public order are directed toward the good.

Chapter Five

Friendship and the Practice of Politics

Friendship in the Polis

This book has traced political philosophy's classic dilemma of how wisdom may positively direct those who hold power in the regime. Chapters three and four showed that Aristotle's solution to this fundamental problem is that of *sunaisthetic* friendship. In this way, he helps ensure that the regime is directed toward the good. Nevertheless, a few things seem to be left unresolved. First, how can a regime made up of disparate parts be ordered toward a single good? Practically speaking, what would it mean for a regime to be ordered toward the good? Furthermore, while Aristotle's account of friendship grounds politics in something other than mere need and so has the potential to make a positive contribution to the life of the polis, it is also true that his account of friendship applies primarily to the friendship between magnanimous individuals and serves primarily as a guide for situations in which public order has broken down. Since this portrait seems rather different from the common account of Aristotle's political writings—that of a self-governing city-state in which citizens take turns ruling and being ruled—we must ask, what are the concrete, practical implications of Aristotle's account of *sunaisthetic* friendship? What does his treatment of magnanimity and friendship mean for us? Or is it the case that the highest type of friendship is simply unattainable for ordinary citizens, and that the exercise of dianoetic virtue is reserved solely for those magnanimous individuals who found cities?

These questions are perhaps even more unsettling in light of the ending of the *Ethics*. Recall that in the very last chapter, Aristotle argues that speeches alone are insufficient to instill virtue in most people. The only thing that "the many" will listen to is "vengeance" (1179b11–13). Aristotle seems to leave us with the conclusion that "the many" need to be habituated, by the coercive force of the law, into leading morally virtuous lives.[1] The manner in which the city obtains the unity necessary to achieve its goal of moral virtue seems limited to the vengeful exhortation of the law, or to force. If we take this to be Aristotle's settled view on the matter, he seems to be calling into question the dignity of the nature and purpose of the city. "The good" to which the city is ordered would be limited to the enforced practice of moral virtue, while the more sublime pleasures associated with the dianoetic virtues are simply beyond the ken of ordinary citizens.

The final paragraph of the *Ethics* seems to reiterate this conclusion. Aristotle states, "Since those prior to us have left undiscovered what pertains to legislation, it is perhaps better for us to investigate it ourselves—and indeed what concerns the regime in general—so that, to the extent of our capacity, the philosophy concerning human affairs might be completed" (1181b13–15).[2] Many have taken this final paragraph to be Aristotle's natural segue into the *Politics* and its discussion of the art of lawgiving (νομοθεσία). The city, it seems, becomes unified and achieves its common goal of producing morally virtuous citizens not primarily through friendship, or even persuasion, but instead through the sanctioned use of force.

As I hope to show, however, the *Politics* reveals that while Aristotle is cognizant of the need for legislation to maintain unity in the city, he does not believe that legislation alone is sufficient for this purpose. Overall, Aristotle devotes very little attention to the role that legislation plays in unifying the regime and in ordering it toward the cultivation of moral virtue. In fact, book II, which serves as a preliminary investigation into the source and extent of the city's unity, exposes the limitations of the law's ability to foster political unity. Book II reveals the crudeness of using legislation to achieve social cohesion, its inability to eliminate faction or to curb the excessive desires of the city's more hubristic inhabitants, and its incapacity properly to incorporate any level of individual judgment or self-government. In turn, books VII and VIII of the *Politics*, both of which concern the best regime, reveal that the source of political unity lies in education—specifically *musical* education. As we shall see, Aristotle argues that musical education remediates the defects associated with law and develops the citizens' capacity to engage in noble judgment. The formative influence of the best regime's educational system renders ordinary citizens capable—to varying degrees—of exercising the dianoetic virtue of prudence. In this way, they learn the art of self-government and come to participate in the *sunaisthetic* friendship of the city's founders.

Unity in the City

Aristotle begins his investigation in book II of the *Politics* by critiquing Socrates's "city in speech" as established in *The Republic*. Underlying this critique is a sustained investigation into the extent to which a regime can be based on friendship. Plato's *Republic* takes the adage "friends have all things in common" to a comic extreme, such that all property and even women and children are held in common.[3] Aristotle treats these proposals as seriously intended and as stemming from Socrates's failure to distinguish friendship from erotic love.[4] Socrates, he asserts, believes the city to be "the work of affection—just as in the discourses on love we know that Aristophanes speaks of lovers who from an excess of affection 'desire to grow together'" (*Politics*, 1262b12–13). Aristophanes's lovers have such an erotic longing for each other that they seek to fuse together and become one entity. In this way, each of the lovers' own good is identified fully with the good of the other. If this model could be taken as the basis for the unity of the city, it would be fully one and would not suffer from factional disputes.

Aristotle notes, however, that if one were to use this model as the basis of the city's unity—that is, if all the friendly relations of the city were treated as relationships of erotic love—the city would not, in fact, grow together. Instead, the city would see a destruction of the natural bonds that hold families and cities together. The reason, relates Aristotle, is that the excessive unity proposed by Socrates does not allow for the proper cultivation of a sense of ownership, or friendship. Socrates's attempt to restructure familial relations in the city, as well as his proposal that all property be held in common, necessarily destroys the exclusivity or "ownness" that accompanies family relations.[5] Destroying this exclusivity or "ownness" has the effect of destroying, in turn, the care that is characteristic of affection. Aristotle explains: "What belongs in common to the most people is accorded the least care: they take thought for their own things above all, and less about things common, or only so much as falls to each individually. For . . . they slight [what is common] on the grounds that someone else is taking care of them" (*Politics*, 1261b33–37). The things held in common, Aristotle explains, are typically afforded less care on the assumption that others are caring for them. Thus, because Socrates's proposal equates friendship with erotic love, it undermines the political unity it seeks to achieve.

Aristotle's critique leaves us wondering whether the city *can* become a unity. If the members of the city are unable to become unified in the manner of Aristophanes's lovers—that is, if they are unable to identify their own good with that of the city—will not the citizens' partiality for their own families and, perhaps with even graver implications, the citizens' partiality for their own desires undermine the unity of the city? How can Aristotle reconcile the citizens' individual good with the good of the whole? Perhaps, if partiality, or man's propensity to factional association, is simply a fact of life, then the only way to ensure that these factions do not utterly destroy the bonds of the city is through the force of legislation. Perhaps coercive force is required to curb or limit citizens' partiality, such that the order of the city may be maintained.

What follows Aristotle's criticism of Socrates's proposals, however, is not an encomium on the power of law. Instead, through an investigation of legislation proposed by Phaleas of Chalcedon and Hippodamus of Miletus, Aristotle reveals the *limits* of the law's ability to curb partiality and factional disputes. The limitations of law first come to the fore in a discussion concerning Phaleas's proposed legislation calling for the equal distribution of property. Phaleas was of the opinion that all factional disputes in the city are the result of inequitable property distribution. To avoid such disputes and to foster a sense of friendship among the citizens, he thought it best to institute a "leveling" program whereby wealth would be redistributed from the wealthy to the poor (1266b1–5). Aristotle likens Phaleas's proposal to Plato's less severe measure in the *Laws*, according to which the discrepancy in property accumulation is limited so that no citizen is "permitted to possess a property five times the size of the smallest one" (1266b6–7). Both measures seek to limit the disparity between the economic classes of the city in the hopes of preventing factional disputes and fostering friendship.

As Aristotle points out, such arrangements are going to be limited in their success, as it is simply not the case that all factional disputes arise from an inequitable distribution of property. Before turning to other sources of political conflict, however, Aristotle points to a pragmatic difficulty that attends "leveling" the property of citizens: its success hinges upon a correct ratio between the size of a property and the number of people that the property is to support. To be effective, any regulation concerning the proper division of property needs to "properly include an arrangement concerning the number of children as well" (1266b10–11). In short, the success of the proposals put forward by Phaleas and Plato are dependent upon further legislation limiting the number of children that citizens will be allowed to have.

In this way, Aristotle hints at the fundamental problem underlying attempts to create social harmony through equalization schemes: no such scheme on its own will ensure social harmony, as the root cause of factional disputes is not material inequality, but desire. The erotic desire that results in procreation leads to, and in fact underpins, the need for extensive property. As he writes a short while later: "One ought to level desires sooner than property" (1266b30–33). By showing that the social cohesion achieved through the leveling of property requires concomitant legislation limiting the citizens' erotic desires, Aristotle reveals the crudeness of seeking to achieve social cohesion through the coercive force of law and leads us to question what other erotic desires—possibly philosophic desires—will be limited or even prohibited when social cohesion is sought through law alone.

Following his claim that factional disputes are the result more of desire than of material inequality, Aristotle points out that the more serious factional disputes that arise in the city stem not from a disagreement concerning the distribution of property, or what he terms the "necessary things," but from the distribution of honors (1266b38–1267a4). Phaleas's crude leveling proposal is ineffective in the face of such disputes. While a scheme creating material equality may have some limited success in countering the envious desires of the many, the nature of disputes concerning honor is different. While "the many" wish for equality in the distribution of honors, "the refined" insist on inequality (1267a1–2). Both "the many" and "the refined" need to be made content in some way with a proportional distribution of honors that is proper to the city. As Aristotle suggests a short while later, the only way to make people content with the distribution of honors proper to the city is through the inculcation of moderation. The desire of the citizenry needs to be tamed and made congruent with the form of the regime. Phaleas's legislative proposal is incapable of resolving such factional disputes.

Aristotle makes the law's inability to curb self-interested desire more explicit when he discusses those who commit the "greatest injustices." These injustices, he states, are committed not out of a desire for necessary things but simply on account of "the enjoyment that comes with pleasures unaccompanied with pains" (1267a6–9).[6] Aristotle even calls into question whether these desires can be excised simply through the inculcation of moderation. Those who harbor such desires are described as asocial individuals, who will "commit injustice" to satisfy their desires. Aristotle goes on to link the commission of these greatest injustices with tyranny. No one, he trenchantly observes, "becomes a tyrant in order to get in out of the cold" (1267a15).

Individuals who commit great injustice are unsatisfied with the common judgment (ὁμογνωμοσύνη) of the political order concerning what is advantageous and just. They are willing to make the choice (προαίρεσις) to subvert the political order to achieve their own ends, and Aristotle suggests they are unlikely to be dissuaded from acting (πράττω) unjustly simply as a result of having been educated with a view to moderation. Thus, neither superficial equalization schemes nor education with a view to moderation can satisfy individuals who harbor tyrannical desires. Instead, Aristotle indicates such individuals should find a remedy for their desires "in connection with philosophy" (1267a13). Echoing his description of philosophy in the last book of the *Ethics*, Aristotle suggests that the practice of philosophy is the most self-sufficient and sublime of pleasures available to man and therefore is a suitable pursuit for those with asocial desires.

Phaleas's equalization scheme is incapable of eliminating all but the most minor of injustices and sources of conflict. While equalization may have some success in resolving disputes concerning the distribution of "necessary goods," it fails to settle the more contentious disputes concerning the distribution of honor, and it also fails to prevent those with "tyrannical desires" from destroying the community. Aristotle suggests that to resolve disputes concerning the distribution of honors requires the inculcation of moderation and that those with "tyrannical desires" should seek to satiate their desire through the practice of philosophy. However, Aristotle does not offer a remedy for individuals with tyrannical desires who have neither the aptitude nor the capacity for philosophic study, which raises the question: is there any place in the city for such individuals? Nonetheless, he is clear in his critique: Phaleas's equalization scheme is ineffective, as it fails to address the source of factional disputes in the city and fails to provide a remedy for these disputes.

Aristotle presents his following critique of the law's ability to act as a source of civic unity in the immediately succeeding chapter, in which he analyzes the various legislative proposals put forward by Hippodamus. While at least two of these seem to concern somewhat trifling matters, a charitable interpretation compels us to conclude that Aristotle focuses on these pieces of legislation on account of the greater principle underlying them. As we shall see, Aristotle's discussion of each of the legislative reforms proposed by Hippodamus highlights the law's general character and reveals the political limitations of using such a crude and general instrument to achieve civic unity.

Aristotle first criticizes Hippodamus's proposed method for judging cases in the appeals court. The standard practice was to judge each case by way of a simple ballot, which provided the jurors with a choice of either upholding the lower court's ruling in its entirety and condemning the accused or overturning the lower court's ruling and acquitting the accused in full. According to Hippodamus, this standard practice was flawed as it provided no way for the jurors to make distinctions when deciding the fate of the accused. The inflexibility of the current administration of justice granted jurors no method to exercise their prudence and, as a result, "compel[led] men to perjure themselves" (1268a5–7). In brief, Hippodamus's complaint was that the current practice relied solely on the general provisions of the law and did not enable the individual jurors to bring their own judgment to bear on the particulars of the case. His proposed change was to reintroduce a level of prudence—or care for the particular—into the judicial system by giving jurors tablets upon which they could write their own personal judgment as to the appropriate verdict, including any distinctions they wished to submit, thereby avoiding the rough generality of the law, which compelled men to perjure themselves.

Aristotle objects that Hippodamus's proposed solution to the generality of law is inadequate. Allowing jurors to write their own personal judgments as to the appropriate verdict, he anticipates, will result in "confused" judgments. Jurors will inevitably differ in their judgments. For example, in a dispute over money, in which the plaintiff "claims twenty minas," one juror may judge "ten minas," "another judges five, another four—it is clear they will split in this way" (1268b12–15). There is no way, Aristotle asserts, that such a method will result in a common judgment.[7] Hippodamus's attempt to offset the rough generality of law by incorporating a level of prudence into the practice of judging is doomed to failure due to the multiplicity of jurors and their differing judgments. Prudence, it seems, is in the eye of the beholder. Aristotle's discussion of Hippodamus's proposal again provides an example of the difficulty in trying to attain unity in the city. On the one hand, enabling jurors to vote in accordance with their own private judgment leads to disagreement as to the correct judgment. On the other hand, using the law to force a level of general agreement amongst the jurors as to the guilt or innocence of the accused may come at the expense of justice and may even force the jurors to perjure themselves.

The second of Hippodamus's proposals also reveals Aristotle's concern with the law's generality. Hippodamus, we are told, thought it beneficial for the city publicly to honor those who "discover something useful to the city" (1268a7–8). In contrast to Phaleas, Hippodamus recognized that honor is very much a driving motivation for some individuals, and he sought to channel this honor in a manner beneficial to the city.[8] Aristotle briefly critiques this proposal, arguing that it may have the profound consequence of leading to a change in the type of regime if someone were to "propose the dissolution of the laws or the regime as something in the common good" (1268b30–32). The brevity of Aristotle's critique again suggests that Hippodamus's specific legislative proposals are not Aristotle's primary concern. Indeed, Aristotle pivots, using the proposal as a launching pad to raise the question as to "whether it is harmful or advantageous for cities to change traditional laws, if some other one should be better" (1268b27–29). Aristotle's principal advice is to remain cautious in changing the law, due to the fact that the law obtains its power from habituation and established usage. Because people obey the law out of a sense of habit that is developed over a period of time, "the easy alteration of existing laws in favor of new and different ones weakens the power of law itself" and ought to be avoided (1269a20–22). As a result, Aristotle's overall suggestion is to avoid unnecessary change in the laws due to the instability it engenders.

Nevertheless, immediately prior to his conclusion that one should avoid needlessly altering the law, Aristotle emphasizes that progress in the law is attainable. As evidence, he points to the "simple and barbaric" nature of the laws that existed in ancient times. Aristotle even goes so far as to ridicule the "ancient ordinances [that] still remain" as being "altogether silly" (1268b39–1269a1). He follows this up with the observation that sometimes laws may need to change, "for . . . it is impossible for everything to be written down precisely; for it is necessary to write them in universal fashion, while actions concern particulars" (1269a9–12). Thus, as part of his inquiry into the question of whether change in the law is good, Aristotle again makes clear that the chief difficulty with the law is its generality. The imprecision and universality that is characteristic of law may, in certain circumstances, undermine the law's purpose or intention when applied.[9] On its own, law is incapable of ensuring that citizens act morally because, as Carnes Lord notes, "moral action, and in particular prudent action, is concerned with particulars, [while] law is necessarily general."[10] Of course, this has implications for the city's unity. If law is overly general and incapable of adequately setting standards to govern moral action, then what is to prevent the city from disintegrating due to the multiplicity of judgments concerning what is right, just, and good? The law's limitations suggest that slavish obedience to the law is not the citizens' highest end.

Overall, Aristotle's account of his predecessors' approaches to political science makes clear that none of them have discerned how to deal with the problem of "the one and the many" as it relates to the city. How can political science bring into being a city comprised of disparate parts that is nevertheless sufficiently unified to make common judgments concerning what is just, beautiful, or good? While the Socrates of *The Republic* believed that the best way to ensure unity in the city was to arrange for the citizens to have *all* things—including families and property—in common, Aristotle argues that this proposal will *destroy* the unity of the city. As we have seen, he maintains that by substituting the bonds of *eros* for the bonds of friendly affection, Socrates ends up destroying the very unity he seeks to create.

The impersonal force of law, however, is equally incapable of fostering the unity necessary for the regime. Phaleas's proposal, which seeks to remove the cause of factional disputes by instituting a leveling program, is insufficient, as it fails to uncover and remove the root causes of the more serious factional disputes. While Phaleas's proposal might have some success in curing people's desire for material goods, it is incapable of responding to people's desire for honor and pleasure. Phaleas, we might say, failed to recognize that people's desires are manifold, and as a result, his overly general, crude leveling proposal was inadequate to deal with these manifold desires.

Hippodamus's political science presents an advance over that of Phaleas due to its recognition of the law's generality and the diversity of men's desires. However, Hippodamus's proposed legislation injects a level of disunion and instability into the regime. His first proposal, as we have seen, attempts to offset the law's generality by permitting the citizens to exercise a level of personal judgment in deciding court cases. However, as Aristotle makes clear, this introduces an element of disunity in the regime, as the citizens' judgments will differ from one another. Hippodamus's second proposal, which encourages useful innovations by publicly honoring those who develop such innovations, has the potential to create such a level of uncertainty and disunity in the regime that it could, in fact, lead to regime *change*. Through his criticism of Hippodamus's proposals, Aristotle argues that the generality of the law is a problem, but that simply granting each citizen free rein to do what is useful or good in his own eyes will put the continued existence of the regime in peril. Thus, none of his predecessors have yet solved the difficulty of maintaining unity in a regime comprised of diverse components.

Education in the Best Regime

The preceding analysis of Aristotle's critique of legislation, along with his recognition of the need for unity in the city, raises a number of questions. First, his focus on the limited capacity of legislation to attain unity in the city seems to stand in stark contrast with his insistence on the necessity of law in the final chapter of the *Ethics*. If the *Politics* is intended to be the counterpart to the *Ethics*, how are we to make sense of the opposing attitudes that Aristotle adopts towards the importance and capacity of law? Furthermore, how can the city attain the unity necessary for common action? If neither Socrates's proposals put forward in *The Republic* nor the coercive force of legislation is able to keep factional disputes at bay, what will ensure that the disparate private interests in the city do not undermine the common good? It seems that some binding power is needed that will enable the members of the city voluntarily to identify with a common good, while at the same time preserving the individuality of the various components of the city.[11]

Aristotle's critique of Socrates's proposal, according to which property and family would be held in common among the members of the city, was grounded in the charge that Socrates mistakes erotic love for friendship. Socrates, he avers, is mistaken in seeking to base all relationships in the city on erotic love. Aristotle's critique seems to suggest that what is needed is to foster friendship—a phenomenon distinct from erotic love. But what sort of friendship ought to be established in the city, and how might the legislator foster such friendship? Aristotle's discussion concerning the limits of law seems to reject the idea that the friendship necessary for the city's unity is founded simply on legal justice. This type of justice, which is marked by equality and reciprocity (*NE*, 1131a10–1134a17), is similar to Aristotle's friendship of utility, according to which the partners love one another "only insofar as they come to have something good from the other" (1156a22–12). As applied to the city, such a friendship would ensure that each citizen contributes in a unique way to the satisfaction of his compatriots' necessities. Aristotle implies that while the utilitarian friendship based on legal justice may be necessary, there needs to be something in addition that binds the city together. He seems to envision a friendship centered on devotion to the common good, or a friendship of the good.

We have seen, of course, that friendship of the good is the *sunaisthetic* friendship shared between the statesman and the philosopher. In book IX of the *Ethics*, Aristotle had described this type of friendship as coming into existence by "living together and sharing in a community of speeches and thought" (1170b12–13). While we have noted the precise way in which this *sunaisthetic* friendship comes to be developed between two magnanimous individuals, Aristotle does not, in the *Ethics*, explain how such a friendship would be fostered in the city. In fact, he does not explain how this occurs until his discussion of the best regime in books VII and VIII of the *Politics*. Here, in his discussion of the best regime, Aristotle makes clear that it is education, and specifically education in music, that can foster the unity and friendship necessary to maintain the city.[12] Music, as we shall see, does not suffer from any of the limitations that prevented legislation from serving as a unifying force in the city. Not only does Aristotle believe that a good education in music makes up for the deficiencies of law, but he shows that it also allows the citizens of the polis to engage in the dianoetic virtue of prudence and to participate in the *sunaisthetic* friendship enjoyed by the philosopher and the statesman.

Once we recognize that Aristotle views music as capable of fostering the friendship of the good that is necessary to maintain the integrity of the city, it becomes possible to reconcile Aristotle's criticisms of law in the *Politics* with the last chapter of the *Ethics*. As we have seen, in the last chapter of the *Ethics*, Aristotle notes that it is "difficult for someone not reared under laws of the requisite sort" to obtain "a correct upbringing with a view toward virtue" (1179b33–34). The implication seems to be that the coercive power of law is needed to habituate children to act in a moral manner. However, the *Politics* does not investigate law in detail; instead, it uncovers the *limitations* of law. As we will see, this apparent contradiction is resolved once we recognize that the Greek word for law or custom—νόμος—is also the word for "melody" or "strain of music."[13] This linguistic detail enables us to read the last chapter of the *Ethics* as suggesting that people need to be reared not only "under *law* of the requisite sort," but also "under *music* of the requisite sort."

This interpretation is bolstered by the fact that in the classical world, analogies between music and politics were commonly developed on the basis of the multiple meanings of the term νόμος. Thomas Mathiesen notes that the various meanings of the term "enables Plato to develop several musico-political analogies in the *Respublica* and the *Leges*, the most famous of which is his statement at *Leges* 799e: 'our songs are our laws.'"[14] Aristotle posits that the varied meanings of the term νόμος arose among preliterate people who "sang their laws" for mnemonic purposes.[15] Thus, Aristotle may himself be playing on the double meaning of the term νόμος to suggest that both law *and* music are important and necessary means by which the city can attain the unity required to keep the polis together. Aristotle may intend νόμος to mean both "law" and "music" in the concluding chapter of the *Ethics*.[16] In light of his extensive discussion of musical education in the last two books of the *Politics*, as well as his discussion concerning the limits of law in book II of the *Politics*, it is likely that Aristotle believes that while law is a necessary component of the city, it is, on its own, insufficient to foster the unity necessary to sustain the city.

The educational system Aristotle develops in the *Politics* is a bifurcated one: it is designed to ensure that the citizens are equipped to acquire the useful goods, or those things that are necessary to their survival; but it is also directed in its overall orientation towards the pursuit and enjoyment of leisure. This division mirrors Aristotle's outlook on life as a whole, where he distinguishes the useful from the noble (*Politics*, 1333a33). The useful, he indicates, ought always to be directed toward, and exist for the sake of, the noble, for in all things "the worse is always for the sake of the better" (1333a22). Just as he does in his *Ethics*, Aristotle criticizes the Spartans for failing to recognize this fact and for orienting the entirety of their educational system toward military training. Doing so, he argues, ensures that the Spartans secure the useful or necessary goods, but they do not pay any attention to educating their citizens with a view to what is leisurely or noble. While the useful art of training for war is necessary to ensure the city is not attacked, defeated, and reduced to slavery, this aspect ought not to constitute the full extent of the city's education. In fact, he states, cities that employ a "crude," utilitarian educational system oriented only toward aggrandizement will eventually decay. Once such a city attains the empire its citizens desire, it comes to ruin, because the legislator failed to educate the citizens in such manner that enables them to be at leisure (1334a10). Education, Aristotle argues, ought to be directed toward leisure, such that individuals can enjoy their leisure in the proper manner and to the extent to which they are able.

In book VIII, the final book of the *Politics*, Aristotle takes up the educational system in detail by investigating the four traditional branches of education: letters, gymnastic, music, and drawing. Music is immediately identified as an anomaly and comes to dominate Aristotle's proposed educational system. While the purpose of teaching children letters, gymnastic, and drawing is relatively straightforward—all have various useful purposes—the purpose of including music in education is not immediately clear (1337b27). Before turning to a discussion of the role that Aristotle posits for music in his educational system, it is necessary to emphasize that he includes poetry in the term *music*. Carnes Lord makes the case that when Aristotle employs the term μουσική, he means it in a "broad and inclusive" sense, so as to incorporate "song and poetry."[17] Thus, in Aristotle's inquiry into the purpose of music, he means to uncover the purpose of not simply melodies or rhythms but also entire theatrical performances.

Aristotle begins his inquiry with a brief preview of some of the difficulties or questions concerning the role of musical education before turning to a discussion of the manner and purpose of education in gymnastic. Why, he asks, ought music to be included in education? While at present most people enjoy music for the sake of pleasure, he states that the original reason people taught music was for the sake of "being at leisure in noble fashion" (1337b32). Thus, the purpose of music is presented as a sort of debate between the view of his contemporaries, which sees music and poetry simply as a means of pleasure, and the older, customary view, which held music to serve leisure. At this point of his inquiry, Aristotle allies himself unambiguously with this older school of thought, noting again that leisure, in contradistinction to occupation, constitutes man's natural purpose or *telos*.[18]

Because leisure constitutes man's natural purpose, Aristotle argues that it is necessary to identify the activity that people ought to undertake in leisure. He initially disparages the idea that this might simply be the activity of "play," as it seems strange to consider play to be the end or purpose of life. As a result, he places play in the category of occupation rather than leisure. While this categorization appears somewhat odd, given the fact that he had earlier identified occupation as that which is concerned with the acquisition of useful and necessary things, Aristotle explains that play forms part of the ordinary cycle of existence. Because the acquisition of the necessary goods involves exertion and strain, the pleasures of play are introduced to allow for a certain level of respite. This respite has a rejuvenating effect, enabling one to resume the strenuous activity characteristic of occupation or labor. Thus, even play is, in a sense, oriented toward securing the necessities of life.[19] In contrast, leisure involves pleasure, happiness, and living blessedly. The purpose of those who originally included music and poetry in education, argues Aristotle, was to educate the citizens "with a view to the pastime that is in leisure" (1338a22). Thus, he ends his initial discussion of music by concluding that music was initially included in education for the purpose of "pastime," without yet identifying what this "pastime" consists of.

Before turning to the manner and extent of gymnastic education, Aristotle leaves us with two separate quotations from Homer's *Odyssey* in support of the contention that music educates with a view to pastime and that the whole of life ought to be ordered toward pastime. However, the quotes, provided one after the other, appear to be somewhat odd. Aristotle introduces them as follows: "Hence Homer wrote thus: 'but [a singer] alone it is needful to invite to the rich banquet,' and then goes on to say that there are certain persons 'who invite a singer, that he may bring delight to all.' And elsewhere Odysseus says that this is the best pastime, when human beings are enjoying good cheer and 'the banqueters seated in order throughout the hall listen to a singer'" (133825–30). Ostensibly, the quotations simply reassert the importance of music and leisure.

The context in which the quotations appear, however, are somewhat puzzling. The first quotation occurs in the context of Odysseus's return to Ithaca. Upon his arrival, disguised as a beggar, Odysseus finds the suitors, all of whom are attempting to woo his wife, engaged in the despicable conduct of gorging on a lavish banquet at his expense. The bard has just finished singing, and the suitors begin mocking the beggar, unaware of his true identity. Why would Aristotle choose this quotation, which conjures up the image of the shameful conduct of the suitors in support of his contention that pastime and leisure are the purpose of life? The second quotation is equally strange. Odysseus makes the comment to King Alcinous of the Phaeacians while he is a guest on their island. The bard, who had been singing of the exploits of Odysseus and his men during the siege of Troy, has been ordered to stop, as King Alcinous notices that Odysseus is weeping. In response, Odysseus reassures the king that the best pastime is, indeed, when all are gathered together to hear the bard sing of great exploits.

Why does Aristotle use these two quotations together? The reason is that he is seeking to remind his readers that while the proper enjoyment of leisure may be the purpose of life, this purpose can be properly enjoyed only after life's necessities have first been attended to. The second quotation reveals that Odysseus cannot properly enjoy the bard's music that extols his virtue while he is still far from home and work remains to be done. When leisure is placed before the necessary work, it will not be enjoyed properly. The first quotation underscores the requirement that leisure be treated as an activity that *supervenes* on the necessary work that merits such leisure. The enjoyment the suitors derive from the bard during their feast is perverse, as they have done nothing to merit the feasting and leisure of which they partake. The proper enjoyment of leisure can be had only once life's necessary deeds have been accomplished.[20] It is on this note that Aristotle turns to the gymnastic education of the best regime (i.e., the necessary work), which serves, in part, to inculcate the virtue of courage necessary for the regime's survival, before investigating in detail the role that music plays in allowing people to enjoy their leisure properly.

The Purpose of Music

After having discussed gymnastic education, Aristotle returns to examine at length the role music ought to play in the educational system of the best regime in the fifth chapter of book VIII. He raises three potential purposes of musical education. Perhaps, he notes, music ought to be studied with a view toward play and rest. In the same way that sleeping and drinking are not excellent but are nevertheless pleasant, so music is pleasant and should be included in education simply because of its capacity to ease life's hardships (1339a15–20). Of course, Aristotle had earlier rejected play as the purpose of life, so the reintroduction of play as a possible purpose for the inclusion of music is somewhat curious. Alternatively, Aristotle suggests, music might contribute to the formation of an individual's moral character. In this scenario, moral virtue takes pride of place, and music is posited as being a useful aid in habituating an individual to enjoy the correct things, in a "correct fashion" (1339a22–25). Lastly, Aristotle states briefly and without further explanation that perhaps music "contributes in some way to pastime (διαγωγή) and prudence" (1339a25). As we shall see, Aristotle eventually comes to the conclusion that music is suitable for all three purposes, while the *ultimate* reason for including music in the educational regime is that it contributes to pastime and prudence. Furthermore, Aristotle is convinced that these purposes make up for the deficiencies in seeking civic unity through the coercive force of law.

In investigating the purpose of music in education, Aristotle seems initially to be dismissive of both play and pastime as purposes of education. Play cannot be the purpose for which musical education is included, as children "do not play when they are learning, as learning is accompanied by pain" (1339a27–28; cf. *NE*, 1173b16–19). Similarly, pastime cannot be the purpose of education, for it is not "fitting to assign pastime to children or those of such ages; for the end is not suited to anything incomplete" (*Politics*, 1339a29–30). Nevertheless, Aristotle holds out the possibility that perhaps children undergo the strenuousness and pain of musical education "for the sake of their play once they have become men and complete" (1339a30–32). This possibility suggests that children learn music not for its own sake, but rather so that they might enjoy music later in life.

Rather than investigate this possibility, Aristotle instead turns to a related question: If it is, in fact, the case that children learn music for the purpose of enjoying it once "they become men and complete," why should children learn to make music themselves? Why can they not simply "have a share in the learning and the pleasures through others performing it, like the kings of the Persians and the Medes?" (1339a34–35). After all, "Zeus himself does not sing and play the lyre" (1339b7–8). If play is the end of life, would it not be best simply to enjoy listening to music and leave to others the difficulty and strain of learning to make music? While Aristotle does not immediately provide an answer, the examples he provides point toward an answer. The kings of the Persians and the Medes were well-known to be tyrannical (cf. *Politics*, 1313a36–37; *NE*, 1160b24–30),[21] and an emulation of their lifestyle is nothing to be pursued. In contrast, while an emulation of Zeus is not similarly problematic, the pleasures enjoyed by the gods are simply beyond the ken of any human being (1154b20–30). Thus, Aristotle suggests, without explicitly stating as much, that humans require a certain level of effort before arriving at the enjoyment of pleasure. Only the gods have the option of simply enjoying life without first putting in the effort and accomplishing the necessary deeds.

While Aristotle leaves to the side precisely *why* the enjoyment of music may be regarded as the end of life, he begins to conflate play and pastime, highlighting the extent to which both involve pleasure. The similarity between the pleasures of play and pastime is underscored a short while later. Play, he indicates, is "for the sake of rest, and rest must necessarily be pleasant . . . and pastime, it is agreed, should involve not only the element of nobility but also pleasure, for being happy derives from both of these" (*Politics*, 1339b15). He continues, noting that because music "belongs among the most pleasant things," this may, on its own, be a reason to include it in education (1339b20–25). Aristotle goes on to grant what Robert Bartlett has called a "remarkably . . . accommodating tone" toward pleasure:[22] "For those pleasures that are harmless are fitting not only with a view to the end but also with a view to rest; and since it happens that human beings rarely attain the end, but frequently rest and make use of play not only for some purpose beyond but also on account of the pleasure, it would be useful thing to have them rest on occasion in the midst of the pleasures that derive from this" (1339b25–32). As Bartlett makes clear, Aristotle, at this point, looks at the function of music not in light of *the end* of education, but simply from the perspective that "human beings rarely attain the end." The end is not attainable for many—perhaps most—human beings, and the pleasure and enjoyment one derives from music can provide relief from life's constant strivings.[23]

Aristotle is quick to add, however, that the *end* for which music is included in education does not involve this type of pleasure: "The end too perhaps involves a certain pleasure—though not any chance pleasure" (1339b34). Because both play and the end or purpose for which music is pursued (an end which has yet to be unambiguously defined) involve pleasure, Aristotle notes that it sometimes happens that people mistake play as the purpose for which music is pursued (1339b34–39). While the pleasures of play are not the *ultimate* reason or purpose for which music is included in the educational regime, they nevertheless constitute a secondary purpose for including music in education.[24]

Aristotle next seeks to determine whether the purpose of music might not have a "more honorable" purpose, which "in some way . . . contributes to the character and the soul" (1340a2–7). He begins by positing strongly that music has the effect of forming our characters. The way in which this happens, he argues, is by listening to rhythms and tunes whose likenesses are "particularly close" to those of "respectable characters and noble actions" (1340a18–20). In the same way that habituation forms moral virtue by training people to take enjoyment in correct or noble actions, so learning to appreciate and enjoy the musical representations of noble actions can positively inform one's character. Commenting on the different types of harmonies that existed in Ancient Greece at the time, Aristotle notes that while some harmonies, such as the mixed Lydian harmony, cause people to be in a state of "grief and apprehension," others, in particular the Dorian harmony, cause people to be in "a middling and settled state" (1340a43–1340b6). In this way, music has the ability to shape one's desires and "render the character of the soul of a certain quality" (1340b12). As a result, Aristotle later concludes that the Dorian tunes are particularly appropriate in educating the young (cf. 1342b13–17).

Reading Aristotle's remarks on the formative power of music in light of his earlier discussion concerning the limits of law reveals the way in which he believes music is able to foster the unity the city requires. Recall that Aristotle had criticized Phaleas's legislative proposal of redistributing property, arguing that this proposal would not achieve political unity. According to Aristotle, the root cause of factional discord in the city is not the unequal distribution of property, but unchecked desire. While Phaleas's proposal might have some limited success in resolving minor disputes concerning the necessary goods, it is incapable of resolving the more serious disputes concerning the distribution of honor. The only thing that can resolve such disputes is inculcating a sense of moderation among the citizenry, such that their desires are consonant with the form of the regime. By making clear that music can have a profound impact on an individual's desires, Aristotle shows that it can do much to prevent any one group from taking action that is contrary to the common good.

Aristotle's proposed solution does not, however, seem problem free. First, it is not clear that music will be capable of completely curbing *all* people's desires. Despite Aristotle's encomium on the power of music, music remains simply a *representation* of respectable characters and noble actions; no one would conflate the act of Napoleon's march across Europe with the simple act of listening to Beethoven's *Sinfonia Eroica*. In fact, as Aristotle continues to elaborate on the way in which a person's character might be formed through listening to music, he begins slowly to reveal that his initially high estimation of music's capacity to form people's characters was somewhat hyperbolic: the "habituation to feel pain and enjoyment in *similar* things is *close* to being in the same condition relative to the truth," but it *is* not the truth (1340a23–24; emphasis added). While music and poetry do have a mimetic function vis-à-vis the moral virtues and can inculcate certain dispositions or passions in the souls of those who listen to it, they cannot form an individual's moral character in the same way as habitual action can. Music may be incapable of adjusting passionate individuals by inculcating the moderation needed to become productive members of the regime.

That music may not be able to moderate such individuals is a potentially serious problem. Recall that in his criticism of Phaleas's redistribution proposal, Aristotle had briefly discussed the danger that such passionate individuals pose to the regime. These individuals, he had noted, may commit the "greatest injustices" in order to satiate their tyrannical desires. He further indicated that these individuals are impervious to the social virtue of moderation. Finally, he suggested that they ought to seek a remedy for their desires in the study of philosophy. We noted, however, that Aristotle's proposed remedy would be ineffective for individuals who have neither the capacity nor the inclination for philosophic study. It seems, therefore, that these individuals will pose a danger to the political community.

While Aristotle is not convinced that music will serve to *moderate* these excessively passionate individuals, he does hold out hope that music will be *cathartic* for them.[25] Aristotle first hints at the cathartic role music might play as he discusses why the flute is not to be used in education. The use of the flute, he explains, not only prevents one from speech, but it can even provoke an irrational "frenzy" in the soul (1341a16–23). At bottom, the flute seems to be an instrument that is more bound up with passionate spiritedness than it is with reason. Nevertheless, Aristotle does not believe it is necessary to omit the use of the flute altogether. Instead, he suggests that it may be "used with a view to those occasions when looking on [θεωρία] has the power of purification [κάθαρσις] rather than learning" (1341a24–25). At this point, Aristotle does not yet elaborate on the manner in which this catharsis will occur, but we are led to the provisional conclusion that the flute is able to purify, or excise, excessive passions.

This reading receives additional support when we turn to the final chapter of the *Politics*, in which Aristotle notes that certain harmonies—specifically the Phrygian harmonies—also are not to be used for the purpose of education, but instead for purification. While those harmonies "most relating to character" can and should be learned for educational purposes, other harmonies—specifically those relating to action and inspiration—should simply be enjoyed by listening to others perform them (1342b1–5). While Aristotle does not here deny the educative value of such tunes, he does note their connection with spiritedness or passion, and he remarks specifically on the ability of such tunes to calm people's passions. He writes:

> For the passion that occurs strongly in connection with certain sorts of souls is present in all, but differs by greater and less—for example, pity and fear, and further, inspiration. For there are certain persons who are possessed by this motion, but as a result of the sacred tunes—when they use the tunes that put the soul in a frenzy—we see them calming down as if obtaining a cure and purification. This same thing, then, must necessarily be experienced also . . . by the generally passionate. (1342a5–10)

Of course, as Lord notes, Aristotle is not opposed to the passions per se.[26] For example, the passion of spiritedness, as Aristotle's discussion of the virtue of courage makes clear, is necessary to maintaining and preserving social life (cf. *NE*, 1116b24–33). Nevertheless, excessive passion can lead individuals to commit the "greatest injustices." Indeed, our earlier analysis of magnanimity in the *Posterior Analytics* has shown that politically magnanimous individuals such as Ajax, Achilles, and Alcibiades are spirited individuals who pose a danger to the political community. The Phrygian harmonies, as well as the flute, are therefore endorsed by Aristotle as means to purge the *excessive* passions from which such individuals suffer.[27] Music, it seems, can potentially integrate these spirited individuals into the political community.

Nevertheless, neither the simple enjoyment of pleasure, nor the inculcation of moral character, nor the purgation of excessive passion constitutes the ultimate purpose of musical education. This becomes evident in chapter six of book VIII, in which Aristotle broaches the question he had raised earlier concerning whether children should learn music by "singing and playing instruments" themselves, or whether it is enough to simply enjoy listening to others make music (*Politics*, 1340b20–23). As we shall see, Aristotle will argue that it is important for children to learn to make music *themselves*. That children need to learn this skill themselves indicates that the true purpose or final end of musical education is neither simply the pleasures of play that music affords, nor the formation of character, nor the purgation of excessive passion. None of these ends requires that children learn to play music themselves. Indeed, one does not need to *learn* music in order to enjoy the pleasures associated with *listening* to it. Similarly, Aristotle had stated that it is simply by *listening* to certain rhythms and tunes that people come to experience the passions associated with moral virtue. Last, the purgation of excessive passion also occurs simply through *listening* to Phrygian tunes, not through *learning* them. All of this suggests that the purpose of including music in education lies elsewhere.

The final end or purpose of teaching children music as a skill that they ought to actively learn is revealed in chapter six of the final book of the *Politics*.[28] We have seen that Aristotle initially provided three potential purposes of musical education: (1) play and rest, (2) character formation, and (3) pastime and prudence. While musical education provides respite from the strains of life, and while it can also contribute to the formation of character by forming and even purging one's passions, it has not yet become clear how musical education contributes to pastime and prudence. Aristotle subtly provides the answer in the context of explaining why children should learn to make music themselves.

Aristotle relates in a somewhat brief manner that "it does indeed make a great difference with a view to becoming a certain quality if one shares in the performance oneself" because it "is an impossible or a difficult thing for [individuals] to become excellent judges without sharing in this way" (1340b23–26). The purpose of learning to make music oneself is to become an "excellent judge." Expanding on this, Aristotle notes that children "should engage in performing when they are young, and when they become older leave off it, and be able to judge the noble things and to enjoy in correct fashion through the learning that occurred in their youth" (1340b37–39). Thus, the end of musical education is to be able to judge and enjoy the noble things *correctly*. Aristotle's explanation as to the ultimate purpose of including music in education might initially appear somewhat underwhelming. The purpose seems akin to simply enjoying music for the purpose of play and respite from care.[29] However, as we shall see, Aristotle's explanation is intimately tied up with the capacity of the regime to engage in the practice of self-government.

By inculcating the capacity to engage in "correct judging," Aristotle's educational system aims at cultivating the intellectual virtue of φρόνησις. Aristotle had described this virtue in book VI of the *Ethics* as a dianoetic virtue that is particularly characteristic of the statesman—although it was not reserved exclusively to the statesman. Aristotle had explained that this dianoetic virtue involves an element of "pure onlooking" or perception (αἴσθησις), by which one judges the "ultimate particular thing" in a given situation. This moment of "pure onlooking" or intuitive grasping of the situation at hand, grants one the ability to discern the correct moment at which he ought to intervene in any given situation.[30]

By presenting the enjoyment of music and poetry as "noble judging," Aristotle makes clear that the educational regime prescribed by the founders of the polis will have an effect on ordinary citizens, such that they will *also* be able to engage in the practice of the dianoetic virtues and will develop the capacity of correct judgment.[31] Of course, we may still wonder what it is about music and poetry that develops this capacity for noble judging. Carnes Lord explains that music and poetry contain a universal philosophic insight that is embodied in, or made clear by means of, a particular action or story. Commenting on Aristotle's statement in chapter 9 of the *Poetics* that poetry is more philosophic than history, due to its emphasis on universals rather than particulars, Carnes Lord relates: "Poetry does not narrate the universals simply: it presents the universals by way of the particulars or as they manifest themselves in particulars. It differs from history by the fact that it is able to present the universals shorn of the unique and contingent particulars which make any historical event inimitable. The universals presented in poetry are universals of 'action' (*praxis*), of human moral, and political action in the broadest sense."[32] For Aristotle, music—and in particular theatrical performances—educates with a view to φρόνησις by combining the universality of philosophy with the particularity required for moral action.

Thus, Aristotle sees the education of citizens with a view to self-rule and moral agency as the primary reason for including music in the educational system. In an excellent exposition of Aristotle's belief in the educational function of Athenian theatrical events, John von Heyking points out the way in which, for Aristotle, the purpose of poetry—in particular tragic poetry, which follows the actions of some noble, virtuous individual who nevertheless suffers on account of some tragic flaw (ἁμαρτία)—is to remind citizens of their own moral failings, and hence their need for other people:

> The characteristic virtue that tragedy teaches . . . is a citizen's *phronesis*: one that is self-critical and communally critical, and one that teaches citizens to bear responsibility together for their choices even when they are mistaken and imperfect. The former is achieved by citizens' reflections on their own tragic flaw (*hamartia*), which they first see in the protagonist; the latter is achieved by reflecting on the way in which that tragic flaw unfolds in the plot (*muthos*). By vicariously becoming part of the plot, citizen-spectators learn the arts of self-rule and moral agency.[33]

Through coming together and witnessing together (*sunaisthesis*) the fate of this tragic hero, whose characteristic virtue (or tragic flaw) proves his undoing, the citizens are reminded of the danger of asocial hubris and the importance of self-knowledge. Through the educative power of music and poetry the citizens come to recognize the way in which the social community can act as a cure for their own flaws in a way that counters the latent causes of faction in every city.

Aristotle's musical education also makes up for the crude generality of the law without sacrificing the city's unity. Recall that in his discussion of Hippodamus's legislative proposals, Aristotle had indicated that while Hippodamus correctly identified the difficulties associated with the law's generality, his proposed solutions encouraged a level of individual judgment that would pose dangers to the regime's unity and stability. Hippodamus sought to inject a level of individual judgment into the regime that would offset the law's crude generality. Nevertheless, he failed to ensure that these individual judgments would not be contradictory to or destructive of the form of the regime. Individual judgment was not guided by a common standard. Aristotle's solution is to follow Hippodamus in allowing for a level of individual judgment, and even self-government, but in order to ensure that the citizens' judgments will be similar to and consonant with the form and purpose of the regime, he institutes a common educational system.

We may yet wonder, however, how Aristotle's musical education relates to *sunaisthetic* friendship. *Sunaisthetic* friendship between the philosopher and the statesman involves a reciprocal process of actualization that enables both the philosopher and the statesman to develop a level of self-awareness. We have seen that the philosopher's potential is actualized by witnessing the noble acts of his friend—acts of which he is the proximate cause—and that the statesman's potential is actualized by perceiving the regime that he has founded with the help of the philosopher. Both the philosopher and the statesman become aware of their own magnanimity through their friendship with the other. How do the citizens partake of this seemingly exclusive *sunaisthetic* friendship?

The answer lies in the shared process of political actualization that the city's musical education enables. On the one hand, once the citizens of the regime have been educated according to the city's νόμος, the philosopher and the statesman are both able to derive some enjoyment from watching their citizens flourish. On the other hand, by having become educated in the music and poetry of the regime, the citizens' potential has also been actualized. They have been formed with a view to self-government. They are not simply inanimate matter that has been given shape, but they have become capable of involving themselves in the administration of the regime by taking ownership and moral responsibility for its direction. In essence, by learning the city's music (νόμος), the people of the city have become citizens capable of partaking in decision and office, and of ruling and being ruled in turn (*Politics*, 1275a23; 1277b14–16). Through the educational system, the citizens have come to "share . . . in a community of speeches and thought" (*NE*, 1170b12–13). The citizens do not "merely feed . . . in the same place" (1170b13–14) as they might in some purely procedural republics but have instead become a unified entity organized for action in history with a shared perception (συναίσθησις) of the good.

Conclusion

Friendship in the American Constitutional Republic

Friendship at the American Founding

Reading the *Lysis* and the *Gorgias* in conjunction with books VIII and IX of Aristotle's *Ethics* reveals a significant and sustained difference in understanding between Socrates and Aristotle of the nature of friendship and, by consequence, of the value and dignity of politics. It has become clear that Socrates views friendship as having a basis in metaphysical lack or need. In contrast, Aristotle holds out the possibility that a *sunaisthetic* friendship might be based on self-sufficiency, according to which each partner appreciates the virtue and goodness of his partner. These divergent conceptions of friendship may, respectively, undermine or affirm the dignity of political life. Indeed, a wholly Socratic approach to friendship may potentially cause one to conclude that the polis is simply a utilitarian association into which individuals enter to compensate for their own individual deficiencies—the sole grounding of political life is found in man's necessitous condition. In turn, an Aristotelian conception of friendship enables us to see the polis as something that is the product or effusion of man's inherent excellence and a place in which citizens can participate in a friendship of *sunaisthesis*. The alliance between wisdom and power effectuated by the means of friendship ensures that the city is oriented toward the good.

The divergent orientations toward political life in classical political thought raises for us the question as to what understanding of friendship forms the foundation of our own polity. Is the American Constitutional Republic founded on an Aristotelian account of friendship according to which philosophy guides and forms politics, ordering it toward the good? Or do we conceive of our republic as a utilitarian association that responds to our necessitous condition? If the American regime is simply a social grouping into which people contract as a means by which they might overcome their individual deficiencies, it would seem the Socratic conception of human nature and friendship is that which underpins our republic. By contrast, if the Constitutional Republic established at the time of the founding is based on a belief in the self-sufficiency and excellence inhering in the American people and the several states with which they identify, the Union would be the product not simply of necessity but could also be said to be recognized as good and beautiful in its own right.

Of course, there are dangers that attend both conceptions of friendship and politics. As the *Lysis* reveals, a Socratic conception of friendship and politics, which focuses on man's necessitous nature can potentially lead us to devalue the other's dignity and ignore what appears to us to be the inherent worth and goodness of our fellow citizens. Adopting such a perspective toward our friendships will necessarily have a destructive effect on our political communities. On the other hand, conceiving of friendship as based on individual self-sufficiency can lead to hubristic attitude and an identification of one's own with the good. Such an account of friendship is not given to self-criticism and, when applied to the realm of politics, can lead to parochial self-satisfaction. Paul Ludwig reminds us of the potential danger of Aristotelian friendship, asserting that it is linked to our capacity for self-assertion and even anger.[1] At its best, an Aristotelian account of politics is oriented *toward* the good, but it is always in danger of identifying its own practices and customs *with* the good in a manner that opens it up to the Socratic charge that such friendships and associations impede one's ability to advance toward the good.

At first glance, we might be inclined to believe that the American founding has more in common with the Socratic conception of friendship and politics. James Madison's famous phrase, "If men were angels, no government would be necessary," reveals with incisive clarity his understanding of man's fallen and necessitous nature.[2] Similarly, John Adams's assertion that the American Constitution was a government of laws, not of men was reflective of his distrust in man's ability to put aside his self-interest for the sake of the common good.[3] While we might be inclined to balance these rather dour accounts of human nature with Jefferson's optimistic belief that the "solid and independent yeomanry" of the country ought to be able to manufacture a new constitution every twenty years, even Jefferson was ultimately convinced of the impracticability of this approach to constitution-making.⁴ The Founding Fathers were under no illusion regarding man's flawed, and hence, necessitous nature. It would seem difficult, therefore, to assert that the *sunaisthetic* friendship based on human excellence characterizes the American founding.

In addition, it does not appear that the American founding evinces the same kind of alliance between philosophy and statesmanship that is operative in Aristotle's account of friendship. According to Aristotle, philosophy ought to have a guiding force on politics that ensures its orientation toward the good, and the manner he saw this union as being practically achieved is through friendship between philosopher and statesman. However, the Founding Fathers responsible for drafting the American system of government at the Constitutional Convention in the summer of 1787 were principally statesmen rather than philosophers. Are we left to conclude that the founding shares no affinity with the Aristotelian conception of friendship and politics?

While the American founders may not have conceived of themselves as philosophers, it is undeniable that they consciously sought to bring the philosophic ideas of the period to bear on politics in an Aristotelian manner. Thomas Jefferson's assertion that the Declaration of Independence received all its "authority" from the "harmonizing sentiments of the day," derived from "Aristotle, Cicero, Locke, Sidney, &c." is perhaps the most well-known example of the manner in which philosophic ideas were leveraged for political action.⁵ However, it was relatively commonplace to appeal to Enlightenment political ideals and the history of antiquity to make the case for one's political positions. For example, after the outbreak of the revolution, John Adams, who had four years earlier penned his *Thoughts on Government*, a massive three-volume study of Montesquieu's insights on the separation of powers in the English Constitution, saw fit to reissue his treatise after receiving multiple requests for copies.⁶ Similarly, Jerome Huyler notes that James Madison requested that Jefferson send "from France the encyclopedic knowledge accumulated on the Continent pertaining to the history of ancient and modern republics" and "with this in hand, . . . prepared for the historic role he would play in 1787."⁷

The Founding Fathers' attempt to use the authority of the philosophic ideas of the day for political action through public discussion also reveals an important aspect of their conception of human nature and friendship. However realistic an account of human nature they may have had, they were sufficiently convinced of their fellow-citizens' intelligence and good sense to entrust political decisions and constitutional design to public discussion and choice. Armed with the political philosophy of the day, as well as with a keen appreciation of the republics of antiquity, the founders sought to persuade one another of the sensibility of their proposals for constitutional design through friendly disputation. In *Federalist 38*, James Madison makes an oblique reference to the important role played by persuasion at the Constitutional Convention in discussing the representatives' unanimous assent to the designed Constitution.[8]

Opening the essay, Madison observes that while every account of the ancient governments established by "deliberation and consent" was undertaken by some "individual citizen, of pre-eminent wisdom and approved integrity," such as Solon of Athens, or Lycurgus of Sparta, the American system was designed by an "assembly of men."[9] The opening remarks of *Federalist 38* appear to highlight the divergence between the American founding moment and those of classical antiquity. However, James Madison deftly parlays this ostensible difference into a suggestion that the American founding is analogous (and perhaps superior) to those of antiquity.

The reason the foundings of antiquity were entrusted to a singular individual, suggests Madison, was a concern for the "discord and disunion" that might result from an assembly of men. For example, the Spartan founding established by Lycurgus, who obtained his understanding of the science of government from the philosopher Thales, would be incompatible with reforms derived from the Pythagorean science of government put forward by Solon of Athens. The establishment of government was seen to require unanimity of mind, which would be threatened by an assembly of men. However, Madison points out that despite proceeding by assembly, the American Founding Fathers were able to secure this unanimity—or *homonoia*—through compromise, cooperation, and above all persuasion. Despite differing interests and starting premises, the representatives at the Constitutional Convention were able to harmonize the prevailing sentiments into a coherent body of principles, thereby securing an alliance between philosophy and politics in a manner similar to that effectuated by the founders of antiquity.[10]

The public and politically oriented friendships among the American founders distinguishes them from the private type of friendship that provided completion for Montaigne and his friend La Boétie. While many of the friendships were founded on the insight and virtue that each party brought to the table, they were oriented toward political action and constitutional design. The correspondence between James Madison and Thomas Jefferson provides a particularly clear example of the way in which the Founding

Fathers' mutual respect and occasional disagreement led to unanimity over constitutional principles and design. In 1787, while Thomas Jefferson was on diplomatic mission to France, James Madison sent him a letter explaining the rationale behind the proposed Constitution. Although Jefferson was gravely concerned that the Constitution did not adequately respect the principle of majority rule, Gordon Wood notes that "Jefferson's growing appreciation of his friend Madison's great contribution to the creation of the Constitution helped him to come around and support the Constitution more enthusiastically than he had at the outset."[11] In turn, Jefferson's concerns induced Madison to revise some of his notes of the proceedings of the Constitutional Convention in a manner that rendered the proceedings more solicitous of democratic input. The friendship between Thomas Jefferson and James Madison is emblematic of the Aristotelian *sunaisthetic* friendship according to which each had a formative impact upon the other, which redounded to the common good of the republic.

The founders' twofold understanding of human nature recognizes that man is subject to necessity even while retaining a level of dignity, value, and excellence upon which it is possible to build a political regime oriented toward that which transcends the merely political. The document drafted at the Constitutional Convention reflects this account of human nature. In acknowledgment of the fact that man is not self-sufficient, driven at times by self-interest, and prone to selfish behavior, the founders established a system of rules and procedures to govern the conduct of politics. At the same time, out of respect for the people's capacity for self-government, they expressly reserved that which was not explicitly granted to the national government to the judgment of the people or state governments. While some procedural justice and attention to bureaucratic policies was recognized as necessary due to man's necessitous and fallen nature, the bulk of substantive policy and value judgments entailed in living together in political community were entrusted to the good sense of the people and the several states.

This approach to constitutional design is remarkably well-encapsulated by Abraham Lincoln's description of the American conception of government in a private note he wrote to himself prior to his inauguration in 1861. Reflecting on a verse from the book of Proverbs, which reads, "a word fitly spoken is like apples of gold in pictures of silver," Lincoln surmised that the Union and the Constitution act as the picture of silver, while the principles of American government operate as the apples of gold: "The picture was made, not to conceal, or destroy the apple; but to adorn, and preserve it. The picture was made for the apple—not the apple for the picture."[12] Paraphrasing Lincoln, we might say that the procedural guarantees and bureaucratic policies espoused in the Constitution operate as the silver frame that surrounds, and is meant to adorn and protect, the substantive value judgments and friendships that are reserved to the people of the several states. The procedural guarantees operate as a response to man's necessitous nature, while the substantive values that the procedural guarantees are meant to protect are entrusted to the friendships and conceptions of justice to which the people freely adhere.

Constitutional Friendship?

The friendship between John Adams and Thomas Jefferson reveals the promise as well as the limit to which the framework provided by the Constitution can protect and guarantee the friendships and substantive conceptions of justice that are the province of practical politics. John Adams and Thomas Jefferson, two of the nation's most revered founders, were close friends during America's Revolutionary period but, due in part to different experiences, values, and understandings of the Constitution, their friendship was cut short in the early period of the 1790s, and it took a decidedly hostile turn after the election of 1800. They were not reconciled until both had retired from political life and were nearing the end of their life by the interposition of their mutual friend, the physician and Founding Father Benjamin Rush.[13]

Adams and Jefferson became familiar with one another at the Second Continental Congress after the battle at Lexington and Concord in 1775. Gordon Wood relates that Adams was impressed by Jefferson's decisiveness and his radical views and, being eight years his senior, regarded him as his protégé, a role that Jefferson seemed to accept.[14] Of the delegates at the congress, the two of them were the most convinced of the necessity for independence, and together they sought to advance this agenda in the face of skepticism from some of the other, more cautious congressional delegates. While Adams did so more forcefully, playing open with his cards in a way that was in keeping with his direct manner, Jefferson was more circumspect.[15] Nevertheless, Jefferson appreciated Adams's forceful approach, later reflecting that Adams "was our Colossus on the floor" of the congress, able to deliver his remarks "with a power, both of thought and of expression which moved us from our seats."[16] Together, the two of them were instrumental in convincing the delegates to vote in favor of a resolution urging the colonies to adopt constitutional reforms. This resolution included in its preamble the momentous declaration that "every kind of authority under the . . . Crown should be totally suppressed" in favor of the "authority of the people of the colonies," a tacit endorsement of independence.[17]

Despite the effectiveness of their alliance and the warm affections they shared for one another, their friendship could not withstand the strong headwinds posed by the political issues of the day and their own headstrong characters. Having very different appraisals of the American public's capacity for independent self-government, and each having great confidence in his own judgment, their friendship eventually faltered. Returning to their respective states with the congressional resolution encouraging the reformation of the colonial governments in hand, both Adams and Jefferson sought to implement changes. Jefferson's optimistic view of human nature led him to adopt more radically liberal and egalitarian political stances that sought, in his words, to ensure that "every fibre would be eradicated of antient or future aristocracy; and a foundation laid for a government truly republican" in the State of Virginia.[18] In contrast, in Massachusetts, Adams's skepticism of egalitarian politics, as well as his belief in man's self-interested nature, led him to emphasize the need for a mixed and balanced Constitution that made room for a republicanized aristocracy capable of mediating between the governor and the people.[19] Adams and Jefferson had very different understandings of the shape that government ought to take, and it is likely to the nation's great fortune that the two of them were away on diplomatic mission—Adams to England and Jefferson to France—during the Constitutional Convention and ratification process.

While their distance from the American political scene kept their disagreements at bay during the crucial summer in which the Constitutional Convention took place, their return to the United States witnessed the subsequent cooling of their former friendship over political disagreements. In 1790–91, John Adams published (anonymously) a series of essays in the *Gazette of the United States* entitled "Discourses on Davila," in which he laid bare his opinions on human nature and the political ramifications of that view. He saw man's innate desire for "superiority and reputation" to be the source of the ongoing French Revolution and, indeed, of "all social upheavals."[20] Gordon Wood reports that in his final essay, Adams seemed to endorse hereditary government as the best antidote to the ambition and desire for superiority that was the source of so much human misery throughout history: "Nearly all the nations of the earth . . . had found 'so much emulation in every heart, so many rivalries among the principal men, such divisions, confusions and miseries' that they concluded that 'hereditary succession was attended with fewer evils than frequent elections.' "[21]

Adams's seeming endorsement of the principle of hereditary government was met with incredulity by Jefferson. While Jefferson's tacit demeanor kept him from seeking to make any public response to Adams's "Davila" essays, he inadvertently got caught up in the controversy in a very public manner to the great detriment of his friendship with Adams. Upon receiving a copy of Thomas Paine's *Rights of Man*, an "impassioned assault on monarchy and hereditary aristocracy," Jefferson forwarded it to a printer in Philadelphia for publication. He included with Paine's pamphlet "a covering note, expressing his pleasure that 'something is at length to be publicly said against the political heresies which have sprung up among us.' "[22] To Jefferson's dismay, this covering note was used by the publisher as a preface to the work, making his disagreements with Adams public. Wood notes that Adams took great offense to Jefferson's note, and he wrote to him, informing him that he considered it "a direct and open personal attack."[23] Adams seems to have evinced an intolerance of insult. Unfortunately, this public disagreement was followed by a host of politically sensitive issues, including most saliently, deteriorating relations with France and the emergence of political parties. While either of these issues on its own would have strained their friendship, together they resulted in its dissolution.

The emergence of party spirit in the latter half of Washington's administration was the result of a variety of factors, but the result seemed inevitable. Events all but ensured that the election of 1796 would be a contest between the Federalists led by John Adams and the Republicans led by Thomas Jefferson. Each candidate represented starkly different constitutional visions, and while the candidates themselves did not openly campaign, the newspapers took up the task on their behalf. For example, the *Aurora*, a Republican paper based out of Philadelphia, presented the election as the choice between "a steadfast friend of the Rights of the People, or an advocate for hereditary power and distinctions."[24] After a bitter election season, the electoral votes were certified in February of 1797, and John Adams came out ahead with seventy-one electoral votes versus Jefferson's sixty-eight votes. Jefferson was magnanimous in defeat, professing a readiness to serve as vice president in Adams's administration, and both men appeared willing to resume their friendship.[25] Reflecting on his sentiments at the time, Adams noted that while they had had their differences "concerning the practicability and success of the French revolution, and some other points, I had no reason to think that he differed materially from me with regard to our national Constitution."[26] Unfortunately, the affairs of the French would encroach on constitutional matters to the detriment of their friendship, despite their best intentions.

Concerned by the growing influence of the French and alarmed by rumors that the French were seeking to undermine his Federalist government, Adams called a special session of Congress to request a buildup of American military forces. Jefferson reacted negatively to this request, believing it to be merely a pretext by the Adams administration to see how far they could push their authority. When this reaction was conveyed to Adams, his earlier suspicions of his vice president were rekindled, laying the ground for further division.

As hostilities between France and the United States grew, the Adams administration undertook a series of measures designed to combat what it perceived to be French aggression and dominance. The first was the passage of the Alien Friends Act, which authorized the government to deport French nationals living in the United States. While Jefferson strenuously opposed the act, it was not until the government passed the Sedition Act in 1798, that he began to openly work against the policies of the government on the grounds that they were "an avowed violation of the constitution."[27] The Sedition Act "made it a crime to 'write, print, utter or publish . . . false, scandalous, and malicious' writings that brought the president or members of either house of Congress 'into contempt or disrepute.'" Jefferson saw this Act as aimed directly at the suppression of the Republican newspapers. In his mind, the federal government had become a foreign government that ought to be challenged by the state governments, and he posited nullification—the theory that each of the several states retained the final authority to void federal law it viewed unconstitutional—as a means of challenging Adams's administration.[28] The two friends' differences over the affairs of the French had emerged as a source of material disagreement on constitutional matters.

The bitter election of 1800 only served to further distance the two former friends. Upon Jefferson's victory, Adams and his fellow Federalists took advantage of the time between the election and Jefferson's inauguration to create a host of new federal positions, filling them with loyal Federalists, a move that angered Jefferson. When the date of the inauguration arrived (March 4, 1801), their relationship had soured to such a degree that Adams refused to greet his successor in office, becoming the first and (until recently) only president not to greet his successor in office. It was not until 1811, well after Jefferson's presidency had ended, that the two statesmen and former friends were reconciled. Had they not been reconciled, their fractured friendship would have cast a pall over the American founding, representing the triumph of factionary party spirit over persuasion and friendly disputation.

The process of reconciliation, however, was a delicate affair, which required the interposition of their mutual friend, the physician Benjamin Rush. Rush had been a friend of both Adams and Jefferson since 1775 and was acquainted with their strengths and weaknesses. In 1809, Benjamin Rush wrote a letter to Adams in which he recounted a dream he had had, in which Adams wrote Jefferson congratulating him upon his retirement. Rush described how this magnanimous act served to reestablish their friendship. Adams was flattered and responded favorably to the letter.[29] Meanwhile, Rush began correspondence with Jefferson as well, informing him of his correspondence with Adams and informing him how he "ardently wished a friendly and epistolary intercourse might be revived" between the two of them. Jefferson eventually responded favorably to Rush's entreaties, expressing his continued warmth toward Adams.[30] Upon receiving this indication from Jefferson, Rush again turned his attention to Adams, telling him of Jefferson's sentiments. He concluded his letter with the following words: "Fellow laborers in erecting the great fabric of American independence!—fellow sufferers in calumnies and falsehoods of party rage!—fellow heirs of the gratitude and affection of posterity!—and fellow passengers in a stage that must shortly convey you both into the presence of a Judge with whom the forgiveness and love of enemies is the condition of acceptance!—embrace—embrace each other!"[31] Benjamin Rush's entreaties were successful, and the two friends were reconciled, enabling them to reflect on the past and express theirs hopes for the future over the course of an epistolary dialogue that lasted through the rest of their lives.

The saga of Adams and Jefferson's friendship provides important insights into the principles underlying American politics. While both statesmen were committed to the republican principles established by the Constitution, they differed as to the exact manner in which these principles ought to operate. Adams's dour and pessimistic understanding of the human condition led him to believe in the necessity of hierarchy and order to keep man's passions in check. In contrast, Jefferson's optimism and sanguine appraisal of the American citizenry led him to favor liberal reforms that prioritized freedom and independence. Adams's account of human nature could be fairly described as Socratic in character, while Jefferson's optimistic belief in the inherent decency of the American people is more Aristotelian. Both strands of thought are therefore operative in the American tradition of politics.

At the same time, the troubled friendship of Adams and Jefferson shows the way in which these two accounts of human nature stand in uneasy tension with one another and can be the source of much acrimony, particularly when these opinions are held by individuals who are resolute and sure in their judgments. On its own, the Constitution is incapable of alleviating this acrimony. Divergent conceptions of social reality are incapable of being synthesized into a harmonious whole solely through legal and procedural means. In fact, Adams's and Jefferson's contradictory conceptions of human nature ultimately led to differing understandings of the Constitution, leading to accusations that one or the other was unfaithful to the spirit of independence. Jefferson's confidence in his own judgment even led him to use the constitutional power delegated to the several states to impede the policies pursued by Adams's administration. Constitutional procedures are, therefore, limited in their ability to reconcile the divergent excellences and insights presented by the heterogeneity of political life.

Ultimately, what served to reconcile their friendship was not an appeal to constitutional procedure, but the wisdom of their mutual friend and physician from Philadelphia. Benjamin Rush, attuned to the character, strengths, and prejudices of his two friends knew what ought to be said, and when it ought to be said, to reunite the former friends. Rush's efforts ensured that the two statesmen, both of whom died on the Fourth of July 1826, passed to their final reward having been reconciled. The saga of Adams and Jefferson's friendship reveals that the modern attempt to establish politics on a scientific basis rather than the fickle ground of friendship first articulated by Thomas Hobbes is unsustainable. While both statesmen were committed to the principles of the revolution and revered the Constitution, their disparate worldviews and headstrong character rendered the procedures of the Constitution a source of acrimony rather than harmony, and only words of friendship from Benjamin Rush served to heal the wounds of their division.

The friendship Rush cultivated over the years with both Jefferson and Adams was based on an admiration of their disparate excellences. We might characterize his friendship with each of them as a friendship of the good, or a *sunaisthetic* friendship. This friendship enabled him to entreat both of them to put aside their differences and be reconciled. When Attorney General William Wirt eulogized the friendship of Jefferson and Adams in an address to Congress as "a lesson of wisdom on the bitterness of party spirit, by which the wise and good will not fail to profit,"[32] he was able to do so through the sage interposition of Benjamin Rush. Benjamin Rush's entreaties to the two former friends became the words fitly spoken that served to pull these statesmen together, providing an instructive lesson for the entire nation.

Notes

Introduction

1. Michel de Montaigne, "Of Friendship," in *The Complete Essays of Montaigne*, trans. Donald M. Frame (Stanford, CA: Stanford University Press, 1958), 135–44.

2. Montaigne, 135–44.

3. Citations to the *Lysis* are taken from David Bolotin's interpretation unless otherwise noted. *Plato's Dialogue on Friendship: An Interpretation of the Lysis with a New Translation* (Ithaca: Cornell University Press, 1979).

4. Montaigne, 135–44.

5. Both Montaigne and Neitzsche attribute the saying to Aristotle. Montaigne, "Of Friendship," 140; Friedrich Nietzsche, *Human, All Too Human: A Book for Free Spirits*, trans. Marion Faber and Stephen Lehmann (Lincoln, NE: University of Nebraska Press, 1984), 194.

6. Unless otherwise indicated all citations to *The Nicomachean Ethics* will be based on the translation provided by Robert C. Bartlett and Susan D. Collins in *Aristotle's Nicomachean Ethics* (Chicago: University of Chicago Press, 2011).

7. H. G. Liddell and R. Scott, *Greek English Lexicon* (Oxford: Clarendon Press, 1996), 1693.

8. Robert D. Putnam, *Bowling Alone: The Collapse and Revival of American Community* (New York: Simon and Schuster, 2000).

9. Adam Smith, *The Theory of Moral Sentiments*, ed. D. D. Raphael and A. L. Macfie (Indianapolis, IN: Liberty Fund, 1982), 223–24 (VI.ii.1.15).

10. Putnam, *Bowling Alone*, 287–95.

11. On the substitution of commercial virtue for traditional virtue in the eighteenth-century Scottish Enlightenment see Christopher J. Berry, *The Idea of Commercial Society in the Scottish Enlightenment* (Edinburgh: Edinburgh University Press, 2013).

12. See P. E. Digeser, *Friendship Reconsidered: What It Means and How It Matters to Politics* (New York: Columbia University Press, 2016); Alexander Nehamas, *On Friendship* (New York: Basic Books, 2016); Ann Ward, *Contemplating Friendship in*

Aristotle's Ethics (Albany: State University of New York Press, 2016); Filippa Modesto, *Dante's Idea of Friendship: The Transformation of a Classical Concept* (Toronto: University of Toronto Press, 2015); Gregg Lambert, *Philosophy after Friendship: Deleuze's Conceptual Personae* (Minneapolis, MN: University of Minnesota Press, 2017); Seow Hon Tan, *Justice as Friendship: A Theory of Law*, (New York: Routledge, 2015); John von Heyking, *The Form of Politics: Aristotle and Plato on Friendship* (Montreal: McGill-Queens University Press, 2016); Alicia J. Batten, *Friendship and Benefaction in James* (Atlanta: SBL Press, 2017).

13. Aelred of Rievaulx, *Spiritual Friendship*, trans. Lawrence C. Braceland, ed. Marsha L. Dutton (Collegeville MN: Liturgical Press, 2010); Thomas Aquinas, *Summa Theologica*, II–II, Q. 23; Q. 114. For an excellent analysis of the manner in which Thomas Aquinas adopts Aristotle's account of friendship while subtly adjusting it to make it amenable with Christian revelation, see Daniel Schwartz, *Aquinas on Friendship* (Oxford: Oxford University Press, 2007); Desiderius Erasmus, *The Education of a Christian King*, trans. Neil M. Cheshire and Michael J. Heath, ed. Lisa Jardine (Cambridge, UK: Cambridge University Press, 1997).

14. Montaigne, "Of Friendship"; Francis Bacon, "Of Friendship," in *Francis Bacon: Essays and New Atlantis* (New York: Walter J. Black, 1942). On the reorientation of friendship from the public to the private realm, see Alexander Nehamas, *On Friendship*, (New York: Basic Books, 2016), 37–65. Lorraine Smith Pangle provides a contrasting account of the history of friendship, according to which the onset of Christianity caused the eclipse of friendship. According to Pangle, Christianity's call to "devote one's heart as completely as possible to God, and to regard all men as brothers made the existence of private, exclusive, and passionate attachments to individual human beings seem inherently questionable," *Aristotle and the Philosophy of Friendship* (Cambridge: Cambridge University Press, 2003), 2. In contrast, Constant J. Mews and Neville Chiavaroli argue that while there was a profound shift in the understanding of friendship from the Classical period to the Medieval period, "classical traditions of friendship never completely disappeared." "The Latin West" in *Friendship: A History*, ed. Barbara Caine (New York: Routledge, 2014), 73.

15. For a considered account of Hobbes's mechanistic political science, see Devin Stauffer, *Hobbes's Kingdom of Light: A Study of the Foundations of Modern Political Philosophy* (Chicago: University of Chicago Press, 2018).

16. Travis Smith, "Hobbes on Getting By with Little Help from Friends" in *Friendship and Politics: Essays in Political Thought*, ed. John von Heyking and Richard Avramenko (Notre Dame, IN: University of Notre Dame Press, 2008), 217.

17. Smith, 243.

18. Michael Walzer, "The Communitarian Critique of Liberalism," *Political Theory* 18, no. 1 (1990): 6–23.

19. Ruth Abbey, "Review Essay: On Friendship." *Review of Politics* 79, no. 4 (2017): 695–707.

20. Catherine H. Zuckert, *Plato's Philosophers: The Coherence of the Dialogues* (Chicago: The University of Chicago Press, 2009) 5–9. Other authors have also sought to gain insight into Plato's views by paying attention to the dramatic details of the dialogue. See for example Thomas G. West, *Plato's Apology of Socrates* (Ithaca NY: Cornell University Press, 1979), 217–21; Richard B. Rutherford, "Problems and Approaches," in *The Art of Plato: Ten Essays in Platonic Interpretation* (Cambridge, MA: Harvard University Press, 1995), 1–38.

21. For the difficulties involved in distinguishing the views of Plato from those of Socrates in the dialogues written by Plato, see Leo Strauss, *The City and Man* (Chicago: University of Chicago Press, 1964), esp. 50–62; see also Catherine H. Zuckert, *Plato's Philosophers*, esp. 1–48.

22. All citations to *The Apology* will be based on the translation provided by Thomas West and Grace Starry West in *Four Texts on Socrates* (Ithaca NY: Cornell University Press, 1979).

23. For example, Georg W. F. Hegel contrasts Socrates's discovery and devotion to the principle of subjectivity with the objective Greek customary morality. *The Philosophy of History* (Mineola, NY: Dover, 1956 [1837]), 269. Hegel goes on to reconcile the principle of subjectivity with objective morality through what he terms the "absolute and universal law." Hegel, 255. Similarly, Jean-Jacques Rousseau despite being estranged from his native city-state of Geneva and describing himself as the "solitary walker," seeks to legitimate the civil order through the notion of adherence to the "general will." See *The Social Contract*, trans. and ed. Victor Gourevitch (Cambridge: Cambridge University Press, [1762] 1997), book 1. This theme is reiterated throughout the history of Western philosophy. The philosopher is presented as largely alienated from the political regime who is able to reconcile his subjective will with that of the political community through devotion to an abstract rule.

24. See Richard Bodéüs, *The Political Dimensions of Aristotle's "Ethics,"* trans. Jan Edward Garrett (Albany: State University of New York Press, 1993); Aristide Tessitore, *Reading Aristotle's Ethics: Virtue, Rhetoric, and Political Philosophy* (Albany: State University of New York Press, 1996); Ronna Burger, *Aristotle's Dialogue with Socrates: On the Nicomachean Ethics* (Chicago: University of Chicago Press, 2008).

25. A. W. H. Adkins, "The Connection Between Aristotle's *Ethics* and *Politics*," *Political Theory*, 12 (1984): 29–41.

26. Paul Cartledge relates that Aristotle gave Alexander a copy of the *Iliad*, and that Alexander carried his "Aristotle-annotated text" with him on his expedition to Asia. Alexander was said to be "so attached to it that at night he allegedly slept with it—and a dagger—under his pillow." *Alexander the Great: The Hunt for a New Past* (New York: Overlook Press, 2004), 227. For a full overview of the relations between Aristotle and Alexander, see Victor Ehrenberg, *Alexander and the Greeks* (Oxford: Oxford University Press, 1938), 62–102.

27. N. D. Arora and S. S. Awasthy, *Political Theory and Political Thought* (New Delhi: Har Anand Publications, 2007), 77: "The two major streams along which the whole Western political thought keeps marching on are: (i) political idealism or as one may see [*sic*] political philosophy, and (ii) political realism, or as one may call it political science. Plato represents political idealism and Aristotle represents political realism."

28. See Leo Strauss, *The City and Man* (Chicago: Rand McNally, 1964); Harry V. Jaffa, *Aristotelianism and Thomism: A Study of the Commentary by Thomas Aquinas on the Nicomachean Ethics* (Westport, CT: Greenwood Press, 1979); Aristide Tessitore, *Reading Aristotle's Ethics*; Ronna Burger, *Aristotle's Dialogue with Socrates*.

29. Allan Bloom argues that the fundamental problem of politics lies in determining how the wisdom of the philosophers may come to influence the gentlemen who have power. In his commentary on *The Republic*, Bloom notes that the first very scene of *The Republic* (327a–328b), in which Polemarchus orders his slave to catch up with Socrates as he leaves the Piraeus, exemplifies the fundamental political problem: "Power is in the hands of the gentlemen, who are not philosophers. They can command the services of the many, and their strength is such that they always hold the philosophers in their grasp. Therefore, it is part of the philosophers' self-interest to come to terms with them. The question becomes: to what extent can the philosophers influence the gentlemen?" "Interpretive Essay" in *The Republic of Plato*, (New York: Basic Books, 1968), 312.

30. Aristide Tessitore writes, "Aristotle attempts to offer guidance for those who are disposed to an active life of political involvement . . . [while] at the same time . . . point[ing] his most gifted students to . . . contemplate something of the radical and more fully satisfying character of the philosophic life." *Reading Aristotle's Ethics*, 20.

31. Leo Strauss seems to suggest as much, when he writes "The only reason why not Socrates but Aristotle became the founder of political science is that Socrates who spent his life in the unending ascent to the idea of the good and in awakening others to that ascent, lacked for this reason the leisure not only for political activity but even for founding political science." *The City and Man* (Chicago: Rand McNally, 1964), 29. Robert C. Bartlett argues that the " 'best regime' " of books VII and VIII of Aristotle's *Politics*, the classic of premodern political science, shows Aristotle to be in no sense naïve or that he knows full well the ways of the world." "The 'Realism' of Classical Political Science" *American Journal of Political Science* 38 no. 2 (1994): 382.

32. This position is encapsulated nicely by the following statement from Aristide Tessitore: "Aristotle's treatment of friendship in books VIII and IX . . . prepares readers for his concluding endorsement of the rare but simply best way of life available to human beings. His subsequent demotion of the life of moral virtue in light of the superior happiness afforded by the contemplative pleasures of philosophy is perhaps less strange and less jarring because it is prefaced with a consideration of friendship." *Reading Aristotle's Ethics*, 95.

33. Friendship is not treated at length in either Plato's *Republic* or *Laws*, nor is it treated forthrightly as a subject in its own right in Aristotle's *Politics*.

34. Cf. Plato, *The Republic*, 369b6–7; Aristotle, *Politics*, 1252a25–b13.

35. Citations to *The Republic* come from the translation provided by Allan Bloom in *The Republic of Plato* (New York: Basic Books, 1968).

36. Citations to *The Politics* come from the translation provided by Carnes Lord in *Aristotle's Politics* (Chicago: University of Chicago Press, 2013).

Chapter One

1. In addition to the four dialogues narrated in their entirety by Socrates, two—*Protagoras* and *Euthydemus*—are narrated by Socrates after an introductory dramatic exchange, and three are narrated by someone other than Socrates—*Parmenides*, *Symposium*, and *Phaedo*.

2. The distinction between Socrates's outward statements (dialectical or otherwise) and his intentions is made most clear toward the end of the *Lysis*. After recounting the various arguments raised throughout the dialogue, Socrates comments, "If nothing among these is a friend, I no longer know what to say" (222e9). However, immediately after this, he suggests to the reader, "But as I said these things, I already had in mind to set in motion someone else among the older fellows" (223a1). While Socrates expresses dismay, it seems that he is not as much at a loss, as he lets on to his interlocutors. On the importance of the narrated dialogues see, Catherine Zuckert, *Plato's Philosophers*, 19; Leo Strauss, *On Plato's "Symposium,"* ed. and with a foreword by Seth Benardete (Chicago: University of Chicago Press 2001), 186.

3. Catherine Zuckert, *Plato's Philosophers*, 482–84 n. 2; 530. Other scholars also suggest that the dialogue might point toward the definition of a friend. Lorraine Smith Pangle comments: "Plato may provide the reader with the outlines of compelling arguments that, though facilely rejected, are not refuted" *Aristotle and the Philosophy of Friendship*, 21. James M. Rhodes points to the subtitle of the dialogue, "On *Philia*: Obstetric," and concludes that "Socrates is practicing the midwife's art. Socrates will not give us a propositional 'theory of *philia*.' Rather, the 'pregnant' characters in the play and we ourselves need to be delivered of the virtue of friendly love" ("Platonic *Philia* and Political Order" in *Friendship and Politics*, ed. John von Heyking and Richard Avramenko [University of Notre Dame Press, 2008], 25–26).

4. Bolotin, *Plato's Dialogue on Friendship*. In my analysis of the dialogue, I am deeply indebted to Bolotin's superb interpretation of the dialogue. However, I seek to further Bolotin's analysis by pointing to some of the deficiencies in Socrates's arguments, which suggest that Plato may have been subtly critiquing Socrates.

5. Cf. Friedrich Ast, *Platon's Leben und Schriften* (Leipzig: Weidmannsche Buchhandlung, 1816) 428–34; Joseph Socher, *Uber Platons Schriften* (Munich: Ignaz Joseph Lentner, 1820), 137–44.

6. Cf. Robert G. Hoerber, "Plato's Lysis," *Phronesis* 4 no. 1 (1959): 15.

7. Diogenes Laertius, *Lives of Eminent Philosophers*, ed. James Miller, trans. Pamela Mensch (Oxford: Oxford University Press, 2018) Bk. III, 35.

8. Gregory Vlastos, *Socrates: Ironist and Moral Philosopher* (Ithaca, NY: Cornell University Press, 1991), 45–46.

9. Zuckert, *Plato's Philosophers*, 3–5.

10. Zuckert, 7.

11. As Lorraine Smith Pangle points out, the trail left by Plato is picked up on by Aristotle in books VIII and IX of *The Nicomachean Ethics*: *Aristotle and the Philosophy of Friendship* (Cambridge: Cambridge University Press, 2003), 36. John von Heyking makes the convincing case that Plato develops his account of friendship in the *Laws*. *The Form of Politics: Aristotle and Plato on Friendship*, (Montreal, QC: McGill-Queen's University Press, 2016), 131–46.

12. The entirety of this dialogue, in which Socrates fails to find a definition of friendship, occurs at the very edge of the city. This fact may be suggestive of Socrates's relation to the city and to politics in general. In contrast, the *Phaedrus*—a dialogue concerning eros—occurs well outside the city.

13. On the connection between wrestling and philosophy, see Clinton DeBevoise Corcoran, "Wrestling and the Fair Fight in Plato," in *Topography and Deep Structure in Plato: The Construction of Place in the Dialogues* (Albany: State University of New York Press, 2016), 119–51.

14. Terry Penner and Christopher Rowe, commenting on the passage in question, note that while the term *Sophist* is ordinarily used in a derogatory sense, here "the term seems to be used in a purely descriptive way; and that . . . is the point: Miccus professes, and teaches, wisdom, and wisdom or knowledge will be one of the chief themes of the main part of the dialogue" (*Plato's Lysis* [Cambridge University Press, 2005], 4n2).

15. Walter Burkert, *Greek Religion: Archaic and Classical*, trans. John Raffan (Cambridge, MA: Harvard University Press, 1985), 156–58.

16. Catherine Zuckert notes that Socrates's entry into the palaestra is itself a transgression of boundaries, as only the older youth were allowed to mingle with the boys, not adults such as Socrates. *Plato's Philosophers*, 513.

17. Arthur Fairbanks, *The Mythology of Greece and Rome* (New York: D. Appleton, 1907), 258–60. According to the myth, once Io has been set free she is not yet free to transform back into a deity, but is pursued by the shade of Argus in the form of a gadfly that stings her incessantly. It is only once Io the cow reaches Egypt that she is finally free to transform back to a deity. If Plato intends for this myth to act as an allegory of Socrates's treatment of friendship, the fact that Io is pursued by a gadfly brings to mind Plato's depiction of Socrates as a gadfly in the *Apology*. Socrates is said continually to alight on the city as a means of waking it from its slumber. It would seem that the change from friendship to eros is a cause of consternation for the city.

18. David B. Robinson notes that the Lysis "is one of five short Platonic dialogues which address themselves entirely to a question of definition. Besides the *Lysis* these dialogues are the *Charmides*, *Laches*, *Hippias Major*, and *Euthyphro*; all of these ask a question of the type 'What is x?' and make this question their sole concern" ("Plato's *Lysis*: The Structural Problem," *Illinois Classical Studies* 11 no. 1/2 [1986]: 63). While I agree with Robinson that the dialogue does seek a definition of friendship, I am of the opinion that the dramatic activity surrounding the question suggests that the purpose of the dialogue is not *simply* to define friendship.

19. This is precisely the definition of friendship that is alluded to but not fully explored in the final sections of the dialogue. See 222b4: "If what is akin differs in some respect from the like, we might be saying something, in my opinion, concerning what a friend is."

20. For dramatic similarities between the *Euthydemus* and *Lysis* see Zuckert, *Plato's Philosophers*, 509–10. Naomi Reshotko points out that Socrates's description of a friend at 212a8–22d8 maps onto his description of the hierarchy of desire found at *Euthydemus* 279 and *Gorgias* 467. "Plato's *Lysis*: A Socratic Treatise on Desire and Attraction" *Apeiron* 30 no. 1 (1997): 1–18.

21. H. G. Liddell and R. Scott, *Greek English Lexicon* (Oxford: Clarendon Press, 1996), 1955–56.

22. Benjamin Rider, "A Socratic Seduction: Philosophical Protreptic in Plato's *Lysis*," *Apeiron* 44 no. 1 (2011): 56.

23. James Rhodes "Platonic *Philia* and Political Order," 27.

24. According to Rhodes, far from seeking to develop a utilitarian conception of friendship, Socrates goal is to *curb* Lysis's utilitarian impulses. Rhodes, 31.

25. Michael Eisenstadt has catalogued a series of connections suggesting that the *Lysis* acts as a counterpart or antithesis to the *Euthydemus*: "In the *Euthydemus*, a pair of sophists interrogate one beautiful boy. In the *Lysis*, Socrates interrogates a pair of beautiful boys. In the *Euthydemus*, Kleinias makes a beeline for Socrates to sit down with and talk to. In the *Lysis*, Socrates must strategize a way to gain access to Lysis. In the *Euthydemus*, a καλός [beautiful] Ktesippos is represented as insistent on keeping in sight the boy he is courting who is indifferent to his attentions. In the *Lysis*, Hippothales, rejected by Lysis, hides himself from the view of his ἐρώμενος [beloved] who cannot bear the sight of him." "Antithesis in Plato's *Euthydemus* and *Lysis*" (unpublished manuscript, last revised July 27, 2020). Available at SSRN: https://ssrn.com/abstract=3624095. Eisenstadt concludes that these connections are philosophically insignificant as they are fortuitous events. However, these events were designed by Plato and are therefore not simply fortuitous but are instead the result of conscious construction. Plato, it seems, wishes to draw our attention to the similarity between the dialogues.

26. Rider, "A Socratic Seduction," 65.

27. Right near the end of the dialogue (223a2–a7), Socrates narrates that the boys' attendants came "like some daemons" and "bade them to leave for home."

Socrates relates that he and the boys had an altercation with the attendants and "tried to drive them away." Socrates's conversation has led the boys to chafe under the authority set over them by their parents.

28. Cf. *Phaedrus* 275d5–e5.

29. Bolotin, 106.

30. Bolotin defends Socrates from this charge, noting that Lysis's desire to chasten Menexenus reveals that their "juvenile friendship was not innocent. We may assume that the shortcomings of their friendship would have come to light eventually with or without the intervention of Socrates" (Bolotin, 106–7). It's not clear to me that this provides an adequate defense for Socrates's behavior, as it underplays the extent to which Socrates's earlier conversation with Lysis prompted Lysis's desire to chasten Menexenus. Furthermore, Socrates encourages, or stokes, Lysis's desire for punishment by pointing to Menexenus's "contentious" character (211c3–5).

31. A. W. Price, *Love and Friendship in Plato and Aristotle* (Oxford: Oxford University Press, 1989), 3–4.

32. The two philosophers who inquire into the whole and are of the view that like is necessarily always a friend to like are Empedocles and Democritus. In *The Nicomachean Ethics*, Aristotle invokes Empedocles in support of the principle "that like *aims* at like" (*NE*, 1155b5–7; emphasis added).

33. Specifically, Aristotle writes, "Socrates, however, was busying himself about ethical matters and neglecting the world of nature as a whole but seeking the universal in these ethical matters, and fixed thought for the first time on definitions" (*Metaphysics*, 987b1–4).

34. In book VIII of *The Nicomachean Ethics*, Empedocles is mentioned as the proponent of the view that "like aims at like." The only other time in the totality of the *Ethics* where Empedocles is mentioned is in book VII, where Aristotle specifically critiques the Socratic thesis that "no one acts contrary to what is best while supposing that he is so acting" (1145b26–27). In this discussion, Aristotle notes that a person may know the words of something but be ignorant of what they mean. Such an individual, Aristotle comments "merely speaks, as a drunk man states the sayings of Empedocles" (1147b12–13). It may be that Aristotle is suggesting that Socrates fails to understand the sayings of Empedocles.

35. Recall that in the *Euthydemus* those who are "skilled at contradicting" are depicted as sophists who engage in the "frivolous part of study" (*Euthydemus*, 277e4–278b5).

36. Bolotin translates κινδυνεύει to be "I am afraid." I have instead translated the term as the more literal "it may be" in order to convey the lack of certainty with which Socrates puts forward this alternative understanding of friendship.

37. Ordinarily, when Socrates attributes his actions to a divine cause, we are told that the source is his "divine sign." Furthermore, Socrates notes that the "divine sign" only ever "tells me to turn away from what I'm about to do, but never prescribes anything" (*Theages*, 128d3–4). This suggests that in this particular instance, Socrates is not speaking under the influence of his divine sign.

38. Socrates does not relate *why* it would be necessary to renounce going on like this. Cf. Aristotle, *NE*, 1094a17–23; Thomas Hobbes, *Leviathan*, ed. Richard Tuck (Cambridge: Cambridge University Press, 1996), 11 (47).

39. In the *Gorgias*, Socrates professes that in his opinion friendship does consist of those who are alike (cf. *Gorgias*, 510b4–6).

40. Specifically, Socrates states, "There will be, then, whatever desires are neither good nor bad, even if the things which are bad cease to be" (221b5–7).

41. Bolotin, 183.

42. Bolotin notes that the notion that the spirited element of the soul is akin to the rational part of the soul is discussed in *The Republic* at 440e. This is also picked up by Aristotle, who states that the nonrational part of the soul shares in reason to the extent it is capable of listening to the rational part of the soul.

43. *Phaedrus*, 267d6–268a6.

44. It is important to note that Socrates does not narrate that Hippothales is the older fellow whom he has in mind to set in motion. This is important as it may absolve Socrates from the charge that he is acting, as Seth Benardete bluntly states, "a pimp." "On Plato's *Lysis*," in *The Argument of the Action: Essays on Greek Poetry and Philosophy* (Chicago: University of Chicago Press, 2000), 198–202.

45. Gary Allan Scott, *Plato's Socrates as Educator*, (Albany: State University of New York Press, 2000), 52.

46. Through the course of the dialogue, all three of these sophistic arguments are walked back (cf. 214c6–d4; 212e6–213a4; 218a7–b1).

47. Bolotin, 197.

48. While Socrates has explored the meaning of friendship with both boys, the conversation appears to have had disparate effects on the two boys. Menexenus did not have all his friendships called into question by Socrates in the same way as Lysis, since he was away undertaking the sacrificial rites of the Hermaea during this portion of the conversation. It could be that as a result Menexenus is featured in other dialogues, most notably *Menexenus*, in which Socrates teaches him the art of rhetoric. Socrates's interest in teaching him the rhetoric of a statesman indicates that Menexenus has undertaken a life devoted to public service rather than philosophy (*Menexenus*, 234a–b). In contrast, Lysis does not appear in any other dialogues. Like Plato (and in contrast to Menexenus) he is not present at Socrates's death in the *Phaedo* (*Phaedo*, 59b). Lysis's absence in the other dialogues may indicate that he has devoted himself to the private life of contemplation, or it could be that Socrates's arguments have led him to enter a private erotic relationship with Hippothales (who also does not appear in any other Platonic dialogue).

49. For a contrary interpretation of this scene, see Mary Nichols, *Socrates on Friendship and the Political Community: Reflections on Plato's* Symposium, Phaedrus, *and* Lysis (Cambridge: Cambridge University Press, 2009), 190–91.

50. Hannah Arendt explains how Socratic questioning of traditional virtues led some of his students to turn against Athenian customs: "In the circle around Socrates, there were men like Alcibiades and Critias—God knows, by no means the

worst among his so-called pupils—who had turned out to be a real threat to the *polis*, and this . . . because they had been aroused by the gadfly. What they had been aroused to was license and cynicism. Not content with being taught how to think without being taught a doctrine, they changed the non-results of the Socratic thinking examination into negative results: If we cannot define what piety is, let us be impious" Hannah Arendt, *The Life of the Mind* (New York: Harcourt, 1977,) 175.

51. H. G. Liddell and R. Scott, *Greek English Lexicon* (Oxford: Clarendon Press, 1996), 1066–67.

Chapter Two

1. Leo Strauss comments, "The individual dialogue is not a chapter from an encyclopaedia of the philosophic sciences or from a system of philosophy, and still less a relic of a stage of Plato's development. Each dialogue deals with one part; it reveals the truth about that part. But the truth about a part is a partial truth, a half truth. Each dialogue, we venture to say, abstracts from something that is most important to the subject matter of the dialogue." *The City and Man*, (Chicago: University of Chicago Press, 1964), 62.

2. The Platonic work that most obviously deals with Socrates's relation to politics is, of course, *The Republic*. In *The Republic*, Socrates and his interlocutors famously construct a "city in speech" to discover the nature of justice. Nevertheless, I have chosen to focus on the *Gorgias* because, like the *Apology*, it focuses on Socrates's way of life. Both the *Apology* and the *Gorgias* concern Socrates's way of life—that is the philosophic life—and examine its relation to the polis. In contrast, the primary investigation of *The Republic* is not Socrates's orientation toward political life, but the city taken as a whole and the way in which it ought to be ordered. In this way, the *Gorgias* is primarily a practical dialogue rather than a theoretical dialogue. The *Gorgias* concerns the practical question of how an individual ought to live, while *The Republic* is a theoretical investigation into the form of justice and the manner in which it might come into being in the city as a whole. Bloom alludes to the theoretical character of *The Republic* by pointing out that only in *The Republic* does Socrates "define justice and elaborate the science which can give ground to such a definition." *The Republic* is, therefore, an apology for the Socratic way of life from the perspective of the science of politics. See Bloom, "Interpretive Essay," 307–8. The *Crito* also deals with Socrates's relationship with the city. However, as Thomas West and Grace Starry West point out, the arguments Socrates employs in that dialogue are developed primarily for the benefit of his admirer Crito, who is guided by the opinions of the city rather than for the sake of their truth. "Introduction," in *Four Texts on Socrates: Plato and Aristophanes* (Ithaca, NY: Cornell University Press, 1998). The *Crito* is, therefore, equally inapposite for uncovering Socrates's relationship with the polis.

3. Further connection between the *Apology* and the *Gorgias* is made clear by Douglas D. Feaver and John E. Hare. They argue that every section of Socrates's main speech in the *Apology* is an "inverted parody" of Gorgias's *Defense of Palamedes*. "The *Apology* as an Inverted Parody of Rhetoric," *Arethusa* 14 no. 2 (1981), 205–16.

4. All citations to the *Gorgias* are taken from the translation provided by James H. Nichols Jr. unless otherwise noted. *Plato Gorgias* (Ithaca: Cornell University Press, 1998).

5. All citations to the *Apology* will be taken from Thomas G. West and Grace Starry West's translation in *Four Texts on Socrates: Plato and Aristophanes* (Ithaca, NY: Cornell University Press, 1998).

6. Specifically, Socrates relates that the politician he questioned "seemed to be wise, both to many other human beings and most of all to himself, but that he was not" (21c). In turn, of the poets, Socrates relates that "they do not make what they make by wisdom, but by some sort of nature and while inspired. . . . For they too say many noble things, but they know nothing of what they speak" (22b). Last, of the manual artisans, or craftsman, Socrates states, "They did have knowledge of things which I did not have knowledge of, and in this way they were wiser than I. But . . . the good craftsmen also seemed to go wrong in the same way as the poets: because he performed his art nobly, each one deemed himself wisest also in the other things, the greatest things—and this discordant note of theirs seemed to hide that wisdom" (22d).

7. Dana Villa, *Socratic Citizenship* (Princeton, NJ: Princeton University Press, 2001), 2.

8. For an extended account of Socrates's negativity see Søren Kierkegaard, *On the Concept of Irony, with Continual Reference to Socrates: Together with Notes of Schelling's Berlin Lectures*, ed. and trans. Howard Vincent Hong and Edna Hatlestad Hong (Princeton, NJ: Princeton University Press, 1992). For a contrary perspective, which emphasizes the positive nature of Socrates's philosophic practice, see Vlastos, *Socrates*; Terence Irwin, "Socrates' Method," in *Plato's Ethics* (New York: Oxford University Press, 1995), 17–30.

9. This is, of course, a truncated description of the activity Socrates undertakes in the *Lysis*, as described in the previous chapter. Cf. *Sophist* 231e; *Meno* 84a–b.

10. Cf. *Republic*, 443b–444a.

11. Thucydides, *History of the Peloponnesian War*, trans. Rex Warner (New York: Penguin, 1972), 147.

12. See e.g., George Kateb, "Socratic Integrity," in *Nomos XL: Integrity and Conscience*, 40, (1998): 77–112; Villa, *Socratic Citizenship*.

13. See e.g., Kateb, "Socratic Integrity," 82; Villa, *Socratic Citizenship*, 25–26.

14. Thomas G. West and Grace Starry West relate the events that comprise the background to Socrates's political activity: "Two years before the end of the [Peloponnesian] war, in 406, the Athenians won a major victory in a naval battle fought near the Aegean island of Arginusae. However, on account of the confusion

following the battle and a storm that arose afterwards, the disabled ships and the Athenians still at the scene of the battle, both alive and dead, could not be rescued as the ten generals had intended. When the generals returned to Athens, eight of them were accused by Theramenes, an unscrupulous and ambitious politician, of neglecting their duty. . . . Theramenes cleverly manipulated the Assembly of the people, and it was led to condemn the eight to death as a group, although it was evident that many or perhaps all of them were innocent of wrongdoing. Socrates . . . maintained that such a procedure was against the law on the ground that the generals should have been tried separately. His protest was ineffectual, for his fellow prytanes easily yielded to the loud threats of the politicians and the Assembly." *Four Texts*, 84 n. 58.

15. George Kateb, "Socratic Integrity" 84.

16. Thomas G. West and Grace Starry West note that "the arrest and execution without trial of Leon, who was reputed to be a perfectly just man, was one of the harshest of the many injustices committed by the oligarchy." *Four Texts*, 84 n. 59.

17. Villa, *Socratic Citizenship*, 26.

18. Hannah Arendt, "Thinking and Moral Considerations: A Lecture," *Social Research* 38, no. 3 (Autumn 1971): 423.

19. Kateb, "Socratic Integrity," 80.

20. Villa, *Socratic Citizenship*, 27.

21. Dana Villa emphasizes his disagreement with Hannah Arendt. He writes that for Arendt, "Socrates cannot serve as a model of citizenship, philosophical or otherwise, precisely because his care for his soul undermines the citizens' care for the (public) world. Socratic conscience is, at bottom, *self*-interest." Villa counters this by positing that Socratic citizenship is a salutary orientation toward the world of politics whereby "one best pursues one's responsibility to the world, to the claims of citizenship, by cultivating a certain distance between the self and the passions and energies of the *demos*." *Socratic Citizenship*, 52–53. Thus, for Villa, Socrates's private actions have a public benefit. However, Socrates never states that he intends to benefit the city as a whole. To be sure, he likens himself to a gadfly who has been "set upon the city by the god, as though upon a great and well-born horse" (*Apology*, 30e). However, he follows this up by reverting to a non-collectivist description of his mission, stating, "I awaken and persuade and reproach *each one of you*" (*Apology*, 30e–31a). The remainder of this chapter will argue that Socrates's negative and private approach stems from a concern that the city interferes with the health of the soul, or that there is a disharmony between the city and the soul.

22. The central role that Socrates's daimonion plays in the *Apology*, along with the relatively scant information we receive about it in the entirety of the Platonic *corpus*, has led to much academic speculation over what precisely Socrates's daimonion is. Today, most scholars assume, in accordance with Hegel, that the daimonion represents Socrates's individuated conscience. See G. W. F. Hegel, *Lectures on the History of Philosophy*, trans. E. S. Haldane, vol. 1, (London: Routledge

& Kegan Paul, 1955), 421–25. For a contrary perspective, which emphasizes the religious character of the Socratic daimonion, see Vlastos, *Socrates*, 158. References to Socrates's daimonion in the works of Plato include *Apology*, 31c–d, 40a–c; *Euthyphro*, 3b; *Republic*, 496c; *Thaeatetus*, 151a; *Phaedrus*, 224b–c; *Euthydemus*, 272e; and *Theages*, 128d–131a.

23. Socrates describes his daimonion's opposition to political as altogether noble (παγκάλως). The noble (καλός) is an important term and in the *Hippias Major* its definition proves elusive.

24. Later in his defense speech, Socrates again subtly implies that he values speech over deeds: "If I say that this even happens to be a very great good for a human being—to make speeches every day about virtue and the other things about which you hear me conversing and examining both myself and others—and that the unexamined life is not worth living for a human being, you will be persuaded by me still less when I say these things" (*Apology*, 38a). As I will make clear, the distinction between speech and deed becomes an important theme in the *Gorgias*.

25. Roger Duncan, "*Philia* in the *Gorgias*," *Apeiron* 8 no. 1 (1974): 23–25.

26. Catherine H. Zuckert, *Plato's Philosophers*, 531. If Zuckert is correct on the dramatic ordering of the dialogues, we can surmise that in the *Gorgias* Plato works out how Socrates's understanding of friendship articulated in the *Lysis* impacts his relation to the political realm.

27. It might reasonably be questioned how Socrates's understanding of friendship causes him both to counsel Polus to return to the city and use rhetoric to purge it of injustice and to counsel Callicles to avoid politics altogether. As I hope to make clear, Socrates's ability to argue in this way hinges upon the different character of each of his interlocutors. While neither Polus nor Callicles is impervious to shame, Callicles proves to be much less sensitive to shame than does Polus.

28. Seth Benardete notes, "The issue in the background of the *Gorgias* is very simple. If Gorgianic rhetoric has the power Gorgias claims for it, it would necessarily follow that the best city in speech of the *Republic* could be realized anywhere on earth and at any time." *The Rhetoric of Morality and Philosophy* (Chicago: University of Chicago Press, 1991), 5.

29. Gorgias was a famous rhetorician who traveled from city to city selling his knowledge. Teresa Morgan, "Rhetoric and Education," in *A Companion to Greek Rhetoric*, ed. Ian Worthington (West Sussex: Blackwell, 2010), 304. The question of Gorgias's relation to the city is, therefore, apposite, as the manner in which Gorgias practices his craft transcends political boundaries and loyalties. Later on, Gorgias will claim that rhetoric ought to be used justly and for the benefit of friends (456a–457c).

30. "Chaerephon, many arts have been discovered among men experimentally through experiences. For experience causes our life to proceed by art, whereas inexperience causes it to proceed by chance. Of each of these arts, various men variously partake of various ones, and the best men partake of the best; among these is Gorgias here, and he has a share in the finest of the arts" (448c).

31. Cf. Aristotle, *Metaphysics*, 981a1–5.

32. This shift is purposeful, and it betrays Socrates's efforts to discover whether rhetoric is capable of aiming towards what *is*, or towards truth. Based on the manner in which Socrates appears to try and redirect rhetoric towards the things "that are," some scholars have suggested that Socrates's purpose is to reform rhetoric. See Devin Stauffer, *The Unity of Plato's "Gorgias": Rhetoric, Justice and the Philosophic Life* (Cambridge: Cambridge University Press, 2006).

33. E. R. Dodds provides the full quatrain. He remarks that "the fourth item is omitted by Plato, since it does not depend on any τέχνη." *Plato Gorgias: A Revised Text with Introduction and Commentary* (Oxford: Clarendon, 1959), 200. However, Dodds does not comment on Socrates's incomplete quotation of the second good. My own view is that Socrates's omission of the fourth good is meant to raise the question of what role friendship ought to play in political life.

34. Some have argued that the self-interest displayed by Socrates is related to his trial. According to this line of argument Socrates is seeking to reform rhetoric so as to make his trial proceed favorably. See Devin Stauffer, *The Unity of the Gorgias*.

35. This primary concern for one's own good is echoed in the *Charmides*: "I am examining the argument mainly for my own sake, but also, perhaps, for that of my other intimates" (166c7–d4).

36. James Nichols writes of Socrates's remark, "Could one imagine a more tactful way of bringing up the rhetor's lack of concern for conveying knowledge about issues of justice?" *Plato Gorgias*, 37 n. 28.

37. We can be skeptical of the extent to which Gorgias, as a traveling rhetorician who sells his wares to the highest bidder, truly believes in the existence of justice and friendship.

38. Polus is likely correct to describe Gorgias's shame as the cause of his refutation, as Gorgias does exhibit a sense of shame at various points of the dialogue (cf. 458d7–458e2).

39. Socrates's response adumbrates what will later be his definition of justice. Justice is refuting others (cf. 505b–c).

40. Cf. *Apology*, 32a.

41. Socrates has implied, earlier in the dialogue that being refuted is best. Cf. *Gorgias*, 458a ("And of what men am I one? Those who are refuted with pleasure if I say something not true, and who refute with pleasure if someone should say something not true—and indeed not with less pleasure to be refuted than to refute. For I consider it a greater good, to the extent that it is a greater good to be released oneself from the greatest evil than to release another. For I think that nothing is so great an evil for a human being as false opinion about the things that our argument now happens to be about"). That Socrates believes that being refuted is the greatest good (greater even than refuting another) explains why Socrates earlier insisted that his primary purpose in pursuing the argument was for his own sake, and not for the sake of his interlocutors. Socrates does not primarily pursue the argument to refute Gorgias, but to test his own opinions.

42. In comparing the rhetor to a common criminal who, according to Polus, deserves punishment, Socrates appeals to Polus's moralistic desire for punishment, which will eventually prove necessary to persuade him that the rhetor is unjust. However, Polus is unwilling to equate the rhetor with the common criminal and, in support of the contention that unjust rhetors are happy, he points to the many unjust deeds that Archelaus the ruler of Macedonia committed in order to attain his station. Socrates never states his agreement with Polus that Archelaus is unjust, or even that he has committed injustices (*Gorgias*, 468e–71d).

43. There is reason to believe that Socrates does not, himself, agree with this argument, as it relies on the claim that the fine or noble is equivalent to the good, a distinction which is challenged in the *Hippias Major*. James Nichols notes that "in the *Hippias Major*, Socrates investigates just what the fine (noble, beautiful) is; it proves very difficult to state." *Plato Gorgias*, 61, n. 54.

44. Nichols, "The Rhetoric of Justice in Plato's *Gorgias*," in *Plato Gorgias*, 139.

45. Cf. *Apology*, 32a–b.

46. Socrates similarly demurs from the statement that "the great king" (i.e., the King of Persia) is unjust, commenting, "I do not know how he stands in regard to education and justice" (*Gorgias*, 470e).

47. Cf. 448b: "I'm asking now. If Gorgias happened to be a knower of his brother Herodicus's art, what would we *justly* name him" (emphasis added). Cf. also 465e–466a: "So then, when you are answering, if I too do not know what use to make of it, you too extend your speech; but if I do, let me make use of it; for that is just."

48. This is finally asserted explicitly toward the end of the dialogue during Socrates's conversation with Callicles. Cf. 522d–e.

49. E.g., Villa, *Socratic Citizenship*, 37: "Public address . . . effectively forbids any fundamental questioning. Oratory is flattery because persuasion, not genuine criticism, is its goal."

50. Nichols relates that Chaerephon' s response "there's nothing like asking the man himself," mirrors Callicles's response to Socrates at the beginning of the dialogue suggesting "that the dialogue is to begin anew here." *Gorgias*, n. 61.

51. The son of Pyrilampes was called *Demos*, which is of course the same word for the Athenian people (*demos*). *Demos* the son of Pyrilampes "was famous for his beauty and also for lack of intelligence." Nichols, *Plato Gorgias*, 70 n. 65.

52. For a convincing analysis of the role of shame in Plato's *Gorgias*, see Richard McKim, "Shame and Truth in Plato's *Gorgias*," in *Platonic Writings, Platonic Readings*, ed. Charles L. Griswold, Jr. (New York: Routledge, 1988), 34–48. McKim argues that Socrates uses the concept of shame as a weapon of psychological warfare in order to maneuver his interlocutors into acknowledging that, deep down, they do hold Socrates's way of life to be superior.

53. There is a wide range of scholarship that interprets Callicles to be a simple immoralist. See Werner Jaeger, *Paedeia*, vol. 2 (New York: Oxford University Press, 1943), 125–41; Eric Voegelin, *Order and History*, vol. 3 (Baton Rouge: Louisiana

State University Press, 1957), 24–45; George Klosko, "The Refutation of Callicles in Plato's *Gorgias*," *Greece and Rome* 31, no. 2 (1984): 126–39. In contrast, Devin Stauffer argues that Callicles's appearance as a cynical immoralist "hides his deepest convictions" and that deep down Callicles does have some standard of virtue. "Socrates and Callicles: A Reading of Plato's *Gorgias*," in *The Review of Politics* 64 no. 4 (2002): 627–57.

54. See 484e, 485e–486a, 486b, 486c.

55. This brief synopsis of the work comes from E. R. Dodds's commentary on the *Gorgias*, 275–76. For a full account of the plot, Dodds directs the reader to N. Wecklein, "Die Antiope des Euripides," in *Philologus* 79 (1923) 51–69; A. W. Pickard-Cambridge in J. U. Powell, ed., *New Chapters in Greek Literature*, 3d series (Oxford, 1933), 105–13.

56. Callicles's commitment to manliness and the ability to help oneself and one's family and friends is explicitly stated at 485c and 486a respectively. His commitment to hard work is intimated by his denigration of childish play at 485b. John Gibert notes that "Zethus advocates hard work, manly strength, care of property, and the ability to help oneself and one's family and friends both privately and publicly" ("Euripides' *Antiope* and the Quiet Life," in *The Play of Texts and Fragments: Essays in Honor of Martin Cropp*, ed. J. R. C. Cousland and James R. Hume [Leiden: Brill, 2009]). The extent to which Zethus is an exact representative of Callicles is debated. Andrea Nightingale points to some apparent differences between Zethus and Callicles by noting that Callicles "does not suggest, as Zethus did, that the life he advocates is for the good of the city, for he would be hard pressed to prove that a self-seeking tyrant is good for a state." "Plato's 'Gorgias' and Euripides' 'Antiope': A Study in Generic Transformation," *Classical Antiquity* 11 no. 1 (1992): 127. However, Devin Stauffer argues convincingly that Callicles is not *simply* a self-seeking tyrant. See n. 53 above.

57. Nightingale, "Plato's 'Gorgias' and Euripides' 'Antiope,'" 127.

58. Nightingale, 128.

59. Gibert, "Euripides' *Antiope*," 34.

60. Specifically, Socrates states "what is akin is something other than the like" (*Lysis*, 222c3–4).

61. The notion that people may be good "in their own nature" is the good that Socrates misquotes in his quotation of the drinking song listing the various things that are said to be good.

62. McKim argues that Callicles does not have any of the three characteristics Socrates ascribes to him. "Shame and Truth," 40; Benardete argues that "Callicles has neither wisdom nor frankness, but he does seem to have goodwill." *Rhetoric of Morality and Philosophy*, 68. Stauffer suggests that "while it may be reasonable to take Callicles' speech as evidence of his outspokenness," he manifestly lacks wisdom, and likely goodwill as well. He concludes that Socrates may mean to indicate by his "proof" that Callicles does not possess what is necessary to pursue the truth

to its attainment, and thus that the truth will not come fully to light in their conversation." *The Unity of Plato's Gorgias*, 93–94; finally, E. R. Dodds holds that while Socrates is being ironic in calling Callicles wise, he genuinely believes that Callicles has goodwill toward him and is outspoken, but that this belief is mistaken.

63. Toward the end of the dialogue Callicles states, "In some way, I don't know what, what you say seems good to me, Socrates; but I suffer the experience of the many—I am not altogether persuaded by you" (513c). Plato's ambiguity in regard to Callicles's character, as well as the way in which Callicles is depicted as not being altogether impervious to Socrates's arguments, may point to Plato's hesitancy or skepticism regarding the relationship between Socrates's way of life and approach to politics.

64. Cf. Aristotle, *NE*, 1140a24–1140b30.

65. Cf. Aristotle, *NE*, 1158a1–1158a12, where Aristotle argues that goodwill is the necessary precursor to friendship, it is not a sufficient condition for the existence of friendship, as friendship requires spending time together. Seth Benardete suggests that the goodwill displayed by Callicles is akin to tolerance: "If push comes to shove, [Callicles] would not help Socrates; but his tolerance insofar as it represents the atmosphere of Athens, suffices to guarantee the survival of Socrates." *Rhetoric of Morality and Philosophy*, 69.

66. Stauffer, "Socrates and Callicles" 640–41. For this next portion of the chapter concerning Callicles's desire for a good that is independent of evil, I am indebted to Stauffer's insights.

67. Aristotle, at the end of book VII of the *Ethics*, seems to agree with Callicles: "Hence the god always enjoys a pleasure that is one and simple, for there is an activity not only of motion but also of motionlessness, and pleasure resides more in rest than in motion. But 'change in all things is sweet,' as the poet has it, on account of a certain defective condition. For just as the defective person is a human being who readily undergoes change, so also the nature in need of change is defective, for it is neither simple nor decent" (*NE* 1154b26–32).

68. Stauffer, "Socrates and Callicles," 644.

69. Stauffer argues that Callicles's desire for a such an unalloyed good indicates that Callicles is not a simple hedonist but has a commitment to virtue. "Socrates and Callicles," 645.

70. Cf. *Republic*, 382c–d. Commenting on this section of the dialogue, Seth Benardete notes, "Philosophy always says the same; Socrates does not." *Rhetoric of Morality and Philosophy*, 90.

71. Cf. *Republic*, 504d, where Socrates indicates that "there is something yet greater than justice."

72. Cf. *Republic*, 382d.

73. According to the myth, during the early portion of Zeus's rule, the fate of individual men was decided while they were still living, and it was decided by other living men. The result was that "the judgments were decided badly." Pluto, the

god of the underworld and those in charge of "the islands of the blessed" informed Zeus that the judges were deciding the fates wrongly and that "unworthy human beings were frequenting them in both places." To rectify this, Zeus ordered that going forward, the men being judged should be dead and naked. For under the previous practice, many "who have base souls are clothed in fine bodies, ancestry, and wealth." Furthermore, the judges were also previously clothed "with eyes and ears and the whole body, like a screen, covering their soul." The problem with the previous practice is that all these coverings—both those of the judges and those of the men being judged—stand in the way and result in poor judgments. Thus, by judging the soul alone, without any of the sensible accoutrements concealing its true state that, the judgments will be made correctly (Cf. 523a–524a).

Chapter Three

1. Nevertheless, as Susan Collins points out, "Aristotle's 'natural beginning' is a bit of a red herring: The city presents its justice as the natural completion of a human being, yet the city is not simply natural in one respect: It must be constituted." *Aristotle and the Rediscovery of Citizenship* (Cambridge: Cambridge University Press, 2006), 19. The fact that justice is not strictly speaking a natural end of the city is hinted at already in book I of the *Politics*. After suggesting that man's capacity for speech or reason is what sets him apart from other "herd animals," Aristotle states that this capacity "is what makes a household and a city" (1253a19). This, of course, suggests that the city is not *distinguished* from the household on account of justice and political virtue. At this point, the distinct end of the polis has not yet been revealed.

2. In a passage that mirrors the division of goods in *The Nicomachean Ethics*, Aristotle divides good things into three: property, the goods of the body, and the goods of the soul. Through a series of arguments, Aristotle concludes that the goods of the soul (i.e., virtue) are superior to other goods. Cf. *Politics*, 1323a24–1323b21.

3. Before turning to the merits and demerits of each life, Aristotle first distinguishes between two *types* of active, or political life. On the one hand, there is a life dedicated to ruling as a master over one's neighbors in a despotic fashion. On the other hand, there is rule in a "political fashion," which seems to be rule in accordance with law. Aristotle lays out three sets of opinions regarding the merits of these two types of active life. Some, Aristotle notes, believe neither type of rule is good; they maintain that while the tyrannical rule over one's neighbors is accompanied by great injustice, rule "in the political fashion" is simply "an impediment to one's own well-being" (1324a36–39). This first opinion encapsulates Socrates's position in the *Gorgias*. Others, Aristotle notes, hold that the "political life" is the only life for a man (1324a40–41). This opinion seems to encapsulate Callicles's assertion that the man who fails to engage in politics will never amount to much. Last, Aristotle

notes, are those who assert that "the mode of regime involving mastery and tyranny is the only happy one" (1324b3–4). Aristotle concludes that while the opinion that rule always involves mastery and tyranny is the most common and even accords with nature to some extent, this is not the city's highest aim. Aristotle will later explain that the city's ultimate aim is, instead, "the actualization and complete practice of virtue" through the institution of laws and education (1332a9–10).

4. Cf. *Gorgias*, 485d–e.

5. Collins, *Aristotle and the Rediscovery of Citizenship*, 116.

6. Collins, 116.

7. Robert Bartlett, "The 'Realism' of Classical Political Science," *American Journal of Political Science* 38 no. 2 (1994): 394.

8. If this conclusion is correct, it may well call into question Aristotle's description of man as a political animal. Indeed, if the end of man is different from the end of the city, it would seem that man is not by nature directed toward participation in the city.

9. Strauss, *The City and Man* (Chicago: University of Chicago Press, 1964), 29.

10. J. L. Ackrill, "Aristotle on *Eudaimonia*," in *Aristotle's Nicomachean Ethics*, ed. Otfried Höffe, trans. Fernbach (Leiden: Brill, 2010), 33–52; John Cooper, *Reason and the Human Good in Aristotle* (Cambridge, MA: Harvard University Press, 1975), 156–77; Thomas Nagel, "Aristotle on *Eudaimonia*," *Phronesis* 17 no. 3, (1972): 252–9; Henry Sidgwick, *Outlines of the History of Ethics for English Readers*, (Indianapolis, IN: Hackett, [1886], 1902),70.

11. See Bodéüs, *The Political Dimensions of Aristotle's "Ethics"*; Burger, *Aristotle's Dialogue with Socrates*; Jaffa, *Aristotelianism and Thomism*; Strauss, *The City and Man*; Tessitore, *Reading Aristotle's Ethics*.

12. See Burger, *Aristotle's Dialogue with Socrates*; Jaffa, *Aristotelianism and Thomism*; Strauss, *The City and Man*; Tessitore, *Reading Aristotle's Ethics*.

13. For example, Strauss writes, "When the philosopher Aristotle addresses his political science to more or less perfect gentlemen, he shows them as far as possible that the way of life of the perfect gentleman points toward the philosophic way of life; he removes a screen." *The City and Man*, 28. Similarly, Tessitore argues that "Aristotle attempts to offer guidance for those who are disposed to an active life of political involvement . . . [while] at the same time . . . point[ing] his most gifted students to . . . contemplate something of the radical and more fully satisfying character of the philosophic life." *Reading Aristotle's Ethics*, 20.

14. For example, Tessitore suggests that Aristotle's reflections on friendship have, "in the measure possible, prepared readers for his concluding endorsement of the rare but simply best way of life available to human beings. His subsequent demotion of the life of moral virtue in light of the superior happiness afforded by the contemplative pleasures of philosophy is perhaps less strange and less jarring because it is prefaced with a consideration of friendship." *Reading Aristotle's Ethics*, 95.

15. David Ross, *Aristotle*, 6th ed. (London: Routledge, 1995), 208.

16. Given Aristotle's famous dictum that the individual "who is in need of nothing through being self-sufficient is no part of a city, and so is either a beast or a god" (*Politics*, 1253a28–29), it would seem that any attempt to invoke the assistance of a magnanimous man who is unbounded by the conventions of the city is, at the very least, fraught with danger.

17. For an excellent rejoinder to the view that Aristotle's listing of the moral virtues in books III and IV is simply an account of the qualities admired by the Greeks during Aristotle's time, see Collins, *Aristotle and the Rediscovery of Citizenship*, 47–52.

18. Aristotle notes that of the five types of courage that merely resemble true courage, "this most closely resembles the courage [in the authoritative sense], because it arises through virtue, that is through a sense of shame and longing for what is noble (since it is for honor) and through avoiding reproach, since it is shameful" (1116a26–29).

19. Homer, *Iliad*, trans. A. T. Murray, vol. 2, (Cambridge, MA: Harvard University Press, 1924) 22:100.

20. Homer, vol. 1, 8:130.

21. W. F. R. Hardie, "'Magnanimity' in Aristotle's *Ethics*," *Phronesis* 23 no. 1, (1978): 63–79; Thomas Aquinas, *Summa Theologica*, trans. Fathers of the English Dominican Province (New York: Benziger Bros., 1948), II–II. Q. 129, Art. 1–3, and *Commentary on the Nicomachean Ethics*, trans. C. I. Litzinger (Chicago: Henry Regnery, 1964), vol. 1, lectures 8–11; Carson Holloway, "Aristotle's Magnanimous Man," in *Magnanimity and Statesmanship*, ed. Carson Holloway (Lanham, MD: Lexington, 2008), 13–28; Jaffa, *Aristotelianism and Thomism* (Chicago: University of Chicago Press, 1952), 121.

22. René Antoine Gauthier, *Magnanimité: L'Idéal de la grandeur dans la philosophie païenne et dans la théologie chrétienne*, (Paris: Vrin, 1951), 104–17; J. A. Stewart, *Notes on the Nicomachean Ethics of Aristotle* (Oxford: Clarendon Press, 1892), 1:334–46.

23. Hardie, "Magnanimity," 70.

24. Gauthier, *Magnanimité*, 106.

25. Tessitore, *Reading Aristotle's Ethics*, 33.

26. For a succinct overview of the debate about whether Aristotle's magnanimous man is a statesman/general or a philosopher, and about whether Aristotle finds fault with the magnanimous man, see Jacob Howland, "Aristotle's Great-Souled Man," *Review of Politics* 64 no. 1 (2002): 29.

27. Jaffa, *Aristotelianism and Thomism*, 140–41.

28. Holloway, "Shakespeare's *Coriolanus* and Aristotle's Great-Souled Man." *Review of Politics* 69 no. 3 (2007): 355.

29. Hardie, *Magnanimity*, 74.

30. I am indebted to Howland's article "Aristotle's Great-Souled Man" for the following discussion concerning Aristotle's reference to magnanimity in the

Posterior Analytics. My own account of Aristotle's discussion of magnanimity takes a similar starting point as that of Howland's—Aristotle views the magnanimous man as tragically flawed and he holds out friendship as the antidote to this flaw. However, my interpretation differs from Howland's in my conclusion regarding Aristotle's appraisal of Socrates.

31. All citations are taken from G. R. G. Mure's translation of Aristotle's *Posterior Analytics* in *The Basic Works of Aristotle*, ed. McKeon (New York: Random House, 1941).

32. While Aristotle provides evidence of the fact that Alcibiades, Achilles, and Ajax are intolerant of insults, he provides no similar evidence regarding the indifference to fortune displayed by Lysander and Socrates.

33. Howland, "Aristotle's Great-Souled Man," 35.

34. Tessitore, *Reading Aristotle's* Ethics, 32.

35. Sophocles, "Ajax," in *The Complete Greek Drama*, trans. R. C. Trevelyan, ed. Whitney J. Oates and Eugene O'Neill, Jr. (New York: Random House, 1938), 1:325.

36. Sophocles, 334.

37. Sophocles, 334.

38. Homer, *Iliad*, vol. 1, 1:160–245.

39. Homer, vol. 1, 9:165–665.

40. Homer, vol. 2, 16:20–45; 780–865.

41. On Alcibiades's failure to listen to Socrates's advice, see Andre Archie, "Listening to Plutarch's Alcibiades in Plato's *Alcibiades Major*," in *Politics in Socrates' Alcibiades: A Philosophical Account of Plato's Dialogue* Alcibiades Major" (New York: Springer, 2015), 101–21. Michael Gargin traces Alcibiades's political failures to Socrates's hubris. See "Socrates' 'Hybris' and Alcibiades' Failure," *Phoenix* 31 no. 1 (1977): 22–37.

42. Plutarch, "Alcibiades," in *The Lives of the Noble Grecians and Romans*, trans. John Dryden, rev. Arthur Hugh Clough (New York: Random House, 1864), 248–50.

43. Plutarch, "Lysander," in *Lives*, 525–26; Plato, *Apology*, 31b–c, 36d; and Xenophon, *Memorabilia*, 1.6. Jacob Howland argues against viewing their easy acceptance of poverty as the basis for Lysander's and Socrates's magnanimity because this trait "is hardly the basis on which one would pick out both Lysander and Socrates as great-souled men." "Aristotle's Great-Souled Man," 36.

44. Howland, "Aristotle's Great Souled Man," 36 ("A more adequate division would separate Socrates from Alcibiades, Achilles, Ajax, and Lysander. These four are all marked by the love of honor and the intolerance of dishonor, but Socrates shares neither trait; he is indifferent to good and bad fortune, and therefore also to the cards that fortune deals him with respect to honor and dishonor"). Lysander's inclusion with Socrates is confusing, given the fact that he does seem to have more in common with Alcibiades, Achilles, and Ajax. However, as I hope to make clear, if we follow Aristotle's instructions on how to come to a common definition,

it is possible to find a commonality between Lysander and Socrates: an ability to persevere in the face of the ill-fortune of an ignoble birth.

45. Tessitore, *Reading Aristotle's* Ethics, 32. Tessitore explains that while Plato never refers to magnanimity, "he does have Socrates speak of philosophic magnificence. As part of his account of philosophic virtue, Socrates explains that nothing human seems great, and that even death itself is not terrible for one who contemplates all being and all time (*Republic*, 486a–b)." Cf. *NE*, 1124b7–9 ("The great-souled man is not one to hazard trifling dangers and he is not a lover of danger either, since he honors few things. But he will hazard great dangers, and when he does so, he throws away his life, on the grounds that living is not at all worthwhile.").

46. For an account of Socrates's poverty and lowbirth see Eduard Zeller, *Socrates and the Socratic Schools*, trans. Oswald J. Reichel (London: Longmans, Green, and Co., 1877), 54, n. 1; Friedrich Nietzsche, *Twilight of the Idols or How to Philosophize with a Hammer*, trans. Duncan Large (Oxford: Oxford University Press, 1998), 11–12. For an account of the way Lysander's birth excluded him from rule in Sparta, see Plutarch, "Lysander," in *Lives*, 541.

47. In the *Apology*, Socrates relates that he is someone who has committed "no injustice," and that as a result of his manner of life he is worthy to be honored with free meals in the Prytaneum, an honor reserved for Olympic heroes (cf. *Apology*, 36d–37a).

48. In the *Apology* Socrates expresses surprise at the closeness of the verdict. After the jury finds him guilty, Socrates states, "Many things contribute to my not being indignant, men of Athens, at what has happened—that you voted to convict me—and one of them is that what has happened was not unexpected by me. But I wonder much more at the number of the votes on each side. For I at least did not suppose it would be by so little, but by much" (*Apology*, 35e–36a). Plato may be indicating that Socrates has underestimated the power of rhetoric.

49. In a passage detailing Lysander's plan to change the constitution, Plutarch relates that Lysander "first attempted and prepared to persuade the citizens privately. . . . Afterwards perceiving so unexpected and great an innovation required bolder means of support, he proceeded, as it might be on the stage, to avail himself of machinery, and to try the effects of divine agency upon his countrymen. He collected and arranged for his purpose answers and oracles from Apollo [so as to] first alarm and overpower the minds of his fellow-citizens by religious and superstitious terrors, before bringing them to the considerations of his arguments" (Plutarch, "Lysander" in *Lives*, 541). The parallel to Socrates's use of the Delphic oracle as recounted by Plato is striking. Socrates also first sought to persuade the citizens of Athens privately to care only for virtue, and eventually used the oracle at Delphi to persuade his fellow citizens. Cf., *Apology*, 36c.

50. Plutarch, "Lysander," 541.

51. Plutarch, 542.

52. Liddell and Scott, *Greek English Lexicon*, 22.

53. Liddell and Scott, 23.

54. Further indication that Aristotle intends the basis for the second type of magnanimity to be an ability to persevere in the face of misfortune is found in his description of the method one ought to employ when seeking to arrive at a "common universal" definition. After noting that it is important to avoid equivocation, Aristotle writes, "We may add that if dialectical disputation must not employ metaphors, clearly metaphors and metaphorical expressions are precluded in definition" (*Posterior Analytics*, 38–40). When describing Lysander and Socrates, Aristotle initially notes that they are both indifferent or steady (ἀδιάφοροι) in the face of good and bad fortune. Shortly after, he notes the same thing, but this time he uses the word ἀπάθεια instead of ἀδιάφοροι to describe their relation to fortune. To be "indifferent (ἀπάθεια) to poverty" is, according to Aristotle, a metaphorical expression. In the *Eudemian Ethics* Aristotle writes, "Again, the man that endures no pain, not even if it is good for him, is luxurious; one that can endure all pain alike is strictly speaking nameless, but by metaphor he is called hard, patient or enduring (κακοπαθητικός)" (*Eudemian Ethics* [*EE*], 2:1221a). The root of κακοπαθητικός is the same as that of ἀπάθεια. Thus, where Aristotle indicates that Lysander and Socrates are "indifferent to fortune," he cannot mean that they are "enduring" poverty, as this is a metaphorical expression and metaphorical expressions are "precluded in definition." We are left with the conclusion that when Aristotle states that Lysander and Socrates are indifferent (ἀδιάφοροι) to fortune, he means that they are capable of persevering in the face of adversity.

55. This is the very first characteristic Aristotle uses to describe the magnanimous man in *The Nicomachean Ethics*. Aristotle writes, "He, then, who deems himself worthy of great things and *is* worthy of them is held to be great souled" (*NE*, 1123b3–4).

56. Plutarch relates that when Lysander "had risen into great renown for his exploits, and had gained great friends and power, was vexed to see the city, which had increased to what it was by him, ruled by others not at all better descended than himself" "Lysander," 541. In the *Apology*, Socrates relates that he is capable of performing "the greatest benefaction" (*Apology*, 36c).

57. Socrates hints that he is well aware of the destructive tendency his way of life has. After the jury has sentenced him, he states, "For you have now done this deed supposing that you will be released from giving an account of your life, but it will turn out much the opposite for you, as *I* affirm. There will be more who will refute you, whom I have now been holding back; you did not perceive them. And they will be harsher inasmuch as they are younger, and you will be more indignant" (*Apology*, 39c–d).

58. Ryan Patrick Hanley, "Aristotle on the Greatness of Greatness of Soul," *History of Political Thought* 23 no. 1 (2002): 5.

59. Ryan Hanley, Carson Holloway, and Harry Jaffa all make this argument, albeit in different ways. Hanley notes, "It is not the magnanimous man but some

other in whose direction the magnanimous man merely nods who is independent of fortune altogether. . . . One has to wait until Book X of the *Ethics* to meet the fully self-sufficient man." "Aristotle on the Greatness of Greatness of Soul," 14–15. Holloway writes that the magnanimous man has a "deficiency" that stems from his "unfamiliarity with philosophy." "Aristotle's Magnanimous Man," 27. Jaffa states, "The traits which Aristotle ascribes to the magnanimous man are those which he evidently believes on the basis of observation actually do characterize the highest human type, as viewed within the dimension of morality. To measure this type by a higher standard is to transcend this dimension. But if we transcend this dimension we no longer see things as they appear within the dimension. The magnanimous man's world is in one respect at least like the world of the child." *Thomism and Aristotelianism*, 140.

60. Howland points out that "At *Iliad* 7.302, Ajax and Hector, having dueled, part 'in friendship.' Hector gives Ajax his sword and receives a belt in exchange. In Sophocles' *Ajax*, Ajax kills himself by falling on Hector's sword. This gesture points toward the death he should have died—death at the hands of his only equal, who is paradoxically both friend and enemy." "Aristotle's Great-Souled Man," 51 n. 40. I would add that this points toward the fact that true friendship can exist only between those who are similar to one another yet differ in point of virtue. Indeed, friendship between those who are identical is unlikely to develop, as neither is able to provide anything the other is lacking.

61. See for example Tessitore, *Reading Aristotle's Ethics*, 74; Smith, *Revaluing Ethics*, 195; Sensen, "On the Nature of Friendship in Aristotle's *Nicomachean Ethics*" in *The Arts of Rule: Essays in Honor of Harvey C. Mansfield*, ed. Sharon R. Krause and Mary Ann McGrail (Lanham, MD: Lexington Books, 2009), 43.

62. Anne Marie Dziob, "Aristotelian Friendship: Self-Love and Moral Rivalry," *The Review of Metaphysics*, 46, no. 4 (Jun. 1993), 798.

63. Patrick Cain and Mary Nichols, "Aristotle's Nod to Homer: A Political Science of Indebtedness," in *Socrates and Dionysius: Philosophy and Art in Dialogue*, ed. Ann Ward (Newcastle, UK: Cambridge Scholars Publishing, 2013), 61.

64. J. David Velleman, "Sociality and Solitude," *Philosophical Explorations* 16, no. 3 (2013): 324–35.

65. The entire line to which Aristotle cites provides further credence to this interpretation: "When two go together, one discerneth before the other how profit may be had; whereas if one alone perceive aught, yet is his wit the shorter, and but slender his device" (Homer. *Iliad*, trans. A. T. Murray. 2 vols. [Cambridge, MA: Harvard University Press, 1967], 10:220–30).

66. Homer, 10:247.

67. Homer, 10:465–540.

68. Some scholars have pointed to the violent nature of the *doloneia* to suggest that Aristotle's citation to the *Iliad* is meant to subtley call into question his encomium to friendship. For example, Ronna Burger relates that the "bloody night

raid" is "a strange choice if one wanted to pick out a single instance to illustrate as clearly as possible how companionship necessarily foster's noble deeds." "Hunting Together or Philosophizing Together: Friendship and *Eros* in Aristotle's *Nicomachean Ethics*," in *Love and Friendship: Rethinking Politics and Affection in Modern Times*, ed. Eduardo A. Velásquez, 37–60 (Lanham, MD: Lexington Books., 2003), 39–40. While it is true that the deeds of Diomedes and Odysseus cannot be described as good in an unqualified sense, this whole episode must be viewed from a political perspective. The night raid advances objectives of the Akhaians within the contingent world of politics, which requires prudential calculations and sacrifices. In the same way that the punishment of a criminal is not unqualifiedly good but can nevertheless be understood to serve the common good, the actions of Diomedes and Odysseus can be said to be in service of the common good.

69. This is made clear in both the *Eudemian Ethics* and the *Magna Moralia*, in which Aristotle provides a brief commentary on the statement by Empedocles that "like aims at like." Aristotle writes in the *Eudemian Ethics*: "The natural philosophers also arrange the whole of nature taking as a principle the movement of like to like; that is why Empedocles said that the bitch sat on the tile, because it had the greatest similarity" (*EE*, 1235a10–12), as quoted in Brad Inwood, *The Poem of Empedocles*, trans. Brad Inwood (Toronto: University of Toronto Press, 1992), 159. Similarly, he writes in the *Magna Moralia*: "They say that there was once a bitch who always slept on the same piece of tile, and when Empedocles was asked *why* the bitch slept on the same piece of tile he said that the bitch was in some way similar to the tile, as though the similarity caused the bitch to go to the tile" (*Magna Moralia* [*MM*], 1208b11–15), as quoted in Inwood, *The Poem of Empedocles*, 159. Finally, near the middle of book VIII of *The Nicomachean Ethics*, at a portion of the argument where Aristotle again lapses into a discussion of nature, Aristotle states, "Yet perhaps one opposite does not aim at the other opposite in itself, except incidentally. Rather, the longing involved is for the middle term, since this is good" (*NE*, 1159b19–21).

70. Further bolstering the possibility that Aristotle views Socrates's inquiry in the *Lysis* to be deficient is the fact that in the entirety of the *Ethics*, the only other time Empedocles is mentioned is in the context of book VII. Here Aristotle explicitly critiques the Socratic thesis that "no one acts contrary to what is best while supposing that he is so acting" (1145b26–27). In this discussion, Aristotle notes that a person who knows the words of something, but is ignorant of what they mean, "merely speaks, as a drunk man states the sayings of Empedocles" (1147b12–13). It may be that Aristotle is suggesting that while Socrates knows the sayings of Empedocles, he fails to understand them. Of course, as we've seen, in the *Lysis* Socrates himself raises the possibility that he does not fully understand the saying "like aims at like." Of the possibility that friendship exists between those who are alike, he states, "Then do you also happen to have come across the writings of the wisest ones . . . namely that what is like is always necessarily a friend to its like?

And they, I suppose, are the ones who converse and write about nature and the whole." Socrates goes on to say that these "wisest ones" may "speak well . . . only we don't understand them" (*Lysis*, 214bff). It was noted above that Plato suggests that Socrates's understanding of friendship is deficient due to his failure to understand the writings of "the wise" (οἱ σοφοί), who inquire into nature and the whole. As Aristotle's discussion of friendship will show, it is precisely this third definition espoused by Empedocles that is capable of elevating friendship from a relationship based on mere necessity to one in which two friends love one another on account of each other's goodness.

71. Aristotle may also be subtly critiquing Socrates's inquiry into friendship by characterizing these possible definitions of friendship as "perplexing questions bound up with matters of nature." As noted above, Aristotle was aware that Socrates "neglect[ed] the world of nature as a whole but [sought] the universal in . . . ethical matters" (*Metaphysics*, 987b1–3).

72. Note that in book II the noble is something that is an object of choice.

73. In contrast to my interpretation, Lorraine Pangle argues that Aristotle is "not making any claim that the simply good is good in some absolute way, wholly apart from its being good or pleasant *for* something, if only for itself." As evidence, she points to the fact that Aristotle includes the pleasant in this discussion, and notes that "it would be absurd to speak of something as being intrinsically pleasant if it were not pleasant for anyone." *Aristotle on Friendship*, 38. However, Aristotle discusses the intrinsically pleasant in book VII of the *Ethics*, where he notes that the existence of the gods is intrinsically pleasant. Specifically, he writes, "Yet the same thing is not always pleasant on account of our nature's not being simple. Rather, something else is present in us as well (hence we are subject to destruction) such that when the one part acts, this is contrary to nature with respect to the other nature; and when both are equally balanced, the action performed seems to be neither painful not pleasant. For if someone's nature were simple, the same actions would always be most pleasant. Hence the god always enjoys a pleasure that is one and simple, for there is an activity not only of motion but also of motionlessness, and pleasure resides more in rest than in motion" (1154b21–28). I suggest that in the same way that the intrinsically pleasant is available only to the gods, so the intrinsically good is also available only to the gods.

74. Laughter is, of course, not a convincing form of refutation (cf. *Gorgias*, 473e1–3). This suggests that Aristotle's full explanation regarding the role that reciprocity plays in friendship has yet to be revealed.

75. Becoming aware of another's existence will prove to be major theme in book IX, in which Aristotle reveals how one becomes a friend to another.

76. Aristotle is quick to add that "friendships of this sort are likely to be rare, since people of this sort are few. Further, there is also need of the passage of time and the habits formed by living together" (1156b25–26). He concludes this chapter with what may be taken as a subtle critique of Socrates's and Callicles's declaration of

friendship in the *Gorgias* (cf. *Gorgias*, 485e3; 485c1; 499c2–5): "Those who swiftly make proofs of friendship to each other wish to be friends but are not such unless they are also loveable and know this about each other. For a wish for friendship arises swiftly, but friendship itself does not" (*NE*, 1156b30–33).

77. This language mirrors Aristotle's discussion of what it is that happiness consists of in book I. In book I Aristotle writes, "The argument, then, is in harmony with those who say that [happiness] is virtue or a certain virtue, for the activity in accord with virtue belongs to virtue. But perhaps it makes no small difference whether one supposes the best thing to reside in possession or use, that is, in a characteristic or an activity" (*NE*, 1098b30–33). This, of course, sets up the fundamental distinction between the moral virtues and the intellectual virtues that undergirds much of the rest of the treatise.

78. At this point, Aristotle is responding also to Socrates's ambiguity in the *Gorgias* regarding the relationship between the good and the pleasant. While Aristotle does not come to a definitive conclusion here, his discussion anticipates his fuller discussion of the difficulty in book X.

79. Cf. *NE*, 1155b25–30; *Lysis*, 212d6–10.

80. Aristotle notes, however, that "people also wish for good things for those who are loved, for the sake of the loved ones themselves, not in reference to a passion but in accord with a characteristic" (1157b32–34). This suggests that even the "active" partner loves not solely in an egotistical way ordered solely towards pleasure, but also for the sake of the other, in so far as the other is good.

81. At this point Aristotle finally answers the Socratic inquiry regarding the reciprocity of friendship.

82. This conclusion points to a further difficulty: the relative inequality of the virtues. The virtue of wisdom (i.e., philosophic virtue) is superior to that of prudence and the moral virtues (i.e., political virtue) (cf. 1143b18–1145a11); for further discussion regarding the superiority of wisdom over prudence, see Richard Bodéüs, "The Gods as Objects of Imitation," in *Aristotle and the Theology of Living Immortals*, trans. Jan Garrett (New York: State University of New York Press, 2000), 168–79. If "friendship is equality," as Aristotle states, how could the wise philosopher and the prudent statesman befriend one another? The answer is hinted at in the following chapter. Aristotle will state that superiority in a point of power can render its practitioner equal to a serious person who exceeds him in virtue (1158a35).

Chapter Four

1. In discussing the giving and receiving of benefits, Aristotle picks up on a theme that he had touched upon in book IV's depiction of the magnanimous man: "[The magnanimous man] is also the sort to benefit others but is ashamed to receive a benefaction; for the former is a mark of one who is superior, the latter

of one who is inferior. He is disposed to return a benefaction with a greater one, since in this way the person who took the initiative [with the original benefaction] will owe him in addition and will have also fared well thereby" (1124b9–13). The magnanimous man's attitude toward the giving and receiving of benefits is rooted in a concern with his own superiority. This attitude initially appears to be at odds with Aristotle's understanding of friendship, which entails an appreciation of the other for his own sake. Book IX of the *Ethics* should be read as Aristotle's attempt to reconcile the magnanimous man's concern with his own superiority with the description of friendship in book VIII.

2. This distinction is made clear both by the concluding sentence of book VIII and by the introductory phrase of book IX. Book VIII concludes: "Let what concerns these matters, then, be spoken of to this extent" (1163b28). "These matters" refers to "homogeneous friendships," or friendships in which both parties to the friendship seek the same goal—for example, usefulness or pleasure. The opening line of book IX reiterates the intention to leave homogeneous relationships behind: "In all heterogeneous friendships, what is proportional equalizes and preserves the friendship" (1163b33–34). Thus, broadly construed, the subject matter of book IX is that of heterogeneous friendships, or friendships in which each party seeks a different goal.

3. Michael Pakaluk notes that this friendship is, strictly speaking, a homogeneous friendship, as both parties seek what is useful. He asserts that Aristotle likely introduces this example by way of contrast with the types of friendship that are to follow. *Aristotle: Nicomachean Ethics Books VIII and IX* (Oxford: Clarendon Press, 1998), 149.

4. In book V, Aristotle notes that the exchange of wares occurs due to the prompting of necessity. Necessity, he argues, prompts people to come together in order to undertake exchange. As a result, an object's worth is measured by necessity, and money acts as the medium of exchange that is capable of equalizing disparate things that have different values (1133a25–b18). Nevertheless, Aristotle states—almost in passing—that some things have their basis in something other than necessity and are incapable of being equalized in this way: "Now in truth, it is impossible for things that differ greatly from one another to become commensurable, but it is possible, to a sufficient degree, in relation to need" (1133b19–21). This may suggest that necessity does not hold *all* things together; some relationships have their basis in something other than necessity and, as such, are beyond being made commensurable via the virtue of justice. In this way, book V's discussion of justice points toward Aristotle's discussion of friendship in books VIII and IX.

5. While Aristotle's evaluation of Protagoras's art is beyond the scope of this project, his distinction between Protagoras and those whom he terms the "Sophists" is striking.

6. Hostility toward philosophers on the part of the political authorities in ancient Greece is well documented, and charges of impiety were brought against

multiple philosophers, including Aristotle himself. Diogenes Laertius, *Lives of Eminent Philosophers*, ed. Jeffrey Henderson, trans. R. D. Hicks (Cambridge, MA: Harvard University Press, 1972), 5.5–8; Peter Ahrensdorf, "The Question of Historical Context and the Study of Plato," Polity 27, no. 1 (1994): 113–32. Less appreciated is the extent to which some philosophers went out of their way to criticize established customs and authorities. Diogenes Laertius relates that many philosophers challenged the established customs and authorities of the time, while the more outspoken of them would hold the authorities in outright disdain (Laertius, Lives 6:38–40 and 9.61–65).

7. Precisely what it means to teach someone the "the political art" and how to become a "good citizen" is not made entirely clear at this point, but Aristotle intimates at various points in the *Ethics* that it means to actualize the potential of an aspiring rule that he may become a statesman worthy of honor (1168a19–22; 1170b11–14; 1180b29–1181a13). In addition, Aristotle also makes clear that the philosopher might also provide more utilitarian benefits for the politician (*Politics*, 1259a5–35).

8. In this way, Aristotle, like Aristophanes, is critical of philosophers who have their heads in the clouds, unaware that they have obligations to their political community. For an analysis of Aristophanes's criticism of Socrates in this regard, see Mary Nichols, *Socrates and the Political Community: An Ancient Debate* (New York: State University of New York Press, 1987), 1–28.

9. According to Aristotle's depiction of magnanimity in book IV of the *Ethics*, to the extent that a philosopher overvalues his self-worth he would fail to be magnanimous. Rather than aiming at and achieving the mean with regard to self-worth, such a philosopher would be guilty of the vice of vanity (cf. 1123b8–9).

10. The difference in approach may be due to the audience Aristotle is addressing. In the first portion of the *Ethics* Aristotle is directing his writing primarily to the politically inclined gentlemen (καλοικάγαθοι), who may initially be suspicious of philosophy. Thus, in order to convince the καλοσκάγαθος to give up what is "his own," Aristotle needs to hold out the possibility of an "objective account" of things. In contrast, in the second half of the *Ethics*, Aristotle seems to be directing his writing to the philosopher who does not need to be reminded of the possibility of obtaining an "objective view" of things. Instead, the philosopher needs to be reminded that he may *not* have such an objective view of things. The political character of Aristotle's audience in the first portion of the *Ethics* is suggested by his remarks on method: "Perhaps it is necessary for us, at least, to begin from the things known to us [i.e., the familiar]. Hence, he who will listen adequately to the noble and just things, and to the political things generally, must be brought up nobly by means of habituation" (*NE*, 1095b3–6). Aristotle's audience is presupposed to have had a noble education. In the second half of the *Ethics*, after stating that it is necessary to "make another beginning" at the outset of book VII (1145a15), Aristotle provides another description of his method: "after positing the phenomena

and first raising perplexities about them, one ought in this way to bring to light especially all the received opinions about these experiences or, failing that, the greatest number and most authoritative of those opinions. For if the vexing questions are solved and the received opinions remain standing as well, then the matter would be adequately explained" (1145b1–7). In what follows, Aristotle engages with several sophistic arguments that would engage his philosophic audience (1146a23–30). For a discussion concerning Aristotle's intended audience, see Tessitore, *Reading Aristotle's Ethics*, as well as Richard Bodéüs, *The Political Dimensions of Aristotle's Ethics*. While Bodéüs contends that Aristotle's primary audience is the lawgiver, whom he hopes to serve by "providing him knowledge of the best political or constitutional rules" (p. 39), Tessitore remarks that Aristotle has a dual audience, comprising of both "non-philosophers and potential philosophers" (p. 20).

11. Ann Ward, *Contemplating Friendship*, 120–23; Lorraine Smith Pangle, *Aristotle and the Philosophy of Friendship*, 135–37; Delba Winthrop, "Aristotle and Theories of Justice," *American Political Science Review*, 72 no. 4 (December 1978): 1214.

12. Ann Ward, *Contemplating Friendship in Aristotle's Ethics* (Albany, NY: State University of New York Press, 2016), 122.

13. Ward, 122.

14. Ward, 122.

15. Aristotle's coyness in this regard stands in stark contrast to Plato's portrayal of Socrates in the *Apology*, where he states—perhaps facetiously—that he ought to be honored in the Prytaneum. (See, Plato, *Apology*, 36e–37a.)

16. Richard Kraut, *Aristotle on the Human Good* (Princeton, NJ: Princeton University Press, 1989), 138.

17. In book IV of *The Republic* Socrates contends that the perfectly just man can be a friend to himself: the just man "arranges himself, becomes his own friend, and harmonizes the three parts [of his soul], exactly like three notes in a harmonic scale. . . . And if there are some other parts in between, he binds them together and becomes entirely one from many" (*Republic*. 443c–e).

18. See for example John Burnet, *The Ethics of Aristotle* (London: Meuthen and Co., 1900), 413. Burnet concludes that Aristotle's argument at this point is "purely dialectical." Both Lorraine Smith Pangle and Aristide Tessitore raise the question as to whether Aristotle views such a friendship as meaningful, but both maintain that Aristotle holds such friendship as possessing a "certain plausibility." Tessitore, *Reading Aristotle's Ethics*, 84; Pangle, *Aristotle and the Philosophy of Friendship*, 153. For a contrary perspective, see Fred Schollmier, *Other Selves: Aristotle on Personal and Political Friendship* (Albany, NY: State University of New York Press, 1994), 53–62; Alexander Grant, *The Ethics of Aristotle*, 4th ed., vol. 2 (London: Longmans, Green, and Co., 1885), 290.

19. The transition from chapter four to chapter five indicates that this may be Aristotle's intention. At the end of chapter four, after having warned that the base

person only seeks to spend time with others so as to escape their own misery, Aristotle tells the reader he must "flee corruption with the utmost effort and attempt to be decent, since in this way he would both be disposed toward himself in a friendly way and become a friend to another" (1166b27–29). In turn, chapter five focuses on good will, which Aristotle defines as "the beginning of friendship" (1167a3).

20. Peter Hadreas, "Εὔνοια: Aristotle on the Beginning of Friendship," *Ancient Philosophy*, 15, no. 2 (Fall 2002): 398.

21. Aristotle's statement raises the question of whether two philosophers will be capable of friendship. In book I, Aristotle notes that he and Plato are friends, but he quickly indicates that it is not necessarily on the basis of their shared philosophic insight (see 1096a11ff). For a contrary perspective finding the basis of Aristotelian friendship to be shared philosophic dialogue, see Burger "Hunting Together or Philosophizing Together," 37–60; Burger, *Aristotle's Dialogue with Socrates*, 183–89.

22. Pangle, *Aristotle and the Philosophy of Friendship*, 157.

23. Aristotle's example also points to a difficulty that will have to be overcome if those who are philosophically magnanimous are to become friends with the politically magnanimous: how will these two individuals, both of whom believe themselves deserving of the greatest honors, decide who ought to rule? This difficulty is addressed, and a solution provided, in chapter 8 of book IX.

24. In book I of the *Metaphysics*, Aristotle provides a further subtle critique of Socrates's interpretation of the phrase "like to like." He writes that "if we were to follow out the view of Empedocles and interpret it according to its meaning and not to its lisping expression, we should find that friendship is the cause of good things, and strife of bad" (*Metaphysics*, 985a3–6). Aristotle may be implying that Socrates's interpretation of Empedocles's view is insufficient.

25. Aristotle's view seems to be similar to that of Protagoras as depicted by Plato in the *Protagoras* (cf. *Protagoras*, 323a4–328c3).

26. Edward C. Halper, *The One and the Many in Aristotle's Metaphysics: The Central Books* (Ohio, IN: Ohio State University Press, 1989), 206. Interestingly, the Megaric position is also described—but not mentioned by name—in the second and third chapters of book VII of the *Ethics*. Here the position is described in the context of a discussion concerning self-restraint. Aristotle asks how it could be the case that "a person, though he forms a correct conviction, lacks self-restraint" (1145b22–23). He goes on to note that on account of this puzzle, Socrates denied that a person "who has scientific knowledge [could] lack self-restraint" (1145b23). The Socratic position holds instead that "nobody acts contrary to what is best while supposing that he is so acting; he acts instead through ignorance" (1145b26–27). This position is identical to the Megaric position; both suppose that when a person has a capacity (in this case, knowledge), he must exercise it; both deny the existence of potentiality. Aristotle rejects this position in chapter three of book VII: "Since we say 'to know' in two senses—both the person who has the science but is not using and he who uses it are said to know—it will make a difference whether someone

who does what he ought not do has the relevant knowledge but is not actively contemplating it, or whether he is actively contemplating it" (1147b31–34). Thus, Aristotle's position differs from Socrates in that he maintains that one can have knowledge but fail actively to exercise it.

27. Halper, *The One and the Many*, 206; Cf. *Metaphysics*, 1047b14–30.

28. This discussion mirrors Aristotle's account in book II of the *Ethics* of the manner in which the intellectual and moral virtues come into being. Aristotle writes, "Both the coming-into-being and increase of intellectual virtue result mostly from teaching—hence it requires experience and time—whereas moral virtue is the result of habit. . . . Neither by nature, therefore, nor contrary to nature are the virtues present; they are instead present in us who are of such a nature as to receive them, and who are completed through habit. Further, in the case of those things present in us by nature, we are first provided with the capacities (δυνάμεις) associated with them, then later on display the activities (ἐνεργείας)" (1103a14–18). Aristotle is clear that while the intellectual and moral virtues come into being through habit and teaching, we have the capacity (δύναμις) for them by nature.

29. Aristotle uses temperature and health as an example of this process at a variety of different places. See for example *Metaphysics*, 1046b18–20, "The wholesome makes health alone, the heat-making potency heat, and the cold-making potency cold" as quoted in Halper, *The One and the Many*, 204; *Physics*, 201a19–24, "The same thing, if it is of a certain kind, can be both potential and fully real, not indeed at the same time or not in the same respect, but e.g. potentially hot and actually cold. Hence at once such things will act and be acted on by one another in many ways: each of them will be capable at the same time of causing alteration and of being altered."

30. Aristotle ends book IX with the same observation in the context of a warning regarding the friendship of base people: "Now the friendship of base people is corrupt: they share in base things and, being unsteady, they come to be corrupt by becoming like one another. But the friendship of decent people is decent and is increased by their associating with one another. They also seem to become better by engaging in activity together and by correcting one another, for they take an imprint from one another of the qualities they find pleasing. Hence the saying, "noble things from noble people" (1172a9–14).

31. Leo Strauss observes that "Aristotle's political science is an attempt to actualize [the gentleman's] potentiality. The gentleman affected by philosophy is in the highest case the enlightened statesman, like Pericles who was affected by Anaxagoras." *The City and Man*, 28.

32. Lorraine Smith Pangle questions why Aristotle begins with courage: "Does [Aristotle] begin with courage because it is traditionally the core meaning of virtue or *arete*? . . . Or is it, to the contrary, because courage is the noblest and most splendid of all . . . ? In beginning with courage, Aristotle begins where the traditional gentleman does without imposing more clarity on his priorities than he

finds there, but with a gentle persistence in querying those priorities." "The Anatomy of Courage in Aristotle's *Nicomachean Ethics,*" *Review of Politics* 80 no. 4 (2018): 571. The fact that Aristotle begins with courage may be explained by his depiction of the development of friendship. In his account of friendship, Aristotle states that goodwill—the beginning and prerequisite condition of friendship—arises "on account of virtue and a certain decency, whenever someone appears to another as noble or courageous or some such thing" (Cf. *NE,* 1167a18–20).

33. While a full investigation of justice is beyond this project, the virtue of justice is also incomplete and points toward friendship.

34. In its most real or highest form, νοῦς is pure actuality, or divine thought thinking itself (Cf. *Metaphysics,* 1072a1–29).

35. Martin Heidegger notes, "Aristotle calls this νοῦς: ὁ καλούμενος τῆς ψυχῆς νοῦς, the "so-called" νοῦς, which means the non-genuine νοῦς." *Plato's Sophist,* trans. Richard Rojcewicz and André Schuwer (Bloomington: Indiana University Press, 1997), 41.

36. Heidegger, 41.

37. The distinction between knowledge attained by pure intellection and knowledge attained through discursive reason is taken up by Thomas Aquinas who makes the case that the angels' knowledge of the truth is obtained through intellection, while man makes use primarily of discursive reason. Aquinas, *Summa Theologica,* I, 58, 3.

38. This translation is adopted from David Corey, "Voegelin and Aristotle on Nous: What is Noetic Political Science?" *Review of Politics* 63, no. 1 (2002): 64–65. Corey's article provides helpful introduction to the operation of νοῦς and on its role in developing the field of political science.

39. Heidegger, *Plato's Sophist,* 110.

40. Heidegger writes, "In Greek geometry the triangle is the ultimate, most elementary plane figure, which emerges out of the polygon by means of a Διαγράφειν, 'writing through.' Διαγράφειν analyzes the polygons until they are taken apart in simple triangles, in such a way that the triangles are the ἔσχατα [outermost limit] where the διαιρεῖν stops. In αἴσθησις, as it occurs in geometry, I see the triangle at one stroke as the most original element, which cannot itself be resolved again into more elementary figures" *Plato's Sophist,* 110–11.

41. Notably, Aristotle distinguishes perception itself from prudence. He writes, "Prudence is concerned with the ultimate particular thing, of which there is not a science but rather a perception, and a perception not of things peculiar to one of the senses, but a perception of the sort by which we perceive that the ultimate particular thing, in mathematics, is a triangle. For here too there will be a stop. But this is perception rather more than prudence, though perception of a form different from that [of one of the senses]" (1142a27–32). Thus, Aristotle conceives perception to be the element of pure onlooking, divorced from action, while φρόνησις involves both the onlooking and the action that follows it.

42. Heidegger, *Plato's Sophist*, 111.

43. Heidegger, 111.

44. Another distinction between φρόνησις and σοφία is that φρόνησις is ordered toward action—that is, it is ordered towards an end beyond itself. In contrast, σοφία contains the end *within* its own activity; contemplation is good for its own sake. As Aristotle will argue explicitly in book X, the very practice, or activity, of contemplation makes one happy or εὐδαίμων. In contrast, φρόνησις, or the intellectual grasping of any given situation that is ordered towards action, is oriented toward bringing this happiness into existence. In this way, φρόνησις is ordered towards an end beyond itself, while σοφία is not. Σοφία is, therefore, architectonic, in that it posits the end for which φρόνησις acts. This same relation between σοφία and the practical affairs governed by φρόνησις is evident in the Thomistic tradition: "wisdom belongs first of all contemplation which is the vision of the Beginning, and afterwards the direction of human acts according to the Divine rules." (*Summa Theologica* [ST] II–II Q. 45 *Art.* 3, *Rep. to Obj.* 3). However, in the Thomistic tradition, φρόνησις, which directs human actions, is governed also by the faculty of *synderesis*, which is absent in Aristotle (*ST* II–II Q. 47 *Art.* 6, *Rep. to Obj.* 3).

45. In the *Politics* Aristotle indicates his disagreement with the conclusion that philosophy is useless by recounting the story told about Thales, who was able to use his knowledge of astronomy to predict a good harvest of olives. Using this knowledge, Thales cornered the olive market by buying up all the olive presses while the olives were out of season. In turn, on the advent of the olive season, he was able to hire out the olive presses for whatever rates he wished. Thales, Aristotle concludes, showed "how easy it is for philosophers to become wealthy if they so wish, but it is not this they are serious about" (*Politics*, 1259a18–19). This example further supports the interpretation outlined above; in book VI of the *Ethics* Aristotle exaggerates the conventional image that people have of philosophers in order to present them in a nonthreatening, almost buffoonish, manner.

46. Cf., *Republic*, 592a7–592b7.

47. Aristotle further notes that the argument "seems to be inconsistent with the sciences" because the various sciences are not concerned with the "knowledge of the good itself." Nevertheless, he concludes, "It is not reasonable for *all* craftsmen to be ignorant of so great an aid and not even to seek it out" (1097a3–7). Aristotle seems to suggest that this pattern of the good may be useful for select few—perhaps one or two—types of craftsmen.

48. In book XII of the *Metaphysics* Aristotle describes the pure activity of the divine νοῦς: "[The First Mover has] a life such as the best which we enjoy, and enjoy for but a short time (for it is ever in this state, which we cannot be) since its actuality is also pleasure. (And for this reason are waking, perception, and thinking most pleasant, and hopes and memories are so on account of these.)" (1072b14–17). For Aristotle, the god, in contrast to human beings, *is* able to undertake action that

is both continuous and pleasurable. Furthermore, the complete activities for which human beings have the capacity—waking, perception, and thinking—are related to the complete activity of the First Mover due to the pleasure involved in these activities. It seems that by engaging in activities such as waking, perception, and thinking (activities that have no end apart from itself), we are—to an extent—able to share in the unqualified pleasure enjoyed by the First Mover or divine νοῦς.

49. Robert Bartlett and Susan Collins note that the term defective (πονέρια) is "usually translated as 'wickedness'; [Aristotle] may here be playing on the fact that the term has both a moral and a nonmoral use." *Aristotle's Nicomachean Ethics*, 162 n. 62.

50. The quotation is taken from Euripides's *Orestes*. In the play, Orestes is suffering from madness brought on by the furies, who are exacting punishment on him for murdering his mother. The line, "change in all things is sweet" is spoken by his sister Electra, who is tending to him and encouraging him to rise from his bed. Orestes responds, "That will I; for that has a semblance of health; and that seeming, though it be far from the reality, is preferable to this" (Euripides, *Orestes*, 235). Aristotle may be suggesting that in response to the painful awareness of the fact that the life of the god is beyond our reach, it is best to embrace the world of appearances, which, though far from reality, can ease our sufferings.

51. Lorraine Smith Pangle, "Friendship and Self-Love in Aristotle's *Nicomachean Ethics*," in *Action and Contemplation: Studies in the Moral and Political Thought of Aristotle*, ed. Robert C. Bartlett and Susan D. Collins (Albany: State University of New York Press, 1999), 198.

52. Pangle, 198.

53. Aristotle's understanding of existence can profitably be contrasted with René Descartes's famous "Cogito, ergo sum." While Descartes's interaction with the sensual world stems from an attitude of skepticism, in which our existence is revealed to us through the use of our mind alone, Aristotle affirms that it is through sense perception that we come to be aware of our existence. Cf. René Descartes, *Meditations, Objections, and Replies*, ed. and trans. by Roger Ariew and Donald Cress (Indianapolis: Hackett Publishing Company, 2006), 14–15.

54. In book VIII, Aristotle had indicated that it is through the exchange of what is good and pleasant that partners in friendship are made equal: "Each one, then, both loves what is good for himself and repays in equal measure what they wish for the other and what is pleasant. For it is said, 'friendship is equality' " (1157b35–37).

55. The equality that characterizes the relationship between the philosopher and the statesman is an equality of returns and not an equality of status. Aristotle intimates that the return one obtains can have the effect of equalizing a relationship that is inherently unequal in status in his discussion of the friendships that exist in the household. He explains that while no amount of affection by a child could make up for the "greatest benefits" that a parent bestows on the child, parents

nevertheless "love children as they love themselves," and that this friendship affords "both what is pleasant and what is useful" (1161b27–34). Thus, it seems that the delight derived from watching an inferior whom one has benefitted in some way is what sustains the relationship. Aristotle also makes clear that pleasure is something whole and complete.

56. Thomas W. Smith, *Revaluing Ethics: Aristotle's Dialectical Pedagogy* (Albany: State University of New York Press, 2001), 118–19.

57. Collins, *Aristotle and the Rediscovery of Citizenship*, 63.

58. See for example Burger, *Aristotle's Dialogue with Socrates*; Pangle, *Aristotle and the Philosophy of Friendship*; Tessitore, *Reading Aristotle's Ethics*.

59. Toward the end of the *Ethics*, Aristotle writes that the political and warlike actions are "without leisure and aim at some end . . . whereas the activity of the intellect [νοῦς], because it is contemplative [θεωρητική], seems to be superior in seriousness" (1177b17–21). On this basis, some have concluded that the life of philosophic contemplation is the only life that is happy in the primary sense. However, "θεωρητική" can also mean "able to perceive." Liddell and Scott, *Greek English Lexicon*, 797. Thus, Aristotle seems to be suggesting that *both* the life of the enlightened statesman and that of the philosopher are characterized by leisure.

60. The friendship between the philosopher and the statesman can also be described as the efficient cause of the polis, as it is the "primary source of the change" between the pre-political and the political state. Mapping the establishment of the polis onto Aristotle's fourfold classification of causes is difficult, "for 'cause' is used in many senses and even within the same kind one may be prior to another" (*Physics*, 194b29–30; 195a29–31).

61. Sarah Broadie, *Ethics with Aristotle* (Oxford: Oxford University Press, 1991), 339.

62. Despite many similarities, significant differences remain between the two accounts of pleasure. Perhaps the most significant discrepancy is that Aristotle seems to provide different definitions of pleasure in the two accounts. In book VII, he concludes that pleasure is an "unimpeded activity" of "the characteristic that accords with nature" (1153a13–14). In contrast, in book X, we are told that pleasure "completes the activity, not as a characteristic that is already inherent in it, but as a certain end that supervenes on it" (1174b33–34). These seem to be contradictory understandings of what pleasure is. As a result, some scholars have concluded that these two accounts are incompatible. According to this interpretation, Aristotle's description of pleasure in book X is simply hortatory, while his account of pleasure in book VII contains his more complete treatment of pleasure. See Smith, *Revaluing Ethics*, 233–45; Aristide Tessitore, "A Political Reading of Aristotle's Treatment of Pleasure in the *Nicomachean Ethics*," *Political Theory* 17 (1989): 247–65.

However, it is not the case that these accounts of pleasure are necessarily contradictory. If we view book X not as providing a definition of the *nature* of pleasure, but instead as a *description* of the way in which we experience pleasure, the two accounts are perfectly compatible. Indeed, in book VII, the definition that pleasure is an "unimpeded" activity suggests that the nature of pleasure—that is, pleasure in its most pure, active form—is the pleasure of contemplation practiced by the god. Given our status as embodied creatures, Aristotle had indicated that our capacity to enjoy such pleasures is limited. As I made clear earlier, this pure, active form of pleasure is presented by Aristotle as a sort of pattern, or model on which we may model our own lives. In book X, we are told *how* one may pursue that pattern or model. By suggesting that pleasure "completes the activity, not in the manner of a characteristic that is already inherent in it, but as a certain end that supervenes on it," Aristotle indicates that it is by pursuing whatever activity accords with our nature that we will experience pleasure. In this way, Aristotle's description of the manner in which we experience pleasure is carefully stated. Thus, while Aristotle's account of pleasure in book X is hortatory in the sense that it compels people to pursue what is good, it is not therefore false or incompatible with his account of pleasure in book VII.

63. In book I, Aristotle writes that "the good will not be good to a greater degree by being eternal either, if in fact whiteness that lasts a long time will not be whiter than that which lasts only a day" (1096b3–4).

64. Viewing the *Ethics* in this way establishes its relationship with the *Politics*, in which Aristotle discusses how regimes can be maintained and reformed. See *Politics*, 1288b21–40.

65. Cf. *Apology*, 38a2–4.

66. Homer, *Odyssey*, ed. Louise Ropes Loomis, trans. Samuel Butler (Roslyn, NY: Walter Black, 1944), 9.105–110.

67. Richard Bodéüs argues that Aristotle's primary purpose in this passage is to align the private education with the public education of the regime. He writes, "Aristotle's injunction upon the heads of household should be understood primarily as providing a way to align children's education, via paternal authority, with the principles of the laws which determine the development of the political community to which the children belong. Thus is removed the possible discontinuity between the household regime and the political regime." *Political Dimensions of Aristotle's Ethics*, 56. Bodéüs continues in a footnote, arguing that Aristotle's point is "not to enact rules of conduct allegedly better than the norms implicitly recommended by the laws, in contradiction with the ends of the constitutional regime in force." Ibid., 166 n. 26. Bodéüs's interpretation does not adequately take into account the context in which this injunction concerning private education is given. Aristotle makes clear that private education ought to be undertaken "when cities utterly neglect the public care" (1180a30–31). This suggests that Aristotle's injunction is not primarily a way of aligning paternal authority with the public education of the regime but is instead a way of reforming a regime that has fallen into a state of disrepair.

68. *Politics*, 1253a30–31: "Accordingly, there is in everyone by nature an impulse toward this sort of community. And yet he who first founded one is responsible for the greatest of goods."

Chapter Five

1. The question of how Aristotle envisions the process by which individuals are made virtuous has received disparate treatments. David Cohen argues that Aristotle's citizens are straightforwardly coerced by the city's magistrates. See David Cohen, *Law, Violence and Community in Classical Athens* (Cambridge: Cambridge University Press, 1995), 41–44. Both Peter Simpson and Robert George argue that the attainment of true virtue is not simply rote obedience to the law, but instead requires reason. According to this interpretation, law has a propaedeutic purpose and prepares people for the rational acquisition of virtue. See Peter L. Phillips Simpson, *A Philosophical Commentary on the Politics of Aristotle* (Chapel Hill, NC: University of North Carolina Press, 1998), 2–4; Robert P. George, *Making Men Moral: Civil Liberties and Public Morality* (Oxford: Oxford University Press, 1993), 23–26. Zena Hitz argues that it is through the process of musical education, detailed in books VII and VIII of the *Politics*, by which Aristotle's citizens become morally virtuous. Zena Hitz, "Aristotle on Law and Moral Education" in *Oxford Studies in Ancient Philosophy: Vol. XLII*, ed. Brad Inwood (Oxford: Oxford University Press, 2012), 263–306.

2. Ronna Burger notes that Aristotle is conspicuously silent about Plato's *Laws* (*Aristotle's Dialogue*, 211). In the *Politics*, Aristotle forthrightly states that legislation has already been covered by Plato (cf. 1265a1–2).

3. Some scholars have argued that the "city in speech" is meant to be taken seriously as an ideal political order. See Dale Hall, "The *Republic* and the 'Limits of Politics,'" *Political Theory* 5 (1977): 293–313; Donald Morrison, "The Utopian Character of Plato's Ideal City," in *The Cambridge Companion to Plato's Republic*, ed. G. R. F. Ferrari (New York: Cambridge University Press, 2007), 232–55. For a contrary interpretation, arguing that Socrates's "city in speech" is an ironic portrayal of the extreme to which politics can be brought, see Allan Bloom, "Response to Dale Hall," *Political Theory* 5 (1977): 315–20; Mary Nichols, *Socrates and the Political Community: An Ancient Debate* (Albany: State University of New York Press, 1987). My own view is that Socrates's proposed city is meant to be ironic.

4. It is my contention that Aristotle's serious treatment of Socrates's proposals in *The Republic* stems, in part, from the fact that he has discerned a basis for friendship that is independent from erotic love. In his critique of Socrates's proposals, Aristotle shows that without friendship the city will not maintain its unity.

5. Aristotle notes that Socrates's statement that "all [will] say 'mine' and 'not mine' at the same time," which Socrates takes to be an indication of the city being completely one, is a fallacy that plays on the double-meaning of the term *all* (*Politics*, 1261b16–30).

6. The enjoyment of "pleasures unaccompanied with pains" is discussed at length in book VII of *The Nicomachean Ethics*, where Aristotle indicates that these

pleasures are "pleasant by nature," but are incapable of being practiced continually by human beings (*NE*, 1154b17–25).

7. Peter Simpson points out that commentators have differed as to what exactly Aristotle criticizes in Hippodamus's proposal. Trevor Saunders (*Aristotle Politics: Books I and II* [Oxford: Clarendon Press, 1995], 144–45) and Franz Susemihl and Robert Drew Hicks (*The Politics of Aristotle: A Revised Text, Books I–V* [London: Macmillan, 1894], 271, 275) argue that Aristotle is "criticizing the idea of making jurors into arbitrators," and that he simply fails to notice the originality of Hippodamus's proposal. In contrast, Simpson argues that Aristotle's objection may be that because Hippodamus is "in effect requiring his jurors to be arbitrators, he ought also to have made it possible for them . . . to confer and make collective decisions." *A Philosophical Commentary on the Politics of Aristotle* (University of North Carolina Press, 1998), 106–7. My own view is that Aristotle's concern regarding the jury practice is secondary; his primary objective is to bring to the fore the difficulty of obtaining unity through legal or institutional change.

8. Michael Davis argues that in this portion of his critique, Aristotle is ridiculing Hippodamus by "accus[ing] him of doing what he does for the sake of ambition—*philotimia*." Davis goes on to suggest that Hippodamus's "plan to reward innovations is . . . a sort of self-glorification." *The Politics of Philosophy: A Commentary on Aristotle's* Politics (Lanham, MD: Rowman & Littlefield, 1996), 39.

9. Thomas Pangle incisively points out that this passage equally shows the danger that theorizing poses to the rule of law. He writes, "civic life, as the life of rational political animals, has a high need for political and legal theorizing, even as civic life is imperiled in its very foundation by the same theorizing." "The Rhetorical Strategy Governing Aristotle's Political Teaching," *Journal of Politics* 73, no. 1 (2011): 85.

10. Carnes Lord, *Education and Culture in the Political Thought of Aristotle* (Ithaca, NY: Cornell University Press, 1982), 156.

11. For a contrary perspective see Bernard Yack, "Community: An Aristotelian Social Theory," in *Aristotle and Modern Politics: The Persistence of Political Philosophy* ed. Aristide Tessitore (Notre Dame, IN: University of Notre Dame Press, 2002), 19–46. Yack that argues that Aristotle develops his conception of community largely to "counter the extreme communitarianism of Plato's *Republic*" (p. 20). However, Yack neither investigates Aristotle's discussion concerning the limitations of law nor looks to Aristotle's description of the best regime.

12. The feasibility of the best regime has long been the subject of debate. Some scholars take the view that Aristotle holds that the best regime can be actualized. See Richard Kraut, *Aristotle: Political Philosophy* (Oxford: Oxford University Press, 2002); Jill Frank, *A Democracy of Distinction: Aristotle and the Work of Politics* (Chicago: Chicago University Press, 2005). Others take the view that the primary purpose of Aristotle's description of the best regime is to highlight the limits of politics. See

Robert Bartlett, "The 'Realism' of Classical Political Science," *American Journal of Political Science* 38, no. 2 (May 1994): 381–402; Stephen Salkever, "Whose Prayer?: The Best Regime of Book 7 and the Lessons of Aristotle's Politics," *Political Theory* 35 (2007): 29–46. In arguing that Aristotle views music as capable of making up for the deficiencies of law, I take the view that he offers his best regime as a model that serves as a guide for legislators to foster unity in their own cities.

13. H. G. Liddell and R. Scott, *Greek English Lexicon* (Oxford: Clarendon Press, 1996), *s.v.* νόμος.

14. Thomas J. Mathiesen, *Apollo's Lyre: Greek Music and Music Theory in Antiquity and the Middle Ages* (Lincoln: University of Nebraska Press, 1999), 59.

15. Aristotle, *Problems* (Cambridge, MA: Harvard University Press, 2011), 19.28 (919b38–920a4). For a recent scholarly account of the origin of the term νόμος see Thanos Zartaloudis, *The Birth of Nomos* (Edinburgh: Edinburgh University Press, 2019).

16. Zena Hitz connects Aristotle's discussion of law in book X of the *Ethics* with his account of music in books VII and VIII of the *Politics*. However, her account does not discuss the ambiguity of the term νόμος, and is limited to an examination of the method by which moral virtue is cultivated. See Hitz, "Aristotle on Law and Moral Education." My own analysis focuses on the Aristotle's use of music as a way of cultivating the dianoetic virtues and maintaining unity in the polis.

17. Carnes Lord argues that modern commentators are incorrect to assume that the word *mousikē* "anticipates if it is not identical with 'music' in its modern sense"; instead, he contends that Aristotle likely understood *mousikē* "to include those forms of poetry which had always had a prominent place in traditional music education." *Education and Culture*, 85–86. Lord goes on to argue convincingly that book VIII of the *Politics* is "fragmentary in nature" and that "poetry *was* explicitly discussed, in the no longer extant portion of book VIII." Ibid., 85, 148–50.

18. While Aristotle allies himself with the older school of thought, we shall see that he makes considerable concessions to the contemporary view.

19. Later, Aristotle will make clear that some people pursue play for its own sake, on account of the pleasures involved (1339b32–33). While this might indicate that the activity of leisure is play, we will see that Aristotle treats play as a leisurely activity that people ought to undertake only if they are incapable of attaining the true end, or incapable of enjoying the activity that is truly proper to leisure.

20. For a contrary perspective, which holds that in citing these Homeric comments, Aristotle is distancing himself from the ancients, see Lord, *Education and Culture*, 81–82. In an observation that somewhat complements my own interpretation, Davis argues that the fact that both Homeric allusions focus on war and occupation proves that leisure is "parasitical upon lack of leisure," and that "music . . . requires the slavish and ugly to be what it is." *Politics of Philosophy*, 134–35.

21. For an overview of the way in which the Greeks commonly conceived of the Persian and Median empires see Kurt Raaflaub, *The Discovery of Freedom in Ancient Greece*, trans. Renate Franciscono (Chicago: University of Chicago Press, 2004).

22. Bartlett, "The 'Realism' of Classical Political Science," *American Journal of Political Science* 38 (1994): 306.

23. Bartlett, 306.

24. In this way, Aristotle makes a concession to the contemporary view, which includes music and poetry for the sake of pleasure, while remaining firmly aligned with the earlier view, which held the purpose of music to be for the sake of leisure.

25. Carnes Lord notes that Aristotle's treatment of catharsis "would seem to owe more than a little to the Pythagorean notion of a musical-poetic education of the passions." The Pythagoreans, Lord asserts, used "a musical therapy of the passions . . . as a preparation for or accompaniment to an education in philosophy." *Education and Culture*, 158–59.

26. Lord, *Education and Culture*, 159.

27. Bartlett suggests that catharsis is the ultimate reason that music is included in the educational system of the best regime. He writes: "Political life seems to require what one might call tragic frenzy to purge, if only for a time, the apprehension and disappointments accompanying that life. . . . The whole discussion of music in book VIII attempts to cope with the limits . . . to even the political life that 'accords with what one would pray for.'" "The Realism of Classical Political Science," 308. My own view is that while Aristotle certainly intends his discussion of catharsis to highlight the way that music can dispel excessive emotions, it is incorrect to assert that the *whole* discussion of music is simply an attempt to cope with the limits of political life. As I point out below, Aristotle's account of music is intended to highlight the way in which music can remediate the deficiencies associated with law and is able to serve as a means of friendship and unity for the city.

28. Even at this last juncture, however, the purpose of including music in the educational system of the best regime is revealed in only a liminal manner. This fact seems to corroborate Lord's suggestion that the *Politics* is an incomplete work. See note 17 above.

29. This is the position of Robert Bartlett, who notes that "according to the third and final enumeration of the ends of a musical education . . . *diagoge* [or leisure, is] . . . given its least intellectual formulation; so far from being linked with prudence and the end of man, it is now indistinguishable from "relaxation and rest." "The 'Realism' of Classical Political Science," 308. Bartlett ignores Aristotle's preceding discussion concerning the way in which learning to play music fosters the capacity for noble judgment, as well as the integral role that judgment plays in the virtue of prudence. Cf. *NE*, 1143a25–1143b15.

30. Cf. *NE*, 1143a25–1143b15.

31. It is important to note that Aristotle provides little information as to the source or basis of the νόμος that the city's founders prescribe for the polis. This raises the frightening possibility that the city's νόμος may not be based on the nature and origin of the universe (Cf. *Timaeus*, 27a), but may simply be the product of the aesthetic judgment of the city's founders. If so, we may with profit search for a source that "takes up the history of the world from its earliest origins,

and shows us by this means, better than all other histories, the original principles which have formed empires." Jacques-Bénigne Bossuet, *Politique tirée des propres paroles de l'Écriture Sainte*, trans. Patrick Riley (Cambridge: Cambridge University Press, 1990), 1.

    32. Lord, *Education and Culture*, 177–78.

    33. John von Heyking, *The Form of Politics: Aristotle and Plato on Friendship* (Montreal: McGill-Queen's University Press, 2016), 77.

Conclusion

    1. Paul Ludwig, *Rediscovering Political Friendship: Aristotle's Theory and Modern Identity, Community, and Equality* (Cambridge: Cambridge University Press, 2022), 26.

    2. James Madison, "Federalist 51," in *The Federalist*, ed. George W. Carey and James McClellan (Indianapolis: Liberty Fund, 2001), 269.

    3. John Adams, "Novanglus," in *Revolutionary Writings of John Adams*, ed. C. Bradley Thompson (Indianapolis: Liberty Fund, 2000), 226.

    4. Thomas Jefferson to William Wirt, 5 Aug. 1815, *The Papers of Thomas Jefferson: Retirement Series*, ed. J. Jefferson Looney, 8:641–46 (Princeton, NJ: Princeton University Press, 2004); Thomas Jefferson to James Madison, 6 Sept. 1789, ed. James Morton Smith, *The Republic of Letters: The Correspondence Between Thomas Jefferson and James Madison, 1776–1826* (New York: Norton, 1995), I:631–36; Gordon S. Wood, *John Adams and Thomas Jefferson: Friends Divided* (New York: Penguin Press, 2017), 230.

    5. Thomas Jefferson to Henry Lee, 8 May 1825, *Political Writings*, ed. Joyce Appleby and Terrence Ball (Cambridge: Cambridge University Press, 1999), 148.

    6. Gordon Wood, *Friends Divided*, 112–13.

    7. Jerome Huyler, *Locke in America: The Moral Philosophy of the Founding Era* (Lawrence, KS: University Press of Kansas, 1995), 261.

    8. James Madison, "Federalist 38" in *The Federalist*, 186–93.

    9. Madison, 186–93.

    10. Madison, 186–93.

    11. Wood, *Friends Divided*, 222.

    12. Abraham Lincoln "Fragment on the Constitution and the Union," in *The Collected Works of Abraham Lincoln*, ed. Roy Basler, vol. 4 (New Brunswick, NJ: Rutgers University Press, 1953), 168–70.

    13. The following remarks on Jefferson and Adams's tumultuous friendship are indebted to Gordon Wood's excellent account in his book *Friends Divided*.

    14. Wood, *Friends Divided*, 105.

    15. Wood, 105–6.

    16. "Eulogy Pronounced at Boston, Massachusetts, August 2, 1826, by Daniel Webster," in *A Selection of Eulogies Pronounced in the Several States in Honor of Those*

Illustrious Patriots and Statesmen, John Adams and Thomas Jefferson (Hartford: D. F. Robinson and Co., 1826), 212.

17. Worthington C. Ford, ed., *Journals of the Continental Congress, 1774–1789* (Washington, DC: Government Printing Office, 1904–1937), I:342, 357.

18. Thomas Jefferson "Autobiography," in *Thomas Jefferson: Writings*, ed. Merrill D. Peterson (New York: Library of America, 1984), 44.

19. Wood, *Friends Divided*, 177–78.

20. Wood, 250–51.

21. Wood, 251.

22. Wood, 257.

23. Wood, 259.

24. Jeffrey L. Pasley, *The First Presidential Contest: 1796 and the Founding of American Democracy* (Lawrence: KS: University Press of Kansas, 2013), 224.

25. Wood, *Friends Divided*, 286; 289–90.

26. John Adams, "Correspondence Published in the *Boston Patriot*," in *The Works of John Adams, Second President of the United States*, ed. Charles Francis, 10 vols. (Boston: Little, Brown, 1856), 9:284–86.

27. Wood, *Friends Divided*, 308–9.

28. Wood, 309; 313.

29. Wood, 357–58.

30. Wood, 358.

31. Wood, 361.

32. William Wirt, "Eulogy Pronounced at the City of Washington, October 19, 1826," in *Selection of Eulogies*, 379.

Bibliography

Abbey, Ruth. "Review Essay: On Friendship." *Review of Politics* 79, no. 4 (2017): 695–707.
Ackrill, J. L. "Aristotle on *Eudaimonia*." In *Aristotle's Nicomachean Ethics*, edited by Otfried Hoffe and translated by David Fernbach, 33–52. Leiden: Brill, 2010.
Adams, John. *The Works of John Adams, Second President of the United States*. Edited by Charles Francis Adams. Vol. 9. Boston, MA: Little Brown, 1854.
Adams, John. "Novanglus." In *Revolutionary Writings of John Adams*, edited by C. Bradley Thompson, 147–284. Indianapolis, IN: Liberty Fund, 2000.
Adkins, A. W. H. "The Connection between Aristotle's *Ethics* and *Politics*." *Political Theory* 12, no. 1 (1984): 29–49.
Aelred of Rievaulx. *Spiritual Friendship*. Edited by Marsha L. Dutton and translated by Lawrence C. Braceland. Collegeville, MN: Liturgical Press, 2010.
Ahrensdorf, Peter. "The Question of Historical Context and the Study of Plato." *Polity* 27, no. 1 (1994): 113–32.
Aquinas, Thomas. *Commentary on the Nicomachean Ethics*. Translated by C. I. Litzinger. Chicago: Regnery, 1964.
———. *Summa Theologica*. Translated by the Fathers of the English Dominican Province. New York: Benziger, 1948.
Archie, Andre. *Politics in Socrates' Alcibiades: A Philosophical Account of Plato's Dialogue Alcibiades Major*. New York: Springer, 2015.
Arendt, Hannah. *The Life of the Mind*. New York: Harcourt, 1977.
———. "Thinking and Moral Considerations: A Lecture." *Social Research* 38, no. 3 (Autumn 1971): 417–46.
Aristotle. *Analytica Priora*. In *The Basic Works of Aristotle*, edited by Richard McKeon and translated by A. J. Jenkinson, 62–186. New York: Random House, 1941.
———. *Metaphysica*. In *The Basic Works of Aristotle*, edited by Richard McKeon and translated by W. D. Ross, 681–926. New York: Random House, 1941.
———. *Nicomachean Ethics*. Translated by Robert C. Bartlett and Susan D. Collins. Chicago: University of Chicago Press, 2011.

———. *Nicomachean Ethics Books VIII and IX.* Translated by Michael Pakaluk. Oxford: Clarendon Press, 1998.

———. *Physica.* In *The Basic Works of Aristotle,* edited by Richard McKeon and translated by R. P. Hardie and R. K. Gaye, 213–394. New York: Random House, 1941.

———. *Politics.* 2nd ed. Translated by Carnes Lord. Chicago: University of Chicago Press, 2013.

———. *Problems.* Edited and translated by Robert Mayhew. Cambridge, MA: Harvard University Press, 2011.

Arora, N. D., and S. S. Awasthy. *Political Theory and Political Thought.* New Delhi: Har-Anand, 2007.

Ast, Friedrich. *Platon's Leben und Schriften: Ein Versuch, im Leben wie in den Schriften des Platon des Wahre und Aechte vom Erdichteten und Untergeschobenen zu scheiden, und die Zeitfolge der ächten Gespräche zu bestimmen.* Leipzig: Weidmann, 1816.

Bacon, Francis. "Of Friendship." In *Francis Bacon: Essays and New Atlantis,* edited by Gordon S. Haight, 109–19. New York: Black, 1942.

Bartlett, Robert C. "The 'Realism' of Classical Political Science." *American Journal of Political Science* 38, no. 2 (May 1994) 381–402.

Batten, Alicia J. *Friendship and Benefaction in James.* Atlanta: SBL Press, 2017.

Benardete, Seth. "On Plato's *Lysis.*" In *The Argument of the Action: Essays on Greek Poetry and Philosophy,* edited by Ronna Burger and Michael Davis, 198–230. Chicago: University of Chicago Press, 2000.

———. *The Rhetoric of Morality and Philosophy.* Chicago: University of Chicago Press, 1991.

Berlin, Isaiah. "Political Liberty and Pluralism: Two Concepts of Liberty." In *The Proper Study of Mankind: An Anthology of Essays,* edited by Henry Hardy and Roger Hausheer, 191–242. New York: Farrar, Straus and Giroux, 2000.

Berry, Christopher J. *The Idea of Commercial Society in the Scottish Enlightenment.* Edinburgh: Edinburgh University Press, 2013.

Bloom, Allan. "Response to Dale Hall." *Political Theory* 5, no. 3 (August 1977): 315–20.

———. "Interpretive Essay." In *Plato's Republic,* translated and edited by Allan Bloom. 307–436. New York: Basic Books, 1968.

Bodéüs, Richard. *Aristotle and the Theology of Living Immortals.* Translated by Jan Edward Garrett. Albany: State University of New York Press, 2000.

———. *The Political Dimensions of Aristotle's 'Ethics.'* Translated by Jan Edward Garrett. Albany: State University of New York Press, 1993.

Bossuet, Jacques-Bénigne. *Politique tirée des propres paroles de l'Écriture Sainte.* Translated by Patrick Riley. Cambridge, UK: Cambridge University Press, 1990.

Broadie, Sarah. *Ethics with Aristotle.* Oxford: Oxford University Press, 1991.

Burger, Ronna. *Aristotle's Dialogue with Socrates: On the Nicomachean Ethics.* Chicago: University of Chicago Press, 2008.

———. "Hunting Together or Philosophizing Together: Friendship and *Eros* in Aristotle's *Nicomachean Ethics*." In *Love and Friendship: Rethinking Politics and Affection in Modern Times*, edited by Eduardo A. Velásquez, 37–60. Lanham, MD: Lexington Books, 2003.

Burkert, Walter. *Greek Religion: Archaic and Classical*. Translated by John Raffan. Cambridge, MA: Harvard University Press, 1985.

Burnet, John. *The Ethics of Aristotle*. London: Methuen and Co., 1900.

Cain, Patrick, and Mary Nichols. "Aristotle's Nod to Homer: A Political Science of Indebtedness." In *Socrates and Dionysius: Philosophy and Art in Dialogue*, edited by Ann Ward, 54–73. Newcastle, UK: Cambridge Scholars Publishing, 2013.

Carrese, Paul. "George Washington's Greatness and Aristotelian Virtue." In *Magnanimity and Statesmanship*, edited by Carson Holloway, 145–70. Lanham, MD: Lexington, 2008.

Cartledge, Paul. *Alexander the Great: The Hunt for a New Past*. New York: Overlook Press, 2004.

Cohen, David. *Law, Violence and Community in Classical Athens*. Cambridge, UK: Cambridge University Press, 1995.

Collins, Susan. *Aristotle and the Rediscovery of Citizenship*. Cambridge, UK: Cambridge University Press, 2006.

Cooper, John. *Reason and the Human Good in Aristotle*. Cambridge, MA: Harvard University Press, 1975.

Corcoran, Clinton DeBevoise. *Topography and Deep Structure in Plato: The Construction of Place in the Dialogues*. Albany: State University of New York Press, 2016.

Corey, David. "Voegelin and Aristotle on Nous: What Is Noetic Political Science?" *Review of Politics* 63, no. 1 (2002): 57–79.

Davis, Michael. *The Politics of Philosophy: A Commentary on the Politics of Aristotle*. Lanham, MD: Rowman & Littlefield, 1996.

Descartes, René. *Meditations, Objections, and Replies*. Edited and translated by Roger Ariew and Donald Cress. Indianapolis, IN: Hackett, 2006.

Digeser, P. E. *Friendship Reconsidered: What It Means and How It Matters to Politics*. New York: Columbia University Press, 2016.

Dodds, E. R. *Plato Gorgias: A Revised Text with Introduction and Commentary*. Oxford: Clarendon, 1959.

Duncan, Roger. "*Philia* in the *Gorgias*." *Apeiron* 8, no. 1 (May 1974): 23–26.

Dziob, Anne Marie. "Aristotelian Friendship: Self-Love and Moral Rivalry." *The Review of Metaphysics* 46, no. 4 (June 1993): 781–802.

Ehrenberg, Victor. *Alexander and the Greeks*. Oxford: Oxford University Press, 1938.

Eisenstadt, Michael. "Antithesis in Plato's *Euthydemus* and *Lysis*" (unpublished manuscript, last revised July 27, 2020). Available at SSRN: https://ssrn.com/abstract=3624095.

Erasmus, Desiderius. *The Education of a Christian King*. Edited by Lisa Jardine and translated by Neil M. Cheshire and Michael J. Heath. Cambridge, UK: Cambridge University Press, 1997.

Euripides. *Orestes*. Translated by E. P. Coleridge. Vol. 2 of *The Complete Greek Drama*. Edited by Whitney J. Oates and Eugene O'Neil, Jr. New York: Random House, 1938.

Fairbanks, Arthur. *The Mythology of Greece and Rome*. New York: D. Appleton, 1907.

Feaver, Douglas D., and John E. Hare. "The *Apology* as an Inverted Parody of Rhetoric." *Arethusa* 14, no. 2 (Fall 1981): 205–16.

Ford, Worthington C., ed. *Journals of the Continental Congress, 1774–1789*. Vol. 1. Washington, DC: Government Printing Office, 1904–37.

Frank, Jill. *A Democracy of Distinction: Aristotle and the Work of Politics*. Chicago: Chicago University Press, 2005.

Gargin, Michael. "Socrates' 'Hybris' and Alcibiades' Failure." *Phoenix* 31, no. 1 (Spring 1977): 22–37.

Gauthier, René Antoine. *Magnanimité: L'Idéal de la grandeur dans la philosophie païenne et dans la théologie chrétienne*. Paris: Vrin, 1951.

George, Robert P. *Making Men Moral: Civil Liberties and Public Morality*. Oxford: Oxford University Press, 1993.

Gibert, John. "Euripides' *Antiope* and the Quiet Life." In *The Play of Texts and Fragments: Essays in Honor of Martin Cropp*, edited by J. R. C. Cousland and James R. Hume, 23–34. Leiden: Brill, 2009.

Grant, Alexander. *The Ethics of Aristotle*. Vol. 2, 4th ed. London: Longmans, Green, and Co., 1885.

Grote, George. *Plato and the Other Companions of Sokrates*. Vol. 2. London: John Murray, 1867.

Hadreas, Peter. "Εὔνοια: Aristotle on the Beginning of Friendship." *Ancient Philosophy* 15, no. 2 (2002): 393–402.

Hall, Dale. "The *Republic* and the 'Limits of Politics.'" *Political Theory* 5, no. 3 (August 1977): 293–313.

Halper, Edward C. *The One and the Many in Aristotle's Metaphysics: The Central Books*. Ohio, IN: Ohio State University Press, 1989.

Hanley, Ryan Patrick. "Aristotle on the Greatness of Greatness of Soul." *History of Political Thought* 23, no. 1 (Spring 2002): 1–20.

Hardie, W. F. R. "'Magnanimity' in Aristotle's *Ethics*." *Phronesis* 23, no. 1 (1978): 63–79.

Hegel, Georg W. F. *The Philosophy of History*. 1837. Translated by John Sibree. Mineola, NY: Dover, 1956.

———. *Lectures on the History of Philosophy*. Translated by E. S. Haldane. Vol. 1. London: Routledge & Kegan Paul, 1955.

Heidegger, Martin. *Plato's Sophist*. Translated by Richard Rojcewicz and André Schuwer. Bloomington: Indiana University Press, 1997.

Hitz, Zena. "Aristotle on Law and Moral Education." In *Oxford Studies in Ancient Philosophy: Vol. XLII*, edited by Brad Inwood, 263–306. Oxford: Oxford University Press, 2012.

Hobbes, Thomas. *De Corpore* Vol. 4 of *The English Works of Thomas Hobbes of Malmesbury*, edited by William Molesworth, 77–228. London: John Bohn, 1839.
———. *Leviathan*. Edited by Richard Tuck. Cambridge, UK: Cambridge University Press, 1996.
Hoerber, Robert G. "Plato's Lysis." *Phronesis* 4, no. 1 (1959): 15–28.
Holloway, Carson. "Aristotle's Magnanimous Man." In *Magnanimity and Statesmanship*, edited by Carson Holloway, 13–27. Lanham, MD: Lexington, 2008.
———. "Introduction." In *Magnanimity and Statesmanship*, edited by Carson Holloway, 1–10. Lanham, MD: Lexington, 2008.
———. "Shakespeare's *Coriolanus* and Aristotle's Great-Souled Man." *Review of Politics* 69, no. 3 (Summer 2007): 353–74.
Homer. *Iliad*. Translated by A. T. Murray. Vol. 2. Cambridge, MA: Harvard University Press, 1924.
———. *Odyssey*. Edited by Louise Ropes Loomis. Translated by Samuel Butler. Roslyn, NY: Black, 1944.
Howland, Jacob. "Aristotle's Great-Souled Man." *Review of Politics* 64, no. 1 (Winter, 2002): 27–56.
Huyler, Jerome. *Locke in America: The Moral Philosophy of the Founding Era*. Lawrence, KS: University Press of Kansas, 1995.
Inwood, Brad. *The Poem of Empedocles*. Translated by Brad Inwood. Toronto: University of Toronto Press, 1992.
Irwin, Terence. *Plato's Ethics*. New York: Oxford University Press, 1995.
Jaeger, Werner. *Paedeia*. Vol. 2. New York: Oxford University Press, 1943.
Jaffa, Harry V. *Aristotelianism and Thomism: A Study of the Commentary by Thomas Aquinas on the Nicomachean Ethics*. Westport, CT: Greenwood Press, 1979.
Jefferson, Thomas. *The Papers of Thomas Jefferson: Retirement Series, Vol. 8*. Edited by J. Jefferson Looney et al. Princeton, NJ: Princeton University Press, 2004.
———. *Political Writings*. Edited by Joyce Appleby and Terrence Ball. Cambridge, UK: Cambridge University Press, 1999.
———. *Thomas Jefferson: Writings*. Edited by Merrill D. Peterson. New York: Library of America, 1984.
Kateb, George. "Socratic Integrity." *Nomos* 40 (1998): 77–112.
Kidd, Thomas. *Benjamin Franklin: Life of a Founding Father*. New Haven, CT: Yale University Press, 2017.
Kierkegaard, Søren. *On the Concept of Irony, with Continual Reference to Socrates: Together with Notes of Schelling's Berlin Lectures*. Edited and translated by Howard Vincent Hong and Edna Hatlestad Hong. Princeton, NJ: Princeton University Press, 1992.
Klosko, George. "The Refutation of Callicles in Plato's *Gorgias*." *Greece and Rome* 31, no. 2 (October 1984): 126–39.
Konstan, David. *Friendship in the Classical World*. Cambridge, UK: Cambridge University Press, 1997.

Kraut, Richard. *Aristotle on the Human Good*. Princeton, NJ: Princeton University Press, 1989.

———. *Aristotle: Political Philosophy*. Oxford: Oxford University Press, 2002.

Laertius, Diogenes. *Lives of Eminent Philosophers*. Edited by James Miller. Translated by Pamela Mensch. Oxford: Oxford University Press, 2018.

Lamb, W. R. M. "Introduction to the *Lysis*." In *Plato*. Vol. 3, *Lysis, Symposium, Gorgias*. Loeb Classical Library 166. Cambridge MA: Harvard University Press, 1925.

Lambert, Gregg. *Philosophy after Friendship: Deleuze's Conceptual Personae*. Minneapolis, MN: University of Minnesota Press, 2017.

Liddell, H. G., and R. Scott. *Greek English Lexicon*. Oxford: Clarendon Press, 1996.

Lincoln, Abraham. "Fragment on the Constitution and the Union." In *The Collected Works of Abraham Lincoln*, edited by Roy Basler, vol. 4, 168–70. New Brunswick, NJ: Rutgers University Press, 1953.

Locke, John. *Second Treatise of Government*. Edited by C. B. Macpherson. Indianapolis, IN: Hackett, 1980.

Lord, Carnes. *Education and Culture in the Political Thought of Aristotle*. Ithaca, NY: Cornell University Press, 1982.

Ludwig, Paul. *Rediscovering Political Friendship: Aristotle's Theory and Modern Identity, Community, and Equality*. Cambridge, UK: Cambridge University Press, 2022.

MacPherson, C. B. "Locke on Capitalist Appropriation." *The Western Quarterly* 4, no. 4 (December 1951): 550–66.

Madison, James. "Federalist 38." In *The Federalist*, edited by George W. Carey and James McClellan, 186–92. Indianapolis, IN: Liberty Fund, 2001.

———. "Federalist 51." In *The Federalist*, edited by George W. Carey and James McClellan, 267–71. Indianapolis, IN: Liberty Fund, 2001.

Mathiesen, Thomas, J. *Apollo's Lyre: Greek Music and Music Theory in Antiquity and the Middle Ages*. Lincoln, NE: University of Nebraska Press, 1999.

McKim, Richard. "Shame and Truth in Plato's *Gorgias*." In *Platonic Writings, Platonic Readings*, edited by Charles L. Griswold, Jr. New York: Routledge, 1988.

Mews, Constant J., and Neville Chiavaroli. "The Latin West." In *Friendship: A History*, edited by Barbara Caine, 73–110. New York: Routledge, 2014.

Modesto, Filippa. *Dante's Idea of Friendship: The Transformation of a Classical Concept*. Toronto: University of Toronto Press, 2015.

Montaigne, Michel de. "Of Friendship." In *The Complete Essays of Montaigne*, translated by Donald Frame. Stanford, CA: Stanford University Press, 1976.

Morgan, Teresa. "Rhetoric and Education." In *A Companion to Greek Rhetoric*, edited by Ian Worthington. West Sussex, UK: Blackwell, 2010.

Morrison, Donald. "The Utopian Character of Plato's Ideal City." In *The Cambridge Companion to Plato's Republic*, edited by G. R. F. Ferrari. 232–55. New York: Cambridge University Press, 2007.

Nagel, Thomas. "Aristotle on *Eudaimonia*." *Phronesis* 17, no. 3 (1972): 252–59.

Nehamas, Alexander. *On Friendship*. New York: Basic Books, 2016.

Newall. Waller R. *Tyranny: A New Interpretation*. Cambridge, UK: Cambridge University Press, 2013.

Nichols, Mary. *Socrates and the Political Community: An Ancient Debate*. New York: State University of New York Press, 1987.

———. *Socrates on Friendship and the Political Community: Reflections on Plato's Symposium,* Phaedrus, *and* Lysis. Cambridge, UK: Cambridge University Press, 2009.

Nietzsche, Friedrich. *Human, All Too Human: A Book for Free Spirits*. Translated by Marion Faber and Stephen Lehmann. Lincoln, NE: University of Nebraska Press, 1984.

Nietzsche, Friedrich. *Twilight of the Idols or How to Philosophize with a Hammer*. Translated and edited by Duncan Large. Oxford: Oxford University Press, 2008.

Nightingale, Andrea. "Plato's 'Gorgias' and Euripides' 'Antiope': A Study in Generic Transformation." *Classical Antiquity* 11, no. 1 (1992): 121–41.

Pangle, Lorraine Smith. "The Anatomy of Courage in Aristotle's *Nicomachean Ethics*." *Review of Politics* 80, no. 4 (2018): 569–90.

———. *Aristotle and the Philosophy of Friendship*. Cambridge, UK: Cambridge University Press, 2003.

———. "Friendship and Self-Love in Aristotle's *Nicomachean Ethics*." In *Action and Contemplation: Studies in the Moral and Political Thought of Aristotle*, edited by Robert C. Bartlett and Susan D. Collins, 171–202. Albany: State University of New York Press, 1999.

Pangle, Thomas. "The Rhetorical Strategy Governing Aristotle's Political Teaching." *Journal of Politics* 73, no. 1 (2011): 84–96.

Pasley, Jeffrey L. *The First Presidential Contest: 1796 and the Founding of American Democracy*. Lawrence, KS: University Press of Kansas, 2013.

Penner, Terry, and Christopher Rowe. *Plato's Lysis*. Cambridge, UK: Cambridge University Press, 2005.

Pickard-Cambridge, A. W. "Tragedy." In *New Chapters in the History of Greek Literature*. 3rd series. Edited by J. U. Powell, 68–155. Oxford: Oxford University Press, 1933.

Plato. *Apology*. In *Four Texts on Socrates: Plato and Aristophanes*. Revised edition. Translated and edited by Thomas G. West and Grace Starry West. Ithaca, NY: Cornell University Press, 1998.

———. *Euthydemus*. Translated by Rosamond Kent Spague. In *Plato: Complete Works*, edited by John M. Cooper and D. S. Hutchinson. Indianapolis, IN: Hackett, 1997.

———. *Euthyphro*. In *Four Texts on Socrates: Plato and Aristophanes*. Revised edition. Translated and edited by Thomas G. West and Grace Starry West. Ithaca, NY: Cornell University Press, 1998.

———. *Gorgias*. Translated and edited by James H. Nichols Jr. Ithaca, NY: Cornell University Press, 1998.

---. *Greater Hippias*. Translated by David R. Sweet. In *The Roots of Political Philosophy: Ten Forgotten Socratic Dialogues*, edited by Thomas L. Pangle. Ithaca, NY: Cornell University Press, 1987.

---. *Lysis*. In *Plato's Dialogue on Friendship: An Interpretation of the Lysis with a New Translation*, translated and edited by David Bolotin. Ithaca, NY: Cornell University Press, 1979.

---. *Phaedrus*. Translated and edited by James H. Nichols Jr. Ithaca, NY: Cornell University Press, 1998.

---. *Protagoras*. In *Plato: "Protagoras" and "Meno,"* translated and edited by Robert C. Bartlett. Ithaca, NY: Cornell University Press, 2004.

---. *Republic*. In *The Republic of Plato*, translated and edited by Allan Bloom. New York: Basic Books, 1968.

---. *Symposium*. Translated by Seth Benardete. Edited by Allan Bloom and Seth Benardete. Chicago: University of Chicago Press, 2001.

---. *Thaeatetus*. Translated by M. J. Levett. Revised by Myles Burneat. In *Plato: Complete Works*, edited by John M. Cooper and D. S. Hutchinson. Indianapolis, IN: Hackett, 1997.

---. *Theages*. Translated by Nicholas D. Smith. In *Plato: Complete Works*, edited by John M. Cooper and D. S. Hutchinson. Indianapolis, IN: Hackett, 1997.

---. *Timaeus*. Translated by Donald J. Zeyl. In *Plato: Complete Works*, edited by John M. Cooper and D. S. Hutchinson. Indianapolis, IN: Hackett, 1997.

Plutarch. "Alcibiades." In *The Lives of the Noble Grecians and Romans*, translated by John Dryden, revised by Arthur Hugh Clough, 233–62. New York: Random House, 1864.

---. "Lysander." In *The Lives of the Noble Grecians and Romans*, translated by John Dryden, revised by Arthur Hugh Clough, 525–45. New York: Random House, 1864.

Price, A. W. *Love and Friendship in Plato and Aristotle*. Oxford: Oxford University Press, 1989.

Putnam, Robert D. *Bowling Alone: The Collapse and Revival of American Community*. New York: Simon and Schuster, 2000.

Raaflaub, Kurt. *The Discovery of Freedom in Ancient Greece*. Translated by Renate Franciscono. Chicago: Chicago University Press, 2004.

Reshotko, Naomi. "Plato's *Lysis*: A Socratic Treatise on Desire and Attraction." *Apeiron* 30, no. 1 (1997): 1–18.

Rhodes, James. "Platonic *Philia* and Political Order." In *Friendship and Politics*, edited by John von Heyking and Richard Avramenko, 21–52. Notre Dame, IN: University of Notre Dame Press, 2008.

Rider, Benjamin. "A Socratic Seduction: Philosophical Protreptic in Plato's *Lysis*." *Apeiron* 44, no. 1 (2011): 40–66.

Robinson, David B. "Plato's 'Lysis': The Structural Problem." *Illinois Classical Studies* 11, no. 1/2 (Spring/Fall 1986): 63–83.

Ross, David. *Aristotle*. 6th ed. London: Routledge, 1995.

Rousseau, Jean-Jacques. *The Social Contract*. Translated and edited by Victor Gourevitch. Cambridge, UK: Cambridge University Press, 1997.
Rutherford, Richard B. *The Art of Plato: Ten Essays in Platonic Interpretation*. Cambridge, MA: Harvard University Press, 1995.
Salkever, Stephen. "Whose Prayer?: The Best Regime of Book 7 and the Lessons of Aristotle's *Politics*." *Political Theory* 35, no. 1 (2007): 29–46.
Saunders, Trevor. *Aristotle Politics: Books I and II*. Oxford: Clarendon Press, 1995.
Schollmier, Fred. *Other Selves: Aristotle on Personal and Political Friendship*. Albany, NY: State University of New York Press, 1994.
Schwartz, Daniel. *Aquinas on Friendship*. Oxford: Oxford University Press, 2007.
Scott, Gary Allan. *Plato's Socrates as Educator*. Albany: State University of New York Press, 2000.
Sidgwick, Henry. *Outlines of the History of Ethics for English Readers*. Indianapolis, IN: Hackett, [1886], 1902.
Simpson, Peter L. Phillips. *A Philosophical Commentary on the Politics of Aristotle*. Chapel Hill, NC: University of North Carolina Press, 1998.
Smith, Adam. *The Theory of Moral Sentiments*. Edited by D. D. Raphael and A. L. Macfie. Indianapolis, IN: Liberty Fund, 1982.
Smith, James M. *The Republic of Letters: The Correspondence between Thomas Jefferson and James Madison, 1776–1826*. New York: Penguin, 2017.
Smith, Thomas W. *Revaluing Ethics: Aristotle's Dialectical Pedagogy*. Albany: State University of New York Press, 2001.
Smith, Travis. "Hobbes on Getting By with Little Help from Friends." In *Friendship and Politics: Essays in Political Thought*, edited by John von Heyking and Richard Avramenko, 214–47. Notre Dame, IN: University of Notre Dame Press, 2008.
Sophocles, "Ajax." In *The Complete Greek Drama*, translated by R. C. Trevelyan, edited by Whitney J. Oates and Eugene O'Neill, Jr., 315–64. New York: Random House, 1938.
Stauffer, Devin. *Hobbes's Kingdom of Light: A Study in the Foundations of Modern Political Philosophy*. Chicago: University of Chicago Press, 2018.
———. "Socrates and Callicles: A Reading of Plato's *Gorgias*." *Review of Politics* 64, no. 4 (Autumn 2002): 627–57.
———. *The Unity of Plato's 'Gorgias': Rhetoric, Justice, and the Philosophic Life*. Cambridge, UK: Cambridge University Press, 2006.
Stewart, J. A. *Notes on the Nicomachean Ethics of Aristotle*. Oxford: Clarendon Press, 1892.
Strauss, Leo. *The City and Man*. Chicago: Rand McNally, 1964.
———. *Natural Right and History*. Chicago: University of Chicago Press, 1953.
———. *On Plato's "Symposium."* Edited by Seth Benardete. Chicago: University of Chicago Press, 2001.
———. *The Political Philosophy of Hobbes: Its Basis and Its Genesis*. Translated by Elsa M. Sinclair. Chicago: University of Chicago Press, 1936.

Susemihl, Franz, and Robert Drew Hicks. *The Politics of Aristotle: A Revised Text, Books I–V*. London: Macmillan, 1984.

Tan, Seow Hon. *Justice as Friendship: A Theory of Law*. New York: Routledge, 2015.

Tessitore, Aristide. "A Political Reading of Aristotle's Treatment of Pleasure in the *Nicomachean Ethics*." *Political Theory* 17, no. 2 (1989): 247–65.

———. *Reading Aristotle's Ethics: Virtue, Rhetoric, and Political Philosophy*. Albany: State University of New York Press, 1996.

Thucydides. *History of the Peloponnesian War*. Translated by Rex Warner. New York: Penguin, 1972.

Velleman, David J. "Sociality and Solitude." *Philosophical Explorations* 16, no. 3 (2013): 324–35.

Villa, Dana. *Socratic Citizenship*. Princeton: Princeton University Press, 2001.

Vlastos, Gregory. *Socrates: Ironist and Moral Philosopher*. Ithaca, NY: Cornell University Press, 1991.

Voegelin, Eric. *Order and History*. Vol. 3. Baton Rouge: Louisiana State University Press, 1957.

von Heyking, John. *The Form of Politics: Aristotle and Plato on Friendship*. Montreal: McGill-Queens University Press, 2016.

Walzer, Michael. "The Communitarian Critique of Liberalism." *Political Theory* 18, no. 1 (1990): 6–23.

Ward, Ann. *Contemplating Friendship in Aristotle's Ethics*. Albany, NY: State University of New York Press, 2016.

Webster, Daniel. "Eulogy Pronounced at Boston, Massachusetts, August 2, 1826." In *A Selection of Eulogies Pronounced in the Several States, in Honor of Those Illustrious Patriots and Statesmen, John Adams and Thomas Jefferson*. Hartford, CT: D. F. Robinson and Co., 1826.

Wecklein, N. "Die Antiope des Euripides." *Philologus*, 79 (1923): 51–69.

West, Thomas. *Plato's Apology of Socrates*. Ithaca NY: Cornell University Press, 1979.

Winthrop, Delba. "Aristotle and Theories of Justice." *American Political Science Review* 72, no. 4 (1978): 1201–16.

Wirt, William. "Eulogy Pronounced at the City of Washington, October 19, 1826." In *A Selection of Eulogies Pronounced in the Several States, in Honor of Those Illustrious Patriots and Statesmen, John Adams and Thomas Jefferson*. Hartford, CT: D. F. Robinson and Co., 1826.

Wood, Gordon S. *John Adams and Thomas Jefferson: Friends Divided*. New York: Penguin Press, 2017.

Xenophon. *Memorabilia*. Translated and annotated by Amy L. Bonnette. Ithaca, NY: Cornell University Press, 1994.

Yack, Bernard. "Community: An Aristotelian Social Theory." In *Aristotle and Modern Politics: The Persistence of Political Philosophy*, 19–46. Notre Dame, IN: University of Notre Dame Press, 2002.

Zartaloudis, Thanos. *The Birth of Nomos*. Edinburgh: Edinburgh University Press, 2019.
Zeller, Eduard. *Socrates and the Socratic Schools*. Translated by Oswald J. Reichel. London: Longmans, Green, and Co., 1868.
Zuckert, Catherine. *Plato's Philosophers: The Coherence of the Dialogues*. Chicago: University of Chicago Press, 2009.

Index

abstention, life of, 46–52
abstentious approach, of Socrates, 48
Achilles, 99, 101, 104
active life, 87, 90, 214n3
"active" partner, 223n80
activity, 146, 147
"activity and an end," pleasure as, 143
actualities, 142, 143
actuality, 130, 156–57
actualization, 150–54, 183
Adams, John, 186, 187, 190, 191, 192, 193
advice, 98, 121, 122
advisor, Aristotle as, 154–60
Aelred of Rievaulx, treatise on friendship, 6
Agamemnon, depriving Achilles of the war prize, 99
Ajax, 98, 101, 104
Ajax and Hector, parting in friendship, 220n60
akin, 41
Alcibiades, 65, 99, 101, 104, 217n41
Alexander the Great, 9, 199n26
Alien Friends Act, 193
ambition and desires, Socrates appealing to Lysis's, 26
American Constitutional Republic, friendship in, 15, 185–95

America's Revolutionary period, John Adams and Thomas Jefferson as close friends during, 190
Amphion, son of Antiope, 67
Anaxagoras, 139
the ancestral, as distinct from the good, 125
animals
  as friends, 32
  sense perception of, 135
"another self," friend as, 126
Antiope (Euripides), 67, 68, 81
Apology (Plato), 8
  connection with the *Gorgias*, 207n3
  on negativity of Socrates, 48
  no definition of either justice or injustice, 50–51
  Socrates's daimonion in, 208n22
  on Socrates's relation to the practice of politics, 13
  trial recounted in, 46
appeals court, Hippodamus's proposed method for, 167
Aquinas, Thomas, 6, 198n13, 229n37
Archelaus, as unjust, 61, 211n42
Arendt, Hannah, 50, 205n50, 208n21
Argus Panoptes, 20. *See also* Panops
Aristophanes, 163, 225n8
Aristotelian friendship, 186

253

Aristotle
  as advisor, 154–60
  critiquing Socrates's inquiry into friendship, 222n71
  as the founder of political science, 200n31
  on friendship, 2, 8, 106, 108, 234n4
  friendship of the good and, 85–116
  on the individual having the same end as the city, 86
  noting that he and Plato are friends, 227n21
  on philosophers as friends, 14
  on Plato's theory of the forms, 109
  on the political life of moral virtue and the philosophic life, 91
  on politics in a favorable light, 10
  on Socrates, 204n33, 204n35, 221n70
  on tension between philosophy and politics, 90
art, as experience conquering chance, 54
art of medicine, Socrates compared justice to, 70
art of rhetoric, Callicles describing, 75
artificial or conventional things, accounting for the existence of, 130
artisan, as fond of his own work, 133
arts and sciences, deliberating about the method, 137
asocial individuals, committing injustice, 165–66
assembly of men, "discord and disunion" resulting from, 188
Athenian people, Callicles in love with, 65
audience, of Aristotle, 225n10
authority
  under the Crown, 191
  friendships of people in, 115
  friendships providing the foundation for, 44
autonomy, granted by the parents of Lysis, 26

bad desires, as detrimental, 39
bad men, obligations to, 123
Bartlett, Robert C., 88, 176, 200n31
base persons
  Aristotle warning regarding the friendship of, 228n30
  as impossible to be friends, 109
  setting ignoble goals, 138
  spending time with others, 127
beautiful as a friend, Socrates suggesting, 35
beautiful things, abstract encounters with the class of, 36
beginning principle, on friendship, 37
being loved, resembling a passive "undergoing," 133
being refuted, as the greatest good, 210n41
belief, 56, 57
beloved
  being akin in some way to, 40
  catching one's, 29
  making "harder to capture," 22
Benardete, Seth, 205n44, 209n28
benefactor, loving the recipient more, 133
benefits
  giving and receiving of, 118, 223n1
  providing to one another, 111
  those performing, 133
best regime
  education in, 170–75, 237n27
  feasibility of, 235n12
"the best thing," pleasure as, 144
binding power, 170
blame and praise, rhetoric assigning, 54

block of wood, potentiality of, 132
Bloom, Allan, 206n2
Bodéüs, Richard, 233n67
Bolotin, David
  defending Socrates, 204n30
  on desire or longing to belong to a larger whole, 40
  on Lysis arranging to have the returning Menexenus chastened, 30
  on the refutation that the good cannot be friends to the good, 41
  on Socrates directing Lysis and Menexenus in a rebellion against guardians, 43–44
  on the spirited element of the soul as akin to the rational part, 205n42
boundaries, Hermes penchant for crossing, 22
Bowling Alone (Putman), 4
Broadie, Sarah, 151
bureaucratic policies, espoused in the Constitution, 190
Burger, Ronna, 220–21n68

Cain, Patrick, 107
Callicles
  agreement with Socrates, 69
  characteristics of, 212n62
  commitment to virtue, 213n69
  on a good, independent of bad, 73
  goodwill for Socrates, 127
  as incomplete and in need, 65
  as much less sensitive to shame than Polus, 209n27
  no longer considered a friend by Socrates, 74
  as not entirely restricted by a sense of shame, 69
  on not pursuing education, 88
  shaming Socrates, 72
  showing goodwill toward Socrates, 70
  Socrates becoming ironic with, 70–71
  Socrates counseling to avoid politics, 13, 82
  on Socrates philosophizing as unmanly, 100
  Socrates's discussion with, 64–65
  struggle with Socrates, 67
  turning the conversation to the question of justice, 71
  urging Socrates to enter the political arena, 52
  urging Socrates to "stop refuting," 67
  as very similar to Socrates, 82
catharsis, 237n25, 237n27
cathartic effect, of music, 178
Chaerephon, asking Gorgias "who he is," 53
chance, rhetoric as a skill conquering, 54
character
  highest type of friendship dependent upon, 3
  music having the effect of forming, 177
  two lovers delighting in one another's, 112
character development, of Lysis, 42
character trait or virtue, as that of real worth, 104
character type, difference in, 82
Charmides, concern for one's own good in, 210n35
children
  learning to make music, 176, 180
  limiting the number of, 165
choice
  stemming from one's characteristic, 114
  subverting the political order, 166

Christianity, causing the eclipse of friendship according to Pangle, 198n14
city (*polis*)
  avoiding strictures and standards of, 105
  coming into being "for the sake of living well," 11–12
  neglecting the law, 155
  not distinguished from the household, 214n1
  as not strictly philosophic, 88
  requiring an individual capable to transcending, 95
  unity in, 163–69
"city in speech," 163, 206n2, 234n3
civic associations and groups, decline of, 4
civic courage, 94–95, 102
civic friendship, 3, 5
civic life, 235n9
civil bonds, 4
classical traditions, of friendship, 198n14
classical world, developed analogies between music and politics, 171
Cleinias, 27–28
Collins, Susan, 87–88, 149
"coming into being," 56, 143
commercial friendships, 2
commercial virtue, substitution of, 5
common good, friendship centered on devotion to, 170–71
common judgment (*homognomosune*), of the political order, 166
commonality, between Lysander and Socrates, 100–101
community, 11, 233n68, 235n11
"community of speeches and thought," establishment of, 149
complementarity
  Aristotle stressing in a friendship, 129
  importance and benefit of in friendship, 107
  importance of in friendship, 126
  as a key ingredient to friendship, 128
  of Lysis and Menexenus, 24
complete actions, 142
"complete activities," pleasure as like, 143
complete friendships, friendships based on the good as, 112
completeness, awakening a desire for, 83
conscience, 51, 208n22
constant activity, life of as impossible, 146
Constitution of the US, 15, 194, 195
Constitutional Convention, 188, 189, 191
Constitutional friendship, 190–95
Constitutional Republic, 186
contemplation
  as good for its own sake, 230n44
  human beings incapable of constant, 146
  pleasure of practiced by the god, 233n62
  pleasures of as "the best thing," 144
  solitary life of as the human good, 91
contemplative type of life, exceeding what is human, 153
correct habits, difficult to obtain without proper laws, 155
correct judgement, developing the capacity of, 181
"correct reason," not defined by Aristotle, 134
corruption, fleeing, 127, 227n19
counsel, rhetoric giving, 56
courage
  Aristotle beginning with, 228n32

Aristotle defining "in the authoritative sense," 93
  as the first moral virtue Aristotle covers in the *Ethics*, 92
  types of resembling true courage, 216n18
  virtue of, 92, 93, 133
courageous individuals, 93, 128, 139
courageous magnanimity, 111
courageousness, of the intelligent and strong, 71
craftsman, for Socrates, 207n6
craftsman of persuasion, rhetoric as, 55
craftsmen
  pattern of the good useful for, 230n47
  political or market friendship between, 117
Crito, guided by the opinions of the city, 206n2
Ctesippus, 20, 21
customs, innovation and, 122
cycle of existence, 173
Cyclops, 155, 156

daimonic voice, 51
daimonion, 208n22, 209n22
death, 93, 218n45
decent people, friendship of, 228n30
decline, of friendship, 3–5
deeds, rhetors capable of accomplishing, 59
defective condition, of humanity, 145
Defense of Palamedes, "inverted parody" of Gorgias's, 207n3
delight, derived from watching an inferior, 232n55
Delphic oracle, Socrates's use of, 218n49
Democritus, 204n32
Demos, 65, 211n51
Descartes, 231n53

desire(s)
  allowing to be as great as possible, 71
  of Callicles, 72, 83
  friendship and, 42–44
  fulfilling for friendship by being friend to oneself, 125
  for a good that is free of evil, 73
  music having the ability to shape, 177
  as really a cause of friendship, 39
  as the root cause of factional disputes, 165
  of Socrates, 83
  stringing together with friendship, 36
  types of, 39
  for what is akin or "one's own," 40
destructive tendency
  of magnanimous men, 102
  of Socrates's way of life, 219n57
development, during the dialogue, 42
dialogues
  analyzing the drama of, 19
  in narrative form by Plato, 17
  not having a happy conclusion, 43
  as partial truths, 206n1
  of Plato, 201n1
dianoetic activity, man having the capacity to engage in, 135
dianoetic virtue, characteristic of the statesman, 181
differentiation. *See* complementarity
Diogenes Laertius, 18, 225n6
Diomedes, 94, 95, 102, 107, 221n68
Dionysodorus, 27
Diotima, 35–36
"Discourses on Davilla" (Adams), 191
dishonor, intolerance of, 97
disputes, on the distribution of honors, 166
disrepute, being fearful of, 93

dissent and noncompliance, Socrates choosing, 49
divination, of Socrates on friendship, 36
divine capacities, 153
"divine sign," 204n37
Dolon, extorting information from, 107
doloneia, 107, 220n68
Dorian harmony, effect of, 177
drinking song, quoted by Socrates, 54
dual audience, of Aristotle, 226n10
Duncan, Roger, on friendship in *Gorgias*, 52
Dziob, Anne Marie, 107

economic classes, limiting the disparity between, 164
education
  Aristotle agreeing with Plato's method of, 155
  in the best regime, 88, 170–75
  of citizens with a view to self-rule and moral agency, 182
  as the source of political unity, 162
educational system, 172, 183, 237n28
educator, 157
Eisenstadt, Michael, on connections between *Lysis* and *Euthydemus*, 203n25
the elderly, unlikely to form friendships, 113
Empedocles, 130, 204n32, 204n34, 221n70, 227n24
enemy, as "a friend to the friend," 34
enlightened statesman, affected by philosophy, 228n31
enlightenment political ideals, 187
equality
  friendship as, 114, 231n54
  relationship between philosopher and statesman, 139, 231n55

equalization schemes, 165, 166
equivocations, 98, 101
Erasmus, Desiderius, 6
eros, characterized by a felt need or desire, 13
erotic desires, 165
erotic friendships, 112, 117–18
erotic individuals, Callicles and Socrates as, 65, 82
erotic love, 35, 39, 42, 170
erotic matters, Socrates's knowledge of, 21
erotic relationships, 42, 106, 118
eschaton, Callicles wishing to immanentize, 74
eternal principles, attaining truth about, 136
Ethics (Aristotle)
  actualizing potentiality of readers appearing to be noble, 129
  actualizing the potentiality of another individual, 133
  Aristotle's presentation of magnanimity in, 14
  Book VIII on self-sufficient friendship, 106–16
  on both the philosopher and the statesman, 96
  concept of friendship developed in, 12
  ending of, 161–62
  on friendship, 10, 150, 157
  as a handbook to establish and to maintain public order, 155
  insistence on the necessity of law, 170
  on moral virtues, 132
  on the philosophic life as the happiest, 87
  relationship with *Politics*, 9
Eudemian Ethics (Aristotle), 219n54, 221n69

Euthydemus, 27, 28
Euthydemus, 13, 27, 203n20, 203n25, 204n35
evil
　first friend remaining a friend in the absence of, 39
　good independent of, 73
evildoer, punishing, 77
excellence, perceiving in the other's character, 3
exchange, between two friends, 148
existence
　Aristotle's understanding of contrasted with Descartes, 231n53
　friendship completing, 153
　human element of, 152
　joint-perception of, 149
　meaning of, 126
　seeking to preserve, 126
existential moment, in Aristotle's *Ethics*, 147
existing, as a choiceworthy thing, 149
experience, 135, 157
external goods
　acquisition of, 71
　Callicles's desire directed solely to, 74
　care for one's soul coming before a concern for, 80

factionary party spirit, triumph of, 194
faculties, independent of reason, 135
fallacious argument, of Socrates, 27
false opinion, as a great evil, 62, 210n41
false start, of Socrates conversation with boys, 23–25
falsity (and flattery), as unjust, 62
family relations, exclusivity or "ownness" accompanying, 163
father, obligation to one's, 122, 123
a feast, Socrates on rhetoric as more like, 53

federal government, Jefferson on, 193
Federalists, led by John Adams, 192
first friend, 37, 38, 39, 109
First Mover, complete activity of, 231n48
flattery, 58, 64, 75
flute, not to be used in education, 178–79
forces, of potentiality and actuality, 129, 130
forming, a friend, 127–39
forms
　Aristotle's critique of Plato's theory of, 121
　of friendship, 109
　Plato's theory of, 109, 144
fortune
　Aristotle's ambiguous treatment of the magnanimous man's relation to, 105
　gifts of connecting to honor, 103
　magnanimous man needing to dispose himself to in a proper manner, 104
　trusting in, 156
Founding Fathers, using philosophic ideas of the day, 187–88
friend(s)
　as another self, 126
　becoming a friend for the sake of a further friend, 37
　forming, 127–39
　having all things in common, 20
　of the philosopher also becoming aware of his own existence, 149
　providing a beneficiary for whom one can perform good deeds, 106
　rendering something to those who were once, 125
　rhetor ought not to use his skill against, 57
　searching for a potential, 128

friend(s) *(continued)*
  senses or usages of, 31
  Socrates's elusive quest for, 2
friendly affection, 114, 133
friendly love, 201n3
friendship
  of Adams and Jefferson, 194
  aiming at the good, 39
  at the American founding, 185–90
  Aristotle on, 110, 161, 229n32
  in Aristotle's discussion of magnanimity, 104
  attributes characteristic of, 125
  of base people as corrupt, 228n30
  basis in deficiency, lack, or need, 39, 40, 151
  as both pleasant and useful, 111
  characterized by a felt need or desire, 13
  characterized by equality, 139–40
  coincidence of power and wisdom and, 81–84
  competitive, or rivalrous aspect of, 107
  concerned both with one's own good and the good of another, 89
  as the cure for socially destructive tendencies, 106
  curing socially destructive tendencies, 14
  decline of, 3–5
  deficiencies of Socrates's understanding of, 10
  definitions of, 30–35, 68, 78, 222n71
  desire and, 42–44
  directed toward the good, 160
  elusive character of, 2
  existing between two individuals similar yet different, 104
  forms of, 109, 110
  fostering, 170
  founded on the virtue of each partner, 74
  of good human beings, 91
  granting dignity to politics for Aristotle, 12
  harsh appraisal of, 38
  Hobbes's attempt to weaken, 6
  impacting the policies of those in power, 117
  as an instantiation of the good, 83
  between John Adams and Thomas Jefferson, 190
  as like a characteristic: friendly affection, 114
  between Lysis and Menexenus, 83
  Lysis questioning his existing, 42
  metaphysical foundations of, 117–60
  of Montaigne and La Boetie, 1
  as "most necessary with a view to life," 106
  necessary to complete our existence, 153
  not arising swiftly, 223n76
  not existing on the basis of the good alone, 113
  not rooted in each friend's deficiencies, 106
  ordinary sense of transformed into love, 31
  of the philosopher and the statesman, 150, 232n60
  Plato and Socrates on, 18
  in the polis, 161–63
  political action and, 45
  politics and, 12
  practice of politics and, 161–83
  as the prescription for the socially destructive propensity of magnanimous men, 102
  problems posed by, 6
  pursued "for the sake of something," 37

qualities of in the person in relation to himself, 140
range of relationships described as, 2
refuting the lie in another's soul, 83
relationship of justice to, 61
removing the lie existing in one's soul, 82
reorienting the magnanimous man's lack of concern with standards for the common good, 97
rhetoric's relation to, 55
of Rush, 195
seeming to be nonpolitical, 5
Socrates bringing out the competitive nature of, 24
Socrates exposing a quality of, 23
Socrates on Callicles's as fraudulent, 74
Socrates's ambivalence about, 81
Socrates's and Aristotle's disparate understandings of, 12
Socrates's understanding of, 53, 209n27
Socrates's wariness of, 20–21
Socratic conception of, 186
strife and, 130
structure of Aristotle's *Nicomachean Ethics* and, 89–91
suitability of between two types of magnanimous men, 105
theme of pervading the *Gorgias*, 52
between those akin to one another, 68
types of, 2, 104
useful for those in their prime, 106
of utility, 2
of utility and pleasure as prone to dissolve, 110
wisdom and, 27
friendship of the good
Aristotle viewing music as capable of fostering, 171
as friendship between two magnanimous individuals cultivating public benefits, 160
pleasure accompanying, 153
as secure against slander, 112
as *sunaisthetic* friendship, 170
friendship via magnanimity, ascent to, 91–102
Funeral Oration (Pericles), 48

gadfly, Socrates as, 208n21
"general will," adherence to, 199n23
generality, Aristotle's concern with the law's, 168
Gibert, John, 68
gift, of philosophy as invaluable, 120
gods
 as the cause of friendship for poets, 32
 enjoying pleasure, 145
 existence of as intrinsically pleasant, 222n73
the good
 being friends to the good, 111
 cannot be a friend of what is bad, 36
 enforced practice of moral virtue, 162
 as friends, 2, 33, 34, 109
 rhetoric aiming toward, 57
 sharing in a friendship of, 14
 as similar to one another, 109
 as sufficient in themselves, 109
 taking priority over one's comrades, 122
 as wholly free of need, 73
the good (virtue)
 as beyond the capacity of a human being to attain, 144
 Callicles's desire for, 82
 desire that Socrates and Callicles have for an unalloyed, 73

the good (virtue) *(continued)*
   doing to a man who's a friend, 62
   friendship impelling one toward, 38
   justice aiming at, 59
   of a nation or city as "nobler and more divine," 91
   overlap with the pleasant, 112
   of people "in their own nature," 212n61
   pursuing in different ways, 109
   pursuing through philosophic contemplation, 84
   "as a sort of model" or pattern, 144
good and bad pleasures, Callicles refusing to distinguish between, 72
the good and the bad, as completely distinct, 73
the good and the pleasant
   exchange of, 231n54
   relationship between, 223n78
   as the same or different, 72
   Socrates eliciting from Callicles as different, 73
good by nature, a friend as, 147
"good citizen," becoming, 120, 225n7
good deliberation, 138
good desires, as beneficial, 39
good human being, as honorable, 105
good laws, 155, 158
good man, as a self-lover, 140
good people, as both beneficial and pleasant to one another, 111
good person, as lovable and choiceworthy to a good person, 113
good sense, 26, 27
goodness
   differentiation in, 112–13
   reciprocal appreciation of another's, 106

goods of the soul (virtue), as superior to other goods, 214n2
goodwill
   alone not sufficient to form a friendship, 110
   arising on account of virtue and decency, 128, 229n32
   as "the beginning of friendship," 127
   of Callicles, 70, 213n65
   distinct from friendship, 70
   friendship involving reciprocated, 110
   not sufficient for friendship, 127
goodwill and friendship, Aristotle's distinction between, 129
Gorgianic rhetoric, directing toward the truth, 56
Gorgias
   exhibiting a sense of shame, 210n38
   the great Sophist, 46
   Part II: Socratic eros and the private life, 64–81
   rhetorician who traveled from city to city selling his knowledge, 209n29
   seeing different cities having different conceptions of justice, 58
   Socrates refuting to remove their false conceptions of what is his, 82
   as "too sensitive to shame," 69
Gorgias (Plato), 7
   foreshadowing Socrates's trial and death, 46
   parts of, 52
   on phantom friends and phantom politics, 52–64
   role of shame in, 211n52
   Socrates refuting Polus and releasing him from his erroneous conception, 63
   on Socrates's daimonion, 51

on Socrates's understanding of
friendship, 19
on Socrates's way of life, 206n2
trial recounted in, 46
witnessing Socrates, 8
greater good, to be released from the
greatest evil, 210n41
greatest harm, turning away, 78
"greatest injustices," committing, 165,
179
"greatest of human affairs," opinions
varying on, 54
"greatest things," 47, 48
great-souled individuals, with a tragic
flaw, 102
great-souled man
Aristotle's depiction of, 91–92
as the philosopher par excellence, 96
portrait of, 95
ground of friendship, getting at, 32

habit, moral virtue as the result of,
228n28
habitual action, potency for, 133
habituation
law obtaining its power from, 168
of music forming moral virtue, 177
Hadreas, Peter, 127
Halper, Edward, 131
Hanley, Ryan, 103
happiness
defining, 223n77
as satisfying desires, 71
as a sort of action, 87
happy person, needing friends, 145
Hardie, on the tragic fault of the
magnanimous man, 96
harmonies, 177, 179
hatred, as the opposite of friendship, 109
healing, doctor already resolved in
favor of, 137

healthy souls, pursuing desires, 75
Hector
excessive concern with honor and
shame, 95
portrayed as a hero with a tragic
flaw, 94
spurning advice, 102
hedonism, Socrates critiquing
Callicles's, 73
Heidegger, Martin, 137, 229n35,
229n40
hereditary government, Adams's
seeming endorsement of, 192
Hermes
entering and restoring order in
Antiope, 81
frustrated Socrates's intentions, 44
god of tricks, 22
receiving a sacrificial victim, 25
reestablishing order, 67
Hesiod, on those most alike, 32
heterogeneous friendships, 117, 224n2
Hippias Major, on the fine or noble as
equivalent to the good, 211n43
Hippodamus
Aristotle ridiculing, 235n8
on honor as a driving motivation,
168
identified the difficulties associated
with the law's generality, 182
legislative proposals put forward by,
166
political science of as an advance
over that of Phaleas, 169
Hippothales
on friendship, 20
gratification of Lysis, 29
inducing Socrates to come inside the
palaestra, 20
revealed to be "in love," 21
Socrates chances upon, 20

Hippothales *(continued)*
   ulterior motives in conversing with Socrates, 22
"historical" Socrates, 17
Hitz, Zena, 236n16
Hobbes, Thomas, 6, 195
Homer's *Odyssey*, 155, 173–74
"homogeneous friendship," 224n2
homonoia, meaning "sameness of mind," 3
honor
   concern for leading to confer great benefits, 98
   courageous man's desire for, 92–93
   fighting for the sake of, 95
   magnanimous man concerned with, 104
   pride and excessive concern for, 94
   relationship with ill-fortune, 93
   underlying basis of, 103
honors
   different relations to be accorded different, 124
   distribution of as a source of factional disputes, 165
   political offices and, 141
household(s)
   existing in order to satisfy "the needs of daily life," 85
   forming, 11
   sufficient to deal with the necessities of life, 150
Howland, Jacob, 97
hubris, 44
hubristic demeanor, 120, 121
human aspect, of friendship, 110
human beings
   arriving at the enjoyment of pleasure, 176
   existence as, 126
   finding completion or perfection in the city, 86
   judgment of in the afterlife, 80
   nonrational and rational potencies, 132
   rarely attaining the end of education, 176
human body, desire for the medical art, 36
human good, 73, 90, 91
human life, limits of, 146
human nature, understanding, 33, 189
human soul, intellect and, 135
human wisdom, Socrates revealing the paucity of, 47
Huyler, Jerome, 187
hypothetical friendship, 125

idealist, Socrates as, 10
identicality, 128, 129
idleness, of the magnanimous man, 148–49
ignorance, 36, 37
Iliad (Homer), 80, 93–94, 199n26
ill-fortune, 92, 93, 94
inanimate objects, 31–32, 110
incidental pleasures, as restorative in nature, 143
incomplete actions, 142
indebtedness to fortune, magnanimous man's inability to recognize, 96
indifferent, two meanings of the word, 101
individual judgment, not guided by a common standard, 182
individual soul and the whole, no natural compatibility between for Socrates, 77
individualism, rise in, 5
individuals
   choosing different activities and pleasures, 152
   committing the "greatest injustices," 178

as the most basic unit of the polis,
    11
  needing the good when some evil is
    present, 36
  uniting with other individuals to
    counter necessity, 85
initiative, taking in giving, 118
injustice
  avoiding, 77, 100
  better to pay the penalty than to
    escape punishment, 62
  doing as worse than suffering
    injustice, 60
  doing but not paying the just
    penalty, 66, 75
  failing to pay the just penalty as the
    greatest evil, 78
  removing from one's own soul and
    from the souls of fellow citizens,
    61
  rhetorician never wishing to do, 57
  Socrates's avoidance of, 50, 51
  unavoidable required by politics, 48
  vulgar conception of suggested in
    the *Apology*, 83
innate potencies, realized through
  practice or habit, 132
innovations, encouraging useful by
  publicly honoring, 169
instability, change in the laws
  engendering, 168
instruction, Socrates in need of, 20
insufficiency, Lysis's awareness of his
  own, 44
insults
  Adams seem to have evinced an
    intolerance of, 192
  those intolerant of, 98
intellect
  concerned with the defining
    boundaries, 136
  defining correct reason, 134

Heidegger explaining, 135
  as pure actuality, 229n34
intellectual capacity, Plato pointing to
  a flaw in Socrates's, 33
intellectual grasping, ordered towards
  action, 230n44
intellectual virtues, 90, 114, 134, 135,
  228n28
intelligence and courage, Callicles's
  admiration for, 74
intemperance, fleeing, 76
intemperate man, 71
interests, rhetoric reconciling opposing,
  53
interlocutors, disparate treatment of by
  Socrates in *Gorgias*, 52–53
intrinsically pleasant, Aristotle on,
  222n73
intuitive grasping, occurring in the arts
  and sciences, 137
Io, 22, 202n17
irony, of Socrates, 17
"isolated city," as active, 87

Jaffa, Harry, 96
Jefferson, Thomas
  adopted liberal and egalitarian
    political stances, 191
  on the authority of the Declaration
    of Independence, 187
  on diplomatic mission to France,
    189
  magnanimous in defeat, 192
  optimistic belief in the "solid and
    independent yeomanry," 186–87
  pushing for independence, 190
  responded to Rush's entreaties, 194
  victory in 1800, 193
"joint perception," *sunaisthesis* meaning,
  14
judgment, learning to play music
  fostering, 237n29

judgments, of citizens differing from one another, 169
jurors, 167, 235n7
just man, 140, 226n17
justice
    aiming at what is best, 59
    allied with the good, 61, 63
    connected to speech, 62
    consisting in refuting a friend, 63
    directed toward the health of the soul, 58, 70
    as the end of the city, 86
    Gorgias allying to friendship, 57
    Gorgias and Polus wedded to conventional conceptions of, 82–83
    Gorgias and Socrates not offering any definition of, 58
    Gorgias's understanding of, 57
    marked by equality and reciprocity, 170
    as not a natural end of the city, 214n1
    Polus's disregard for as feigned, 60
    in relation to the good and friendship, 58
    rhetoric pretending to be, 58
    seeking to administer, 61
    Socrates on, 58, 59, 62
    virtue of as incomplete, 229n33

Kateb, George, 49, 50
kings of the Persians and the Medes, pleasures of, 176
kinship, between Socrates and Callicles, 74
knowledge
    Aristotle not dismissing Sophists' claims of, 158
    Aristotle's position differing from Socrates on, 228n26
    attained by pure intellection versus discursive reason, 229n37
    of Callicles called into question by Socrates, 69
    Lysis not having any, 27

La Boétie, Étienne, 1, 188
"ladder of friendship," Socrates establishing, 37
"ladder of love," of Diotima, 35–36, 37
laughter, as refutation, 222n74
law
    changing traditional, 168
    Hippodamus's attempts to offset the generality of, 167
    incapable of ensuring that citizens act morally, 168
    life as a whole in need of, 155
    limitations of, 171
    limited ability to curb partiality and factional disputes, 164
    preparing people for the rational acquisition of virtue, 234n1
    rule in accordance with, 214n3
    selection of which to implement requiring particular skill, 158
law of nature, 66
law or custom, Greek word for, 171
the lawful, as a tool of the weak, 66
lawgiver, 157, 226n10
learning to make music, purpose of, 180–81
Leges, on songs as our laws, 171
legislation, alone not sufficient to maintain unity in the city, 162
legislative art, sophistry pretending to be, 58
leisure
    characterizing both the life of the enlightened statesman and that of the philosopher, 232n59
    in contradistinction to occupation, 173
    supervening necessary work, 174

Leon the Salaminian, arrest of, 50
Leviathan, Hobbes's embrace of, 6
life
  of contemplation, 29–30
  of philosophy, 87
  of politics, 79
  types of, 87
the like
  as a friend to like, 33, 38, 109
  as most hostile to its like, 34
  as useless to its like insofar as there is likeness, 41
"like aims at like," 108
like and akin, as the same, 41
like to like, 78, 129, 227n24
like-mindedness, 128
limitations
  causing us to engage in friendship, 145
  of law, 164, 171
  posed on us as human beings, 153
Lincoln, Abraham, 189
living, defined, 147
living together, 113, 149
living well, 86, 130
Lord, Carnes, 168, 173, 181
love
  reciprocating as a matter of choice, 114
  taking primacy over friendship, 21
love objects, incapable of reciprocating love, 108–9
loved one, as a friend, 32
lover, not loved in return, 31
lover and beloved
  capacity of Socrates to recognize, 21
  relationship of, 112
loving oneself most, 140
loyalty to one's own, of Gorgias, 57
Ludwig, Paul, 186
Lycurgus of Sparta, 188
Lydian harmony, effect of, 177

Lysander
  commonality with Socrates, 99–100, 218n44
  excluded from rule on account of their status in society, 100
  in the face of good and bad fortune, 219n54
  indifference to fortune displayed by, 217n32
  lowborn status of, 100
  plan to change the constitution, 218n49
"Lysis," translated as "to loosen" and "to destroy," 44
Lysis
  Hippothales songs of praise about, 21
  inducing into conversation, 22
  Menexenus and, 30, 83
  moral failing of, 29
  as more thoughtful, 42
  not appearing in any other dialogues, 205n48
  pondering Hippothales's passionate love, 40
  questioning all his existing friendships, 25
  Socrates refuting, 63
Lysis (Plato), 1–2, 7
  addressing a question of definition, 203n18
  authenticity of no longer disputed, 18
  conclusion of, 81
  introduction of, 19–23
  presenting Socrates as giving short shrift to friendship, 45
  presenting Socrates with interlocutors, 8
  Socrates conversation with two young boys about friendship, 17–18

Lysis (Plato) *(continued)*
   Socrates directing away from the topic of age, 26
   Socrates driving to resent his parents, 25
   Socrates's conception of justice and approach to Polus mirroring, 63
   Socrates's understanding of friendship, 12, 78
   the wise invoked in, 77

Madison, James, 188, 189
magnanimity
   of Alcibiades, 115
   Aristotle on, 13, 91–92, 97, 217n30, 219n54, 225n9
   ascribed to the apex of the moral life, 96
   first type of as at root, political, 98
   friendship between those characterized by, 91
   genera of, 97
   pointing toward friendship, 133–34
   as at root a philosophic virtue, 96
   types of, 13, 96, 101, 111
magnanimous individuals, 145, 146, 161, 171
magnanimous man
   Aristotle indulging, 105
   concerned with great actions, 96
   curing, 102–6
   "deficiency" of stemming from his "unfamiliarity with philosophy," 220n59
   describing, 95, 219n55
   identity of Aristotle's, 92
   as incapable of living only with a friend, 104
   as independent of fortune, 220n59
   invoking the assistance of, 216n16
   perceiving the regime he has formed, 150
   as a statesman/general or a philosopher, 216n26
   as tragically flawed and needing friendship, 217n30
   viewing most things as beneath him, 148
magnanimous men, types of, 111
magnanimous philosopher, 140, 142, 160
magnanimous statesman, 119, 138, 160
man, defined by his capacity for speech, 134
manliness, Callicles's commitment to, 212n56
master and slave, conjoining of, 85
Mathiesen, Thomas, 171
Megaric position, 227n26
Megaric school, potency and act as unified and indistinct, 131
Menexenus, 23, 30, 34, 42, 205n48
Menexenus and Lysis, belonging to one another in some way, 40
metaphors, metaphorical precluded in definition, 219n54
metaphysical foundations, of friendship, 117–60
Metaphysics (Aristotle), 134
   on actuality as the opposite of potentiality, 142
   clarifying discussion of friendship in the *Ethics*, 133
   criticism of the Megaric school, 131
   inquiry into the nature of "being" in, 129
   on Socrates ignoring the study of nature, 33
Miccus, as a capable sophist, 20
middle approach, 108
moderate man, life of as like that of a stone, 72
moderate soul, as good, 76

moderating advice, incapacity to heed, 99
moderation
 in distribution of honors, 165
 inculcating among the citizenry, 178
 not chosen simply for its own, 75
 Socrates turning to the question of, 71
 as virtue of the soul, 76
money, capable of equalizing disparate things, 224n4
Montaigne, Michel de, 1, 188
moral character, music contributing to the formation of, 175
moral failings, reminding citizens of, 182
moral integrity
 of Socrates, 48, 49
 Socrates's examples of, 51
moral virtue(s)
 Aristotle on, 10, 90, 216n17
 as characteristics marked by choice, 114
 cultivating, 236n16
 exemplifying, 114
 fundamental distinction with intellectual virtues, 223n77
 goal of, 162
 pointing toward philosophic virtue, 90
 present in those with a nature as to receive them, 129
 relating to the life of philosophic contemplation, 90
morality, 66
motion, contrasting pleasure with, 151
mousikē, including forms of poetry prominent in traditional music education, 236n17
movements, as actions having a definite end, 143

music
 Aristotle on, 172, 236n12, 237n27
 contributing to pastime and prudence, 175
 contributing to the character and the soul, 177
 cultivating the dianoetic virtues, 236n16
 delight from interfering with other more rational activities, 154
 final end or purpose of, 180
 good education in, 171
 impact on an individual's desires, 178
 integrating spirited individuals into the political community, 180
 and law as important and necessary means, 172
 not completely curbing all people's desires, 178
 purpose of, 175–83
 taught for the sake of "being at leisure in noble fashion," 173
musical education, 162–63, 175, 180, 182, 234n1
myth, 77–78, 79, 80

natural harmony, 77, 86
natural justice, 66, 83
natural philosophy, Socrates on, 33
natural purpose, leisure constituting man's, 173
nature
 of friendship, 46
 friendship's connection to, 108, 113
 as nasty and brutish, 156
 potentialities from as nonrational, 131
necessity
 as the basis for the development of the polis, 85
 man subject to, 189

necessity *(continued)*
  prompting people to come together, 224n4
  Socrates on friendship's basis in, 12
need, causing one to befriend another, 34
negative and private approach, of Socrates, 48, 208n21
negativity
  extended account of Socrates's, 207n8
  Socrates's emphasis on, 47
the neutral
  being a friend to the good, 37
  as friends with the good, 109
  seeking out the good, 36
neutral state, between good and bad, 36
Nichols, James, 80
Nichols, Mary, 107
Nicomachean Ethics (Aristotle), 3, 8
  on friendship, 7, 89–91
  on life of theoretical contemplation, 88
  on philosophic life as superior to the political life, 87
  types of friendship, 2
Nightingale, Andrea, 67, 212n56
"no injustice," committed by Socrates, 218n47
the noble, 128, 172
noble acts, the philosopher witnesses his friend's, 148
noble and courageous, philosophers befriending, 120
"noble judging," enjoyment of music and poetry as, 181
noble things, 181, 228n30
noncompliance, of Socrates, 50

"objective account" of things, possibility of, 225n10
objectivity, 121–22
obligations, 123, 124
Odysseus, 107, 221n68
Odyssey (Homer), 155, 173–74
older fellows, 43, 44
one's own, desiring, 40, 121–22
oneself, characteristics of friendship pertaining to, 125–26
onlooking, as the statesman's ultimate activity, 150
opposite sorts of men, 28
opposites, 32, 34
"oppositional" conception of friendship, 35
oracle at Delphi, 47
orderly and moderate man, 71–72
ordinary friends, 37–38
ordinary friendships, of Lysis, 42
Orestes, 231n50
Orestes (Euripides), 145–46, 231n50
outspokenness, of Callicles, 70

Pakaluk, Michael, 224n3
palaestra, as a place of instruction, 20
Pangle, Lorraine Smith, 128, 146, 198n14, 222n73, 228n32
Pangle, Thomas, 235n9
Panops, 20, 22
paromologia, Aristotle employing, 122
"partial associations," inclined toward self-interest, 6
passionate love, 43, 114
passionate lover, 40
passionate philosopher, 114
passions, Aristotle not opposed to, 179
pastime, 175, 176
pastime and prudence, musical education contributing to, 180
paternal authority, 156, 233n67
Patroclus, death of, 99
penalties, inducing men to fight, 95
penalty, suffering for injustice, 60

perception
  Aristotle distinguishing from prudence, 229n41
  in Aristotle's definition of man, 147
  of a friend, 148
  life of, 150
  pleasure accompanying, 153
  of the ultimate particular thing, 137, 181
Pericles, 48, 139, 228n31
persuasion, 55, 62, 155
Phaedo (Plato), 33
Phaleas, 164, 169
phantom friends, 63, 109
phantom friendships, 63, 64, 65
phantoms, of the "first friend," 37
philosopher(s)
  ability to form another individual, 132–33
  acting like an artisan by dispensing advice, 133
  Aristotle directing his writing to, 225n10
  Aristotle exhorting to be patient, 123
  becoming aware of existence, 149
  capacity to write treatises and laws, 158–59
  as the cause of noble actions, 148
  coming to terms with gentlemen in power, 200n29
  criticizing established customs and authorities, 225n6
  engaging and gratifying the authoritative, 152
  ensuring personal preservation, 126
  forming character of the statesman, 139
  friendship with those who hold power, 119
  grounding in community, 120
  as incapable of friendship, 127
  lacking experience in political affairs, 66
  on like as always necessarily a friend to its like, 32–33
  need for friendship, 145, 146
  obligations toward the political community, 124–25
  obtaining something in return from the statesman, 141–42
  possessing the knowledge of political science, 138
  practicing the highest form of friendship, 119
  taming, 119–27
  tension with the polis, 8–10
philosopher's friend, actualizing the potential of the philosopher, 142
philosophic contemplation, private activity of, 88
philosophic education, Aristotle's views on, 88
philosophic ideas, leveraged for political action, 187
philosophic life
  of contemplation as the highest life, 90
  examining its relation to the polis, 206n2
  fulfilling one's desire for the good, 37
  giving up for the political life, 66
  maintaining the superiority of, 9
  as the most active life, 87
  of Socrates as superior to the active life, 65
philosophical virtue, 10, 223n82
philosophically magnanimous man, 115, 141, 227n23
philosophy
  always saying the same thing, 65–66
  animating and orienting the city toward, 88

272 / Index

philosophy *(continued)*
    Callicles on, 68, 69
    finding a remedy for desires, 166
    having a guiding force on politics, 187
    practice of, 166
    recourse to on friendship, 32
    Socrates on, 10, 65, 100
phronesis, as the characteristic virtue that tragedy teaches, 182
Phrygian harmonies, 179–80
Plato
    allusion to Zeus's banishment of Poseidon, 81
    ambiguity in regard to Callicles's character, 213n63
    aware of the dangers of Socrates's approach, 44
    on a complementary way of life, 83
    on the danger that Socratic understanding of friendship poses for politics, 84
    on friendship between two people, both good, 83
    hinting at sloppy reasoning by Socrates, 41
    on *Lysis* pointing toward a more complete understanding of friendship, 19
    on a potential reconciliation between Callicles and Socrates, 68
    on a reconciliation between politics and philosophy through friendship, 84
    showing Socrates to be somewhat hasty about friendship, 43
    on the similarity between Socrates and Callicles, 72
    as skeptical of Socrates's approach to friendship, 45
    on Socrates as uncertain of the soundness of philosophers, 33
    on Socrates failing to give friendship the proper regard, 19
    on Socrates not fully understanding "wisest ones," 77
    on Socrates using eristic arguments and sophisms, 12
    on Socrates's approach to politics and philosophy, 79–80
    on Socrates's skepticism, 21
    on Socrates's understanding of friendship, 8, 38–39, 79, 209n26, 222n70
    on Socrates's way of life as deficient, 69
    as subtly critiquing Socrates, 201n4
    suggesting that Callicles's character is a linchpin, 69
play
    Aristotle places in the category of occupation, 173
    as a possible purpose for the inclusion of music education, 175
    pursuing for its own sake, 236n19
    as for the sake of rest, 176
play and pastime, both involving pleasure, 176
the pleasant
    distinguishing from the good, 74
    done for the sake of the good, 76
    as friends, 109
the pleasant and the painful, as mixed, 73
pleasure
    Aristotle elevating friendships of, 111–12
    Aristotle providing different definitions of, 232n62
    Aristotle's extended account of, 143
    completing activities bound up with, 154
    deprecating as being less than the good, 143

differences between two accounts of, 232n62
existing for the sake of some other end, 143
experiencing, 151, 233n62
friendship needing, 113
friendships of, 2, 110
human incapacity to experience continuously, 145, 151, 152
human limitations in achieving, 144
as necessarily mixed with pain, 73
philosopher receiving in return for philosophical advice, 148
of play, 177
received from witnessing good or noble acts, 146
self-love and, 139–50
as something whole and complete, 152
types of, 143
unaccompanied with pains, 234n6
wholeness or completeness of, 151
Plutarch, 100, 218n49, 219n56
poetry, 173, 181
poets, 32, 207n6
Polemarchus, 200n29
polis (city)
citizens participating in a friendship of *sunaisthesis*, 185
classification of causes and, 232n60
differing stances of Socrates and Aristotle toward, 10–12
emergence of, 11, 85
establishment of, 149
existence of, 130
friendship in, 161–63
Gorgias's relation to, 46–47
having an end, 86
making safe for philosophy, 10
philosopher and enlightened statesman as cocreators of, 150
Socrates's relation to, 47

political abstention, 48–49
political activity, 48, 207n14
political affairs, Socrates's failure to take seriously, 100
political animal, Aristotle's description of man as, 215n8
"the political art," 118, 120, 225n7
political art, as prudence, 136
political benefits, attaining, 107
political boundaries, friendships transcending, 5, 11
political communities, 12, 46, 124
political conflict, sources of, 164
political consequences, of friendship between the philosopher and the statesman, 149
political disagreements, of Adams and Jefferson, 191
political effects
  attending the Socratic approach to friendship, 45
  of the highest type of friendship, 159
political fashion, rule in, 214n3
political idealism, Plato representing, 200n27
political interpretations, of the *Ethics*, 90
political life
  effects of Aristotle's *sunaisthetic* account of friendship on, 14
  exploring friendship's relationship to, 7
  as an impediment to one's own well-being, 87
  role friendship ought to play in, 210n33
  Socratic objection to, 88
political or market friendship, as easily equalized, 118
political oratory, advice regarding, 119
political parties, emergence of, 192

political philosophers of antiquity, on friendship, 6
political philosophy
  analyzing friendship, 7
  classic dilemma of, 161
political realism, Aristotle representing, 200n27
political reformation, Plato gave up on, 45
political reforms, tailoring to the circumstances on the ground, 159
political relationships, as difficult to equalize, 118
political rule, life of, 88
political society, markers of, 138
political unity, limitations of the law's ability to foster, 162
political view, of friendship, 6
politician
  philosopher turning toward virtue, 119
  philosophers providing utilitarian benefits for, 225n7
  questioned by Socrates as not wise, 207n6
politics
  of abstention and negation of Socrates, 50
  Aristotle making his peace with, 9
  Aristotle's twofold account of, 159
  as the art directed to the soul, 58
  friendship and the practice of, 161–83
  fundamental problem of, 117, 200n29
  parts of, 58
  phantom art of, 58
  phantom friendships of, 84
  Plato's depiction of the Socratic approach to, 45, 46
  pre-political relationships having an important effect, 11
  relationship with philosophy, 118
  requiring the leavening effects of prudence and friendship, 15
  Socrates and Aristotle adopting differing stances to, 12
  Socrates not concerned with unjust practices of, 61
  Socrates's complete avoidance of conventional, 63
  Socrates's negative approach to, 50, 53, 63, 81–82
  Socrates's unwillingness to involve himself in, 13
Politics (Aristotle), 9
  on the ability of impersonal institutions to achieve unity, 14
  on cities partaking in the action of thought, 87
  on the emergence of the polis, 85, 150
  on friendship, 7
  as an incomplete work, 237n28
  origins of the polis, 130
  on philosopher's estrangement from the city, 89
  political advice contained in, 12
politics and philosophy, unresolved tension, 85–89
Polus
  on the good and the pleasant as the same, 73
  moralistic desire for punishment, 211n42
  praising Gorgias's art as "the best," 54
  questioning Socrates on what rhetoric is, 58
  refutation of Socrates showing why rhetoric is unjust, 64
  Socrates partially reintegrating into the city, 61
  Socrates's discussion with, 53

as "too sensitive to shame," 69
  on what is peasant opposed to what is best, 59
Poseidon, 80
positive nature, of Socrates's philosophical practice, 207n8
Posterior Analytics (Aristotle)
  Aristotle's on magnanimity in, 13, 92, 96, 101, 104, 111
  on man's capacity for intellect-like activities, 135
potency and actuality, account for movement and becoming, 131
potential, of friendships to spur one on to higher friendships, 38
potential friend, 127, 133
potentialities
  coming into contact, 132, 142
  pairs of, 131
potentiality
  as an originative source of motion, 130
  of a philosopher, 142
poverty
  bearing the ill-fortune of with equanimity, 100
  easy acceptance of, 217n43
power
  good sense alone as not enough to obtain, 26
  necessary to avoid suffering injustice, 78
  obtaining over the artisans using rhetoric, 55
  of rhetoric using only against one's enemies, 57
  Socrates refuting Polus's conception of, 59
  those in not disposed to become friends with philosophers, 117
power and wisdom, coincidence of, 68, 115–16

the powerful, as unlikely to befriend the wise, 115
pre-political relationships, giving rise to the polis, 11
preservation, hinging on the virtue of prudence, 126
pre-Socratic answers, to why things manifest goodness or beauty, 130
Price, A. W., 31
private actions, of Socrates having a public benefit, 208n21
private association, friendship analyzed as, 7
private education, 157, 233n67
private friendships, as foundational to conventional politics, 7
private manner, active life as practiced in, 87
private setting, of *Gorgias*, 51–52
private sphere, relegating friendship to, 6
property distribution, 164
Protagoras, 118, 224n5
Protagoras (Plato), 227n25
providence, trusting in, 156
prudence
  Aristotle describing the statesman's, 148
  Aristotle emphasizing, 126
  Callicles possessing, 70
  coming in a variety of forms, 136
  dealing with everyday existence, 136
  governed by wisdom, 69
  incorporating a level of, 167
  oriented and directed toward action, 139
  taking direction from wisdom, 138
prudent man, perceiving how he ought to act, 137
public discussion and choice, 15
punishment
  administering, 61

punishment *(continued)*
  ensuring that false convictions are refuted, 62
  releasing one from "badness of soul," 60
  Socrates appealing to Polus's desire, 60, 61
pursuit of the good, Socrates on, 10
Putnam, Robert, 4
Pythagorean science of government, 188
Pythagoreans, musical therapy of, 237n25

rapprochement, between two individuals, 65
rational being, man as, 137
rational potency, of a philosopher, 132–33
"real philosophy," Lysis pursuing, 29
realist, Aristotle as, 10
rebellious streak, Socrates instilled within Lysis, 44
recipient
  of the advice determining its worth, 148
  loving his benefactor, 133
reciprocal nature, of friendship, 110
reciprocity, Socrates raised the problem of, 108
recklessness, of Socrates, 30, 43
reconciliation
  of Adams and Jefferson by Benjamin Rush, 194
  between power and wisdom, 68, 83–84
"the refined," insisting on inequality in the distribution of honors, 165
refutation
  as a greater good, 210n39
  as painful process leaving one better off, 63

regime
  forming or reforming, 160
  founding, 158
relationships, disappearance of meaningful, 4
repayment, for political advice, 120
representation, of music, 178
reproach, 140, 216n18
The Republic (Plato)
  adage "friends have all things in common," 163
  as an apology for the Socratic way of life, 206n2
  comparison of the tyrannical man and the just man, 140
  countering extreme communitarianism of, 235n11
  dealing with Socrates's relation to politics, 206n2
  as an investigation into the form of justice, 206n2
  Polemarchus's definition of justice, 57
  Socrates on a city coming into being, 11
  Socrates on the tyrannical soul, 25
rest, must necessarily be pleasant, 176
returns, equality of, 231n55
rhetor
  allowing healthy souls to pursue their desires, 75
  Gorgias as, 54
  under the mistaken belief that he is doing something good, 59
  as persuasive only, 56
rhetoric
  "able to persuade by speeches," 54–55
  aiming at what is most pleasant, 59
  as all-powerful, 57
  allying with friendship, 59
  as capable of aiming towards truth, 210n32

commanding all other arts and
sciences, 55
containing a conflict with one side
victorious, 53
designated as an experience rather
than an art, 75
dissolving people's false conceptions
of justice and of what is, 64
pretending to be justice, 58
proving the power of, 56
relation to friendship, 55
Socrates attempting to use, 100
Socrates on, 54, 55, 61, 210n32,
218n48
as a sort of flattery for Socrates, 58
switching from art to science and
back, 55
using justly and for the benefit of
friends, 209n29
using to punish oneself, one's
friends, and one's fatherland, 65
Rhetoric (Aristotle), 119
rhetoric skills, using against "enemies
and doers of injustice," 57
rhetorical display, Socrates not truly
believing his, 76
rhetorician, having two incompatible
goals according to Gorgias, 57
Rhodes, James, 29
Rider, Benjamin, 28, 29
right reason, 137
Rights of Man (Paine), 192
Rousseau, Jean-Jacques, 199n23
rule, always involving mastery, 215n3
Rush, Benjamin, 15, 190, 194

safety, of Socrates, Callicles's concern
for, 69
"sameness of mind," according to
Aristotle, 3
science
compared to intellect, 134
of politics, 158
scientific knowledge, as sufficient by
itself for the Sophists, 158
Scottish Enlightenment, writers of
sought to refashion virtues, 5
self-contemplation, of the
magnanimous man, 149
self-deprecation, of Socrates, 17
self-government, capacity of the regime
to engage in the practice of,
181
self-interest, 55, 208n21, 210n34
self-interested desire, Aristotle on the
law's inability to curb, 165
self-love
making compatible with friendship,
140
pleasure and, 139–50
self-lovers, 140
self-restraint
Aristotle's praise of, 140
Socratic position on, 227n26
self-sufficiency, 33, 145, 150–54, 186
self-sufficient friendship, 83, 110
self-sufficient individuals, 33, 34
sensation, capacity for, 152
sense perception, present in some
animals, 135
serious man
actions of, 146
serving a friend, 122
"serious people," magnanimous man's
concern for honor, 106
serious person
doing many things for the sake
of both his friends and his
fatherland, 141
finding his existence to be both
desirable and good, 126
not rendered equal [to the person of
greater power], 115
role of, 141

shame
    causing Gorgias and Polus to shrink, 66
    as the corollary of honor, 95
    of Polus and Gorgias, 82
    Socrates appealing to Gorgias's sense of, 58
    Socrates using the concept of, 211n52
shameful things, defined by pain and badness, 60
sight, perceiving that we have through the sense of, 147
similarities, of Socrates with Callicles, 65
slavish obedience, to the law, 169
Smith, Adam, 4
Smith, Travis, 6
social community, acting as a cure for their own flaws, 182
social contract theories, 6
social order, accepting the existing, 105
social reality, divergent conceptions of, 195
social virtues, 134, 138
socially destructive manner, acting in, 102
society, friendships posing a danger to for Hobbes, 6
Socrates
    charge of corrupting the youth and, 23
    distinction between outward statements and intentions, 201n2
    engaging in more than a verbal dispute, 43
    ensuring unity by having all things in common, 169
    eschewed the practice of politics, 9
    in the face of good and bad fortune, 219n54
    failing to understand the sayings of Empedocles, 204n35
    as a gadfly in the *Apology*, 202n17
    identifying himself with Amphion, 67–68
    investigating just what the fine is, 211n43
    justifying his way of life to the jurors, 100
    Plato presenting as raising serious arguments, 19
    portrait of the "real," 17
    questioning the Athenian citizens' settled convictions, 13
    remaining cryptic about what justice is, 59
    as representative of the second type of magnanimity, 99
    sending Polus back into the city with a rhetoric designed to refute the city, 82
    teaching Menexenus the art of rhetoric, 205n48
    unending ascent to the idea of the good, 200n31
    on "the unexamined life," 8
    valuing speech over deeds, 209n24
    viewing his manner of life to be superior to the political life, 100
    way of life as shameful, 66
    as young and beautiful, 17
Socrates (Callicles and)
    ironic with Callicles, 70–71
    proclaiming Callicles to be a touchstone, 69
    refuting Callicles by distinguishing the pleasant from the good, 74
    shaming Callicles, 72
Socrates (friendship and)
    definition of friendship, 35, 45, 104, 129
    desire for a friend, 1–2
    difficulties associated with friendship, 110

difficulties in defining friendship, 108
disclamation of any knowledge regarding friendship, 30
failure to distinguish friendship from erotic love, 163
on friendship consisting of those who are alike, 205n39
on the meaning of friendship, 205n48
negative understanding of friendship, 10
not in a position of superiority on friendship, 20
subsuming friendship into the ambit of erotic desire for the good, 84
switching between various meanings of the term friend, 31
transforming friendship into love, 23, 42
Socrates (Lysis and)
encouraging Lysis's desire for punishment, 204n30
inability to match Lysis with one of the older fellows, 44
led Lysis to the conclusion that he is not wise, 29
setting Lysis against his family, 25
using Lysis's penchant for eristic games, 29
Socratic approach, to politics as negative and destructive, 82
Socratic citizenship, 45–84, 208n21
Socratic Citizenship, as Socrates's stance toward the polis, 48
Socratic friendship, 17–28, 35–42
Socratic justice, 62, 64
Socratic life, as avoiding committing injustice, 79
Socratic method, seeming to be entirely negative, 47
Socratic opinion, on self-sufficiency and friendship, 145
Socratic paradox, Aristotle resolving, 153
Socratic sophisms, sacrificial victim and, 25–30
Socratic stance, not conveying the totality of the phenomenon of friendship, 146
Socratic understanding of friendship, negatively impacting his relation to the polis, 80
Solon, 32
Solon of Athens, 188
sophism, Socrates engaging in a deliberate, 27
sophistic arguments
of Aristotle engaging his philosophic audience, 226n10
in *Lysis*, 18
Plato presenting Socrates as using, 29
of Socrates to Lysis, 29, 37
sophistry, pretending to be the legislative art, 58
Sophists
professing to teach "the political art," 158
Protagoras distinguished from, 118
in a purely descriptive way, 202n14
soul
alone of importance, 81
gratifying the nonrational part of, 140
improvement of, 88
judging only, 214n73
as a microcosm of the whole, 77
nonrational part sharing in reason, 205n42
Spartan founding, established by Lycurgus, 188
Spartans, educational system oriented toward military training, 172
species, defining to the universal from, 97–98

specious argument, equivocating on the term "to understand," 43
specious courage, examples of, 94
speeches
  Gorgias adapting to the city he is visiting, 58
  rhetoric of, 54
spiritedness, passion of, 179
stability, of philosophy, 65
"stable" friendships, of those who are good and alike in point of virtue, 110
statesman
  actualizing the innate potentiality of, 142
  actualizing the potentiality of the philosopher, 147
  Aristotle convincing the philosopher to engage with, 14
  engaging and gratifying his most authoritative part, 152
  having capacity to bring a particular action to completion, 159
  potential actualized by perceiving the regime he has founded, 149
  receptivity to the formative advice of the philosopher, 134
statesman and the philosopher, transcending mere nature, 154
status, equality of, 231n55
Stauffer, Devin, 71, 73, 212n56
Strauss, Leo, 9, 206n1, 228n31
strengths, recognizing differing as complementary, 24
study, frivolous part of, 28
substantive policy, bulk of entrusted to the good sense of the people and several states, 189
suicide, Ajax committing, 98
sunaisthetic, meaning "joint perception," 3

sunaisthetic friendship
  Aristotle's, 5, 161, 183
  basing on self-sufficiency, 185
  citizens coming to share in, 14
  participating in, 163
  unifying influence on the city, 14
Symposium (Socrates), recounting how Diotima sought to initiate him into erotic matters, 35–36
synderesis, faculty of absent in Aristotle, 230n44

taming, the philosopher, 119–27
Tecmessa, attempting to dissuade Ajax, 98
tension
  between the philosopher and the city, 89
  between philosophy and politics, 8–10
Tessitore, Aristide, 98, 200n30, 200n32, 215n14
Thales, 139, 188, 230n45
theatrical events, Aristotle on the educational function of, 182
theatrical performances, including as part of music, 173
theoretical virtue, as the best life, 103
things in common
  friends having, 24
  given least care by most people, 163
  typically afforded less care, 163–64
"thoughtful"
  ambiguity of the term, 37
  meaning of the term, 28
Thoughts on Government (Adams), 187
time and trust, friendship requiring, 127
to learn, equivocating on, 28
"to think," thoughtful meaning, 28
"to understand," thoughtful meaning, 28

touchstone, Callicles as for Socrates, 69
traditional authority, difficulty that Socrates's approach poses to, 44
tragedy, magnanimous man able to avoid, 106
tragic flaw (*hamartia*)
  citizens' reflections on their own, 182
  of magnanimous men, 111
transformation
  of friendship into passionate love, 40
  from friendship to erotic love, 36
true characteristic, bound up with action and accompanied by reason, 136
true friend, Socrates acting as, 63
truth
  as just, 62
  pursuing on argument for the sake of, 56
  taking precedence over political and familial loyalties, 123
tyrannical desires, 166
tyrannical man, 140
tyrannical rule, 214n3
tyrannical soul, 25–26
tyranny, 166, 215n3
tyrant, 60, 78

"ultimate particular thing," perception of, 137
unalloyed good
  on Callicles's desire for, 74, 76
  as friendship between two individuals who are good, 74
  independent of any evil, 71, 82
  Socrates not believing in, 77, 79
  transcending the present life for Socrates, 73
unexamined life, as not worth living, 209n24

"unimpeded" activity, definition of pleasure as, 233n62
unity
  in the city, 163–69
  obtaining through legal or institutional change, 235n7
universal good, distinction from what is good for each individual, 110
universals, poetry presenting, 181
unjust deed, bringing into the open, 61
unjust practices, Polus conveying a litany of, 61–62
unlike, being friends with each other, 34
"unqualified pleasures," as pleasant in and of themselves, 143
untutored nature, as nasty, brutish, and short, 155
the useful, 33, 109, 172
utilitarian educational system, 172
utilitarian impulses, Socrates goal to curb Lysis's, 203n24
utility, friendships of, 2, 4, 110

value judgments, 189
"vengeance," "the many" will listen to, 162
Villa, Dana, 47, 50, 208n21
village
  households join together to constitute, 85
  as self-sufficient, 130
  sufficient to deal with the necessities of life, 150
violence, 152
virtue
  Aristotle on possessing and making use of, 154
  Aristotle on the process making individuals virtuous, 234n1

virtue *(continued)*
  city's ultimate aim as the practice of, 215n3
  deprioritized in favor of utility, autonomy, and profit, 5
  differential in, 115
  expressing in different ways, 112
  friendship of, 2–3
  relative inequality of, 223n82
  Socrates defining, 47
  of the soul as moderation, 76
virtuous individuals, desiring each other's company, 111
Vlastos, Gregory, 19
von Heyking, John, 182
vulgar justice, as unjust, 63

Walzer, Michael, 6–7
want or lack, as not considered to be bad, 40
Ward, Ann, 123, 124
water, potential to assume an altered state, 131–32
way of life
  Callicles serving as the touchstone for Socrates's, 79
  most choiceworthy, 86
  of Socrates, 46, 47
wealth, redistributing from the wealthy to the poor, 164
who or what a friend is, 24
the whole
  as prior to the part, 86
  Socrates not having a full grasp of, 34
the wicked, cannot be friends with one another, 33
"wickedness," defective usually translated as, 231n49
wine, as an antidote to hemlock, 38
Wirt, William, 195

wisdom
  beyond merely human concerns, 136
  Callicles may not have, 69
  comparing with the eminent practicality of prudence, 139
  concern with the outermost limits of correct reason, 136
  directing those who hold power, 161
  as a formative or guiding force, 139
  involving an intellectual grasp of things, 136
  Lysis's love of, 24
  of a mutual friend, 195
  not like the other things about which friends compete, 24
  Socrates driving home Lysis's lack of, 27
  superior to moral virtues, 223n82
  taking priority over, 138
  those not yet either good nor bad loving, 36–37
  the wise, understanding of nature and the whole, 77
wise man, honor due to, 124
wise person, as "the most self-sufficient," 146
wisest, Socrates as, 47
"wisest ones," not understood, 222n70
wood, block of, 132
Wood, Gordon, 189, 190, 191
world
  of appearances, 231n50
  of the magnanimous man, 220n59
  of politics, 64
worthiness, recognition of another's, 127
wretchedness, of those needing to satiate desires without end, 71

young man, in love beginning the dialogue on friendship, 21

Zethus, 67, 212n56
Zeus, 22, 80–81

Zuckert, Catherine, 18, 19, 52, 209n26

www.ingramcontent.com/pod-product-compliance
Lightning Source LLC
Chambersburg PA
CBHW060825080825
30784CB00002B/9